EXPANDING
THE NEW AUDIENCE
FOR THEATRE

The History of ASSITEJ
The International Association Of Theatre For Children And Youth
Volume II
(1976–1990)

EXPANDING THE NEW AUDIENCE FOR THEATRE

The History of ASSITEJ
The International Association Of Theatre For Children And Youth
ASSITEJ / l'Association International
du Théâtre pour l'Enfance et la Jeunesse)
Volume II
(1976–1990)

NAT EEK, PhD
College of Fine Arts
University of Oklahoma
Honorary President of ASSITEJ
President of ASSITEJ, 1972–75
Santa Fe, New Mexico, USA
with

ANN M. SHAW, EdD
Queens College
Department of Theatre and Communication Arts
City University of New York
Honorary Member of ASSITEJ
1st Vice-President of ASSITEJ, 1981–87
Santa Fe, New Mexico, USA
with

KATHERINE KRZYS, MFA
Curator, Child Drama Collection
Arizona State University
Curator, ASSITEJ/USA & ASSITEJ
1985 to present
Tempe, Arizona, USA

SANTA FE

On the Cover: *Peer Gynt* by Henrik Ibsen. Adapted by Bertil Herzberg & Björn Samuelsson. Directed by Björn Samuelsson. Set Design and Puppets by Gunilla Pantzar. Music by Peder Nabo and Tomas Forsell. Actors: Stephen Holström, Lars Sonnesjö, Ann-Catherine Fröjdö, and Lilian Gustavsson. Performed by Byteatern at the Xth World Congress of ASSITEJ in Stockholm, Sweden/19–27 May 1990. Photography by Bertil Herzberg. Courtesy of Niclas Malmcrona, ASSITEJ/Sweden.

Funded in part by a grant from the Children's Theatre Foundation of America.
Photo preparation by Konrad S. Eek.

© 2011 by Nat Eek, PhD.
All Rights Reserved.

No part of this book may be reproduced in any form or by any electronic or mechanical means including information storage and retrieval systems without permission in writing from the publisher, except by a reviewer who may quote brief passages in a review.

Sunstone books may be purchased for educational, business, or sales promotional use. For information please write: Special Markets Department, Sunstone Press, P.O. Box 2321, Santa Fe, New Mexico 87504-2321.

Book and Cover design ▷ Vicki Ahl
Body typeface ▷ WTC Our Bodoni
Printed on acid free paper

Library of Congress Cataloging-in-Publication Data

Eek, Nat, 1927-
  Discovering a new audience for theatre : the history of ASSITEJ, the International Association of Theatre for Children and Youth / by Nat Eek, with Ann M. Shaw, and Kaerine Krzys.
      v. cm
  Includes bibliographical references.
  Contents: v. 1. 1964-1975
  ISBN 978-0-86534-660-4 (v. 1 : pbk. : alk. paper)
  1. International Association of Theatre for Children and Young People–History.
I. Shaw, Ann M. (Ann Marie), 1930- II. Krzys, Katherine. III. Title.
  PN2015E45 2008
  792.02'2609–dc22
                        2008010550
  Contents: v. II. 1976-1990
  ISBN: 978-0-86534-798-4 (v.11 : pbk. : alk. paper)

Published in

WWW.SUNSTONEPRESS.COM
SUNSTONE PRESS / POST OFFICE BOX 2321 / SANTA FE, NM 87504-2321 /USA
(505) 988-4418 / ORDERS ONLY (800) 243-5644 / FAX (505) 988-1025

This History has been dedicated to ASSITEJ, to its leaders, and its National Centers and their members who gave of their time, their money, and their devotion to a firm belief in the art of the theatre for young people, making it an artistic equal to adult theatre.

Volume II is dedicated especially to the two Michaels—Ramløse and FitzGerald—whose voluminous emails, constant communication, remarkable information, and incredible support made this volume accurate and readable.

CONTENTS

Volume II
(1976–1990)

FOREWORD / 11
INTRODUCTION / 25

PART III:
THE EUROPEAN CONSOLIDATION (1975–1984) / 31

The World at the Time / 31
The Status of ASSITEJ—June 1975 / 31
Bureau of ASSITEJ Meeting/Paris, France/13–18 October 1975 / 34
Executive Committee of ASSITEJ Meeting/Milan and Rome, Italy/8–16 May 1976 / 36
Bureau of ASSITEJ Meeting/Sophia, Bulgaria/4–5 October 1976 / 44
Executive Committee Meeting of ASSITEJ/Calgary, Banff, Montreal, and Ottawa, Canada/12–20 May 1977 / 50
Bureau of ASSITEJ Meeting/Paris, France/October 1977 / 57
Executive Committee of ASSITEJ Meeting/Moscow, USSR/26–30 March 1978 / 60
VIth International Congress of ASSITEJ/Madrid, Spain/10–17 June 1978 / 63
A Summary of 1975–1978 / 72
Interim/1976–1979 / 79
Bureau Meeting of ASSITEJ/Paris, France/October 1978 / 81
Bureau Meeting of ASSITEJ/Moscow, USSR/10–13 June 1979 / 84
Executive Committee of ASSITEJ Meeting/Šibenik, Yugoslavia/25–28 June 1979 / 85
Executive Committee of ASSITEJ Meeting/Washington, D.C., USA/ 9–14 April 1980 / 90
Bureau Meeting of ASSITEJ/Dortmund/FGR/28–30 November 1980 / 98
Executive Committee of ASSITEJ Meeting/Prague, Czechoslovakia/17–20 March 1981 / 99
VIIth International Congress of ASSITEJ/Lyon, France/13–20 June 1981 / 106

PART IV:
THE OPEN CLASH OF POLITICS / 119

The World of 1981–1990 / 119
Bureau of ASSITEJ Meeting/Lille, France/11–13 October 1981 / 121

Executive Committee of ASSITEJ Meeting/Havana, Cuba/5–11 April 1982 / 125
Bureau of ASSITEJ Meeting/Paris, France/12–13 October 1982 / 132
Interim/ASSITEJ/USA—1983 / 134
Executive Committee of ASSITEJ Meeting/Lisbon, Portugal/28–30 June 1983 / 136
Bureau of ASSITEJ Meeting/London, Great Britain/31 October–3 November 1983 / 148
Interim—June 1984 / 152
Executive Committee of ASSITEJ Meeting/Munich, FGR/9–17 June 1984 / 155
VIIIth International Congress of ASSITEJ/Moscow, USSR/19–27 September 1984 / 162
A Summary of 1978–1984 / 179
Bureau of ASSITEJ Meeting/Paris, France/2–3 February 1985 / 193
Executive Committee of ASSITEJ Meeting/Šibenik, Yugoslavia/22–29 June 1985 / 196
Bureau of ASSITEJ Meeting/Prague, Czechoslovakia/4–5 October 1985 / 207
Bureau & Executive Committee Meetings of ASSITEJ/Helsinki, Finland and Stockholm, Sweden/3–10 May 1986 / 208

PART V.
HIGH CONFLICT AND INTERNATIONAL EXPANSION / 215

Executive Committee of ASSITEJ Meeting/Berlin, GDR/6–11 January 1987 / 215
IXth World Congress of ASSITEJ/Adelaide, Australia/8–16 April 1987 / 219
Interim—1987 / 230
ASSITEJ Commission on Themes & Artistic Activities Meeting/Modena, Italy/3–8 November 1987 / 231
Executive Committee of ASSITEJ Meeting/Odense, Denmark /15–22 May 1988 / 233
Bureau Meeting of ASSITEJ/Moscow, USSR/16–18 November 1988 / 244
Executive Committee Meeting of ASSITEJ/Lyon, France/3–6 June 1989 / 248
Bureau Meeting of ASSITEJ/Warsaw, Poland/4–10 November 1989 / 254
Bureau & Executive Committee Meeting of ASSITEJ/Havana, Cuba/4–11 February 1990 / 258
Xth World Congress of ASSITEJ/Stockholm, Sweden/19–27 May 1990 / 262
A Summary of 1985–1990 / 279

CONCLUSION / 293
THE AUTHORS / 294

APPENDICES

APPENDIX A—List of Officers and Honorary Members (1965–1990) / 295
APPENDIX B—Biographies of Principal Officers, Leaders, and Members (1976–1990) / 297
APPENDIX C—List of International/World Congresses of ASSITEJ (1965–1990) / 329
APPENDIX D—List of Executive Committee Meetings of ASSITEJ (1965–1990) / 330
APPENDIX E—List of Members of the Executive Committee of ASSITEJ by Terms (1965–1990) / 332
APPENDIX F—The Constitutions of ASSITEJ (1965 and 1990) / 335
 The 1965 Constitution / 335
 The 1990 Constitution, as amended / 340
APPENDIX G—History of the Formation & Suspension of National Centers—1976–1990 / 347
APPENDIX H—The Current Election Process of ASSITEJ (2005) / 350
APPENDIX I—Speeches / 353
 "Children and the Art of the Theatre" a speech by Dr. Nat Eek, Past President of ASSITEJ, given at the Yugoslav Festival of the Child in Šibenik, Yugoslavia on 25 June 1979 / 353
 "Welcoming Speech" by Dr. Ilse Rodenberg, President of ASSITEJ, given at the VIIIth International Congress in Moscow, USSR in 20 September 1984. / 356

NOTES / 360
BIBLIOGRAPHY / 372

FOREWORD TO VOLUME II
by
Michael Ramløse
Administrative Director of Theatre Fair Play, Denmark
Chairman, Executive Board, 17th ASSITEJ World Congress &
Performing Arts Festival for Young Audiences, 2011
Secretary General of ASSITEJ (1990–1996)

Article 1 in the ASSITEJ Constitution states—and has always stated:
1. This Association proposes to unite theatres, organizations and individuals throughout the world dedicated to theatre for children and young people.
2. This Association is dedicated to artistic, humanitarian, and educational efforts and no decision, action, or statement of the Association shall be based on nationality, political conviction, cultural identity, ethnicity, or religion.

Point Two is of special interest, when reading Volume II of *The History of ASSITEJ*, authored by Nat Eek, with Ann Shaw, and Katherine Krzys. It highlights just how important this political dimension has actually been to the organization in the particular period under discussion.

The authors have painstakingly trawled through the archives (both the official and the personal), corresponded with a great many of the people involved in the incidents and events of this period, sifted and sorted through a wealth of material to present us with a thoroughly well researched, objective account of the actual circumstances within ASSITEJ from 1975 until 1990. It offers (at least at times) a subjective assessment of the developments within the organization and of the motives of those concerned.

What is so striking when reading Volume II is the huge extent to which the geo-political dimension has influenced the organization in this period of time. The world was divided into east and west—clearest, of course, as symbolised in Europe by the Berlin Wall. ASSITEJ resembles, at times, a "mini United Nations", and even though those involved attempted to live up to the spirit of the Constitution and remain non-political, they seldom achieved this in practice. This can be clearly seen in the choices, the voting, and the elections to the Executive Committee—and most clearly at the 1984 Moscow Congress.

One can say that Europe's history from the end of the Second World War until the 1990s is also ASSITEJ's history. Until the 1990s, the rest of the world hung on and followed, while the power of decision making within ASSITEJ was centered in Europe—here where east and west clashed and had a vested interest in maintaining the internal balance of power (without unnecessary disturbance from any "foreign" influence).

So ASSITEJ's history is also the history of international "bloc" politics.

BUT it is decidedly also a story about people. Dedicated, committed and hard-working, visionary theatre people, the great, as well as the eccentric, personalities, who have left their memories and their mark, and will not be forgotten. And then there are the stories of the "hangers-on", those who have occasionally held office and not achieved anything more than personal gain and who are, luckily and quickly, forgotten again.

It is the history of the starting of the ASSITEJ centers in many different countries, and of the "ghost centers" that represented nobody at all, apart from the individuals who saw the benefit of ASSITEJ membership for themselves, while they held the rest of their country and colleagues outside of the international fellowship.

It is in this Volume II that we see what happened to an originally progressive organization which gradually stagnated and refused to keep up with the development of the times, got left behind, only saw too late how the world outside was changing, and failed to heed "the writing on the wall".

It is a period of centralization in ASSITEJ—decisions were often taken only by a few—the Bureau (which according to the Constitution, should only meet in matters of extreme urgency between the Executive Committee meetings) met regularly, completely independent from the Executive Committee. In other words, decision-making was centralized and controlled by a small number—there may have been many reasons for this, but the result nevertheless was a weakening of the already fragile democracy in the organization, causing (as the book so clearly describes) growing unrest and dissatisfaction amongst the membership.

It is the authors' great achievement, that in this volume they document and comment upon the disagreements, the political struggles, the breakthroughs and the retreats, the important individuals and their influence for better and for worse, the motives (both the noble and ignoble), the great visions and the mistaken projects . . . in short, everything which has driven the development of the organization onwards and which, with this history beside us and with a clear focus on the future, will enable us to face the challenges of the twenty first century.

So, therefore, let this acutely relevant quotation serve as a guide for ASSITEJ: "We will not fear the future—we will create it!"

—/s/ Michael Ramløse

FORORD TIL BIND 2

Artikel 1 i ASSITEJs vedtægter fastslår—og har altid (med lidt varierende ordlyd) fastslået, at:
1. This Association proposes to unite theatres, organizations and individuals throughout the world dedicated to theatre for children and young people.
2. This Association is dedicated to artistic, humanitarian, and educational efforts and no decision, action, or statement of the Association shall be based on nationality, political conviction, cultural identity, ethnicity, or religion.

Især punkt 2 er naturligvis af interesse, når man læser Nat Eek's 2. bind af ASSITEJs historie, for det er slående i hvor høj grad netop den politiske dimension er allestedsnærværende i organisationen i den periode, der beskrives i dette bind.

Forfatteren har med vanlig omhu og præcision dykket ned i arkiver (officielle såvel som personlige), korresponderet med et stort antal af periodens aktører, øst af selvoplevede begivenheder og episoder, vægtet og sorteret og kan præsentere os for en på samme tid grundigt researchet objektiv fremstilling af de faktiske forhold i ASSITEJ i tiden 1975 – 1990 og en (i hvert fald til tider) subjektiv vinkel på organisationens udvikling og nogle af aktørernes bevæggrunde.

Det er slående, når man læser dette bind af historien om ASSITEJ, i hvor høj grad den geo-politiske dimension har haft betydning i organisationen på denne tid: Verden er delt i øst og vest—klarest, selvfølgelig, symboliseret i Europa med Berlin-muren. ASSITEJ minder i disse år om et mini-FN— og selv om aktørerne på ASSITEJ-banen ser ud til at forsøge at leve op til organisationens vedtægter om at være upolitiske, lader det sig sjældent gennemføre. Det viser sig blandt andet i afstemninger og valg til EC—tydeligst ved kongressen i Moskva i 1984. Man kan sige, at Europas historie—delingen efter 2. verdenskrig—indtil omkring 1990 også er ASSITEJs historie. Indtil 1990 "hang resten af verden på", men magten i ASSITEJ lå i Europa—det var her øst og vest stødte klarest sammen og havde en interesse i at bevare den interne balance (og nødig så den forstyrret af "udefrakommende").

Først da den kolde krig sluttede i 1989 kunne Europa "gøre plads" til resten af verden i ASSITEJ.

Så historien om ASSITEJ er—også—historien om storpolitik.

MEN det er så sandelig også historien om mennesker. Dedikerede, arbejdsomme, visionære teaterfolk, store—og excentriske—personligheder, hvoraf nogle har efterladt sig varige spor og minder, der ikke vil blive glemt. Og det er også historien om "døgnfluer", om folk der har haft positioner i organisationen, men sjældent har udrettet noget udover, hvad der måtte have gavnet dem selv—og de er heldigvis hurtigt glemt igen.

Det er historien om ASSITEJ-centres opståen, uddøen og genopståen i forskellige lande, om "ghost-centres", som ikke repræsenterede/ repræsenterer noget som helst i deres land—udover en person, der kunne se en egen fordel i at tilslutte sig ASSITEJ og holde resten af kollegerne udenfor dette fællesskab.

Det er (i dette bind) historien om en fra starten progressiv organisation, der efterhånden gik i stå og nægtede at følge med tiden og erkende, at verden "udenfor" ændrede sig meget hurtigt, og som derfor for sent så skriften på væggen.

Det er en periode med centralisering i ASSITEJ—beslutningerne samles på færre hænder—Bureauet (som ifølge vedtægterne kun skal mødes "for urgent matters" mellem EC-møderne) holder helt regelmæssige, fastsatte møder uafhængigt af EC—med andre ord: beslutningerne i ASSITEJ centraliseres og varetages af færre personer—der kan have været mange grunde hertil, men resultatet var jo ikke desto mindre en svækkelse af det i forvejen skrøbelige demokrati i organisationen—og det skabte da også—som bogen så forbilledligt beskriver—en voksende utilfredshed i medlemsskaren.

Det er Nat Eek's store fortjeneste i denne ASSITEJ-historie, at han dokumenterer og kommenterer de uenigheder, politiske kampe, fremskridt og tilbageslag, enkeltpersoners betydning på godt og ondt, motiver (af ædel og af mere dubiøs karakter), store visioner og fejlslagne projekter—alt det, som har drevet og driver udviklingen frem i en organisation, som med denne historie i ryggen og blikket fast rettet mod fremtiden også vil stå godt rustet til at løse sine opgaver i det 21. århundrede.

Så derfor: lad dette—aktuelle—citat stå som ledetråd for ASSITEJ: "Vi vil ikke frygte fremtiden—vi vil skabe den!"

—/s/ Michael Ramløse

PREFACE AU VOLUME II
Par Michael Ramløse
Directeur Administratif du Théâtre Fair Play, Danemark
Président, Conseil de direction, 17ième Congrès mondial de l'ASSITEJ et du Festival des arts du spectacle pour jeunes publics
Secrétaire général de l'ASSITEJ (1990-1996)

L'Article I de la Constitution de l'ASSITEJ constate, et a toujours constaté que:
1. Cette association se propose de réunir les théâtres, organisations et individus partout dans le monde qui se consacrent au théâtre pour enfants et pour la jeunesse.
2. Cette association se consacre aux efforts artistiques, humanitaires et pédagogiques, et aucune décision, action ou déclaration de l'association ne peut être fondée sur des convictions politiques, une nationalité, une identité culturelle, une ethnicité, ou une religion.

Ce dernier propos intéressera particulièrement les lecteurs du Volume II de l'histoire de l'ASSITEJ, écrit par Nat Eek avec Ann Shaw et Katherine Krzys qui soulignent tous l'importance de cette dimension politique pour l'organisation pendant l'époque étudiée.

Les auteurs ont soigneusement examiné les archives officielles et privées, ont pris contact avec un grand nombre de personnes qui ont participé aux incidents et événements de l'époque, ont passé au crible et trié une profusion de documents pour nous offrir un compte-rendu solidement étayé et objectif des circonstances au sein de l'ASSITEJ entre 1975 et 1990. Le texte présente (au moins par moments) une évaluation subjective des développements au sein de l'organisation ainsi que des motivations des personnes concernées.

Le Volume II met en valeur pour le lecteur l'influence très importante au sein de l'ASSITEJ de la dimension géopolitique. A l'époque, le monde était divisé entre l'Est et l'Ouest, séparation symbolisée clairement en Europe par le mur de Berlin. L'ASSITEJ ressemble parfois à une "mini-Organisation des Nations Unies," et bien que ses membres aient essayé de respecter l'esprit de la Constitution en restant apolitiques, en pratique ils n'ont pu y arriver que rarement. On le comprend bien en regardant les choix et les votes du comité exécutif ainsi que les élections de ses membres, surtout lors du Congrès de Moscou en 1984.

On peut dire que l'histoire de l'Europe dès la fin de la Deuxième Guerre Mondiale jusqu'aux années 90 est aussi l'histoire de l'ASSITEJ. A cette époque, pendant que le reste du monde attendait et suivait, c'est en Europe qu'était basé la prise de décision au sein de l'ASSITEJ, car c'est là que l'Est et l'Ouest se confrontaient et avaient tout intérêt à maintenir l'équilibre du continent (sans l'intrusion inutile des influences "étrangères").

Ainsi, l'histoire de l'ASSITEJ est aussi l'histoire de la politique internationale des "blocs".

MAIS, il s'agit aussi de l'histoire des gens ordinaires du milieu théâtral, des personnes convaincues, engagées, et travailleuses, parfois visionnaires, qu'il s'agisse des grands ou des excentriques ainsi que des personnalités qui ont laissés leurs souvenirs et leurs marques, et qui ne seront pas oubliés. Et puis il y a les histoires des «crampons», ceux qui ont à l'occasion occupé des postes à responsabilité sans accomplir grand chose mais en ont tiré des bénéfices personnels et qui seront (heureusement et rapidement) oubliés.

C'est l'histoire des débuts des centres de l'ASSITEJ dans plusieurs pays et des "centres fictifs" qui ne représentaient personne sauf les individus qui ont profité de leur statut de membre de l'ASSITEJ, tout en tenant leur pays et leur collègues éloignés de la sphère de cette association internationale.

Le Volume II révèle ce qui s'est passé à l'intérieur d'une organisation à l'origine progressive mais qui a peu à peu stagné en refusant de se moderniser, qui s'est retrouvée à la traîne, ne s'est rendu compte que trop tard que le monde avait changé et n'a pas su reconnaître l'ampleur et l'imminence de ces transformations.

Durant cette époque de centralisation au sein de l'ASSITEJ, des décisions ont souvent été prises par un groupe restreint—le Bureau (qui selon la Constitution, ne devait se réunir entre deux rencontres du Comité Exécutif qu'en cas d'extrême urgence) se réunissait régulièrement, tout à fait indépendamment du Comité Exécutif. Autrement dit, la prise de décision était centralisée et contrôlée par un petit groupe. En dépit des nombreuses raisons qui peuvent expliquer cela, en est résulté un affaiblissement de la démocratie (déjà fragile) de l'organisation qui a conduit (comme les auteurs le décrivent clairement dans leur ouvrage) à des troubles croissants et au mécontentement général des membres.

La grande réussite des auteurs a été de documenter et commenter les mésententes, les luttes politiques, les avancées et les reculs, le rôle des personnalités et leur influence, bonne ou mauvaise, les mobiles (nobles ou ignobles), les grandes visions et les projets ratés . . . bref, tout ce qui a propulsé le développement de cette organisation, et qui nous permettra de faire face aux défis du 21ième siècle, en nous concentrant clairement sur le futur, ce passé désormais derrière nous.

Laissons donc cette citation ô combien pertinente servir de guide à l'ASSITEJ: "Nous n'aurons pas peur du futur, nous le créerons!"

—Translated by Jeanie Fleming

ПРЕДИСЛОВИЕ к II тому

Микаэль Рамлезе
Административный директор Театра Фэа Плей, Дания;
Председатель Исполнительного совета XVII Всемирного Конгресса АССИТЕЖ и Фестиваля исполнительского искусств для юных зрителей (2011 год): Генеральный секретарь АССИТЕЖ (1990–1996).

Первая Статья Устава АСИТЕЖ неизменно гласила и гласит:
1. АССИТЕЖ объединяет театры, организации и отдельных людей, посвятивших себя театру для детей и молодежи в разных странах мира.
2. АССИТЕЖ занимается художественной, гуманитарной и образовательной деятельностью и ни одно решение, действие или заявление Ассоциации не может быть совершено или принято на основе национальных или политических убеждений, либо в зависимости от культурной идентичности, этнической или религиозной принадлежности.

При чтении второго тома истории АССИТЕЖ, составленной Натом Иком совместно с Энн Шоу и Кэтрин Крис, особенно интересным представляется то, что в нем подчеркивается, насколько важной была политическая составляющая в жизни Ассоциации в тот период, о котором идет речь.

Авторы не пожалели усилий для проработки архивов, (как официальных, так и личных), переписывались со многими людьми, участвовавшими в событиях того времени, отсортировали и разобрали груды материалов, чтобы представить нам тщательно проанализированный и объективный отчет о деятельности АССИТЕЖ с 1975 по 1990 год. В то же время, иногда, книга предлагает субъективную оценку происходившего внутри организации и мотивов действий тех, кто их совершал.

Читатель II тома будет поражен, какое большое влияние гео-политика оказывала на деятельность ассоциации в то время. Тогда мир был разделен на западный и на восточный, и наиболее четким символом этого разделения была Берлинская стена в Европе. Иногда АССИТЕЖ была похожа на «мини-Организацию Объединенных Наций». И хотя ее члены старались сотрудничать в духе Устава и быть вне политики, им это редко удавалось на практике. Это отражалось в выборе действий, в голосовании, в составе Исполнительного Комитета.

Особенно ярко это проявилось на Московском Конгрессе АССИТЕЖ в 1984 году.

Можно сказать, что история Европы с конца Второй мировой войны и до начала девяностых—это и история АССИТЕЖ.. До начала девяностых весь остальной мир оставался где-то в стороне, в то время как все решения, принимавшиеся в АССИТЕЖ, были сосредоточены на Европе, там, где сталкивались восток и запад и где их интерес состоял в сохранении внутреннего силового баланса (без ненужного вмешательства «иностранного» влияния).

Итак, история АССИТЕЖ—это также история международной политики «блоков».

НО, это, прежде всего, история о людях. О преданных делу, без устали работающих визионерах, людях театра. О великих, эксцентричных, оставивших о себе память, людях, которые не будут забыты.

Кроме того, это и история о «попутчиках», о тех, кто попал в ассоциацию случайно, ничего не привнес в ее работу, но использовал это в своих интересах и кто, к счастью, был скоро и легко забыт.

Это история становления центров АССИТЕЖ в разных странах мира. А также история «центров-призраков», чьи руководители никого не представляли, но извлекали личную выгоду из членства в АССИТЕЖ в то время, как коллеги в их стране находилась вне международных контактов.

В этом втором томе мы читаем о том, что произошло с изначально прогрессивными организациями, стагнация которых помешала им соответствовать духу времени, они отстали от остальных и слишком поздно обнаружили, как изменился окружающий мир, пока они не обращали внимания на «письмена на стене».

Это был период централизованного управления в АССИТЕЖ—когда решения принимались всего лишь несколькими людьми—членами Бюро АССИТЕЖ (которое, согласно Уставу должно собираться только в случаях чрезвычайной необходимости в период между заседаниями). Бюро же заседало регулярно и совершено независимо от Исполкома АССИТЕЖ. Иными словами принятие решений было централизованным и контролировалось небольшой группой. Наверное, тому было много причин, однако результатом было ослабление в Ассоциации и так хрупкой демократии, что вызывало (как это очень хорошо описано в книге) растущее беспокойство и неудовлетворенность среди членов ассоциации.

Большим достижением авторов книги является то, что они и рассказывают и спорят о разногласиях, о политической борьбе, о прорывах и отступлениях, об известных творческих деятелях, об их хорошем и плохом влиянии, о мотивах их поступков, (благородных и нет), об их предвидениях и ошибочных проектах . . . То есть, обо всем том, что двигало Ассоциацию вперед и о том, что мы можем теперь изучать как историю, что поможет нам сосредоточиться на будущем и ответить на вызовы двадцать первого века.

Поэтому, пусть вот эта очень злободневная цитата станет знаковой для АССИТЕЖ: «Мы не боимся будущего,—мы создаем его!»

—Микаэль Рамлезе

Translated by Galya Kolosova

Prefacio a Volumen II
Por
Michael Ramlose
Silletero de la Comisión Ejécutiva

Artículo I de la constitución de ASSITEJ dice—y siempre ha dicho:
1. La Asociación propone unir a teatros, organizaciones e individuos por todo el mundo dedicado al teatro para niños y jóvenes.
2. Esta asociación está dedicado a los esfuerzos artísticos, humanitarios y relativos a la enseñanza y no sería fundado ninguna decisión, acción ni declaración de la Asociación en la nacionalidad, la convicción política, la identidad cultural, la étnica, ni la religión.

El punto dos es de interés especial cuando leyendo Volumen II de La Historia de ASSITEJ, escrito por Nat Eek, con Ann Shaw y Katherine Krzyz. Se eleva en efecto tan importante ha sido esta dimensión política a la organización en la época preciso bajo discusión.

Los autores han investigado laboriosamente por los archivos (ambos los oficiales y los personales), han correspondido con muchas personas quien estaban enrollado en los incidentes y eventos de esta época, han separado y clasificado por una riqueza de material para presentarnos con un cuento bien investigado, un cuento objetivo de las circunstancias actuales dentro de ASSITEJ de 1975 hasta 1990. Se ofrecen (por lo menos a veces) un amillaramiento subjetivo de los desarrollos dentro la organización y de los motivos de los a quien se pertenece.

Cuando se lee Volumen II lo que es tan notable es la gran amplitud que ha influido la organización en esta época. El mundo estaba dividido en el este y el oeste—más claro, por supuesto, como simbolizado en Europa por la pared de Berlin. ASSITEJ a veces se parece a una mini Naciones Unidas—y aunque los que estaban implicados trataron vivir en conformidad al espíritu de la constitución y quedarse falta de política, en práctica ellos raramente lo llevaron a cabo. Esto se puede ver en las selecciones, la votación y las elecciones a la Comisión Ejécutiva—y más claramente en el Congreso de Mosco en 1984.

Se puede decir que la historia de Europa desde el fin de la Segunda Guerra hasta los años 1990 también es la historia de ASSITEJ. Hasta los años de 1990, lo demás del mundo atendió y siguió, cuando el poder de decidir adentro de ASSITEJ estaba centrado en Europa—aquí donde el este y el oeste se batieron y tuvo un interés vestido en mantener el equilibrio interna del poder (sin molestar inútilmente de cualquiera influencia "extranjera").

Así, la historia de ASSITEJ es también la historia de los "bloc" políticos internacionales.

PERO absolutamente es un cuento de gente también. Gente visionaria del teatro dedicada, cometida e industriosa, los grandes tan bien como las personalidades excéntricas quien ha dejado sus memorias y su marco y nunca se los olivaran. Y luego hay los cuentos de los pegotes, ésos que de vez en cuando han estado colocados y no han ganado nada más que beneficio personal y otra vez a quien se los olvidan afortunadamente y rápidamente.

Es la historia de la comienza de los centros de ASSITEJ en muchos países distintos, y de los "centros sombrados" que no representaron a nadie, aparte de los individuos quien vio el beneficio de la comunidad de ASSITEJ para si mismos, cuando guardaron al resto de su país y sus colegas afuera de la confraternidad internacional.

Es en este Volumen II que vemos lo que pasó a una organización originalmente progresiva, que gradualmente se estancó y se negó mantener el desarrollo de los tiempos, se dejo atrás, viendo demasiado tarde como el mundo afuera estaba cambiando, y faltó prestar atención a "la escritura en la pared".

Es una época de centralización en ASSITEJ—muchas veces decisiones fueron hecho por unos cuantos (aunque según la Constitución solamente debiera encontrar en novicios de urgencia extremada entre las reuniones de la Comisión Ejécutiva, la Agencia se reunió regularmente, completamente independiente de la Comisión Ejécutiva. En otras palabras, estaban centralizadas y mandadas las deciciones por pocos. Posiblemente había muchas razones por esto, pero sin embargo, el resultado fue la debilitación de una democracia ya frágil en la organización—causando inquietud creciendo y descontento entre los individuos (como tan claramente describe en el libro).

Es la gran realización del escritor que en este volumen documentaron y comentaron sobre los desacuerdos, las luchas políticas, las estropeadas y las retiradas, los individuos importantes y su influencia por lo mejor o lo peor, los motivos (ambos el noble y el innoble), las grandes visiones y los proyectos equivocados. En corto, todo que ha manejado el desarrollo de la organización adelante y cual con esta historia al lado de nosotros y con un foco claro en el porvenir nos falicita hacer cara a las demandas del siglo veintiuno.

Por eso, permite servir como guía para ASSITEJ, esta cita muy aplicable: "No tendremos miedo del porvenir—lo creáramos."

—Firmado por Michael Ramlose

Translated by Anneke Chittim

VORWORT ZU BAND II
von
Michael Ramløse
Verwaltungsdirektor am Theater Fair Play, Denmark
Vorsitzender, Präsidium, 17 ASSITEJ World Congress &
Performing Arts Festival for Young Audiences, 2011
Generalsekretär der ASSITEJ (1990–1996)

Artikel 1 der ASSITEJ-Satzung lautet—und hat schon immer gelautet:
1. Diese Vereinigung beabsichtigt, Theater, Organisationen und Einzelpersonen aus der ganzen Welt, die sich dem Theater für Kinder und Jugendliche widmen, zusammenzuführen.
2. Diese Vereinigung widmet sich künstlerischen, humanitären und pädagogischen Bestrebungen, wobei keine Entscheidung, Handlung oder Erklärung der Vereinigung auf Nationalität, politischer Überzeugung, kultureller Identität, Ethnizität oder Religion beruhen soll.

Der zweite Punkt ist von besonderem Interesse, wenn man Band II des Buches The History of ASSITEJ, geschrieben von Nat Eek in Zusammenarbeit mit Ann Shaw und Katherine Krzys, liest. Hier wird die Bedeutung der politischen Dimension der Organisation im dargelegten Zeitraum besonders unterstrichen.

Die Autoren durchkämmten sorgfältig die Archive (sowohl die offiziellen als auch die privaten), korrespondierten mit einer Vielzahl von Menschen, die die Ereignisse dieser Zeit erlebt haben, sichteten und sortierten eine Fülle von Material, um uns nun einen gut und gründlich recherchierten, objektiven Bericht über die tatsächlichen Gegebenheiten innerhalb der ASSITEJ von 1975 bis 1990 zu präsentieren. Dieser liefert zuweilen auch subjektive Einschätzungen der Entwicklungen innerhalb der Organisation sowie einen Einblick in die Beweggründe der Betroffenen.

Besonders fällt an Band II das enorme Ausmaß, in dem die geopolitische Dimension die Organisation zu dieser Zeit beeinflusst hat, auf. Die Welt war in Ost und West aufgeteilt—mit der Berliner Mauer als offensichtlichstem Symbol in Europa. ASSITEJ gleicht in mancher Hinsicht einer Miniaturausgabe der Vereinten Nationen—obwohl alle Beteiligten sich bemühen, die Satzung zu befolgen und unpolitisch zu sein, können sie dies nur in den seltensten Fällen in die Praxis umsetzen. Deutlich wird das an den Entscheidungen, der Abstimmung sowie der Wahl des Präsidiums und ganz besonders beim Kongress von 1984 in Moskau.

Man kann sagen, dass die Geschichte Europas vom Ende des Zweiten Weltkrieges bis hinein in die 90er Jahre auch die Geschichte der ASSITEJ ist. Bis zu den 90er Jahren folgte der Rest der Welt einfach, während die Beschlussfassung innerhalb der ASSITEJ in Europa erfolgte—hier, wo Ost und West aufeinander trafen und reges Interesse daran hatten, die internen Machtverhältnisse aufrechtzuerhalten (ohne unnötige Störungen von „außerhalb").

Insofern ist die Geschichte der ASSITEJ auch die Geschichte internationaler Blockpolitik.

DENNOCH wird auch eine Geschichte von Menschen erzählt. Von engagierten, fleißigen, vorausschauenden Theaterleuten, von großartigen sowie exzentrischen Persönlichkeiten, die ihre Erinnerungen und Spuren hinterlassen haben und nie vergessen werden. Und dann gibt es noch die Geschichten der „Mitläufer", die ab und an ein Amt innehatten und nicht mehr als persönlichen Nutzen erreichten, die, glücklicherweise und sehr schnell, wieder vergessen wurden.

Es ist die Geschichte der ersten ASSITEJ-Zentren in vielen verschiedenen Ländern und der „Geisterzentren", die bis auf diejenigen, die in einer ASSITEJ-Mitgliedschaft einen persönlichen Vorteil sahen, während sie den Rest ihres Landes und ihrer Kollegen außerhalb des internationalen Zusammenschlusses hielten, niemanden repräsentierten.

In Band II sehen wir, was mit einer ursprünglich progressiven Organisation passierte, die langsam stagnierte und sich weigerte, mit dem Lauf der Dinge Schritt zu halten, zurückblieb, erst viel zu spät erkannte, wie sich die Welt veränderte und es nicht verstand, die Zeichen der Zeit zu lesen.

Es ist eine Zeit der Zentralisierung für die ASSITEJ—Entscheidungen wurden häufig nur von einigen wenigen getroffen—das Büro (welches nach der Satzung zwischen den Sitzungen des Präsidiums nur in äußerst dringen Fällen zusammenkommen sollte) tagte regelmäßig und komplett unabhängig vom Präsidium. Die Beschlussfassung war also zentralisiert und wurde von einer kleinen Zahl Mitglieder kontrolliert. Dafür mag es Gründe gegeben haben, aber nichtsdestotrotz wurde dadurch die ohne schon fragile Demokratie der Organisation weiter geschwächt, was wiederum (wie im Buch sehr deutlich beschrieben) zunehmende Unruhen und Unzufriedenheit unter den Mitgliedern nach sich zog.

Die größte Errungenschaft der Autoren in diesem Band ist Dokumentation und Kommentierung der Unstimmigkeiten, der politischen Machtkämpfe, der Durchbrüche und Rückzüge, der wichtigen Persönlichkeiten und deren Einfluss auf die Wendung zum Besseren oder Schlechteren, der Beweggründe (sowohl der ehrenhaften als auch der niederen), der großen Visionen und der verfehlten Ziele... kurzum, aller Dinge, die die Entwicklung der Organisation vorangetrieben haben und die es uns ermöglichen, uns den Herausforderungen des 21. Jahrhunderts zu stellen, nun, da dieser Abschnitt der Geschichte hinter uns liegt und wir uns ganz klar auf die Zukunft konzentrieren.

Daher sollten dieses treffende Zitat als Leitspruch der ASSITEJ verstehen: „Wir werden die Zukunft nicht fürchten—wir werden sie schaffen!"

/s/ Michael Ramløse (Translated by Gisa Schönfeld)

第 2 巻 の 発刊 に よ せ て

ミケル・ラムローズ

世界アシテジ規約の第1章第1条に次の項目がある。
1) 本協会は児童青少年演劇に携わる全世界の個人、組織、劇団の結合を目的とする。
2) 本協会は芸術的、人道的、教育的活動を目的とし、いかなる政治的、宗教的、人種的主義主張にも関与しない。

ナット・イーク、アン・ショウ、キャサリン・クルジス諸氏の編纂による「アシテジの歴史」第2巻を読み終えて、あらためて上記の第2項がいかに重要であるかを痛感した。

編纂者たちは実に多様な公的、私的文献や緻密な文通連絡により世界アシテジの1975年～1990年間の資料を綿密に蒐集し、なしうる限り完璧で客観的な史実を提供している。

本書によってこの時期の世界の政治情勢がアシテジにいかに大きな影響を与えていたかに驚かされる。当時の世界は「ベルリンの壁」に象徴されるように東西二つに分かれており、アシテジはまさに「ミニ国連」的様相を呈していた。そして上記第2項の精神の具現を願う多くの人々の努力も殆ど成果をあげないままに、1984年のモスクワ大会を迎えた。

第2次世界大戦終結の1945年以降1990年代までのヨーロッパの歴史は、そのままアシテジの歴史ともいえる。つまり1990年代までのアシテジの諸決議はヨーロッパ中心であり、東西の二大勢力が拮抗しつつ争う国際政治の場であった。

しかし、アシテジはまた人間の物語でもある。演劇に献身し、夢を抱く個性的な人々がそこに歴然と足跡を残している。また一時的に関わった無名の多くの人々の物語でもある。

それは世界各国のアシテジセンター発足の歴史であるが、その中には「ゴーストセンター」とよばれる、個人的に私物化されたものもあった。

第2巻を見ると、私たちは発足当初は進歩的であった組織が、次第に沈滞して時代におくれ、危機的兆候に鈍くなり、世界の変化に取残されていった状況を知ることができる。

この時期はまたアシテジの中央集権化の時代で、多くの事項が少数の役員会のみで決定された。規約では、役員会とは定期理事会外の緊急事態に対処する臨時機関であったが、理事会と無関係に定期役員会を開き諸事項を決定した。それは様々な理由があるにせよ、結果として本書が明示した通り、民主主義の停滞と、会員の中に不満と動揺をもたらした。

本書の大きな成果は、そのような不都合な事例を含むあらゆる事実を、編纂者ができる限り正確に提示したことである。不一致、政治的葛藤、前進、後退など、その全てが相俟ってこの組織を発展させる原動力、私たちを21世紀の未来へ向かわせる力となるのだ。

次の言葉をアシテジの指針として進んでいこうではないか：
　　「私たちは未来を恐れず、未来を創っていこう！」

ミケル・ラムローズ（Michael Ramlose)
フェアプレイ劇団代表（デンマーク）、前世界アシテジ事務局長（1990～1996)

　　　　　　　　　　　　　　　　　　—Translated by Fusako Kurahara

INTRODUCTION

Sources

Shaw wrote in her original document on the first years of ASSITEJ:[1] "Writing the history of the first thirty years in the life of an international organization is a daunting task. Much of the documentation needed has either vanished or rests in the files of individuals and national centers. . . . Much of this history has been written while doing research in both Eek's and Shaw's documents in the ASSITEJ Archives in the Library at Arizona State University."

Eek began his association with ASSITEJ in 1965 at its Founding Conference in Paris, continued it through his Presidency to 1975, and has attended all but one of the World Congresses up to and including that in Montreal, Canada in 2005. Only the Moscow Congress of 1984 was missed.

Shaw first attended ASSITEJ in 1972 at the Canada/USA joint Congress in Albany, New York, USA. As a member of the US Center she attended the Spanish Congress in 1978. Then as President of ASSITEJ/USA, she began attending all ASSITEJ meetings in 1978 as an elected Member of the EXCOM and one of its Vice-Presidents. She went off the EXCOM in 1988, but continued attending all the Congresses up to and including Montreal, Canada in 2005.

These attendances provide a compendium of personally witnessed activities and events of ASSITEJ International. Between Eek and Shaw, the years of ASSITEJ from 1965–75 and 1978–2005 have been personally witnessed, and all of the Assemblies and Congresses have been attended. Joyce Doolittle (Canada) who was Vice-President from 1972–1981 has been relied upon extensively to fill in the years 1975–1981. Notes and Minutes taken by Patricia Snyder as President of the US Center during 1975–1978 and the Archives of Harold Oaks during 1987–1990 have been extremely helpful.

The authors specifically wish to express their profound gratitude to the following people who were involved significantly in ASSITEJ, and who have both contributed to and helped edit the manuscript for Volume II: Michael Ramløse for his instant responses, corrections of facts, and eternal support; to Michael FitzGerald for his critical reading of the MS and cheering us on to the end; to Harold Oaks for the excellence of his files; to Moses Goldberg for his critical reading of the MS and appropriate corrections; to

Joyce Doolittle for completing the Canadian contributions in the '70s; to Fusako Kurahara for her finding and translating the information needed from ASSITEJ/Japan; to Meike Fechner for her finding, copying, and forwarding of precious materials from the German Archives; to Galina Kolosova for her translations and her biographies of Russian leaders; to friend Gerald Tyler, son of the first ASSITEJ President, for his instant finding of biographical sources for British leaders; to Nena Stenius for her account of the harrows of planning international meetings; to Marjorie E. MacLean, Vickie Ireland, Paul Harman, Patricia Snyder, Niclas Malmcrona, and Iviča Simič for their quick responses to a myriad of questions; and to all those who responded to our constant e-mails—the miraculous method of contact in the 21st Century. Without the willing assistance of all these people, and many others un-named, Volume II could never have been written.

Organizational Pattern of the History

Overview: This History ultimately will be in three volumes. Volume I covered the first ten (10) years of the existence of ASSITEJ, the time when Eek was an officer and most active in the organization, and was published in April 2008. Now Volume II covers the next fifteen years of ASSITEJ, the time when Shaw was an officer and most active in the organization, and has been published in 2011.

These two volumes have been written in chronological order starting with the early informal meetings of 1957. They continue on through 1990, the first twenty-five years of the existence of ASSITEJ, and conclude in 1990 with the Congress in Stockholm, Sweden. Volume III will cover the final fifteen years of this History, ending with the Canadian Congress in Montreal in 2005. Then it will up to other writers and scholars to continue the History of ASSITEJ, as well as correct our errors.

Volume II covers all the major meetings as well as the International Congresses. The major agenda items and the ensuing discussions at each gathering are included, a list of the conference activities, and the election results of each congress are listed in detail where possible.

There is a narrative of all the Executive Committee and Bureau meetings over these years, as well as the results of those meetings. Anything significant that occurred between meetings is also listed, which includes major world events that affected the tenor of the meetings and the activities of ASSITEJ.

Occasionally there are Interim sections between major meetings that describe the activities of the Association as well as the state of the world. At the end of every few years there is a Summary listing the salient points, achievements, failures, disappointments of that time in the progressive history of the Association. Comments on historical events and personal experience and observations are added primarily in the Summaries whenever pertinent and appropriate.

If the reader wishes to get a complete but simplified overview of the History of ASSITEJ, it is recommended that one should go from Summary to Summary, thus avoiding many of the finer details. Hopefully the reader will then want to go back and read this History in greater detail.

Volume II of this history concludes with a summing up of the past and future of ASSITEJ as of 1990, its current status at that time, and its possible future direction.

Appendices: Separate Appendices list the dates of meetings, locations, major individual participants, and countries participating. Also in the Appendices are copies of the original and current Constitutions of ASSITEJ (1965 and 1990 as amended), plus other items too lengthy to include in the body of the History. Of particular interest is the continuing listing of the Formation and Suspension of the National Centers.

Conference Titling: Consistency in terminology has been difficult in that many different terms were used interchangeably and in some cases indiscriminately. Many times this was a result of improper translation. In terms of titling, the archives show a mixture of terms—conference, general assembly, congress, world congress. The initial meetings to form ASSITEJ were called conferences. Since the organizational structure of ASSITEJ was patterned after the United Nations, the word General Assembly began being used for the proposed future gatherings. That in turn was abandoned for the term International Congress by the Prague meeting in 1966.

For clarity in this History, the Paris meeting is called the Constitutional Conference. Meetings after Paris are designated as International Congresses, and then World Congresses after 1987 in Adelaide, Australia. The term World Congress emerged with the Adelaide meeting, undoubtedly prompted by the incredible increase of national centers around the world promoted by the Nordic Centers as well as the Centers of Australia, Japan, and the USA, plus the fact it was the first Congress being held in the Asian hemisphere. The governing rules of the Association are called both the Statutes and the Constitution.

The meetings within a Congress have been called Plenary Sessions, General Assemblies, Discussion Sessions, etc. For clarity the term General Assembly has been used whenever all the delegates at the Congress met together.

Abbreviations: To avoid writing out terms each time, the following abbreviations have been used. As countries were consolidated, separated, and/or changed in name, the new name has always been used with a single identification of the old name at the time of the change. Then the new name is used consistently. For example: USSR became Russia, Georgia, Ukraine, etc.; Czechoslovakia became the Czech Republic and Slovakia; Ceylon became Sri Lanka; FGR and GDR became Germany; and Yugoslavia became Croatia, Serbia, etc.

Participants are first mentioned by their full name, and after that the narrative primarily uses only their last name. Usually no formal titles are used, only the titles of the elected officers of the ASSITEJ Association.

ASU—Arizona State University
ATA—American Theatre Association
EXCOM (1965–1990) or EC (after 1990)—Executive Committee
FGR—Federal Republic of Germany
GDR or DDR—German Democratic Republic
UNESCO—United Nations Educational, Scientific, and Cultural Organization
IATA/AITA—International Association of Theatre Amateurs
ITI—International Theatre Institute, a division of UNESCO
TYA—Theatre for Young Adults
UNIMA—International Association of Puppeteers
USSR—Union of Soviet Socialist Republics
USA—United States of America

Meeting Narrative: Each meeting's narration begins with a listing in bold type of dates, locations, officers, participants, countries represented, members absent, and special items of information. The notes on the meeting itself usually follow this order: agenda, discussion, motions or decisions, special presentations, special events or performances seen, and finally a brief evaluation.

Summaries: Personal brief biographies, anecdotes, historic notes, comments and evaluations on the meetings and performances presented are all given in the Summaries to put the actions taken in proper perspective. More complete Biographies of the current ASSITEJ World Leaders in Volume II (1976–1990) are in Appendix B.

Notes: Notes are placed at the end to avoid interrupting the narrative.

Authors' Caveat: This History is written from the perspective of three citizens of the United States of America, and should be judged accordingly. However, the authors have tried to be as objective as possible in their observations and judgments, while keeping an international perspective.

Also, we have tried to keep the narrative human and personal, and any errors of fact are certainly not deliberate but those of the authors.

The authors hope that Volume II will continue to become a rich and accurate resource of the history of an important international theatre organization, and we are grateful for the privilege of attending the actual events and recording their history in writing.

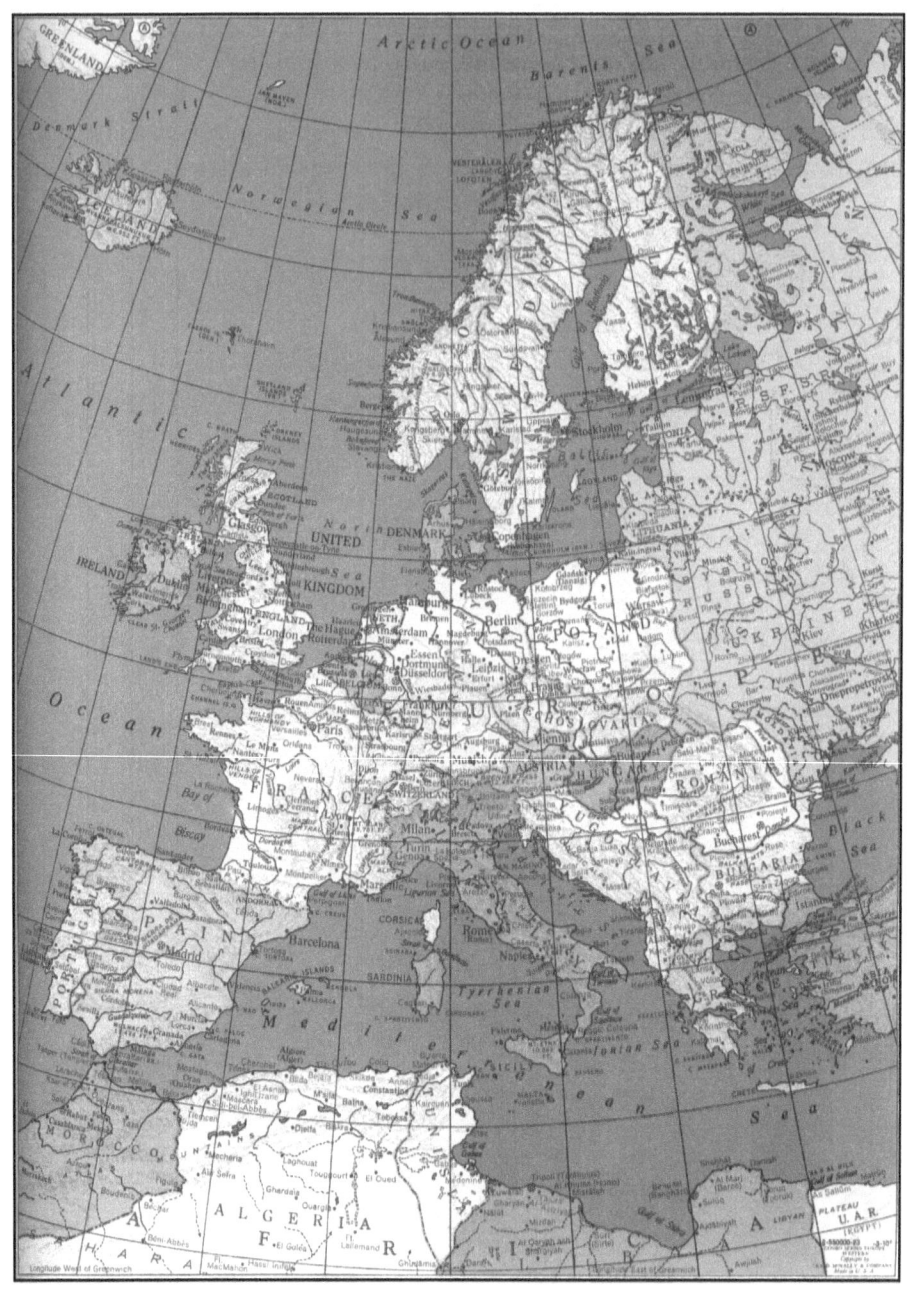

Europe in the 1980s

PART III:

THE EUROPEAN CONSOLIDATION
(1975–1984)

The World at the Time

The decade from 1970 to 1979 was essentially a period of disillusionment. In the USA from 1975 on there were gasoline shortages, a sluggish economy, and environmental problems which led to slow growth. The Watergate scandals forced President Richard Nixon's resignation in 1974, and his country's moral and economic leadership were being questioned world-wide.

With the death of Mao Tse Tung and Chou en Lai, China entered a period of power struggles between the orthodox Maoists and the pragmatists. By 1976 the pragmatists had won, and the "Gang of Four" was arrested.

The conservative, colonialist government of Portugal was overthrown in 1974. In Greece the military dictatorship was defeated, and Sweden voted out its Socialist government after 44 years of being in power. All of non-Communist Europe was under democratic rule after free elections were held in Spain in 1976, seven months after the death of Francisco Franco. However, the European Economic Community (EEC) had continuing monetary problems.

In the arts, traditional modes in painting, architecture, and music returned to popular and critical attention in the 1970s. The pictorial emphases in neorealist and photorealist painting, the return of many architects to detail, decoration, and traditional natural materials, and the concern with ordered structure in musical composition were novel experiences for artistic consumers after the exhaustion of experimental possibilities. However, the new conservative styles were able to co-exist with modernist works with variety and tolerance. [2]

The Status of ASSITEJ—June 1975

At the Vth International Congress in Berlin, GDR in April of 1975 Vladimir Adamek (Czechoslovakia) was elected President of ASSITEJ for the next three years (1975-1978). Following that election Nat Eek stepped out of active participation in the organization as well as his attendance at the EXCOM Meetings representing the USA. He was succeeded by the election of Patricia Snyder as the President of the US Center for ASSITEJ. Eek continued his attendance at the Congresses every three years up to 2005, only missing the Moscow Congress in 1984. However, he remained a dues-paying Member of the US Center and in turn a Member of ASSITEJ International.

At the Berlin Congress in 1975 it was announced that there were 28 official Centers for ASSITEJ. Volume I of this History listed them as below. The Czech Bulletin No. 3 issued in June 1975, two months after the Berlin International Congress, listed them as below.[3]

The spaces with asterisks (*) were not listed as active centers. For example, Argentina was missing from the Czech Bulletin list. From past history some of these centers were not dues-paying, but did have a corresponding member as well as an official address. Others may not have been credited with their dues yet, and were not listed.

It seemed best to combine the two lists of national centers as published in Volume I and the Czech Bulletin. The Bulletin has been consistently accurate, and along with the official one from the Vth Congress, there were a total of 33 centers as of June 1975.

Volume I	Czech Bulletin #3 (June 1975)
Algeria	Algeria
Argentina	*
Australia	Australia
Austria	Austria
Belgium	Belgium
*	Bulgaria
Canada	Canada
Cuba	Cuba
Czechoslovakia	Czechoslovakia
Denmark	Denmark
Federal German Republic (FGR)	Federal German Republic (FGR)
Finland	Finland
France	France
German Democratic Republic (GDR)	German Democratic Republic (GDR)
*	Great Britain
Hungary	Hungary
Ireland	Ireland
Iran	Iran
Israel	Israel
Italy	Italy
Japan	Japan
Netherlands	Netherlands
Peru	Peru

Portugal	Portugal
Romania	Romania
Spain	Spain
Sri Lanka	Sri Lanka
*	Switzerland
*	Turkey
USA	USA
USSR	USSR
Venezuela	Venezuela
*	Yugoslavia

When President Vladimir Adamek (Czechoslovakia) came into office at the Vth International Congress in Berlin, GDR in April 1975, he approached his leadership with caution, incisiveness, professionalism, and fairness as long as it did not conflict with political survival.[4]

He immediately had plans to create Commissions, to organize a Working Agenda, and the desire to professionalize the Association.

Since he spoke French fluently, he and Secretary General Rose-Marie Moudoués (France) formed a close association, and soon the Bureau became the dominant decision maker for ASSITEJ. Of course, all of their decisions were presented to the EXCOM for approval, but the EXCOM never reversed any of them. This manner of management was more in keeping with the traditional "Eastern Bloc" approach, and continued through Moudoués' tenure until 1990.

Paris, France

**1975
BUREAU MEETING
Paris, France/13–18 October 1975**

The Bureau of ASSITEJ met in Paris, France on 13–18 October 1975. Vladimir Adamek (Czechoslovakia) presided as President, Ilse Rodenberg (GDR) as 1st Vice President, Joyce Doolittle (Canada) as 2nd Vice President, Maria Sunyer (Spain) as 3rd Vice President, Rose-Marie Moudoués (France) as Secretary General, and Ion Lucian (Romania) as Treasurer. Also, attending was Don Raffaello Lavagna (Vatican, Italy) as an Observer.[5]

President Vladimir Adamek outlined his program for the next three years. It would be the function of the Bureau to "prepare all administrative and organizational measures for solving the respective problems" of the organization, which in turn would be presented to the EXCOM for their approval and action. Accordingly, he stated that all previous appointments were cancelled and established the following committees with their Chairs.
- Publications—Ion Lucian
- Contact with IATA,UNIMA—Joyce Doolittle
- Statutory and Editorial—Vladimir Adamek
- Terminology—Rose-Marie Moudoués
- Creative Themes—Maria Sunyer
- Coordination on Activities of National Centers and Publicity—Ilse Rodenberg

For the sake of simple identification, this History has standardized the names of the Commissions as: Publications, Liaison w/IATA, UNIMA, & UNESCO, Statutes, Terminology, Creative Activity & Themes, and Promotion & Publicity. Although the Minutes indicate variations in the titles over time, their charges remained basically the same.

Adamek then presented a draft of a plan to formalize the inviting of single representatives of national centers to attend future meetings of the EXCOM with an advisory vote, instead of nominating permanent advisors or co-options. They also discussed various organizational problems, and requested the Secretary General to put their solutions into action.

There were reports from Rodenberg on her visits to Denmark, FGR, and Yugoslavia, and from Moudoués on hers to Czechoslovakia. There was also discussion on how to speed up the acceptance procedure of new centers.

They also requested the Secretary General and the Treasurer to demand the settlement of all debts of the individual centers, as well as asking them to increase their subscriptions to *The Revue*.

There was unanimous agreement in requesting the Centers to send in their suggestions for increasing the intensity of activities of ASSITEJ as an organization by February 1976. The purpose would be to aim towards high artistic standards of theatrical art for children and young people and the development of those standards.

Under New Business, they approved having the next EXCOM meeting for 10 days in Milan and Rome, Italy in May 1976. The Bureau and the new Committees would also meet at the same time. Also, specific representatives from Algeria, Belgium, Denmark, Finland, Hungary, and Iran would be invited to attend the meetings. Other centers would be invited to future meetings. They decided to have a Bureau meeting in France in the fall of 1976 to prepare the program for the EXCOM Meeting in Canada in 1977. They also selected the theme of the Spanish Congress in 1978 as "Search for New Aesthetic Forms in Theatre for Children and Young People."

Lastly, Adamek presented a report on discussions with representative George Malvius of the International Association of Amateur Theatres (IATA) in Prague. The result was that those members of ASSITEJ who were most interested in the inclusion of "creative dramatics" as part of ASSITEJ, should instead join IATA, while ASSITEJ would concentrate on the theatrical activities of "grown-ups".

Under **News from the Centers:**
- **FGR** reported their World Festival of Theatres for Children took place in Hamburg, FGR on 21-28 September 1975. Productions came from Israel, Scotland, Poland, Yugoslavia, Iran, USSR, Japan, and Turkey.
- **USSR** reported that Natalya Satz had been named "National Artist of the USSR".
- **Great Britain** announced in honor of the 10th Anniversary of ASSITEJ a six week "Autumn Season" of productions was celebrated throughout the country.
- **France** announced that the National Theatre of Chaillot in cooperation with the French ATEJ had presented plays for young people from Lyon, Nancy, and Caen.
- **The Czech Center** reported a celebration of the 40th Anniversary of the permanent professional theatre for young people in Czechoslovakia, with a variety of performances attended by Rose-Marie Moudoués and Natalya Satz.

Rome, Italy

1976
EXECUTIVE COMMITTEE MEETING
Milan and Rome, Italy/8–16 May 1976

The Executive Committee of ASSITEJ met in Milan and Rome, Italy on 8–16 May 1976. Vladimir Adamek (Czechoslovakia) presided as President, Ilse Rodenberg (GDR) as 1st Vice President, Joyce Doolittle (Canada) as 2nd Vice President, Maria Sunyer (Spain) as 3rd Vice President, Rose-Marie Moudoués (France) as Secretary General, and Ion Lucian (Romania) as Treasurer.

Other members attending were: Victor Georgiev (Bulgaria), Benito Biotto (Italy), Patricia Snyder (USA), Ivan Voronov (USSR) for Natalia Satz, and Zvjezdana Ladika (Yugoslavia). Don Raffaello Lavagna (Vatican, Italy) stood in for Benito Biotto as the Italian representative when Biotto was absent.[6]

Observers who had been invited to attend were: Algeria, Belgium, Finland, Iran, Denmark, and Hungary. Iran, Denmark, and Hungary accepted the invitation, but at the last minute Iran and Hungary were not able to attend. Jean-Yves Gaudreault (Canada) was also welcomed as an Observer.

As a result of the election at the Vth International Congress in Berlin in April, 1975, only eleven centers had been elected to the EXCOM, although the Constitution allowed a total of fifteen. Although nominated, Great Britain and the Netherlands failed to get a majority of the votes. Things had been politically manipulated by some centers voting for less than fifteen centers (See Volume I, p. 284)

1st Meeting of the EXCOM

At the request of President Adamek, Vice-President Ilse Rodenberg thanked the Italian Center for hosting their meeting, and special written greetings came from Past Presidents Tyler and Shakh-Azizov. They then approved the Minutes of the EXCOM meetings in Berlin.

Treasurer's Report: Ion Lucian distributed copies of the Financial Report listing assets and expenditures, indicating that many countries do not state what their checks were for. Turkey, Peru, and Sri Lanka were cited for non-payment of dues.

He also cited that the USA had not yet paid for the many copies of the *Review* which they had received. Moudoués commented that both ITI and UNIMA have trouble collecting dues, but stated that if they enforced the required payments, they would have many fewer members. Their advice was not to exclude the non-paying members, but deprive them of a vote, or nomination for office. Finally she suggested waiting a month, and then writing the USA for immediate payment. The Report was accepted.

Secretary General's Report: given in two parts—matters requiring a vote, and miscellaneous discussion.

The 6 Commissions: these were created by Adamek with the approval of the Bureau to respond to questions raised by the various meetings in the course of regular business. Moudoués defined them as follows:

Statutes: to examine and propose changes in the Constitution as required.
Terminology: to create a glossary of frequently used theatre terminology, define in translation to avoid misunderstandings.
Publications: all ASSITEJ printed and published matter.
Liaison w/IATA, UNIMA, & UNESCO: specifically with UNIMA and IATA. Especially defining the parameters of theatre for young audiences and creative dramatics.
Creative Activity & Themes: most specifically Spain in 1978.
Promotion & Publicity: to foster communication among centers, and encourage the founding of new centers.

The EXCOM approved the creation of these Commissions.

Moudoués then reported the recommendations of recent Bureau meetings:
- VP Rodenberg had represented ASSITEJ at recent meetings in Šibonek, Yugoslavia and Hamburg (FGR). She also visited Denmark to help in establishing the Danish Center.
- Doolittle suggested enlarging the EXCOM from 11 to 15, but they accepted Adamek's suggestion that they invite representatives of other member centers to fill those four places.
- The Bureau in Paris also recommended inviting Members of Honor to all Congresses, and all centers have been asked for their opinions. Moudoués also asked that news of all festivals be sent to the Secretariat. The EXCOM delegated powers to the Bureau to accept new centers when the EXCOM was not meeting.

All recommendations made by the Bureau were approved by the EXCOM.

Doolittle raised the question of the place of Honorary Members in the organization. In The Hague Congress Past President Gerald Tyler (Great Britain) was named Honorary President and didn't that entitle him to hold a place on the Executive Committee, unless the title was revoked by the General Assembly? Adamek and Moudoués stated that the title was for life, but it did not carry a seat at every meeting. This ended the discussion.

Annual Reports: Moudoués reported receiving annual reports from Czechoslovakia, Hungary, USSR, Australia, GDR, Bulgaria, Canada, France, Romania, and Spain. She reminded everyone that it was the responsibility of each center to send in this annual report in 30 copies.

New Centers:
- **Japan** had an association of professional dramatists, and had requested a copy of the Statutes, which had been sent.
- **Argentina** had not yet sent in the Statutes of their Center.
- **Mexico** had made contact through Galya Kolosova (USSR) which seemed promising.
- **Egypt** had been contacted by Moudoués through their Ministry of Culture, but had received no further correspondence.
- **Ireland** had not corresponded for some time.
- Conversations with **Poland** were continuing through Moudoués and Henry Jurkowski (Poland) of UNIMA.
- Doolittle had received a letter of inquiry from **Greece**, which she forwarded to Moudoués, who in turn sent the necessary information.

ITI Conference: Moudoués as the ASSITEJ representative attended a 5-day ITI conference on "Problems of the Third World". She led a session of theatre for youth, which was unknown in most Third World Countries. Most had a culture imposed on them by the colonialists; their indigenous theatre was yet to appear. Usually there were strong oral and dance traditions which could be the starting point for their theatres.

Moudoués proposed further collaboration with ITI to pursue theatre for young audiences in the Third World, and the EXCOM approved her involvement.

VIth International Congress plans: Sunyer announced that the VIth Congress would be held in Spain in the spring of 1978, and spoke to the theoretical, practical, and public relations aspects of the Congress plans.

The theme chosen was "Research for new aesthetic levels of theatre for children." A competition has begun for a poster designed by a child. The performing companies would come from Spain, with one invited from Europe and one invited from the USA. On the first day there would be conference sessions in the morning and performances in the afternoon. This same pattern would be repeated for most days. As an experiment delegates would be grouped by language hoping to promote more spontaneous discussion.

Each center would be invited to make a visual presentation using film, video tape, and there would be optional visits to observe creative drama.

In public relations there would be a reception, two luncheons, and a visit to a 17th century theatre at the end of the Congress. The Congress would last six days in the first week of June 1978.

Commission on Statutes: Adamek (Chair), Moudoués, Snyder, and Voronov: Adamek reported that they plan to examine the text of the Constitution in each of the three languages, in order to update and adjust the documents.

Commission on Terminology: Moudoués (Chair), Tyler, Voronov: Moudoués reported that Tyler was trying to find a younger member from Great Britain to take his place, but would continue to serve in the meantime. Each center has been requested to make a specific list of terms that pose problems in translation, and she would like to receive them in October for the Bureau meeting.

Commission on Publications: Lucian presented the following suggestions:
1. Send a letter to all Centers asking for information on their current publications.
2. Encourage co-operation with existing publications.
3. Invite all Centers to publish their annual Reports in the form of a magazine.

4. Establish an international library.
5. All publications need to be sent to the Secretariat for archival documentation.

There was further discussion about *The Review* of ASSITEJ published by the French Center. Moudoués indicated that 4,000 subscriptions were needed to sustain it financially. At the present time there were 500 subscriptions in France, a probable 100 in the USA, and 120 in all other countries. Italy suggested requiring a fixed number of subscriptions per center, but the proposal was opposed by the EXCOM.

Adamek reported on the compilation of "Who is Who in ASSITEJ", and cited the need for biographies on Charlotte Chorpenning (USA), Nat Eek (USA), Hanswalter Gossmann (FGR), Sara Spencer (USA), Patricia Snyder (USA), and Zvjezdana Ladika (Yugoslavia). He also stated that the *Czech Bulletin* would come out only once a year, but would continue to be free.

Moudoués reported that the book about "best plays" was at the printers, and new material for *The Review* needed to be received by December 1. Rodenberg reported that the history book on children's theatre being published in the GDR would cover 26 countries, 120 theatres, and have 144 pictures and 250 photographs.

Commission on Liaison w/IATA, UNIMA, & UNESCO: Doolittle (Chair), Georgiev, Ladika, Inga Juul and José Géal as advisors: Doolittle stated that this Commission was primarily a result of inquiries from IATA, and recommended that it:
1. Develop a calendar of national festivals and events
2. Create a bibliography and survey of creative dramatic activity in each member nation.

It was vitally important that these three organizations make contact with each other within their own countries. The audiences are the same but the art is different. It was finally suggested that a comparison of the constitutions of the three organizations be made to identify common goals and problems.

Commission on Creative Activity & Themes for Congresses: Sunyer (Chair), Lucian, Rodenberg: Gaudreault (Canada) was welcomed as an observer: Sunyer gave the following report announcing the proposed theme "What do we consider to be a theatre of high [artistic] level?" for the 1978 Congress in Spain. Questions arising from the discussion were:
1. What is the role of dramatization of classics; can they help in a developing theatre?
2. What are the advantages and disadvantages of the classics?

3. What are the responsibilities of new drama for children?
4. Can we present reality without reticence [censorship]?
5. Are we looking for entertainment or education?

After considerable discussion the theme was reworded and accepted as "A search for new forms in a theatre of high quality."

Commission on Promotion & Publicity: Rodenberg (Chair): Rodenberg reported the need for more information from each of the centers, and more information from Third World countries that are just starting theatres. The brochure about ASSITEJ, distributed at the Berlin Congress is a start, but there needs to be more. Snyder is preparing a slide show which includes slides from all the centers. Doolittle was instructed to inquire about its availability.

There was considerable discussion about "Why ASSITEJ?", and it was decided that its main function was to help other countries found theatres and in turn to create ASSITEJ Centers.

Future Work of ASSITEJ: President Adamek made a major speech outlining the purposes of ASSITEJ and its function in creating and sustaining other national centers.

To clear up the confusion between children's theatre and creative dramatics he stated that those involved in creative drama should join IATA rather than ASSITEJ. Everyone from all forms of theatre helped establish ASSITEJ, but now after ten years it was time to concentrate on creating the highest form of theatre, professional and amateur. The ASSITEJ Statutes specify this concept as our common interest. If this concentration is not paramount, in some countries ASSITEJ could be dissolved, because of its multiplicity of interests and organization.

Considerable discussion followed the President's speech, with Lucian summing up the result. The only direction ASSITEJ can go is "to support professional theatre for children, but we should not eliminate amateur groups, but help them to raise the quality of their work."[7]

When the EXCOM reconvened they turned to a variety of questions.

It was suggested that each center bring 30 posters to the Spanish Congress, and then exchange them among the other centers. Snyder requested 5-10 slides from other centers along with the appropriate text, so these could become archival. Iran and Algeria asked for visiting lecturers. Canada asked for a directory of names of resource people to be compiled by each center.

Future Meetings: The EXCOM approved the following meetings:
- Bureau Meeting in Sophia, Bulgaria in October 1976
- EXCOM Meeting in Banff & Calgary, Canada in May 1977
- Tentative Bureau Meeting in Paris, 1977

- Tentative Bureau Meeting in Paris in January or February 1978, prior to the next Congress in Spain

The EXCOM approved the meetings in Bulgaria and Canada.

2nd Meeting of the EXCOM

The next meeting of the EXCOM involved the presentation of Reports from various national centers.

Denmark: Inga Juul reported that Denmark has 40 theatres for young people, but they are individualized by being created to perform for specific age groups. Creative drama has its own amateur organization. When asked she replied that most of these companies used professional actors. The Danish Center provides workshops for the various companies to help raise their quality. Finally the Danish Center was in the process of reorganization.

In the discussion which followed Adamek pointed out that some people feel that ASSITEJ only wants formal theatre and is too traditional, but work in the schools with professional actors is within the province of ASSITEJ. When Juul indicated that workshops, lectures, and demonstrations in theatre for children were important to have, Moudoués replied that such workshops must be requested from the Bureau in Paris in order to be considered as an ASSITEJ Workshop.[8]

Hungary: A representative from Hungary was not present, but a 30-page paper had been sent to the Secretariat. It reported that 70% of the members of their national center were actors, so in 1977 they will be holding a meeting of actors from many countries. Next season their magazine "Friends of the Theatre" will focus on theatre for children. There will also be a children's theatre festival in their country, and one of their companies is performing at the Šibenik Festival in Yugoslavia in June. They also plan a photograph exhibition of productions from ASSITEJ companies.

French Canada: Observer Jean-Yves Gaudreault of Montreal was invited to report on theatre in French Canada. He stated there are four categories of company currently playing:
1. Companies of adults offering some plays for children
2. Professional companies specializing in theatre for young audiences. The two most notable are La Nouvelle Compagnie, whose theatre children attend in Montreal, and Les Pissenlits, which plays only in elementary schools and tours all of Canada.
3. Marionette Theatre.
4. Amateur and semi-professional groups performing for children.

He has also proposed a national Theatre for Children to the Quebec Minister of Culture.

After the report when asked for his major problem, he replied that since there are no theatrical traditions, it is difficult for the artist to agree upon basic criteria. Lucian added that he had worked with their theatre, and had found them serious and professional.

Italian Center: Three major problems: organization, artistic, and planning for the future. Several large theatres who do not belong to ASSITEJ receive the largest governmental subsidies. As usual a few people do all the work. Moudoués commented that the work she had seen in Italy was excellent with fine acting. High quality is possible with minimal resources. Even small children paid attention to the actions on the stage.

In discussion Moudoués still felt that children should not perform for children. Lucian commented that the countries that complain most about lack of subsidy and facilities are often the countries that have creative dramatics in abundance. Could subsidies be withheld from theatre for children because the bureaucrats can say "but you have theatre [in creative dramatics]!"?

Sunyer commented that in Spain the budgets for professional theatre and creative dramatics are totally separate in philosophy and substance. One budget comes from the Ministry of Culture, the other from the Ministry of Education.

Miscellaneous: When asked for a list of names and addresses from the Berlin Congress, Rodenberg replied that they were not available. When Sunyer was asked for such a list at the Spanish Congress, she replied that it would be available. Moudoués noted that Australia had asked for an ASSITEJ ID Card for travel abroad to facilitate the individual being identified to other ASSITEJ centers. If the Board approved, Moudoués would see that such cards were made available.

Voting proxies were discussed, and Moudoués replied they were permitted as long as the request was in writing, and requested far enough in advance of the next Congress.

It was announced that Ladika was the new head of the Yugoslavia Center, and Hans Snoek (Netherlands) in a letter introduced the new head of the Netherlands Center [name not included in the Minutes].

On a final note President Adamek asked various members of the EXCOM to reply in giving thanks to the various Italian authorities for their hospitality.

The last meeting was adjourned. However, the Doolittle document did not indicate the separate days of the meetings nor the date on which the meeting ended.

1976
BUREAU MEETING
Sophia, Bulgaria/4–5 October 1976

The Bureau of ASSITEJ met in Sophia, Bulgaria on 4–5 October 1976. Vladimir Adamek (Czechoslovakia) presided as President, Ilse Rodenberg (GDR) as 1st Vice President, Joyce Doolittle (Canada) as 2nd Vice President, Maria Sunyer (Spain) as 3rd Vice President, Rose-Marie Moudoués (France) as Secretary General, and Ion Lucian (Romania) as Treasurer.[9]

EXCOM Members Shaun Hennessey (Great Britain), Ottorino Negri (Italy), Inga Juul (Denmark), Ivan Voronov (USSR), Zvjezdana Ladika (Yugoslavia), and Patricia Snyder (USA) all were in attendance at the Festival, but were not allowed to attend the Bureau meetings.

Sophia, Bulgaria

President Vladimir Adamek established the Agenda to deal with the following problems:
- Accepted the Minutes of the meeting of the EXCOM and the Bureau in Italy in 1975.
- Accepted the Treasurer's Report and urged him to collect past dues from Algeria, Israel, Sri Lanka, and Turkey. Snyder reported that 19 countries had yet to pay their dues.

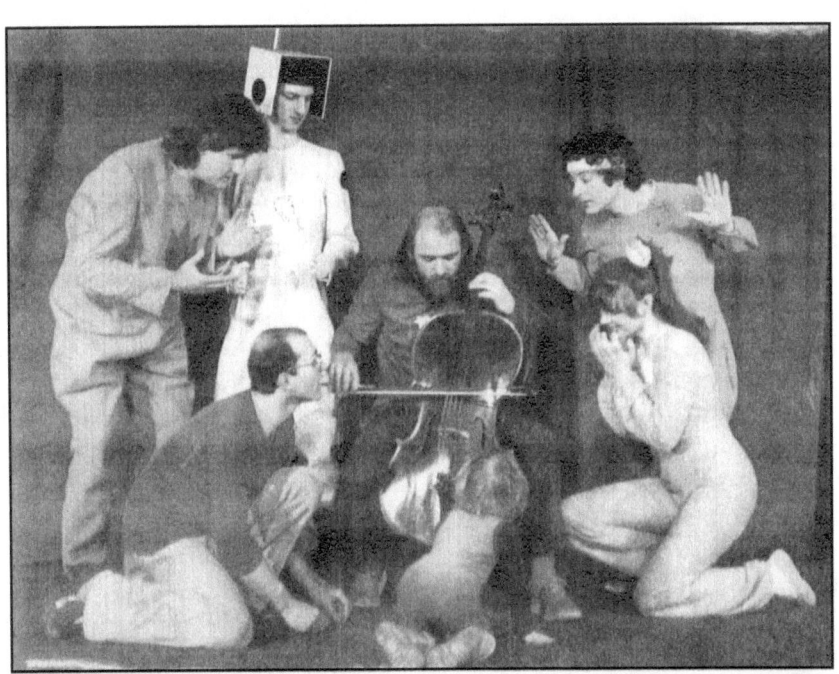

Performances seen of the Children's Theatre of Bulgaria by the EXCOM at their meeting in Sophia, Bulgaria in October 1976. Courtesy of the Archives, ASU, AZ, USA.

Secretary General's Report: In Moudoués' Report she cited the following problems with some of the national centers: The Irish Center is practically non-existent. The Belgian and Netherlands Centers are both in a state of reorganization, and the new Chair of the Belgian Center is Edgard Verhoven. Both the Mexican and Japanese Centers have established contact. The new Chair of the USSR Center is Natalya Satz. The new Chair of the Yugoslavia Center is Zvjezdana Ladika. The Swiss ASSITEJ Center has been reported as excellent. Several people including the Secretary General attended their recent festival.

The new Constitution as approved at the Berlin Congress will be mailed within a short time. She will also be issuing a new list of ASSITEJ Centers.

She was also entrusted with the continuing correspondence with the Committee on Youth of the ITI. In addition she will represent ASSITEJ in an ITI Third World Conference in Paris. Lastly, the Secretariat was to urge each Center's compliance with sending in a Report on their activities in 1976, and the Secretariat was to distribute 60 "free" copies of *The Review* in an effort to boost subscriptions among the Centers.

EXCOM Meeting in Canada: Doolittle's Report on the up-coming EXCOM in Canada was presented. 12-13 May 1977 would be in Calgary; 14-16 May would be in Banff; and 17 May would be in Calgary. 17-23 May the EXCOM would travel to and stay in Ottawa for the Festival. Since the second half of the meetings will be held in Ottawa in conjunction with the CCDYA conference, Doolittle was unable to make arrangements in Montreal. Accordingly, the US Center would not be co-hosting the EXCOM Meeting. Subsequently, Monday was added to the sites of the EXCOM Meeting in Canada.

The Secretary General was instructed to send all the pertinent materials from the recent Bureau Meeting to the Members of the EXCOM so they could discuss and approve of the recommended decisions. She was also to invite representatives of Australia, Cuba, Israel, Peru, Sri Lanka, and Venezuela to attend the Canadian EXCOM Meeting and to present a report on the activities of their respective centers.[10]

VIth International Congress: Sunyer presented the proposed program for the Spanish Congress in 1978 which included the Bureau Meeting, a meeting of all the Commissions, sessions of the General Assembly, and the meetings of the old and new EXCOM. It would be up to the Spanish Center to determine the rules for the intended exhibitions.

The Bureau then heard reports from the various Committees:
- Rodenberg showed examples of publicity brochures, and urged a Calendar of ASSITEJ Events for 1979, and asked each center to send in 2-3 colored slides.

- Sunyer reported that no replies had been received related to the proposed discussions at the 1978 Congress.
- Doolittle reported on the continuing correspondence and relationships with UNIMA and IATA, which essentially stated that continued communication was desirable by all parties concerned.
- Moudoués reported that the Terminology Committee should only concern itself with specialized terms of theatre for children and youth, not those of a general theatrical character.
- Lucian reported that he had not heard from Past President Eek in relationship to the preparation of the "Ten Years of ASSITEJ" document.
- Adamek reported that the Statutes Committee had both official French and English versions of the Constitution and the Russian version was being prepared by the Soviet Center.
- The Bureau decided that all Committee correspondence should go through the Secretariat.

Miscellaneous business: The Bureau accepted the Soviet invitation for an EXCOM meeting in the USSR in February of 1978, taking place at a time of a festival, and would last 6-10 days. Also, they entrusted the GDR Center to prepare a drawing of a "Membership Card in ASSITEJ" for identification of single members of ASSITEJ traveling abroad.

News of the centers: There were the following reports:
- **Canada** had recently published the book "The Child and Dramatic Expression."
- **Bulgaria** reported on its October Festival 1976 for Children and Youth, and commented that the most important event was hosting ASSITEJ representatives from Canada, Cuba, Czechoslovakia, Denmark, France, FGR, GDR, Great Britain, Hungary, Italy, Yugoslavia, Romania, Spain, USA, USSR, as well as the members of the Bureau.
- **Switzerland** reported their 5th Biennale of La Chaux-de-Fonds from 14-20 October 1976 with companies performing from France, Belgium, and Turkey.
- **The USSR Center** reported 37 members from many republics in the Soviet Union, and that Natalya Satz was its new President.
- **The Spanish Center** reported that the 6th issue of the Ibero-American Bulletin of the Theatre for Children and Young People is devoted to the problems of youth theatre in Cuba.
- **The GDR Center** helped celebrate Dr. Rodenberg's 70th birthday, and her Theater der Freundschaft performed at the Jiří Wolker Theatre in Prague.

- **The French Center** had just published a booklet on the activities of theatres for children and youth in France for the 1976-77 season.
- The Theatrical Organization of **Cyprus** has started performing plays for children.
- **The Belgium Royal Theatre for Youth** produced a new version of *Pinocchio* in Antwerp.
- **The Australian Center** reported that the Iranian Children's Theatre Troupe, under the direction of Don LaFoon, had performed in several places in Australia in plays and pre-plays, and participated in discussions and workshops.
- **Czechoslovakia** reported production of a new opera for children *Sly Fellows* by the Slovak Theatre, and new productions of *Cinderella*, *The Snow Queen*, and *King Jörg* at the Jiří Wolker Theatre in Prague.

On an informal basis Snyder polled the members of the Bureau since she was perturbed that the centers from Great Britain, Italy, Denmark, USSR, Yugoslavia, and the USA were not permitted to attend the two official Bureau Meetings. She told Adamek that if members of the EXCOM had traveled great distances to attend the Bulgarian Festival, it was ridiculous for them to be excluded from meetings of their own organization.

In her report she stated that Sunyer, Rodenberg, Doolittle, and Adamek suggested she put her request in the form of a proposal to be presented at the Canadian EXCOM Meeting in 1977. She was not able to poll Moudoués.

John English (Great Britain) reported that he was having great difficulty with his center as well as ITI. He commented that the state of youth theatre in Great Britain was in a bad way, but he was determined to bear down.

The new Chair of the Italian Center was Ottorino Negri, and Snyder reported him as "a well organized, highly intelligent humanitarian."[11] Biotto was now the Public Relations officer for the Italian Center

Snyder met with Sunyer and presented two companies in nomination to appear at the VIth Congress: The Children's Theatre of Minneapolis and The Magic Carpet Company in San Francisco. Sunyer stated that she had asked Past President Eek to present a report on children's theatre in the USA as part of the VIth Congress,[12] needing the Report by January 1978 for the necessary translations. The dates of the Congress were set as 9-17 June 1978 in Madrid, and she told Snyder she hoped the USA would send a large delegation.[13]

Snyder also reported that the Bureau approved the concept of slide packages, and Rodenberg was charged with collecting slides from all of the Centers.

Snyder also explained to both Adamek and Moudoués that the US Center would only be ordering as few as 10-20 copies of *The Review* in the future, and the two commented this was no problem, and that all the Centers operated in this fashion.[14]

Lastly it was suggested that all Centers distribute Membership Cards in ASSITEJ to help identify members traveling abroad.

The meeting concluded with Adamek thanking Georgiev and the Bulgarian Center for their support of the Bureau Meeting, and congratulating them on the success of Bulgaria's 3rd International Festival for Young People.

1977
EXECUTIVE COMMITTEE MEETING
Calgary, Banff, Montreal, and Ottawa, Canada/12–20 May 1977

The Executive Committee of ASSITEJ met in three locations in Canada on 12–20 May 1977: Banff, Calgary, and Montreal.[15] Vladimir Adamek (Czechoslovakia) presided as President, Ilse Rodenberg (GDR) as 1st Vice President, Joyce Doolittle (Canada) as 2nd Vice President, Maria Sunyer (Spain) as 3rd Vice President, Rose-Marie Moudoués (France) as Secretary General, and Ion Lucian (Romania) as Treasurer.

Members of the EXCOM in attendance were: Don Rafaello Lavagna (Vatican) for Ottorino Negri (Italy), Patricia Snyder (USA), Ivan Voronov (USSR), and Zvjezdana Ladika (Yugoslavia).

Absent was: Victor Georgiev (Bulgaria).

Proxy: Natalya Satz for Victor Georgiev.

Advisors: Gerard Fernandez (Cuba).

Also attending by invitation were representatives from: Great Britain, FGR, Netherlands, Portugal, Switzerland, and Turkey.

Other Invitees: Australia and Sri Lanka sent their materials in writing. Peru and Venezuela did not respond.

Observers: Jean-Yves Gaudreault (Canada), Klaus Urban (GDR), and Yuri Berjukov (USSR).

The EXCOM Meetings were held in Banff, Calgary, and Montreal, with the delegates moving by bus from city to city. President Adamek presided at all the meetings.

1st Meeting of the EXCOM

The Minutes of the EXCOM meeting in Milan/Rome, Italy in 1976 were approved.

Financial Report: It was presented by Ion Lucian, Treasurer, indicating an Income of 9,763.55 US$, Expenditures of 6,691.30, leaving a Balance of 3,072.25 in US$. The French Center continued its subsidy of Rent.

There was concern expressed on checks arriving at the Secretariat without specifying what they were for. This was particularly true of the USA's remittance of funds.

Those countries that have not paid their dues for 1977-78 would not be allowed to vote at the VIth Congress.

Secretary General's Report: The Secretary General stated that the following countries were in the process of forming Centers: Argentina, Belgium, Brazil, Dahomey, Egypt, Guatemala, India, Ireland, Japan, Jordan, Mexico, Poland, Tunisia, and Uruguay.

Members of the EXCOM at Heritage Park. (Standing left) Vladimir Adamek (Czechoslovakia), (unidentified). (Sitting on bottom row of steps, left to right) Orna Porat (Israel), Ilse Rodenberg (GDR), Joyce Doolittle (Canada), Don Rafaello Lavagna (Vatican); (sitting on top row, left to right) Zvjezdana Ladika (Yugoslavia), Rose-Marie Moudoués (France), and Patricia A. Snyder (USA). (Standing on porch) 2 unidentified women, Fernando Gerardo (Italy), (unidentified), Ruth Frost (behind), Maria Sunyer (Spain), Klaus Urban (GDR), Ion Lucian (Romania). EXCOM Meeting, Calgary, Alberta, Canada, 11–23 May 1977. Photo courtesy of Joyce Doolittle

The EXCOM approved Reports of the Secretary General and the Treasurer, accepted the Future Agendas of the ASSITEJ Centers, and then discussed the proposed program for the Congress to be held in Madrid, Spain.

Madrid Congress in 1978: Maria Sunyer (Spain) submitted the program and invitation for the VIth International Congress to be held in 1978 in Madrid. She asked each center to give her input on each of the three areas of proposed discussion at the Congress: 1) dramatization of classical works; 2) complexity of a play's language; and 3) the use of improvisation (collective creation).

Sunyer also informed Snyder that invitations of performance had been issued to the USA Children's Theatre of Minneapolis, Minnesota and The Magic Carpet of San Francisco, California. However, they would only be able to feed and house ten (10) members of the Minnesota Company, and provide no subsidy for the California company.

Snyder wrote that Sunyer seemed rather uneasy at the meetings, and attributed it to the fact that there was an upcoming election in Spain on 15 June[16], and she was concerned about losing her funding. However, she said she was determined to host the VIth Congress.

It was reported that efforts at communication with the International Amateur Theatre Association (IATA) and the International Puppeteers Association (UNIMA) were slow. It was recommended that the three organizations co-sponsor a common calendar of activities as well as an international bibliography of theatrical books, excluding plays. It was decided to invite representatives of the two organizations to attend the Spanish Congress in 1978, and to be given a place on the program for a 10-minute presentation.

The EXCOM also considered the agenda for their next Meeting to be held in Moscow in 1978, along with the International Exhibitions and Festival of Soviet Theatres for Children.

They accepted reports from the Commissions, and the Report of the Canadian Center.

Resolution on ASSITEJ Membership: Importantly the EXCOM approved the sending of the entire text of a Resolution made by them at the meeting of 16 May 1977 in Canada. That text said in part:
- Companies playing for children primarily with puppets do not belong in the national centers of ASSITEJ, but to UNIMA.
- ASSITEJ supports all activity which raises the standards of theatre for children and youth. Since "creative dramatics" is primarily to develop the individuality of the child, organizations which engage exclusively in this activity are directed to join the International Association of Amateur Theatres (AITA/IATA).

National Center Activities: The Secretary General reported the following activities in the national centers:
- **The Swiss Center** had established a materials center at their library in Zurich in order to lend out items to teachers and administrators for youth events.
- **The Belgian Center** had been split in two (French and Flemish) with two presidents serving alternately every year. All inquiries are to be addressed to Edgard Verhoeven.
- **Australia** has lost its governmental subsidy and Margaret Leask will go on half-time.
- **Great Britain** will have a play festival in Wales in July with several foreign troupes performing.
- **France** will be hosting a festival from 2-18 July in Lyon. Participating theatres are from Chile, Belgium, West Germany, and France.

- **Mexico** is forming its center, and its constitution will be presented at the next EXCOM Meeting of ASSITEJ.
- **The Argentinean Minister of Culture** has written that he is amenable to the establishment of an ASSITEJ Center in that country. The Secretariat is awaiting a copy of their constitution.
- Mr. Oti-ai of **Japan** announced the formation of the Japanese Center in October 1976, and the Secretariat is awaiting a copy of their constitution.
- **Greek Cyprus** has just started an organization for children.
- **ITI/Brazil** has written that it is interested in starting a national center for ASSITEJ.
- **USA**—noted the death of Sara Spencer, noted playwright, author, and publisher, and one of the founding members of ASSITEJ.
- **GDR**—the 1st International Seminar for Directors of Theatre for Children took place in Berlin in October 1976. There was also a seminar for eight Asian and African countries. In December 1976 the Leipzig "Theatre of the Young World", being the oldest children's theatre in the GDR, celebrated its thirtieth anniversary.
- **Lyon, France** held its 1st International Meeting of Theatre for Children and Youth under the direction of Maurice Yendt, along with a theatre Festival featuring performances from three French theatres as well as companies from Belgium, FGR, Switzerland, and the Chilean Theatre in Exile, currently in the GDR.
- **USSR**—the Ministry of Culture decreed that each adult theatre was to present each year at least one performance for children. The Moscow Musical Theatre for Children under the direction of Natalya Satz toured Hungary.
- **Belgium**—Edgard Verhoeven became the new official correspondent of their National Center, replacing José Géal.
- **India**—produced three significant new plays for children: *Treasure Hunt* by Pragji Dissa, *Indrana Asan* by Nancy Lahute, and *Ali Baba and the 40 Thieves* by Sudha Karmarkar.
- **FGR**—the new heads of their national center are Kathrin Türks from Dinslakenü and Peter Möbius from Dortmund.
- **Czechoslovakia**—the Jiří Wolker theatre under the management of Karel Richter produced the Bulgarian play *Who's Better Than Who?* Ladislav Knížátko became the new Chairman of their national center with Karel Richter as Vice-Chairman. Vladimir Adamek directed the students of the Academy of Arts in their first performance designed for children.

Additional reports were made as follows:
- Inga Juul (**Denmark**) announced the reorganization of the Danish Center which has started a program for young people.
- Orna Porat (**Israel**) reported that Don Lafoon, the President of the Iranian Center, has left Iran.
- Rodenberg announced that the GDR book *Children's Theatres of the World* will be available for purchase at the Spanish Congress in 1978 for approximately 25 US$.
- There was need for a codification on terminology, and each center was encouraged to send in its suggestions.

Commissions: Promotion & Publicity: Rodenberg reported that the book "Children's Theatres of the World" would be ready for purchase at the VIth Congress. The GDR is preparing a calendar of youth theatre events planned for September 1978 through August 1979 to be distributed at the Congress. The Secretariat has requested each center to list its children's theatre activities for 1979. The list will be submitted in turn to UNESCO, since it considers the year 1979 as a year for Young People in the Arts.

Terminology: Each center must send in its list of terminology used in its theatre activities for and with children by 1 July 1979.

Publications: Under Publications there was considerable discussion about the value of *The Review*, but it was acknowledged that the last two issues had better material, and as long as the quality improved, it would be continued. There was the usual request for more materials to be sent in.

Statutes: There would be several changes in the Constitution to be voted upon at the Spanish Congress.

Art. 5, Rights and Obligations: No. 3 to read as follows:
All members have the obligation to work to achieve the aims defined by the Association, to maintain its statutes, to act upon the decisions taken by the Association, to pay their membership fees payable to ASSITEJ, to send the checks to the Secretary General, and to send once a year a written report to the Secretary General.

Art. 9, Function of the General Assembly, No. 13 to read as follows:
The General Assembly shall elect the Executive Committee and from the Committee's Membership, a President and three Vice-Presidents shall be elected. Nominations for the Executive Committee must be submitted by each Center for itself to the Secretary General three months before the date of the meeting of the General Assembly in order to circulate the nominations with the membership. The General Assembly appoints the Secretary

General and the Treasurer on the recommendation of the outgoing Executive Committee.[17]

Future Meetings: the 1979 EXCOM Meeting will take place in Šibenik, Yugoslavia, and the 1980 EXCOM Meeting in Havana, Cuba.

President Adamek closed the meetings with the recommendations that:
- All theatres should establish better communication with IATA, UNIMA, UNESCO, and ITI.
- Those interested in Creative Dramatics should join UNIMA which has a special section on drama in education.

There being no further business, the meeting was adjourned.

Activities witnessed: Most meetings were held in Calgary and Banff where the business of ASSITEJ was conducted. While there the members attended many performances of Canadian theatres for young people, as well as meeting significant members of the Canadian theatre.

Highlights of the Calgary sessions[18] included a social evening at the home of Vice-President Joyce Doolittle, and her husband Quenten, a famous award-winning composer of contemporary Canadian music. They were also hosted by the Alberta Government at Calgary's Professional Club, given a tour of Heritage Park (a recreation of Pioneer life in the late 19th century in Canada), and a performance of *The History* Show at the historic Canmore Opera House in Heritage Park. The EXCOM also attended a performance of *Alice in Wonderland* at the Pumphouse Theatre on the Bow River, a theatre that had been dedicated in honor of Doolittle who had succeeded in raising the funds for its restoration as a professional theatre.

The EXCOM then traveled to Banff for an overnight stay at the Banff Centre for the Arts, and enjoyed spectacular views of the Rocky Mountains at their final Alberta Province meetings. "Finally, members flew across Canada—first to Montreal and then to Ottawa where additional opportunities to see Canadian theatre for the young were abundant."[19]

Snyder stated that the EXCOM had met a total of six times, with each meeting lasting two and a half hours. She felt that a great deal was accomplished, and the general attitude was positive.

At the end of the meetings Adamek on behalf of ASSITEJ thanked Joyce Doolittle, Jean-Yves Gaudreault, and the Canadian Center members for making their entire stay in Canada interesting and most successful.

Members of the EXCOM at Heritage Park. Bar at the Wainwright Hotel. (Left to right) Klaus Urban (GDR), Ilse Rodenberg (GDR), Ion Lucian (Romania), Orna Porat (Israel), Vladimir Adamek (Czechoslovakia), Rose-Marie Moudoués (France), (hidden by hand) Maria Sunyer (Spain) and Patricia A. Snyder, (unidentified), Joyce Doolittle (Canada). (Standing) (unidentified), Fernando Gerardo (Italy), Don Rafaello Lavagna (Vatican), Zvjezdana Ladika (Yugoslavia). EXCOM Meeting, Calgary, Alberta, Canada, 11–23 May 1977. Photo courtesy of Joyce Doolittle.

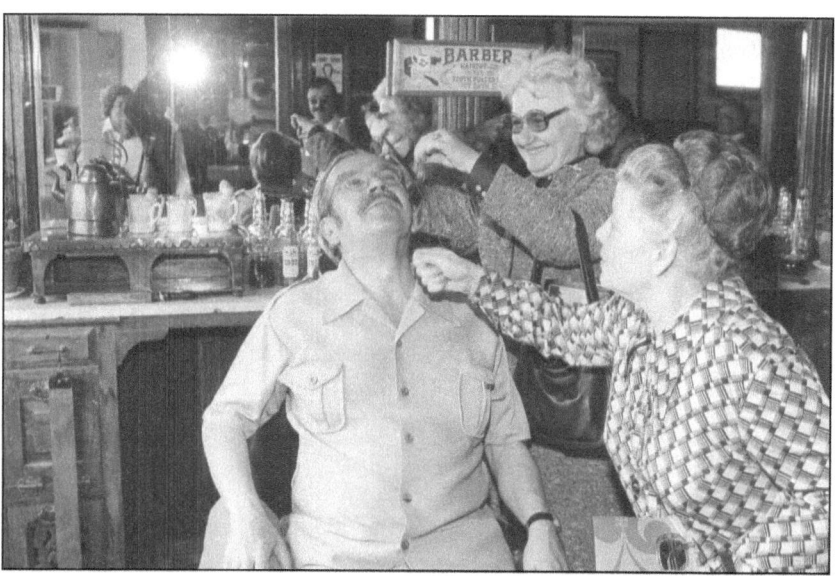

Giving the President of ASSITEJ a shave and haircut. (Left to right) Vladimir Adamek (Czechoslovakia), Rose-Marie Moudoués (France), and Ilse Rodenberg (GDR). Heritage Park, Calgary, Alberta, Canada, 11–23 May 1977. Photo courtesy of Joyce Doolittle.

1977
BUREAU MEETING
Paris, France/October 1977

The Bureau of ASSITEJ met in Paris, France in October 1977. Vladimir Adamek (Czechoslovakia) presided as President, Ilse Rodenberg (GDR) as 1st Vice President, Maria Sunyer (Spain) as 3rd Vice President, Rose-Marie Moudoués (France) as Secretary General, and Ion Lucian (Romania) as Treasurer.[20]
Absent: Joyce Doolittle (Canada).

Moudoués announced that she would send the Minutes of this Bureau Meeting to all the Centers of ASSITEJ.
The following items were dealt with:
- Approval of the Minutes from previous meetings
- Accepted the Treasurer's Report, noting those non-payers of dues
- Secretary General's Report
- Accepted the Uruguay Center as a member of ASSITEJ
- Prepared a future plan of activities
- Prepared the VIth International Congress in Madrid, Spain in 1978
- Prepared the Bureau and EXCOM Meetings in Moscow, USSR in March 1978 with invitations to Observers from Great Britain, Turkey, Portugal, FGR, Iran, and Switzerland
- Accepted reports from the Commissions
- Discussed suggestions for ITI and UNESCO for events associated in 1979 with the International Year of the Child

News from the Centers included:
- **USSR**—Past President Konstantin Shakh-Azizov died in Moscow on 20 November 1977. Shakh-Azizov was a founding member of ASSITEJ, and served as its President from 1968-1972. He was named an Honorary President in 1972.
- **Great Britain**—Wales hosted an International Festival of Theatres for Children and Young People including puppets, and featured performances from Great Britain, Australia, Canada, France, Iran, Italy, Norway, Netherlands, Poland, and Romania.
- **Japan**—Theatre Center for Boys and Girls in Tokyo published the third issue of a brochure entitled "Theatre All Over the World" featuring activities in the USA, Canada, and Australia.
- **FGR**—Their ASSITEJ Center continues to publish their bulletin "Grimm + Grips" detailing the work of theatre for children in the FGR.

- **Romania**—The Municipal Theatre of Ploiesti took a three month tour to 42 cities and towns of Japan presenting *Tales with Masks* by Ion Lucian and V. Puicea. The performances were attended by more than 80,000 people.
- **France**—Colmar's L'Atelier Lyrique du Rhin presented performances of *Flights Above the Ocean*, inspired by the work of Antoine de Saint-Exupéry, collaborating with 2600 children.
- **Israel**—Their National Theatre for Children and Young People concluded their seventh season where more than half a million children viewed eight different productions of which six were original local plays.
- **GDR**—On 14 October 1977 Rolf Büttner died. He was Director Emeritus of the Young Generation Theatre in Dresden for many years, and was an influential person in the early creation and founding of ASSITEJ (see Volume I). In the fall of 1977 the 2nd Seminar of Producers of young people's theatres was held. Representatives came from Bulgaria, Cuba, Czechoslovakia, GDR, France, Hungary, and Yugoslavia. Playwright Hans-Dieter Schmidt made the opening address.
- **Australia**—In November and December 1977 the Adelaide Festival produced a number of plays for young people, including *Alice in the Deep*.
- **Netherlands**—A new spacious theatre for children is to be built in Amsterdam. The Association of Theatre Directors has founded the "Hans Snoek Award" named for Dame Hans Snoek, Head of the Netherlands ASSITEJ Center for many years, and the first Award was granted to the group Wederzijds for their performance of *The Indians*.
- **Canada**—Joyce Doolittle and Jean-Yves Gaudrault now head their ASSITEJ Center, one for English-speaking and one for French-speaking.
- **USA**—The Children's Theatre Association of America (CTAA) in their annual August Convention had as a major topic of presentation: "ASSITEJ: An International View of Theatre for Young Audiences." In Washington D.C. the JFK Center for the Performing Arts in 1976–1977 sponsored a Children's Art Series featuring theatre, dance, and musical groups from all over the country. The Empire State Youth Theatre in Albany, New York just concluded its first year of performances, conceived and directed by Patricia Snyder. Also in Washington D.C. the first "White House Conference on Arts in

Education" was held in conjunction with the U.S. Office of Education in the Department of Health, Education, and Welfare.

Special recognition was made of the following theatres: Common Sense and The Great American Children's Theatre Company of Milwaukee, Wisconsin; The Nashville Children's Theatre in Tennessee; the Magic Carpet Play Company in San Francisco; The Children's Theatre Company of Minneapolis; Eastern Michigan University's Theatre for the Young in Ypsilanti; The Free Theatre of the Germantown Theatre Guild in Philadelphia; Helen Avery's Adventure Theatre in Maryland; and the Center Theatre Group of the Mark Taper Forum in Los Angeles.

- **Czechoslovakia**—The Czech Center announced that this was the 30th issue of the Bulletin, which was started in 1966. Great thanks are due to those who write and publish it as well as those national centers that contribute information. Ostrava-Poruba sponsored the 4th National Festival of amateur theatre for children from 7-14 October 1977. Performing were six Czech ensembles and one from Estonia.

This concluded the items on the meeting's agenda.

1978
EXECUTIVE COMMITTEE MEETING
Moscow, USSR/ 26–30 March 1978

The Executive Committee of ASSITEJ met in Moscow, USSR on 26–30 March 1978. Vladimir Adamek (Czechoslovakia) presided as President, Ilse Rodenberg (GDR) as 1st Vice President, Joyce Doolittle (Canada) as 2nd Vice President, Maria Sunyer (Spain) as 3rd Vice President, Rose-Marie Moudoués (France) as Secretary General, and Ion Lucian (Romania) as Treasurer.[21]

Members attending: Victor Georgiev (Bulgaria), Kathrin Türks (FGR), John English (Great Britain), Ottorino Negri (Italy), Patricia Snyder (USA), Ivan Voronov for Natalya Satz (USSR), and Zvjezdana Ladika (Yugoslavia).

Observers: Egmont Elschner (FGR), A. Randle (Great Britain), Lilia de Fonseca (Portugal), and Natalya Satz, J. Berjukov (USSR).

Invitees: Turkey and Iran did not respond.

The Secretary General will send Minutes of the meetings to all the centers in the near future.

The EXCOM made the following decisions:
- Noted the death of Past President Konstantin Shakh-Azizov, a significant founding leader of ASSITEJ
- Approved the decisions of the past Meeting of the Bureau in October 1977
- Accepted Uruguay as a new member of ASSITEJ
- Approved the Treasurer's Report
- Emphasized that non-dues-paying members did not have the right to vote, could not be elected, and could only attend meetings with an advisory vote
- Accepted the Report of the Secretary General and noted that her contacts with other international organizations had been greatly strengthened
- Recognized the 15 member centers nominated for election at the VIth International Congress in Madrid, which had been received in accordance with the Statutes
- Approved reports from the Commissions, and noted that there were no recommended changes to the Statutes
- Approved the preparations for the VIth International Congress in Madrid
- Discussed the themes serving as a basis for reports on ASSITEJ activities at the Madrid Congress, recognizing that 1979 had been declared the Year of the Child by UNESCO

- Heard and discussed reports from the centers in Great Britain, FGR, Portugal, and the USSR, and made recommendations
- Stated that in the past three years a higher level of international contacts had been attained among theatres for young people
- Sent warm greetings to Gerald Tyler, Honorary President of ASSITEJ, on the occasion of his 70th birthday

Bolshoi Theatre, Moscow, USSR, Courtesy of Dr. Harold Oaks, Archives, ASU, AZ, USA.

Before the EXCOM began its meetings, all the six Commissions met and deliberated. Enigmatically the Czech Minutes then state "Before the meetings of the Executive Committee and after them, a number of decisions were accepted by the Bureau of ASSITEJ concerning administrative problems with a view to safeguarding further work of the respective ASSITEJ bodies." Regrettably the Minutes state that decisions were made or accepted, but do not say what they were! For example, they accepted the names of the 15 nominated centers for election, but do not list them by name!

During the EXCOM Meeting the delegates attended a rich variety of performances, visited an exhibition of historic and contemporary documents on Soviet and foreign theatres for children, and viewed the working room of V.I. Lenin in the Kremlin.

News of the Centers were as follows:
- **Great Britain**—Lots of activity at all levels from small amateur performances to the highest level of professional theatre. The National Theatre included a "family" production which ran for one month for the first time. Money is a problem even though every level of government contributes—regional arts associations, education, municipalities, and national budgets. Grants have not kept up with the inflation. Costs have doubled in the past five years. Thirty percent of the population is young; therefore thirty percent of subsidies should go to the arts for young people.[22]
- **Yugoslavia**—26 January-3 February 1978 Prof. Ljubisa Djokič organized a national seminar on the theme "New Trends in Theatre for Children and Young People." The Theatre of the Youth in Zagreb achieved great success with the play *The Invisible Leonard* by Norma Shermentova, written by a university student, given over 100 times, dealing with parents who are too occupied by work and public activities.
- **GDR**—On 7 March 1978 Prof. Hans Rodenberg, husband of Ilse Rodenberg, died. He was the first Director of the Theater der Freundschaft in Berlin, and helped popularize the founding of theatres for young people in the GDR.
- **France**—Prof. Raoul Carrat, creator of several international exhibitions, requested all centers to send him their materials.
- **Czechoslovakia**—Director Karel Richter of the Jiří Wolker Theatre in Prague produced two new plays, and in March 1978 eight best companies participated in the VIth Selective Festival of Amateur Theatres in Prague.

At the end of the meeting President Adamek thanked the representatives of the Ministry of Culture and those of the Pan-Russian Theatrical Company for their support and hospitality during their productive meeting.

Following the meeting Adamek and Moudoués were taken on a tour of Azerbeijan, Armenia, and Georgia as guests of the Soviet Center to see performances at their theatres for children and meet with their artists.

1978
VIth INTERNATIONAL CONGRESS OF ASSITEJ
Madrid, Spain/10–17 June 1978

The VIth International Congress of ASSITEJ met in Madrid, Spain on 10–17 June 1978. Vladimir Adamek (Czechoslovakia) presided as President, Ilse Rodenberg (GDR) as 1st Vice President, Joyce Doolittle (Canada) as 2nd Vice President, Maria Sunyer (Spain) as 3rd Vice President, Rose-Marie Moudoués (France) as Secretary General, and Ion Lucian (Romania) as Treasurer.[23]

Members of the EXCOM in attendance were: Victor Georgiev (Bulgaria), Patricia Snyder (USA), Ivan Voronov for Natalya Satz (USSR), and Zvjezdana Ladika Yugoslavia).

Absent: Kathrin Türks (FGR), John English (Great Britain), Orna Porat (Israel), Ottorino Negri (Italy), and Elisabeth Cozona (Switzerland).

A total of thirty-six (36) countries attended with twenty-four National Centers of ASSITEJ represented.

he Theme of the Congress was "In Search of New Aesthetic Forms in Children's and Youth's Theatre." The Spanish Center, under Maria Sunyer, offered the utmost in hospitality, and the week began with a Reception opening the ASSITEJ exhibit in the Crystal Palace of the Retiro Park. Several troupes of Spanish folk dancers provided the entertainment.[24]

Palacio De Congresos, Madrid, Spain. Personal photograph.

The Bureau Meeting/9 June 1978

Attending were: Adamek presiding as President, Rodenberg, Doolittle, Sunyer, Moudoués, and Lucian.

They approved the Minutes of the previous Bureau Meeting in Moscow as distributed.

There was considerable discussion when the USA Center claimed that their 1978 dues were credited instead to the subscription fees of *The Review*, which would make them ineligible to vote. The Secretary General stated that apparently there had been an error in the proper crediting, but the Bureau deplored the furor created by the US Center over the incident.

The Secretary General had been informed that an association had been formed under the guidance of the Ministry of Culture in Denmark, and wish to be admitted to ASSITEJ, and wished to know what the situation was with Inga Juul. Moudoués announced that Juul had announced her participation in the Congress as the representative from Denmark, and they decided to accept her accordingly with the necessary payment of dues.

The Peruvian Center requested to be represented by Uruguay, since they could not attend because of economic difficulties.

Doolittle announced the new status of the Canadian Center: Joyce Doolittle, Honorary President; Jean Yves Gaudreault (French representative); Barbara McLauchlin (English representative) as Presidents in rotation; Magda Rundle as Secretary with the Center based in Ottawa.

The Bureau then set the following Agenda:
- Speech by Gerald Tyler
- Announce the list of participants
- Announce the list of those with the right to vote
- Election of the Voting Commission—the 3 tellers
- Distribution of all the written materials of the Congress, primarily the Secretary General's Report and the Treasurer's Report
- Report of the Commissions:
    1. Commission on Creative Activity & Themes
    2. Commission on Terminology—Henri Lagrave
- Announce the list of candidates for election to the EXCOM
- Proposal of the following Members of Honor: Caryl Jenner (Great Britain), Hans Rodenberg (GDR), and Sara Spencer (USA), all in memoriam.
- The Presidency: Adamek announced he would not be a candidate. The Bureau proposed Ilse Rodenberg as President, and as Vice-Presidents: Joyce Doolittle, Natalya Satz, and Maria Sunyer. They also proposed the re-election of Rose-Marie Moudoués as Secretary General and Ion Lucian as Treasurer.

The Executive Committee Meeting/10 June 1978

Attending as officers were: Adamek presiding as President, Rodenberg, Doolittle, Sunyer, Moudoués, and Lucian. As Members: Georgiev, Snyder, Voronov, and Ladika.

The agenda was set as follows:
- Approval of the minutes of meetings since the 1975 Congress
- The Report of the Secretary General; the Organization of the Congress
- The Organization of the General Assemblies
- Miscellaneous questions

The EXCOM approved the Minutes of all the previous meetings since the 1975 Congress in Berlin, making two corrections of dates.

The Bureau decisions related to the Danish and Peruvian Centers were approved.

The US payment of dues was corrected, and its Center allowed to vote.

ASSITEJ was represented last May (1977) at the UNESCO Conference of Organizations. As a result ASSITEJ is now a well-known part of that organization.

The Commission of Themes at their meeting on 10 June decided to separate the delegates into 7 discussion groups at this Congress: 2 on dramaturgy; 2 on scene design; 2 on directing; and 1 on open discussion.

In the General Assembly: the Treasurer would announce the definitive list of Centers with the right to vote; the name of each nominated Center and its representative would be announced; approved admittance of Japan as a Member, with the proviso that they pay their dues and submit a report of activities at the next EXCOM Meeting.[25]

Announced that correspondence with Elisabeth Kullenberg who promised the formation of a Swedish Center in the near future.

Recommended that with the devaluation of the US$ dues be raised to 125 US$.

Recommended the retention of Cornel Popa and Eléna Vladutzi as Auditors.

Recommended the acceptance of the new Logo for ASSITEJ (a world globe with an olive branch) be approved at the next EXCOM Meeting.

Proposed Caryl Jenner (Great Britain), Hans Rodenberg (GDR), and Sara Spencer (USA) as Honorary Members of ASSITEJ.

Proposed that a plaque be given to Natalya Satz commemorating the occasion of her 60 years of activity in theatre for children.

Adamek announced that he did not wish to run again for President, so the EXCOM recommended Ilse Rodenberg as President, Natalya Satz, Joyce

Doolittle, and Maria Sunyer as Vice-Presidents, and the re-appointment of Rose-Marie Moudoués as Secretary General and Ion Lucian as Treasurer. The vote was for this slate, except the USA voted against it.

General Assembly/Opening Session/ 12 June 1978

President Adamek opened the Congress by welcoming the delegates and thanking the Spanish Center for their hosting the event. He also congratulated Honorary President Gerald Tyler on the occasion of his 70th birthday, and Natalya Satz for her 60 years of service in theatre for children. He then paid homage to the memories of Konstantin Shakh-Azizov, Honorary President of ASSITEJ, Hans Rodenberg, and Sara Spencer.

The Spanish Minister of Culture, Pio Cabanillas Gallas, welcomed the delegates stating the major importance of theatre for young people, and how important it was for those in authority to support it since it is an essential element in the education of future generations.

The Secretary General announced the presence at the Congress of representatives from major theatre organizations, including ITI (Secretary General Jean Daconte), UNIMA and IATA.

Three reports were given based on the theme of the Congress: "New Aesthetic Forms in Theatre for Children and Youth". The presenters were Nat Eek (USA), Carmen Bravo Villasante (Spain), and Ion Lucian (Romania).

General Assembly/14 June 1978

The General Assembly first approved the Minutes of the General Assembly at the Congress in Berlin in 1975.

The Secretary General gave her Report.

- Eek asked if the Year of the Child in 1979 could be celebrated by a gathering of playwrights, each presenting selected plays from their centers. The question was referred to the EXCOM.
- Snyder remarked that the co-opted members and the Past Presidents had not been introduced to the Assembly. Eek was instructed to do so at the end of the session.
- A Spanish delegate protested violently against the exclusion of puppets and marionettes from membership in ASSITEJ, which was answered by the fact that puppeteers had their own professional organization—UNIMA, and ASSITEJ had constant contact and cooperation with them.
- Rodenberg announced a seminar for scene designers in the GDR which would accept 10 from the GDR and 10 from foreign countries. She asked centers to make recommendations from their countries. Adamek mentioned that the last Czech seminar for actors had 15 foreign members.

- Gaudreault (Canada) asked Hungary to clarify their playwriting project for the Year of the Child. G. Karpathy (Hungary) stated that the seminar for playwrights would invite 15-20 from around the world and would have an international festival at the same time.
- Egmont Elschner (FGR) observed that he had spoken with the West German Center and was told that it did not exist anymore.

The Secretary General's Report was accepted.

The Treasurer presented his Report, and distributed it to the delegates. He commented:

- *The Review* is expensive and there are too few subscriptions. He requested greater efforts to get subscriptions.
- He also mentioned the trouble in identifying what checks are for what payment. He requested that each center inform the Secretariat in Paris exactly for what payments they are, and when they are sent include a photo-copy for the Treasurer in Romania. Also send the checks in francs rather than US$ or other currency since those checks were difficult to cash.
    1. Cornel Popa and Eléna Vladutzi were accepted as Auditors by a majority vote with 4 abstentions.
    2. Snyder requested that the Treasurer send an Invoice for the following year before the 31 December of that year. The proposition was approved.
    3. The Financial Report was approved with only the USA abstaining.
    4. The General Assembly approved the increase of dues to 125 US$ as a result of the devaluation and inflation.

The Treasurer's Report was accepted.

- There were no requests for changes in the Statutes.
- Caryl Jenner (Great Britain), Hans Rodenberg (GDR), and Sara Spencer (USA) were named Members of Honor in ASSITEJ.
- Sunyer nominated Moudoués for reelection as Secretary General and Ion Lucian as Treasurer. From a possible 60 votes they received the following votes: Moudoués—46 for, 9 against, 10 abstentions; Lucian—46 for, 12 against, 2 abstentions.
- At the end of the session Satz protested that the written documents had not been translated into Russian, which was the 3rd official language of ASSITEJ. Moudoués responded that from the beginning the Russian delegation had accepted the fact they would be responsible for the translations, since it would be too expensive for the Association otherwise.

This ended the session.

General Assembly/Elections/15 June 1978

At the beginning of the session Egmont Elschner (FGR) thanked the EXCOM for all their excellent activity on behalf of the centers and the association.

The Secretary General announced that delegates from two centers were not present at the first session, but were now present, so that the total number of votes which could be cast was now 65.

Patricia Snyder (USA) proposed that the list of candidates be approved by acclamation in its totality. This proposal was based on the fact that there were 15 places in the EXCOM and there were only 15 nominations. The proposal was rejected as being in conflict with the Statutes.

In the election a total of 65 votes could be cast. 33 votes were the majority needed for election. The results of the election of the new EXCOM in rank order were as follows:

John English (Great Britain)—64; Patricia Snyder (USA)—63; Ottorino Negri (Italy)—62; Victor Georgiev (Bulgaria)—62; Maria Sunyer (Spain)—60; Kathrin Türks (FGR)—61; Vladimir Adamek (Czechoslovakia)—58; Zvjezdana Ladika (Yugoslavia)—57; Joyce Doolittle (Canada)—57; Ilse Rodenberg (GDR)—57; Elisabeth Cozona (Switzerland)—57; Natalya Satz (USSR)—49; Orna Porat (Israel)—47.[26]

Rose-Marie Moudoués was reelected as Secretary General and Ion Lucian as Treasurer.[27]

EXCOM Meeting during the Election/15 June 1978

In the election process after the new Executive Committee was elected, they retired to discuss and recommend a slate of officers for the new Bureau.

In this discussion Türks proposed Adamek as Vice-President, but he declined. Ladika nominated Ion Lucian as Vice-President when she was reminded that he had been elected as Treasurer. She then nominated Patricia Snyder as a Vice-President, and Rodenberg nominated Victor Georgiev, commenting that now they would have a large number of candidates. This made 5 candidates for the 3 Vice-President positions: Doolittle, Snyder, Sunyer, Satz, and Georgiev.

General Assembly/Elections *Cont'd.*

The results of this election were: Ilse Rodenberg as President—53; Joyce Doolittle—47, Maria Sunyer—43, and Natalya Satz—31,[28] as Vice-Presidents. Patricia Snyder—30 and Victor Georgiev—29 were not elected.

The French Center proposed to hold the 1981 Congress in Lyon, France on the occasion of its celebrating the 3rd International Meeting of Theatre for Children and Youth. The proposal was accepted by the Assembly.

Miscellaneous discussions: The following points were raised:
- The Peruvian Center requested that as an ASSITEJ rule a new Program of projects should be written for the new EXCOM.
- Hans Snoek (Netherlands) requested on behalf of the Magic Carpet Theatre Company (which performed at this Congress) that the children of the world send letters to that group to be included in their next playbills.
- Both the Portuguese and Australian Centers proposed hosting an EXCOM meeting in their respective countries at a date to be determined. The Czech Center invited the EXCOM to have a meeting in Prague in the spring of 1981.
- Y. Berjukov asked that everyone in the theatre for children and youth intensify their work along humanistic principles.
- Nat Eek requested that 1) a calendar of festivals be published in advance, and 2) the work of the General Assembly be open to all participants in the Congress, that they be designated as observers, and that the official delegates only have the right to speak and vote. Moudoués responded that few centers have responded to the request for such dates, and such dates are not just dependant on ASSITEJ but also ITI.
- A Finish delegate asked for an open meeting place for the delegates to gather to exchange ideas, opinions on the themes of the Congress, and talk with groups about their work. The request would be given to the organizers of the next Congress.
- Doolittle requested that a place be reserved for the presentation of materials from the various centers. This request also would be referred to the organizers of the next Congress.

The Congress was closed with thanks from the EXCOM and the Bureau, and President Rodenberg commended the Spanish Center for their excellent hospitality and the fine organization of the entire Congress. She also thanked Vladimir Adamek for his activity on behalf of ASSITEJ. To loud applause for all concerned the meeting was then adjourned.

Performances: During the meeting the delegates were able to attend a variety of productions. "We saw two parodies by the U Of Cuc, a Barcelona Company performing in Catalan. *The Dream of Baghdad* caricatured desert film epics; *Supertot* satirized the superheroes of films and comic strips.

"The Jiří Wolker Theatre of Prague, Czech presented a folk-art production of *How the Devils Got Married,* notable for its excellent lead actor. The Madrid School of Dramatic Arts, La Gaviot, offered a very eclectic production of Strindberg's *The Journey of Lucky Peter.* The company of

Lauro Olma, one of Spain's foremost contemporary playwrights for the adult theatre, presented *General Assembly*, a rock musical version of a La Fontaine fable.

"The USA was represented by two very different companies working in very different styles. The Magic Carpet presented its improvisational works, stemming primarily from the writings of children. The Nashville Academy Theatre mounted *Really Rosie*, a musical based on works of Maurice Sendak with music by Carole King.

"The last production was *Puss in Boots*, staged by an amateur group from Madrid. Developed by improvisation, and given an environmental staging that required the audience to stand in the middle, it was either loved or hated by delegates, with no middle ground on which there was agreement. . . .

"After this last performance, delegates viewed demonstrations from various Centers of Dramatic Creativity. . . . We saw children performing songs, dances, and playlets that had been developed improvisationally in some cases and had been memorized in others. . . . the entire focus was on performance. . . .

"In general, the productions did not seem to set ever-higher artistic standards, demonstrate new aesthetic forms, or challenge delegates to thoughtful discussions with colleagues. A common view expressed seemed to be an attitude of disappointment about specifics, but an enthusiasm for international congresses."[29]

The New EXCOM Meeting/16 June 1978

President Ilse Rodenberg presided.
- Confirmed the results of the elections with the new Bureau and EXCOM
- Confirmed the Chairs of the 7 Commissions
- Miscellaneous discussion
- Confirmed the next Congress to be held in Lyon, France in 1981
- Set the next meeting of the Bureau in Paris, France in October 1978
- Stated that Minutes of EXCOM Meetings and the Congress would be distributed to all the Centers
- Approved the next EXCOM Meeting to be held in Šibenik in conjunction with the International Festival celebrating the Year of the Child in June 1979
- Discussed two invitations for EXCOM meetings: FGR in Dortmund and the USA in Washington, D.C. Accepted the USA invitation for the EXCOM, and stated that the Bureau would meet in Dortmund

- Portugal and Australia accepted their invitations to attend a future EXCOM Meeting. The Czech Center extended an invitation for spring of 1981
- Adamek announced a Festival in Hungary in 1979 to which the EXCOM was invited, and their Center is interested in establishing a Center of Documentation of Plays for Children
- Satz informed them that the Musical Theatre in Moscow would be dedicated during the Festival in Šibenik
- Rodenberg recommended that they continue the rotation of invitations to centers who did not belong to the EXCOM

At the end of the Congress the delegates were taken to a small village in La Mancha which had preserved their 17th Century theatre (corral), and saw a performance of one of Miguel de Cervantes entremeses. This was followed by the witnessing of a paseo in the village plaza (central square).[30]

A SUMMARY OF 1975–1978

1975

The decade of 1970–1980 was, in many ways, a decade of disillusionment. The world economy was sluggish, governments were becoming more chauvinistic, and the east-west split was intensifying. However, all of non-Communist Europe was under democratic rule after free elections were held in Spain in 1976, seven months after the death of Francisco Franco. This in turn forced the "eastern" governments to become more closed, more isolated, and more rigid in their restrictions. It would not be until 1989 with the fall of the Berlin Wall that countries removed many travel restrictions, and the world was much more open to free interchange.

One cannot overlook the incredible influence of computers and e-mail in the open transfer of information. The proliferation of e-mail occurred so rapidly that it was almost impossible for any government to monitor totally the sending and receiving of electronic mail. One Chinese official stated that they only monitored those e-mails sent *from* China, not those sent *into* China. They obviously wanted information from the rest of the world.

As ASSITEJ moved into its next three-year term between congresses, there was a total of 33 national centers, which included all six continents. This number was almost doubled after the Stockholm, Sweden Congress in 1990.

When President Vladimir Adamek (Czechoslovakia) came into office at the Vth International Congress in Berlin, GDR in 1975, he approached his leadership with caution, incisiveness, professionalism, and fairness as long as it did not conflict with political survival.[31] He was well organized, and immediately established a series of goals for the organization which he began to implement.

Since Adamek spoke French fluently, there was a constant interchange of information between him and Secretary General Rose-Marie Moudoués (France). Usually included in these exchanges was Ilse Rodenberg (GDR) as 1st Vice-President, and the next President in line of succession. Along with Treasurer Ion Lucian (Romania) this gave the "east" dominant representation on the Bureau. The "west" was only represented by Maria Sunyer (Spain) and Joyce Doolittle (Canada). This made for a clique of five Europeans to one North American, and an east-west vote of 4 to 2.

Soon the Bureau became the dominant decision maker for ASSITEJ, and the number of their separate meetings greatly increased. While all these decisions were presented later to the EXCOM for approval, the EXCOM never reversed any of them. This manner of management, which was more in keeping with the traditional "eastern" approach, was reinforced under President Rodenberg's tenure starting in 1978, and continued through Moudoués' tenure until 1990.

At the first Bureau meeting in October 1975 President Adamek outlined his proposed program of action, and established six Commissions, each headed by a member of the Bureau, to deal with the administrative problems of ASSITEJ. They were Commissions on Statutes, Terminology, Publications, Creative Activity & Themes, Liaison w/IATA, UNIMA, & UNESCO, and Promotion and Publicity.[32] This last one was the most important and was chaired by Rodenberg. Second in importance was that of the Statutes headed by Adamek, which would recommend amendments to the Constitution that echoed the new administrative approach.

Over the years the names of the Committee varied, but essentially they covered the same territory. Also, as members of the EXCOM changed, their Chairs changed. Ultimately some of the Commissions went out of existence, but in their early years they provided a valid and efficient means of getting the Association's work done by committee.

Politically speaking, appointment to Chair a Commission could have power or not depending on which Commission. Promotion and Publicity gave its Chair opportunities to visit and recruit new centers. Terminology was essentially "an elephant graveyard", prestige but no effective power. It was a convenient way to give members responsibilities while keeping them off the power brokering Commissions.

Also, Adamek established the concept of inviting heads of various national centers to attend the EXCOM meetings as observers without vote instead of appointing advisors or co-opting centers. An excellent concept, this allowed more centers to be involved in the administration of the Association, to give reports of their Centers, and to witness personally the Association in action, instead of locking in only a few centers for all three years. Unfortunately many times those countries invited were not able to attend the meetings, either because of travel restrictions, soft currency, or just lack of funds.

There was major concern about the lack of payment of dues, and the Treasurer was urged to demand the settlement of all debts.

The next Bureau Meeting was set for the fall of 1976 in France to prepare the agenda for the next EXCOM Meeting in Canada in 1977.

Lastly, Adamek presented a report on discussions with representative George Malvius of IATA in Prague. The result was that those members of ASSITEJ who were most interested in the inclusion of "creative dramatics" as part of ASSITEJ, should instead join the International Association of Amateur

Theatres (IATA), while ASSITEJ would concentrate on the theatrical activities of "grown-ups". This report was the first step in eliminating creative dramatics as a possible component of ASSITEJ, which had been a long festering wound.

1976

The first EXCOM Meeting of the new administration was held in Milan and Rome, Italy in May 1976.

Of major concern according to Moudoués was the fact that the US Center had not paid their dues or for their copies of *The Review*, considering that they were the largest purchaser (100 copies) of all the centers. Part of this confusion was created by the fact that when checks arrived from a center, there was no identification for what it was intended. There was fault on both sides: the Secretariat did not send invoices, and many checks from the centers covered dues and subscriptions in a lump sum.

Moudoués commented that ITI had told her if they enforced the required payments, they would have many fewer members. Their advice was not to exclude the non-paying members, but deprive them of a vote, or nomination for office. She recommended waiting a month and then writing the US Center requesting immediate payment.

Apparently there was no immediate action. However, as a result of this, there ensued a blistering correspondence in May 1978 between Ann Shaw, then Secretary of the US Center, and Moudoués, which was resolved by identification of the checks which had already been sent and cashed, and an apology from the Secretariat. However, to Shaw the whole incident was designed to discredit the US Center and perhaps deprive them of a seat and a vote at the Madrid Congress in 1978.

Doolittle suggested since the EXCOM had the power to appoint replacement members to the EXCOM, they should bring the number up to the appropriate 15. It was ignored. Instead the EXCOM approved Adamek's recommendation that centers be invited to attend the meetings. A valid suggestion, but while it expanded the voices at the EXCOM Meetings, it narrowed the control of the Association.

Doolittle also raised the question of the "perks" of Honorary Members of ASSITEJ, and their attendance at Meetings. Their attendance at Congresses was not questioned, but sitting in on Bureau and EXCOM Meetings was. Once more the Secretary General made a decision to her advantage without any precedent. Honorary President Gerald Tyler (Great Britain) had been sitting in on EXCOM meetings, and in many cases entered into the discussions keeping them fair and even-handed, even challenging some of the Secretary General's automatic decisions. Her decision that Honorary Members had no "right" to attend EXCOM Meetings eliminated Tyler's effectiveness as a senior counselor, and in the future Honorary Members appeared only when invited.

At this meeting Adamek made a major speech outlining the purposes of ASSITEJ. To clear up the confusion between children's theatre and creative dramatics he stated that those involved in creative drama should join IATA rather than ASSITEJ. "Everyone from all forms of theatre helped establish ASSITEJ, but now after ten years it was time to concentrate on creating the highest form of theatre, professional and amateur. The ASSITEJ Statutes specify this concept as our common interest. If this concentration is not paramount, in some countries [an] ASSITEJ [center] could be dissolved, because of its multiplicity of interests and organization."[33]

Considerable discussion followed the President's speech, with Lucian summing up the result. The only direction ASSITEJ can go is "to support professional theatre for children, but we should not eliminate amateur groups, but help them to raise the quality of their work."[34] The creation of the Commission on Co-operation with IATA and UNIMA was the first step in directing those interested in creative drama to transfer their interest to an organization other than ASSITEJ. ASSITEJ now was to be "professional" theatre only, although "amateur" or educational theatre was acceptable since they used professionally trained personnel.

There were no new centers reported, but there was continuing contact with Japan, Argentina, Mexico, Egypt, Poland, and Greece. Ireland was apparently defunct.

Sunyer presented extensive plans for the 1978 Congress in Madrid, Spain. The theme was "Research for new aesthetic levels of theatre for children". A competition had begun for a poster designed by a child. The performing companies would come from Spain, with one invited from Europe and one invited from the USA. There would be conference sessions in the mornings and performances in the afternoons. Delegates would be grouped by language to promote more spontaneous discussions. Centers were invited to make visual presentations using film, video tape, and there would be optional visits to observe creative drama. There would be a reception, two luncheons, and a visit to a 17th century theatre at the end of the Congress. The Congress would last six days in the first week of June 1978.

The Bureau met for a second time in Sophia, Bulgaria in October. Its main purpose was to discuss problems with some of the centers, and finalize plans for the EXCOM Meeting in Canada in 1977 and the Madrid Congress in 1978.

The Irish Center had all but disappeared, both the Netherlands and the Belgian Centers were reorganizing, Natalya Satz was the new head of the Soviet Center, and Zvjezdana Ladika was the new Chair of the Yugoslav Center. The Swiss Center was alive and active.

Moudoués indicated that the Constitution with the Amendments passed at the Berlin Congress would be mailed out soon, as well as a new list of national centers. The programs for both the 1977 Canadian meeting and the Madrid Congress were presented and approved.

Finally it was strongly emphasized that all Committee and Commission correspondence must go through the Paris Secretariat. While there was an obvious need for the Bureau to know everything that was going on and to be informed intelligently, it could also create a stumbling block since correspondence from the Secretariat many times was slow or non-existent. It also underlined the growing paranoia of the Bureau needing greater control on everything that the Association did and wrote about. However, ASSITEJ was no longer an elite organization of the chosen few. It had grown much larger and needed broader management, which the current leadership was not willing to grant.

1977

Canada hosted the next EXCOM Meeting in May 1977, and had them meet in Banff, Calgary, and Montreal.

While the Secretariat listed 14 centers in process of forming, there were still no new centers. The Belgian Center had been split in two by language—French and Flemish; Australia had lost its governmental subsidy; Lyon was holding its 1st International Festival for Young People under Maurice Yendt's leadership, which would become the centerpiece of the 1981 Congress; and the Soviet Ministry of Culture decreed that all adult theatres must present at least one play for children each year.

Perhaps the most important thing to occur was the EXCOM's approval of the Resolution on ASSITEJ Membership at their meeting of 16 May 1977, and that its text be sent to all centers. That text said in part:
- Companies playing for children primarily with puppets do not belong in the national centers of ASSITEJ, but to UNIMA.
- ASSITEJ supports all activity which raises the standards of theatre for children and youth. Since "creative dramatics" is primarily to develop the individuality of the child, organizations which engage exclusively in this activity are directed to join the International Association of Amateur Theatres (AITA/IATA).

The dissemination of this Report put an end to any further consideration of "creative dramatics" as a viable component of ASSITEJ. The professional European centers regarded creative drama as strictly amateur despite the fact that there were extensive professionally taught programs in the Netherlands, Spain, Yugoslavia, the Scandinavian countries, Canada, and the USA.

The question had been a vital argument at the 1964 London Conference which helped create ASSITEJ, was revived and discussed extensively after the 1972 joint Canada-USA Congress, had a Resolution denied at the London EXCOM Meeting in 1973, and this broadcast statement completely finished the controversy. It has never been revived despite the use of young non-professional actors in many of the third world countries.

At the time it seemed like a slap in the face to many members, but in the long run it strengthened the organization, gave it a stronger artistic focus, gave it credibility among its peers, and helped raised the level of performance in all countries.

Most importantly it raised the importance and prestige of the profession of theatre for young audiences in the "adult" theatre world. In the USA it brought their professional theatres to the attention of the Theatre Development Fund and the National Endowment for the Arts (similar to a Ministry of Culture).

This particular meeting in Canada was remarkable in its breadth and variety, and the committee had responded with delight. In a sense it was Doolittle's farewell, since she would resign her Vice-Presidency the next year, step down from her administrative position of the Canadian Center, and would only attend a few Congresses in the future.

On a sad note Konstantin Shakh-Azizov (USSR), a Founder and the second President of ASSITEJ from 1968-1972, died in Moscow in November 1977. He was a professional artist and administrator of the theatre, and was long remembered for appearing unannounced at the 1964 London Conference with 30 delegates to participate in the discussion on forming the new association. According to Tyler, this gave an imprimatur of importance to the entire international proceedings.

1978

The VIth International Congress of ASSITEJ was held in Madrid, Spain from 10-17 June 1978. A total of 36 countries participated with delegates from 24 National Centers present. The Congress opened with a reception in the Crystal Palace of the Retiro Park, and the entertainment was provided by several troupes of Spanish folk dancers.

In the elections a total of thirteen countries were chosen as the new EXCOM: Bulgaria (Victor Georgiev); Canada (Joyce Doolittle); Czechoslovakia (Vladimir Adamek); FGR (Kathrin Türks); GDR (Ilse Rodenberg); Great Britain (John English); Israel (Orna Porat); Italy (Ottorino Negri); Spain (Maria Sunyer); Switzerland (Elisabeth Cozona); USA (Patricia Snyder); USSR (Natalya Satz); and Yugoslavia (Zvjezdana Ladika).

From among these, the following officers were elected: Ilse Rodenberg as President; Joyce Doolittle, Maria Sunyer, and Natalya Satz as Vice-Presidents. Patricia Snyder and Victor Georgiev, who had been nominated as Vice-Presidents, were not elected. Rose-Marie Moudoués as Secretary General and Ion Lucian as Treasurer were re-elected.

It was at this Congress that Snyder informed Shaw that she would have to take over as head of the US Center, since Snyder had to devote full time to heading the development and the building of her theatre at the State University of New York at Albany, NY. However, she would like to continue as the USA representative on the international EXCOM of ASSITEJ. Shaw informed her that she felt it was absolutely essential that the international EXCOM representative and the head of the National Center be one and the same person. Accordingly, as Shaw became President of the US Center, she took her place on the international EXCOM. A little later for her excellent past service Snyder was appointed as an Advisor to the EXCOM.

With President Rodenberg presiding the new EXCOM confirmed that the next Congress would be in Lyon, France in 1981, and that the next EXCOM would be held in Šibenik in conjunction with the International Festival celebrating the Year of the Child in June 1979. They also accepted the USA invitation to hold an EXCOM Meeting in Washington, D.C. in 1980.

During the past few years Spain had worked hard to become acquainted with Spanish speaking leaders of theatre for young audiences in Mexico, Central America, and South America. With Spain's assistance a few of these people were able to attend the Congress, and it provided the long established centers of Europe and North America with an opportunity to expand their world view.

Perhaps the most memorable event of this Congress was the long six hour bus trip through the countryside of La Mancha to a village which prided itself on its *El Corrale de Almagro*—a theatre from the 17th Century set in a courtyard among houses where windows on the upper floors were used as box seats. A talented company presented Miguel de Cervantes' entremeses, *Retablo de las Maravillas*, directed by José Osumn. All of the actors were men dedicated to honoring the tradition of grand gesture and voice.

The delegates joined the enraptured villagers as audience to this marvelous theatre event, and to the authentic *paseo*[35] which took place in the village square following the performance.

As usual politics had raised its head at the Spanish Congress in the General Assembly, but it was tame compared to what was to come in Moscow, Australia, and Stockholm in the next twelve years.

INTERIM (1976–1979)

1976

In the fall of 1976 the Board of the US Center for ASSITEJ asked Ann Shaw to complete Nicholas Wandmacher's term as Executive Secretary-Treasurer. Wandmacher had resigned to accept the office of Treasurer of the American Theatre Association (ATA). Shaw had been told membership had fallen off some.

Shaw recalls, "I arrived at Nick's home on Long Island. I found that 'some' applied to the remaining 27 members, 2 of whom kept neglecting to pay their dues but were 'good for it.' . . . The amount of money remaining in the US Center account was in dispute as it was held in the coffers of ATA, and our separate account books didn't agree. . . . And then there was the matter of ASSITEJ International billing us for several hundred US dollars for the 300-400 back issues of a dismal publication in three languages which had arrived the worse for postal wear and reposed in Nick's basement.

"Nick offered to carry these gems to my rented car, and ever after enjoyed telling people: 'Ann's response was to collapse on the basement stairs and say something profound like Oh, Brother!' I persuaded Nick to keep the publications until we solved the problem.

"Happily we found a copy of the letter that Nick had sent to Paris reducing our order to 30 or so over a year before this lot was mailed. The Paris office said it had not received our letter. Hmmm. Patricia Snyder, then President of the US Center and our international representative, was able to persuade the international EXCOM that the error in numbers and the delay in receipt of publications was not the fault of the US Center. I think Nick incinerated the publications."[36]

This incident and change of leadership is what prompted the exchange of letters and thorough discussions at the ASSITEJ meetings of this time.

1977

In 1977 the Czech Center issued in mimeographed form "Who's Who in ASSITEJ". It listed short biographies of the major leaders in ASSITEJ as submitted by their national centers.[37] The brief biographies were written either in French or English. Three years in the making, it was divided into three sections: 1) Honorary Members; 2) major ASSITEJ Leaders; and 3) names of those to be included in a future edition. It tried to include biographical information on these leaders up through 1977.

It first listed those who had been elected as Members of Honor in

1975: Alexander A. Bryantsev (USSR), Léon Chancerel (France), Charlotte Chorpenning (USA), Míla Mellanová (Czechoslovakia), and Victor Popa (Romania). Then Honorary President: Gerald Tyler (Great Britain).

Then the biographies of the other notables: Vladimir Adamek (Czechoslovakia), Margareta Barbutza (Romania), Myra Benson (Great Britain), Benito Biotto (Italy), Orlin Corey (USA), Ljubisa Djokič (Yugoslavia), Joyce Doolittle (Canada), John English (Great Britain), Jean-Yves Gaudreault (Canada), Hanswalter Gossmann (FGR), Victor Georgiev (Bulgaria), Caryl Jenner (Great Britain), Inga Juul (Denmark), Ján Kákoš (Czechoslovakia), Yuri P. Kiselyov (USSR), Galina Kolosova (USSR), Ian Cojar (Romania), Zvjezdana Ladika (Yugoslavia), Wolker D. Laturell (FGR), Rafaello Lavagna (Italy), Ion Lucian (Romania), Stanislav Mičinec (Czechoslovakia), Rose-Marie Moudoués (France), Eberhard Möbius (FGR), Milka Natcheva (Bulgaria), and Orna Porat (Israel).

It was an accurate and valuable document.

1978

Rebuilding the US Center for ASSITEJ was the new goal of the USA leadership. By the time of the International Congress in Spain in June 1978, the membership had increased dramatically, and the US delegation to the Madrid Congress numbered 72.

1979

In November 1979 the following countries were listed as having ASSITEJ Centers, a total of 27 national centers. Denmark and Japan were listed as possible new centers,[38] making a total of 29.

Algeria
Australia
Belgium
Bulgaria
Canada
Czechoslovakia
Cuba
FGR
Finland
France
GDR
Great Britain
Hungary
Ira

Ireland
Israel
Italy
Netherlands
Peru
Portugal
Romania
Spain
Sri Lanka (Ceylon)
Switzerland
USSR
USA
Yugoslavia

1978
BUREAU MEETING
Paris, France/October 1978

The Bureau of ASSITEJ met in Paris, France in October 1978 five months after the VIth International Congress in Madrid, Spain. President Ilse Rodenberg (GDR) presided as President, Joyce Doolittle (Canada) as 1st Vice President, Maria Sunyer (Spain) as 2nd Vice President, Natalya Satz (USSR) as 3rd Vice President, Rose-Marie Moudoués (France) as Secretary General, and Ion Lucian (Romania) as Treasurer.[39]

President Rodenberg presided and established the Agenda to deal with the following items:
- Materials from the VIth International Congress in Madrid would be published in the Review.
- The following Commissions would continue their work:
    Statute and Official Documents—Moudoués as Chair
    Publications and Terminology—Sunyer as Chair
    Themes—Lucian as Chair
    Publicity and Coordination—Rodenberg as Chair
    Co-operation with AITA/IATA and UNIMA—Doolittle as Chair

They approved the next meeting of the EXCOM at Šibenik, Yugoslavia 25 June-1 July 1979 during their International Festival (23 June-7 July 1979). Representatives from the national centers of Denmark, Finland, Sri Lanka, Turkey, and Japan would be invited to attend. Meetings of the Bureau and the Commissions would precede the EXCOM Meeting.

With Maurice Yendt (France) in attendance they approved the basic principles for the preparation of the VIIth International Congress to be held in Lyon, France in 1981.

Dealt with problems of the centers in Denmark, Algeria, and Peru.[40]

The Bureau accepted the Center in Poland provided it would fulfill all necessary duties and obligations.

National Centers: Celebrating the Year of the Child, under news of the national centers:
- **Great Britain**—Announced the April 1979 International Festival in Cardiff, Wales, a Festival at the Young Vic in London in October 1979, and the publication of an article by Honorary President Gerald Tyler on "Searching for New Aesthetic Forms in Children's and Youth Theatre."
- **USSR**—Announced tours in Europe by Natalya Satz' State Musical Theatre for Children of Moscow, Zinovy Korogodski's Leningrad

Theatre for Young Spectators performed in Moscow, many theatres for children around the USSR participated in the spring of 1978 in the Pan-Russian Festival of Theatrical Art of the Nations of the USSR, a birthday celebration for Natalya Satz—her 75th year and her 60th year of creative activity in theatrical art for children.

- **Switzerland**—The Swiss Center's Newsletter carried a detailed report on the 1978 Madrid Congress.
- **France**—The 2nd International Meeting of Theatres for Children and Youth will be held in Lyon, France from 1-17 June 1979.
- **Spain**—Is offering a competition for the best play written by children and for children in honor of the International Year of the Child. The 10th Number of the Boletino Ibero-americano presented materials on the history and activity of children's theatre in Catalonia, which date back to the beginning of the 20th century.
- **Netherlands**—"Scapino", a ballet for children, was awarded first prize at the 1977 Forum of Dance in the Theatre des Champ-Elysées in Paris, and toured to FGR, Italy, and Yugoslavia, and Dame Hans Snoek has created a new association dedicated to bringing children of the Netherlands and children of foreign workers in the Netherlands together through theatrical means. The Netherlands Center is continuing its process of reorganization.
- **GDR**—The GDR held its well known International Seminar of Directors of Theatre for Children and Young People in Berlin in November 1978. This was its third iteration. The book "Theatre for Children and Young People in the World" was published in 1978 to great acclaim. Comments for a future edition are asked for.
- **Belgium**—The Royal Theatre for Young People in Antwerp, Belgium presented a new play about the artist Rubens "Pietro Paolo of Antwerp", an opera "The Man from the Cake", and a new dramatization of "Tom Sawyer" after Mark Twain.
- **Norway**—Elisabeth Gording of Oslo sent 20 years of materials of the theatre Barn og Ungdomsteatret to the Secretariat in Paris.
- **Canada**—Vice-President Joyce Doolittle was awarded the Province of Alberta Achievement Award. In 1978 in Montreal the Théâtre des Pissenlits of Jean-Yves Gaudreault celebrated its eleventh year of production—over two thousand performances for more than a million young spectators. New performances are being prepared for 1979.
- **Czechoslovakia**—Listed many performances of new plays as well as translations of familiar works around the country.

- There was no news listed from the **USA Center**, which was reorganizing and going through the throes of a diminished membership as well as its attendant lack of finances.

From this Bulletin it is clear that Past President Adamek along with Secretary General Moudoués had been using the meetings of Bureau, not just for formulating agendas for the future meetings of the EXCOM, but using it for decisions before the input of the EXCOM.

In this first ASSITEJ Meeting since the spring 1978 Congress in Spain when Rodenberg replaced Adamek as President, the discussions showed that President Rodenberg was consistently following Past President Adamek's practice of using the Bureau both for making decisions as well as using his excellent concept of Working Groups to forward the business of ASSITEJ.

1979
BUREAU MEETING
Moscow, USSR/10–13 June 1979[41]

The Czech Minutes state that "It was attended by all its members and counselors." These would probably have been: Ilse Rodenberg (GDR) presided as President, Maria Sunyer (Spain) as 2nd Vice President, Natalya Satz as 3rd Vice-President, Rose-Marie Moudoués (France) as Secretary General, and Ion Lucian (Romania) as Treasurer.

Vladimir Adamek (Czechoslovakia) as Counselor was present.

Absent: Joyce Doolittle as 1st Vice-President and the Canadian representative had resigned in 1978.

The Bureau met at this time because of the opening of the new building of the State Children's Theatre of Music, a building later named in honor of Natalya Satz. Foreign guests from France (Moudoués), Bulgaria (Georgiev), Romania (Lucian), USA (Snyder), Czechoslovakia (Adamek), Spain (Sunyer), Yugoslavia (Ladika), GDR (Rodenberg), Canada (Rubes), Hungary, and Poland. They met representatives of the Soviet ASSITEJ Center, and were received by P. Barabash, the USSR Deputy Minister of Culture.

Items discussed were as follows:
- Rodenberg reported on her trips to various national centers, Reports of the Secretary General, and the Treasurer
- Preparations for the EXCOM Meeting in the USA/9-17 April 1980
- Problems about the VIIIth Congress in Lyon in 1981
- A plan of ASSITEJ activities, and the possibility of holding the next Congress in the USSR, a Bureau Meeting in the autumn 1980 in the FGR
- Proposals for changes in the Statutes

1979
EXECUTIVE COMMITTEE MEETING
Šibenik, Yugoslavia/25–28 June 1979

The EXCOM of ASSITEJ met in Šibenik, Yugoslavia on 25–29 June 1979 in conjunction with the 19th Yugoslav Child's Festival which ran from 21 June to 7 July 1979. The Festival was sponsored by UNESCO.

Ilse Rodenberg (GDR) presided as President, the position of 1st Vice President was vacant, Maria Sunyer (Spain) as 2nd Vice President, Natalya Satz as 3rd Vice-President, Rose-Marie Moudoués (France) as Secretary General, and Ion Lucian (Romania) as Treasurer.[42]

Members present: Victor Georgiev (Bulgaria), Susan Rubes (Canada), Vladimir Adamek (Czechoslovakia), Kathrin Türks (FGR), Mrs. Penny Francis for John English (Great Britain), Orna Porat (Israel), Elisabeth Cozona (Switzerland), Ann Shaw (USA), Natalya Satz (USSR), and Zvjezdana Ladika (Yugoslavia).

Absent: Ottorino Negri (Italy).

Invitees: Inga Juul (Denmark), Nena Stenius (Finland). Japan, Turkey, and Sri Lanka did not send any invited delegate.

Observer: Ladislav Knižátko (Czechoslovakia).

Several changes were noted: Joyce Doolittle (Canada) had resigned leaving a Vice-Presidency vacant, and now Susan Rubes represented Canada. Ann Shaw had replaced Patricia Snyder as the representative from the USA Center. The British Center had sent Mrs. P. Francis to be its representative at the Šibenik meeting.

1st Meeting of the EXCOM

Ilse Rodenberg (GDR), presiding as President, welcomed the delegates and thanked Drago Putnikovič and the Festival's executive committee for their excellent hospitality.

Joyce Doolittle (Canada) announced her resignation as 1st Vice-President, and introduced Susan Rubes, an actress and producer from Young People's Theatre in Toronto, as the new official Canadian delegate.

Adamek announced his intention to retire as the Czech delegate, which gave reason for the presence of Ladislav Knižátko as an Observer.

Japan had officially opened its Center on 12 May 1979, and because of this occasion they were not able to attend the meeting.

The EXCOM approved the following items on the Agenda:
- Accepted the Minutes from the last session, accepted the Report of the Bureau and of the Commissions, and the Reports of the Secretary General and the Treasurer.
- Approved the transfer of the ASSITEJ Account to another Paris bank,

since there had been a bank crisis in France two years before, and instructed the Treasurer to inform all the centers accordingly. Also urged the Treasurer to press those centers in arrears to pay their back dues immediately.
- Accepted Japan, Ecuador, and Iraq as new Centers.
- Discussed issues pertaining to publicity for theatre art for young people, and a proposal for a joint conference with the International Organization of Theatre Critics.
- Noted Presidential trips to FGR, Denmark, and Belgium to assist with problems of their centers.
- Endorsed the USA proposal of fund raising through the sale of theatre posters.
- Requested that all centers inform the Secretariat in advance of their important events.
- Approved the basic outline of the program for the VIIth International Congress in Lyon in June 1981.
- Discussed reports on the work in the centers of Denmark, Finland, and Yugoslavia.
- Accepted the USA invitation and program for an EXCOM Meeting in April 1980, and recommended holding an EXCOM Meeting in Prague in the spring of 1981.
- Endorsed the Bureau's proposal to invite representatives of centers in Austria, Cuba, Peru, Venezuela, Ecuador, and Uruguay to the EXCOM in the USA.

Two days were set aside for papers and discussion of the theme: Art—A Tie of Friendship between the Children of the World. A total of ten papers were presented. The Secretary General was to distribute information on the sessions to all the centers.

News from the National Centers included:
- **USA**—The Empire State Youth Theatre under the direction of Patricia Snyder featured 18 different productions in the past three seasons in its new theatre building.
- **Spain**—The National Center of Initiation of Children and Youth to Theatre, an ensemble supervised by the General Theatre Management of the Ministry of Culture met with great success in the Year of the Child. Plays were presented in Madrid, Alicante, Seville, and Cadiz. The events in Alicante alone were attended by over 10,000 children. Performances included workshop sessions with teachers, local theatrical ensembles, and the like.
- **Finland**—In addition to 5 professional theatres and 3 amateur

theatres, the Finish Center had 27 individual members in the spring of 1979. In celebration of the Year of the Child a Festival of Theatre Performances for Children is being planned for October of 1979. The Center has begun to publish its own Bulletin, and seeks to establish a wider Scandinavian base for its cooperative efforts.

- **France**—The Théâtre des Jeunes Années of Lyon, Maurice Yendt Director, held its 2nd International Meeting of Theatre for Children and Young People from 5-17 June 1979, with the participation of 5 French and 5 foreign theatres (Poland, Portugal, Canada, USSR, and Spain), including workshops and public discussions. *The ASSITEJ Review*—Nos. 1 and 2, 1978 carry materials from the VIth International Congress of ASSITEJ in Madrid in 1978.
- **Canada**—The Young People's Theatre of Toronto, Directed by Susan Rubes, included a new version of *Treasure Island* by Robert Lewis Stevenson, *The Curse of the Werewolf* by Ken Hill, and a play on the life of Hans Christian Andersen, directed by Brian McDonald. L'Université du Montréal plans an international conference on Utilization of the Arts in August 1980. Joyce Doolittle and Zina Barnieh have published their book *A Mirror of Our Dreams: Children and the Theatre of Canada*, with a chapter on Quebec theatre for the young by Hélène Beauchamp.
- **FGR**—The ASSITEJ Center continues to publish its *Grimm+Grips* Bulletin. The Spring 1979 issue features events on the occasion of the International Year of the Child, including an article by Ilse Rodenberg on international trends in theatre for children and youth. Wolker D. Lauterell (Munich), well known for his ASSITEJ activities, has received the Order of Merit of the FGR from the Bavarian Ministry of Culture and Education.
- **GDR**—The 3rd International Seminar of Directors of Theatre for Children (9-14 November 1978) is featured in Issue No. 7 of the GDR ASSITEJ Review. The fourth International Seminar of Directors will be held in November 1980. An exhibition held in the Theater der Freundschaft in Berlin commemorated Dr. Hans Rodenberg, the theatre's founder and an Honorary Member of ASSITEJ.
- **Romania**—A Festival held in Bucharest titled "The Arts and the Child" featured many productions by professional and amateur theatres.
- **Australia**—*Lowdown*, a voluminous publication contains information on the organizational structure and activities of theatre for children and youth in Australia. "Kids-Train" is a project scheduled to tour

various Australian towns for several weeks presenting productions for children. A Festival of the Arts is to be held in Adelaide in 1979 with foreign troupes presenting plays for children.
- **USSR**—Many events celebrated the International Year of the Child: the Pan-Russian conference "Theatre and Village Children", a Revue of the 1979 and 1980 productions for children, a joint conference of theatres for young audiences and marionette theatres on "Specifics of Development and Art in Today's Soviet Theatre for Children", a working session of dramaturges of theatres of music, a joint conference of the heads and pedagogues of theatres for young audiences, and featured programs on national television and radio networks. The Leningrad Theatre for Young Spectators, headed by Zinovy Korogodski, performed *Our Circus, Bambi, A Public Lesson*, and Shakespeare's *A Comedy of Errors* in Poland in 1979.
- **Belgium**—The Royal Youth Theatre in Antwerp featured a new play by Jean Colette and Rid Olivier *Come to the Table, Julian, Shut Up and Eat the Bananas.*
- **Yugoslavia**—A new record on the Jugoton label features the musical *Genghis Khan the Tomcat and Miki Trasi*, performed by the Theatre for the Young of Zagreb.
- **Czechoslovakia**—the Jiří Wolker Theatre in Prague has added several plays to its repertory, including 3 classics—*The Taming of the Shrew* of Shakespeare, *The Insect Comedy* of Karel Capek, and *Balzaminov's Wedding* by Ostrovsky.

The EXCOM also held a joint meeting with representatives of UNIMA and AITA/IATA which was attended by Secretary Generals Henry Jurkowski of UNIMA and Jan Ytteborg of AITA/IATA. The session analyzed their joint contributions to the International Year of the Child, and they agreed to the principles of contacts, mutual invitations, and exchange of information on the international scale as well as within the countries.

Performances: The members were also able to see many events as part of the Šibenik Festival. Performances were presented from the following countries: 61 from Yugoslavia, 2 from Belgium, 18 from Bulgaria, 24 from Czechoslovakia, 5 from Great Britain, 3 from Finland, 17 from France, 3 from Israel, 1 from Korea, 3 from Madagascar, 1 from the Netherlands, 7 from GDR, 5 from FGR, 5 from the USA, 46 from Poland, 18 from Romania, 18 from the USSR, 11 from Spain, and 6 from Sweden.[43] In addition there was an international exhibition of posters and children's drawings, an arts conference, and many marionette and film showings.

Outdoor performance, Festival of the Child, Šibenik, Yugoslavia, June 1979.
Courtesy of Archives, ASU, AZ, USA.

Of particular interest were puppet productions which were part of the Festival. The Zagreb Puppet Theatre presented a fairy tale entitled *Bas-Celik* ("Bad-Iron"), a black metal bullet-headed monster with copper teeth and two bull horns, black drapery body, no hands, and riding a 7-foot horse with a shiny black head. The horse stomped him to death at the end of the puppet play.

The company used rod-puppets—a carefully crafted head on a metal rod with shoulders attached. The body was draped fabric with the hands at the end of the fabric supported by two rods, one for each hand. The actor speaking the lines moved the head, while another manipulated the two hands.

The Drak Puppet Theatre of Czechoslovakia presented a very adult and highly political *Circus Unicum* ("The Greatest Circus on Earth") featuring an evil Ringmaster (Premier Brezhnev?), his dwarf son (a puppet country?), a dancing bear (Russia?), a blond magician (corrupt youth?). The company's cry for freedom and simple honesty was almost audible.[44]

Events: Members of the EXCOM were received at the Šibenik Town Hall, attended receptions organized by the Yugoslav state authorities and the Festival management, and took part in an outing to the waterfalls on the river Krka.

At the conclusion the EXCOM voiced its thanks to Zvjezdana Ladika, Berislav Frkič of the Yugoslav Center, and Festival Director Drago Putnikovič for their great care devoted to the organization of the sessions and their exceptional hospitality.

1980
EXECUTIVE COMMITTEE MEETING
Washington, D.C./9–14 April 1980[45]

The Executive Committee of ASSITEJ met in Washington, D.C., USA from 9–14 April 1980.

Ilse Rodenberg (GDR) presided as President, the position of 1st Vice President was vacant, Maria Sunyer (Spain) as 2nd Vice President, Rose-Marie Moudoués (France) as Secretary General.

Members attending were: Sara Lee Lewis (deputized for Susan Rubes—Canada), Wolfgang Wöhlert (deputized for Vladimir Adamek—Czechoslovakia), Kathrin Türks (FGR), Shaun Hennessey (Great Britain), Orna Porat (Israel), Ottorino Negri (Italy), Elisabeth Cozona (Switzerland), Ann Shaw (USA), and Zvjezdana Ladika (Yugoslavia).[46]

Members absent: Bulgaria, Romania, and USSR.

Invited members: Joan Pope (Australia), Eddy Socorro (Cuba) and his interpreter, and Shin Shikata (Japan). Invited but not attending were: Peru, Uruguay, and Venezuela.

Presenters: Maurice Yendt, Michel Dieuaide (France) had been invited to discuss preparations for the VIIth International Congress in Lyon in 1981.

Washington, D.C., USA

Since the EXCOM meeting was being sponsored by the US Center, the Center had also invited all members of its Center, at their own expense, to attend the annual conference held by the Kennedy Center in conjunction with their Imagination Celebration. That conference was scheduled from 11-13 April 1980, and it focused on issues and approaches involved in management, directing, and pedagogy related to theatres for young audiences. The attendees were also hosted at the reception being held for the EXCOM during their meeting. Most of the 60 members of the US Center accepted the invitation.

Dr. Ann Shaw (1st Vice-President of ASSITEJ) in the center introduces Mrs. Jean Kennedy Smith (Sister of Former U.S. President John F. Kennedy Jr.) to Mme. Rose-Marie Moudoués—Secretary General of ASSITEJ (France); seated at the left, are Maurice Yendt (France) and Patricia Whitton (USA) looking on at the EXCOM Meeting in Washington, D.C., USA, April 1980. Photo courtesy of the Archives, ASU, AZ, USA.

Dr. Nat Eek, Past President of ASSITEJ (1972–1975) welcoming the delegates at the EXCOM Meeting in Washington, D.C., USA, April 1980. Photo courtesy of the Archives, ASU, AZ, USA.

Dr. Ilse Rodenberg (GDR) President of ASSITEJ at the EXCOM Meeting in Washington, D.C., USA, April 1980. Photo courtesy of the Archives, ASU, AZ, USA.

Zjvezdana Ladika (Yugoslavia) attending the EXCOM Meeting in Washington, D.C., USA, April 1980. Photo courtesy of the Archives, ASU, AZ, USA.

1st Meeting of the EXCOM

After the sessions of the Bureau and the Commissions, the EXCOM approved the following:
- Approved the Minutes of the Šibenik Meeting in 1979 (only in French), the Report on the Bureau's activities, the Financial Report, and the Reports of the President and Secretary General
- Accepted new centers in Sweden, Turkey, and Argentina as members
- Heard the Report of the Secretary General on the centers in Peru, Netherlands, Portugal, Iraq, and Ecuador
- Discussed the complicated situation in Denmark and suggested solutions to the problem
- Endorsed suggestions for improving contacts and cooperation with centers in Latin America
- Heard the reports by the representatives from Australia and Japan on their contacts with other countries in Asia and the Pacific area
- Noted the report by the Secretary General on cooperation between ASSITEJ, UNIMA, IATA/AITA and AICT (International Association of

Theatre Critics), and on the UNESCO Conference on theatre in Paris in March 1980
- The Poster sale had started, but Centers were not sending in bibliographic materials

Recommendations for changes in the Statutes were being received, and the Committee will draw up comprehensive materials before the next Congress in Lyon. Publications still needed more material. Suggestions on Terminology will be published for the next Congress.

The EXCOM received reports from Australia, Cuba, Japan, and USA. Endorsed the plans for the Lyon Congress and endorsed the theme: "The Role and Place of Theatre for Children and Young People in Contemporary Theatre Art."

They also set the next meetings of the Bureau and the EXCOM in Prague in mid-March 1981. Received invitations to have an EXCOM meeting in Cuba in 1982; to hold the VIIIth International Congress in Moscow in 1984; and an invitation to hold the same Congress in Birmingham, Great Britain in 1984.

The Secretariat promised to send the Minutes of the Meetings to all the Centers.

Performances: The EXCOM viewed the preview performance of *Maggie Megalita* by Wendy Kesselman, the first play for young audiences produced by the John F. Kennedy Center for the Performing Arts. The play ". . . dealt with the way a young girl trying to assimilate into American teen-age culture faced the crisis of her Spanish-speaking grandmother's arrival into her home and life."[47]

President Rodenberg presented an address "International Perspectives on Theatre for Young Audiences" following the performance.

They also viewed *Analysis of Mineral No. 4* by Moses Goldberg as produced by the Louisville, Kentucky Children's Theatre.

Special Events: The EXCOM and delegates and observers were treated to a special buffet at the home of Mrs. Sally Smith, a well-known Washington hostess. The feast, with dishes named for the various states of the union featured Maryland shrimp, New Mexico nachos, Virginia pumpkin soup, Georgia baked ham, Wyoming lemon chicken, Florida key lime tarts, and a red-white-and-blue cordial to complete it, was prepared by Nat Eek, Patricia Snyder, and Bill Gleason of the US Center.

Jean Kennedy Smith (sister of the former U.S. President) presented bronze medallions from the Kennedy Center to all the international delegates at a special luncheon, and in return the US Center gave Mrs. Smith a collection of international theatre posters.

Excursions: While in Washington, the delegates visited several performances for children and young people, a puppet theatre, and the American Ballet Theatre. There were discussions on stage directing, pedagogies and management, and all delegates were invited to tour the White House, the Capitol, and the Hirschorn Art Gallery.

The officials of the Kennedy Center and the US Center for ASSITEJ hosted several receptions. The Closing Ceremony Luncheon was hosted by Jean Kennedy Smith, and on behalf of the EXCOM, President Ilse Rodenberg thanked all those involved in making the meetings so successful, particularly Ann Shaw, Chair of the US Center.

After the Washington meeting, many of the delegates and their interpreters accepted the invitation of Patricia Snyder to visit the Empire State Theatre in Albany, New York, where she gave an instructive review of their Institute's art and educational work. They were also hosted at the Empire State Theatre's performance of *Sleeping Beauty* followed by a reception at Snyder's home. This production was later invited to appear at the Lyon Congress in 1981.

News of the Centers included:
- **Spain**: The Ministry of Culture published a volume of extensive materials on the VIth International Congress of ASSITEJ held in Madrid in 1978. Issue No. 16 of the *Boletino Ibero-americano*, published by the Spanish Center, was distributed to Spanish-speaking countries in March 1980.
- **USSR**: The Soviet Union now has some 200 theatrical companies for young audiences, with performances in 40 languages, which are seen by over 70 million children. The premiere in the new building of the Moscow State Musical Theatre for Children, later named in honor of Natalya Satz, was the opera *Little Red Riding Hood* by M. Rauchverger, newly edited by Natalya Satz. For adult spectators they staged Puccini's *Madame Butterfly*.
- **Denmark**: The Cooperative Committee of theatres for children and youth under the leadership of Jorgen Melskens organized the 10th Danish Festivals of Theatre for Children. At Aabenraa in April 1980 some forty companies participated. Admission fees to about 80 performances were subsidized by the Ministry of Culture.
- **Japan**: *Theatre for Children in Japan 1979* edited by Sozaburo Otiai featured 85 theatres and 12 organizations involved in the art (including puppet theatres). In one year theatre companies staged

15,500 performances for an audience of 8.5 million children. The Japanese ASSITEJ Center plans to publish information on its activities in English for distribution abroad.
- **Cuba**: An exhibition on the Development of Theatre for Children and Young People in Cuba was part of the January 1980 Theatre Festival. President Ilse Rodenberg visited Cuba at the invitation of their ASSITEJ Center for two weeks.
- **Australia**: As part of their celebration of the Year of the Child, eight troupes toured the outback giving performances where none had ever been staged before.
- **Canada**: 13 Canadian companies and foreign theatres participated in the 7th Quebec Children's Theatre Festival in Montreal in August 1980.
- **Israel:** The National Theatre for Children and Young People last season staged 1,372 performances in 122 towns, villages, and settlements for an audience of over 500,000. Orna Porat, its director and founder, was awarded the 1979 Israel Prize.
- **FGR**: The ASSITEJ Center has just published a handbook and directory plus descriptions of all theatres for children and young people in the FGR.
- **GDR**: Materials from the 4th International Seminar of Directors of Theatres for Children have been published in No. 8 of the GDR ASSITEJ Bulletin. 27 scores from 13 countries were entered in the international music competition for musical theatre for children. Awards went to composers from Switzerland, Netherlands, GDR, USSR, Yugoslavia, and Austria. President Rodenberg was a guest at the Children's Theatre Festival in London.
- **USA**: The Paris Secretariat has received a directory of names and addresses of publishers of plays and literature on theatre for children in the USA.
- **Uruguay**: The EXCOM of Uruguayan ASSITEJ met in the autumn of 1979 to discuss ways of expanding its activities, sponsoring festivals, and opportunities for contact with theatres in Argentina and Brazil.
- **Sweden**: Unga Clara (Young Clara), a prominent children's theatre in Stockholm, organized a festival of its productions in autumn 1979. It was founded in 1975.
- **Switzerland**: Following the success of the 1979 International Festival of Theatre for Children, other festivals are being planned for Geneva and Lugano in 1981.
- **Belgium**: An article in *Brabant Magazine (No. 1/1980)* by R. Deldime

analyses the problems of theatre for children on the occasion of their international festival, held in Brussels from 13-17 November 1979.
- **Czechoslovakia**: Prague's National Theatre premiered "The Nutcracker Ballet" by Tchaikovsky for children the end of 1979, directed with high originality by M. Kůra. Students of the theatre faculty of Prague's Academy of Performing Arts chose Maurice Yendt's play *Machine à Théâtre* for their mid-term exams in January 1980. Many new titles have been added to the 1979-1980 season, including premieres of plays from USSR, Great Britain, Italy, France, USA, GDR, and other countries.

1980
BUREAU MEETING OF ASSITEJ
Dortmund/FGR/28–30 November 1980[48]

The Bureau of ASSITEJ met in Dortmund, FGR from 28–30 November 1980. President Ilse Rodenberg presided, Maria Sunyer (Spain) and Natalya Satz (USSR) as Vice-Presidents, Rose-Marie Moudoués (France) as Secretary General, Ion Lucian (Romania) as Treasurer, and Vladimir Adamek (Czechoslovakia) as Counselor.

The Bureau was warmly welcomed by Kathrin Türks, President of the FGR ASSITEJ Center, and Egmont Elschner. In addition to the meetings, they offered the Bureau the opportunity to see three productions, one each in Dortmund, Düsseldorf, and Essen, as well as meeting with the theatre staffs, other artists, representatives of municipal institutions, and trade unions. Directors of Municipal Theatres also attended the meetings.

The Bureau dealt with the following items:
- Preparations for the next EXCOM Meeting, including the Bureau and the Commissions, in Prague from 16–20 March 1981
- Preparations for the VIIIth Congress in Lyon from 13–20 June 1981
- Non-payment of dues by centers, which need to be reminded that they cannot vote nor be elected at the next Congress without their paying of all dues
- Dealing with Spain's suggestion to organize a Latin-American Centers meeting prior to the Lyon Congress in early 1981. This was accepted unanimously.

1981
EXECUTIVE COMMITTEE MEETING
Prague, Czechoslovakia/17–20 March 1981

The Executive Committee of ASSITEJ met in Prague, Czechoslovakia from 17–20 March 1981. President Ilse Rodenberg (GDR) presided, with Maria Sunyer (Spain) and Natalya Satz as Vice-Presidents, Rose-Marie Moudoués (France) as Secretary General, and Ion Lucian (Romania) as Treasurer.

Members attending were: Victor Georgiev (Bulgaria), Dennis Foon for Sara Lee Lewis (Canada), Kathrin Türks (FGR), Egmont Elschner (GDR), Shaun Hennessey (Great Britain), Orna Porat (Israel), Ottorino Negri (Italy), Elisabeth Cozona (Switzerland), Ann Shaw (USA), and Zvjezdana Ladika (Yugoslavia).

Advisors: Vladimir Adamek (Czechoslovakia) and Patricia Snyder (USA).

Invitees: J. Nyilassi (Hungary). Portugal and Belgium declined, Netherlands and Algeria were absent. Maurice Yendt and Michele Dieuaide were invited to present the 1981 Congress Program in Lyon.

Other invitees: Gabriel Vessigault (France), Eddy Socorro (Cuba), Elisabeth Gording (Norway), Francis Fluhman (Switzerland), Irina Godiridze (USSR), Wolfgang Wöhlert (GDR), and Ladislav Knižátko and Karel Richter (Czechoslovakia).[49]

The members were welcomed by M. Klusák, Minister of Culture, and Ms. O. Janská, Chair of the Trade Union Association of Workers in Art, Culture, and Social Organizations. The Bureau and the Commissions met prior to the EXCOM Meeting.

City Gates, Old Town, Prague, Czechoslovakia. Personal photograph.

1st Meeting of the EXCOM/17 March 1981

President Ilse Rodenberg opened the meeting at 3:05 PM on 17 March 1981 at the Jiří Wolker Theatre Club. The Agenda as proposed by the Bureau was accepted without change.

- Approval of the Minutes of the 1980 EXCOM Meeting in Washington, D.C.
- Secretary General's Report
- Question's from Centers: USA and Spain
- Financial Report
- Preparations for the 1981 International Congress
- Commission Reports
- Reports from the invited centers
- Report from the Czech Center
- Other business

Rodenberg then announced that the EXCOM would first consider the preparations for the 1981 International Congress in Lyon, France, since Yendt and Dieuaide could only be there for that day.

Meanwhile papers were handed out for study: Statutes of the Danish Center and a letter of explanation from Inga Juul. Also, they received copies of a new Danish Center's Constitution from another source [Melskens].

Presentation of the Program for the VIIth International Congress in Lyon, France: Yendt and Dieuaide had tried to incorporate the suggestions made by the EXCOM to them at the Washington, D.C. meeting. With the help of President Rodenberg, Moudoués, and the Lyon authorities, considerable technical assistance was obtained. All the municipal theatres of Lyon will participate.

Performances: 6 foreign companies (USSR, GDR, USA, Czechoslovakia, Italy, and Sweden) and 7 French companies would present 14 productions for a total of 76 performances. The repetition of performances would allow all those at the Congress to see every play presented. The productions had been chosen to fit into the theme of the Congress ("The Role and Place of Theatre for Children and Young People in Contemporary Theatre Art") which would serve as a basis for discussion, while showing-off companies which operate under very different material circumstances.

Companies were selected not only that illustrated the theme of the Congress, but that 1) would provide some controversy, 2) companies which exist and work under different circumstances in their countries, and 3) a selection of plays which the participants in the Congress would like. The choice of foreign companies was based on reciprocity with the Théâtre des Jeunes Années in Lyon.

The foreign companies selected were: "Little Red Riding Hood" from Natalya Satz' Musical Theatre for Children (USSR); a production from the Theater der Freundschaft (GDR); "Sleeping Beauty" by the Empire State Youth Theatre Institute, directed by Patricia Snyder (USA); "With Bonds and Chains" from Turin Theatre (Italy); and "The Little Beast" by the National Theatre of Goteberg (Sweden).

From Lyon would come "Pebbles of the Stars"—Le Companie Grinet; "Einstein"—Careme Company; "Labors of Hercules"—L'Opera de Lyon; and "History of a Calendar"—The Red Ink Company.

French National Theatre Companies "Come In and Turn the Page"— The Theatre of Green Apple; "The Cat's Dance"—The Big Pebble Theatre; and "The History of Red Hair" and "A Graffiti on the Subway"—Le Théâtre des Jeunes Années.

Shaw asked if all invitations were extended with a reciprocal engagement in mind? Yendt replied that it was not systematic since it was very difficult to obtain money from the French Ministry of Culture to develop an exchange policy.

Meetings: There was to be a meeting hall for the official sessions, an exhibition hall, a library, and a hospitality location for everyone to meet and use. All Congress activities would be in one place in the center of Lyon: Le Palais Bondy. In one room each center would be provided with an exhibition stand for the display of information and publications. They requested centers to send technical information relative to the display material, and hoped that the displays would be colorful and lively, and in the three languages of ASSITEJ. A video tape room would be available for showings, technical information will be sent to the centers, and they needed to know who will be in charge from each center.

The opening session would be on 13 June with discussion papers to be presented by Natalya Satz, Shin Shikata, and Maurice Yendt. The mornings would be given over to Commission meetings and critiques of the productions. There would be four working groups: Sources of the server: dramatic writing; Theatre: a factor for integration or emancipation?; Does a young audience impose limits on the creative development of the artist?; and The school, a venue for performance.

The EXCOM would be housed at a hotel only a few yards away from the Congress location, and it and the Bureau would meet on 12 June. Simultaneous translation would be available for the Plenary Sessions, the General Assemblies, and the Commissions. Performances would be in various venues in the afternoons and evenings. There would be four receptions and A Celebration on the last evening.

The EXCOM would meet on Friday morning, 12 June at 2 PM, with the Official Opening Session on Saturday 13 June at 10 AM, which session all should attend.

As of 10 March 267 persons from 27 countries had registered. These included: Argentina, Australia, Belgium, Brazil, Bulgaria, Canada, Czechoslovakia, Denmark, FGR, Finland, France, GDR, Great Britain, Guatemala, Israel, Italy, Japan, Mexico, Portugal, South Africa, Spain, Sri Lanka, Sweden, USA, USSR, and Yugoslavia. There was concern that fewer had registered to attend than expected, and of those all have not yet paid the registration fee. They had expected 400 participants, based on the attendance at the 1978 Madrid Congress. That estimate probably did not take into account that Spain had just become a constitutional monarchy, was not often frequented by tourists, and costs were considerably lower.

Exhibition Guidelines: Each exhibit would be given a small stand. They do not want a formal aesthetic exhibit, but a lively one where every country would display what is happening. They hoped for everyone's very active participation.

Someone would need to be present to put up the exhibit, and all materials for putting up the exhibit would need to be sent with the exhibit. Photographs, posters, and printed materials of no value, and not for sale, would be admitted by Customs. However, centers could sell books at their stands.

Admittance: A Congress Membership Card would provide admittance to every session, to 14 productions, and to the receptions. The EXCOM would attend as guests. The 235 members, actors and technicians, of the producing companies would be guests of the Congress, and would be free to attend all meetings and performances. All attendees must pay a small fee (20 French Francs—approximately 4 US$) by 30 April. After that date hotel costs would rise.

Videoteque: Let them know immediately if you were planning to bring video tapes, the length of them, and verify permission to show the materials. Details would be sent in 10 days time, and the deadline for answers was 1 May. You must indicate on all Videotapes: contents, slides, length, projection time, and name the person in charge, and whether an interpreter is needed. Tape showings would be continuous and a part of the Congress Program. People can come and go as they wish.

Seminars: The EXCOM of the International Association of Theatre Critics and La Mission d'Animation Culturelle with the Ministry of Education have invited those interested in animation from other countries to participate in the Congress. The Critics' EXCOM would organize the play critiques.

The Commissions: Terminology. The question was raised how to move the current results forward to be presented at the next Congress. Moudoués asked Sunyer if the material already in hand be duplicated and sent to all the Centers in three months? Sunyer replied she would have to look into it in Madrid. **Translation:** Yendt asked about progress, and Moudoués replied that the Commission must make the first step, and then the National Centers would respond.

The Congress Program would allow Commission Reports for 10-20 minutes in length, and asked that they be sent in the 3 languages by the end of April for editing and rewriting for distribution at the Congress.

Speakers: The three main speakers at the Congress who would speak on the main theme would be: Natalya Satz (USSR), Shin Shikata (Japan), and Maurice Yendt (France).

1st Working Group: Sources of Contemporary Dramatic Writing; Reporter: Israel; Discussion Moderator: Yugoslavia.

2nd Working Group: Factors of Interpretation—a factor for integration or emancipation? Reporter: Portugal; Moderator: Spain.

3rd Working Group: Does a young audience impose limits on the creative development of the artist? Reporter: Wolfgang Wöhlert (GDR); Moderator: Canada.

4th Working Group: The school, a venue for performance. Reporter: Great Britain; Moderator: Italy.

Each Working Group would have three hours for their meeting. The invitations to the Reporters and the Moderators have been sent, and they have been asked to find the most suitable person to make the final Report and coordinate it.

The work of the Working Groups will start on the 2nd day. On the first day, they will meet with the coordinators and the interpreters, so they must be informed of who are the people chosen.

This concluded the presentation.

2nd Meeting of the EXCOM/18 March 1981

President Rodenberg explained to the EXCOM that Egmont Elschner would replace Kathrin Türks for the rest of the meeting. Ann Shaw, in the name of Jean Kennedy Smith, gave bronze medallions from the Kennedy Center to those absent from the Washington EXCOM Meeting (Ion Lucian, Victor Georgiev, and Natalya Satz).

The EXCOM proceeded to act on the following:
- Approved the Minutes of the meeting in Washington, D.C.
- Accepted the Secretary General's Report which listed the Bureau's preparation of the Prague Meeting, the questions for the Lyon

Congress, and the Agenda for the Congress General Assembly
- **New Centers: Egypt** planned to come to Lyon as an observer; **China**—Mme. Xiao, an envoy had received information about ASSITEJ, and has sent statutes to her Ministry; **Panama** through Eugenio Fernandez had asked for statutes and registration forms for the Lyon Congress as an observer; and **Zaïre** had not sent sufficient information for membership, but would have an observer at Lyon.

The ASSITEJ Centers reported the following information:
- **Norway**: Admitted as a Corresponding Center much to Elisabeth Gording's surprise. The Secretary General suggested she contact the corresponding center, and if theatres group around, then it could become a regular center. There is always the danger of a center being monopolized by one person, e.g. Denmark.
- **Belgium**: Edgard Verhoeven had not answered any correspondence. He had paid dues for one year, which was credited to 1979. 1980 and 1981 were in arrears. Belgium had a great deal of theatrical activity. A number of people were working under Roger Deldine, and it was recommended that he be contacted to reorganize the Belgian Center. The Swiss Center suggested that on the occasion of the Geneva Festival, where three Belgian companies would appear, that the opportunity be taken to find out their position *vis à vis* ASSITEJ. The motion was to be sent to Edgard Verhoeven. A liaison had been reestablished with an address for the new center.
- **Japan**: their center was very active, and the EXCOM should study ways to have them gather information from the Asiatic Continent.
- **Denmark**: there was considerable discussion to find out what exactly was the situation. Adamek proposed that the Secretary General of ITI intervene to find an accord between the current Danish Center of ASSITEJ and the companies united within Samarbejdsudvalget. 9 voted for, 5 against, 1 abstained.

In further discussion Adamek proposed that Moudoués write Melskens (Denmark) that the companies in membership of Samarbejdsudvalget should ask individually for admission to the Danish Center, and they should inform the Secretary General of the response. The Secretary General should demand that Melskens cease calling his group the Danish Committee of ASSITEJ since it was not affiliated with ASSITEJ. A copy of this letter was to be sent to Inga Juul. The proposal was passed unanimously.

There being no further business the meeting was adjourned.

In 2008 at Eek's inquiry and request Michael Ramløse replied: "Inga [Juul] did not accept the applications from the companies that wanted to join which led to the formation of an 'alternative' centre of about 20 companies (the leading professional companies in the country) and they gathered in a way under the auspices of Samarbejdsudvalget (later TEATERCENTRUM) of which Jørgen Melskens was the head. There was a meeting between Inga and the representatives of the 'Danish Committee of ASSITEJ'—a meeting that lasted about 10-15 minutes as Inga saw no point in talking to—let alone—allowing membership [to] companies whose only aim was to destroy the Danish Centre and take it over. At this time the official Danish Centre represented Inga Juul's theatre plus 3 personal members who were all drama pedagogues."[50]

1981
VIIth INTERNATIONAL CONGRESS OF ASSITEJ
Lyon, France/13-20 June 1981[51]

The VIIth International Congress of ASSITEJ was held in Lyon, France from 13-20 June 1981. Ilse Rodenberg (GDR) presided as President, Maria Sunyer (Spain) and Natalya Satz (USSR) as Vice Presidents, Rose-Marie Moudoués (France) as Secretary General, and Ion Lucian (Romania) as Treasurer.

Members of the EXCOM in attendance: Victor Georgiev (Bulgaria), Sara Lee Lewis (Canada), Ladislav Knižátko (Czechoslovakia), Kathrin Türks (FGR), John English (Great Britain), Orna Porat (Israel), Ottorino Negri (Italy), Elisabeth Cozona (Switzerland), Ann Shaw (USA), and Zvjezdana Ladika (Yugoslavia).

Advisors: Vladimir Adamek (Czechoslovakia) and Patricia Snyder (USA).

Countries attending were; Australia, Austria, Belgium, Brazil, Bulgaria, Canada, Cuba, Czechoslovakia, Denmark, FGR, Finland, France, GDR, Great Britain, Guatemala, Hungary, Israel, Italy, Japan, Mexico, Namibia, Netherlands, Norway, Panama, Paraguay, Poland, Portugal, Romania, South Africa, Spain, Sweden, Switzerland, Uruguay, USA, USSR, and Yugoslavia.

A total of 36 countries attended with most of the National Centers of ASSITEJ represented.

"The setting was France, in Lyon, one of the gourmet capitals of the world. The franc had just gone down enough to make *cafe au lait* and *croissants* a comparative bargain. . . . so the delegates gathered from around the world for 9 days of seeing plays and mingling with some 300 of our counterparts. . . . The sunshine was brilliant and the roses in bloom . . . the city beautiful with its Roman theatre and the Cathedral nestled in the hills above, and its two rivers, the Rhone and the Saone, intertwining among the red-roofed buildings, intersected by bridges and lined with quais. The food ranged from inexpensive to wildly extravagant—and it was all good. The public transportation was punctual and efficient, and the walking was even better, because of its abundant opportunities for stopping at outdoor cafes or shopping in open-air markets and talking, talking, talking."[52]

The Executive Committee Meeting/12 June 1981/after 5:00 PM

President Ilse Rodenberg presided. The EXCOM approved the following Agenda:
- Approval of the Minutes of the Prague EXCOM
- Candidature of Brazil/ Information on Poland

- Problem of Ecuador
- Explanation of votes in the General Assembly
- Discussion of the Secretary General and the Treasurer
- Voting on the Secretary General and the Treasurer
- Selection of the Official Auditors
- Subscriptions—dues
- Problem of the Danish Center

View of Lyon, France

The most serious discussions centered upon the following:

Brazil and Portugal: Brazil had sent a letter in Portuguese [the language of that country] which was translated into French requesting to be admitted as a member of ASSITEJ. The letter gave names of theatre groups and people concerned. They had an organization in Sao Paulo to which 20 theatres and teachers and critics belonged. Their representative was present at the Congress and ready to pay their dues. Could they be admitted?

Ecuador: Their ASSITEJ correspondent has left for Chile, and he has found no one to replace him. The center is therefore moribund.

Belgium: Cozona was asked to investigate the situation in Belgium. She found three theatre groups, but they had little contact with the Secretariat, and didn't know about the Lyon Congress. They would try to attend and straighten matters out.

Denmark: Moudoués had sent a letter to Denmark stating that the Melskens' companies should apply to Inga Juul for admittance to the Danish Center, and to send copies of her response to the Secretariat, and meanwhile asked them to remove ASSITEJ from their letterhead.

Melskens replied saying the meeting between Juul and them had been broken off. Juul called to say the door was open and she would welcome them, but nothing has been done.

The main problem was that in Lyon Juul, as the Danish representative, had brought an exhibit of the 5 theatres in the center. Melskens had also brought an exhibit that represented the other centers. When they came to the Exhibit Hall, they were told that they couldn't make their display without approval from the EXCOM since a Danish exhibit was already there. Melskens' group then asked the Swedish Center to give them space. The question of the EXCOM was: would they accept the Swedish exhibit distributing materials from the Melskens group? They were told that this was illegal. The discussion was quite heated.

The final decision was: 1) that the Melskens' materials not be allowed, and 2) an official committee be appointed from the EXCOM to attempt to get to the bottom of the controversy, and recommend a solution to the New EXCOM at this Congress. They appointed a committee of Nat Eek, Shaun Hennessey, Dennis Foon (Canada), and Orna Porat (Israel).

Moudoués said that Melskens was to call her tomorrow morning and she would inform him that 1) they could not accept his exhibit, and that neither could Sweden, and 2) that a committee of four had been appointed to find a solution.

In 2008 Ramløse wrote Eek as follows: "The illegal delegation consisted of Michael Ramløse (Theatre BANDEN) Anne Josephsen (representing the Association of Children's Theatres), Birthe Løkso (Theatre FONIX), Ray Nusselein (Paraplyteatret)—all members of the board of the illegal Danish ASSITEJ Committee plus Marie Brandt representing Samarbejdsudvalget and Jørgen Melskens. . . . Sweden—being a new member of ASSITEJ did not want to take part in these illegal activities, [and] actually the exhibition was set up in the Dutch exhibit space. . . ."[53]

New Appointment: As a final bit of business they recommended that the New EXCOM appoint Shaun Hennessey (Great Britain) as a Financial Counselor, without vote.

The meeting was adjourned.

The General Assembly/15 June 1981

According to Michel Dieuaide's letter of 24 October 1980, he states there are 1) only 3 official delegates from each center who shall have the 3 votes; 2) participants are theatre people who will participate in all except the General Assembly; and 3) observers who attend the events on their own.

This is a decision that has no basis in the Statutes. It essentially says that only the 3 official delegates may attend the General Assemblies, and participate in the discussions and the voting. In the past all members were allowed to attend the Assemblies, but only the official delegates could speak and vote. Apparently this letter was sent with the complete approval of the Secretary General. This decision may have been made because of the small size of the Assembly Room. However, more likely it was another attempt to control the organization and eliminate observation. There should have been a strong protest against this decision, but there was none.

President Ilse Rodenberg opened the Meeting of the General Assembly by proposing the following Agenda for the Congress:

- Approval of the Minutes of the General Assembly of the Madrid Congress in 1978
- Secretary General's Report of Activities from 1978-1980
- Financial Report
- Amendments to the Statutes
- Questions raised by the National Centers
- Honorary titles
- Location of the next General Assembly
- Nomination of the Secretary General and the Treasurer
- Nomination of the auditors
- Election of the Executive Committee
- Recess for Meeting of the New Executive Committee
- Election of the President and Vice-Presidents
- Miscellaneous questions

The Agenda was approved, and the Treasurer verified the votes of the Centers present. There was a total of 80 votes, which would require a majority of 41 votes for election.

The President asked for nominations as tellers. The following three people were proposed and elected: Else Mazure (Netherlands), Shin Shikata (Japan), and João Luis Pereira de Souza (Portugal).

The Assembly then voted to accept the Minutes of the Madrid Congress in 1978.

The Secretary General presented her Report for 1978-80 and plans for 1981-83. The Report had been distributed in advance, and with no objections, the USA moved to accept the Report, seconded by Great Britain, and the Report was accepted unanimously.

National Centers: Of particular interest in the Secretary General's

Report to the General Assembly was that on Membership. Moudoués stated that since the Madrid Congress in 1978 these countries had joined, bringing the total affiliate centers to 36: Japan, Ecuador, Iraq, Sweden, Argentina, and Poland. Norway was trying to establish a Center, and negotiations were underway with Austria, Egypt, Mexico, Zaïre, Panama, and China. She stated that much more recruiting needed to be done in Asia, the Pacific, Africa, and Latin America.

The Spanish Center had organized a Latin American conference in Madrid prior to the 1978 meeting; Australia was sending information to New Zealand and New Guinea; and Japan was assisting with Asia.

Publications: Moudoués reported the following official publications: *Theatre, Childhood, and Young People* (a semi-annual review published by the Secretariat); *ASSITEJ Bulletin* (published by the Czech Center); *Boletino Iberoamericano* (published and distributed by the Spanish Center).

In addition, she cited *Terminology, Volume I* (prepared by the Terminology Commission and published by the Spanish Center); *Bibliography* (at the printer's from the Secretariat); *Theatre for Children in the World* (published and distributed by the GDR); National publications are available from Canada, Australia, USA, France, Italy, Switzerland, Portugal, GDR, FGR, and Japan.

Altogether this was an impressive list of official publications. In addition, for some time ASSITEJ had needed and wanted to print a brochure that listed all the appropriate information about the organization, which in turn could be used as a promotional tool. Shaw had organized a sale of theatrical posters from the various ASSITEJ theatres, which in turn had earned $1,008.63 for the Association. For the moment that money was pledged to the printing of the brochure in Romania. Later these monies proved to be insufficient for the cost of printing, and the money went into the general fund and was used elsewhere.

The Financial Report: Ion Lucian, Treasurer, presented the Financial Report, which had been distributed in advance. It contained a financial statement for the three previous fiscal periods, a projected budget for 1981-83, and the Auditors' Report.

This was the first time within memory that such a complete financial report was presented. The bank had been transferred to Great Britain, and Shaun Hennessey appointed as a Financial Counselor. Even one of the Auditors was English now. This completeness was a result of Hennessey's objectiveness and efficiency as Financial Counselor.

A series of questions were asked: Geoffrey Brown (Australia) asked why the costs of translation were so significant, having been non-existent at the Madrid Congress. The answer was that for the first time all the documents had been translated, printed, and distributed to the delegates in advance.

Ann Shaw (USA) observed that the projected increases in office costs and communication seemed insufficient. In response it was stated that the projections were only an approximation, based on an average increase of 10% per year.

Maurice Yendt (France) stated with regret that the budget was clearly insufficient. Considering the important projects of ASSITEJ, he urged research into fund-raising and other sources. On a motion by the USA, seconded by France, Italy, and Czechoslovakia, the projected Budget for 1981-83 was adopted unanimously.

Membership dues: There was considerable debate over a dues increase. Rodenberg stated that any increase would create hardships for many of the National Centers with soft currency.

Australia, Canada, and Great Britain proposed that those centers with more considerable means pay an augmented dues. Moudoués commented that ASSITEJ from its inception refused to establish monetary discrimination among the centers. She suggested that those with means could always make a donation.

Israel recommended that a fixed date be established for the submission of dues. France suggested an annual progressive membership fee of an additional 15 US$ which would bring the dues to 150 US$ by 1983. The Treasurer proposed the setting of 150 US$ for 1982-84. John English (Great Britain) proposed supporting the motion. The increase was approved by 59 votes for and 21 abstentions (included were Cuba, Portugal, USSR, Spain, Czechoslovakia, and Uruguay).

Finally, on a motion from France and seconded by Great Britain, Italy, and Portugal, the Financial Report was accepted unanimously.

Amendments to the Constitution: The EXCOM had recommended that the following changes be made to the Constitution, primarily for the sake of clarification:

- To Ch. IV, Art. IX, 13 (passed unanimously)
- To Ch. IV, Art. X, 1.(59 for, 10 against, 11 abstentions) increased EXCOM to 17 members
- To Ch. IV, Art. X, 2 (76 for, 4 abstentions) added: *except in the case of the President where the replacement shall be from amongst the Vice Presidents and in the case of the Vice Presidents where the Executive Committee is authorized either to leave the place vacant or, if it judges it necessary, to elect a replacement from amongst its own members.*
- To Ch. IV, Art. X, 4 (passed unanimously) may appoint a deputy *from his or her national center*, by giving notice . . .

- To Ch. IV, Art. X, 5 (passed unanimously): by a deputy *from their own national center* the presence of . . .
- To Ch. IV, Art. XI, 3 (tabled)
- This last amendment provoked the most discussion, whether counselors should have a vote or not. The vote was postponed until the 2nd Session of the General Assembly the next day.

2nd General Assembly Session/18 June 1981

The first item of business was consideration of the final amendment to the Constitution. The wording was changed to *without voting rights* for counselors and specialists. The new text was put to the vote without discussion—71 for, 2 against, 4 abstentions. (For all the new texts in the Constitution see Appendix F.)

Questions from the Centers: USA: proposed utilizing the profits from the sale of theatre posters for the publication of a brochure designed to promote ASSITEJ, its goals, its achievements, and its projects. The proposal was accepted unanimously.

Cuba: requested the dissemination of the works of young Third World authors, as well as the involvement of Third World groups in ASSITEJ. Cuba also proposed the development of relations with Third World countries by ASSITEJ in the form of dramaturgy and the circulation of scripts.

In the discussion which followed the Spanish Center mentioned its publication of the *Boletino Ibero-americano* which could contribute to this development, but that Centers must contribute material.

The Australian Center was equally concerned with problems of dissemination of information, and offered publication prospects.

The Secretary General proposed:
- the establishment of a Commission to devise a working plan
- the organization of seminars with the Third World countries
- research on authors who might adapt proposed works

Honorary Titles: Sunyer (Spain), in the name of the EXCOM, moved that the General Assembly award the following honorary titles:
- Hans Snoek (Netherlands)—Honorary Member
- Sozaburo Ochiai (Japan)—Honorary Member (posthumously)
- Vladimir Adamek—Honorary President

The granting of these titles was approved.

1984 Congress: Three countries proposed to the General Assembly to hold the next Congress in 1984: USSR (Moscow), Portugal (Lisbon), and Belgium. The votes were: USSR—46; Portugal—20; Belgium—8; with three abstentions for a total vote of 77. Moscow became the site of the 1984 Congress.

They also approved retaining the Portuguese invitation of Lisbon which had been received at the Prague EXCOM for a possible Congress in 1987. Also, they acknowledged the invitation from the Belgium Center, signed by both the French and Flemish Centers.

Nomination of the Secretary General and the Treasurer: Upon the recommendation of the EXCOM, the General Assembly voted upon whether the Secretary General and the Treasurer should be retained. The vote was as follows: Rose-Marie Moudoués—67 for, 6 against, 4 abstentions; Ion Lucian—69 for, 4 against, 4 abstentions.

The Auditors were elected unanimously by a show of hands: Cornel Popa (Romania), and an auditor to be designated by the British Center.

The Elections: Prior to the elections the EXCOM considered the problem of Portugal as a voting National Center. Its candidacy for nomination to the EXCOM was turned in on time, but the language suggested that the candidacy was tied to Portugal being selected as the site for the next Congress. According to the Secretary General, this was an error in translation, and after discussion Portugal's candidacy was accepted unanimously by a show of hands with one abstention.

Portugal, which was leftist in its political sympathies, had not been active in ASSITEJ at this point. Its nomination and possible election was possibly a ploy for a more leftist EXCOM. The total number of votes which could be cast—77—was certified by the Secretary General. This meant that a majority of 39 was required for election.

With the amendments to the Statutes passed by the General Assembly at this VIIth Congress in Lyon, France the EXCOM was increased from 15 to 17 members. This meant that with the automatic seating of the Secretary General and the Treasurer, who also represented their countries, 15 seats were left for other countries with no duplication. Accordingly, the General Assembly elected the following EXCOM for 1981–1984.

FGR (Kathrin Türks): 64; Czechoslovakia (Ladislav Knížátko): 64; Australia (Geoffrey Brown): 63; Canada (Sara Lee Lewis): 63; GDR (Ilse Rodenberg): 62; Yugoslavia (Zvjezdana Ladika): 62; Cuba (Eddy Socorro): 59; Great Britain (Shaun Hennessey): 59; USA (Ann Shaw): 59; Portugal (João Luiz Brites): 58; Spain (Maria Sunyer): 56; Bulgaria (Victor Georgiev): 55; Switzerland (Elisabeth Cozona): 54; USSR (Natalya Satz): 54; and Italy (Ottorino Negri): 43. Israel (Orna Porat): 26; and Denmark (Inga Juul): 5; were not elected.

The Secretary General called for a recess to allow the new EXCOM to meet and vote on a slate of officers. After this meeting the EXCOM proposed the re-election of Rodenberg as President, and named four candidates for the positions of the 3 vice-presidents: Natalya Satz, Ann Shaw, Eddy Socorro, and Maria Sunyer.

For this ballot, a total of 74 votes was declared, making the majority required for election as 38 votes. Rodenberg was elected president with 66 for, 1 against, 4 abstentions, and 3 spoiled ballots.

The first round of voting for the vice-presidents was: Shaw: 56 for (elected); Sunyer: 48 for (elected); Socorro: 35 for; and Satz: 32 for. Since neither Socorro nor Satz had the required majority, there was a second round of balloting: Socorro: 37 for (elected); and Satz: 29 for (not elected) and 8 spoiled ballots![54]

Following the elections, the General Assembly considered various Miscellaneous Questions:

Statute Modification: The FGR Center asked for a Statute change that would allow two new members to be added to the Bureau, the sole purpose of which would be to allow new members to benefit from the experience of meeting with more long-term members. This request was tabled, since it could not be voted upon until the meeting of the next Congress in 1984.

ASSITEJ Center for Young People's Theatre: Hennessey (Great Britain) in the name of Commission No. 5 requested the establishment of a structure with outside financial support to promote the exchange of information and ideas of youth theatre among all countries. Specifically he made the following request: [55]

1. "That structures to support Young People's Theatre wishing to effect exchanges should be investigated and setup in each country;
2. "That each government be asked to fund an ASSITEJ Centre, open to all Young People's Theatres, and give it the job of coordinating the exchange of information on Young People's Theatre;
3. "That the Executive Committee of ASSITEJ takes on the task of setting up the necessary full-time specialist support for the international exchange of information and seek funds for this purpose from international organizations, foundations and other sources."

This proposal was adopted unanimously by a show of hands, with 4 abstentions.

Theatres of the World: Georgiev (Bulgaria) proposed the idea of a Theatres of the World for young spectators. Since RITEJ of Lyon occurred every 2 years, he proposed to discuss with his government the organization of international meetings to occur alternately with the RITEJ Festival.

Report from South Africa: ASSITEJ/USA requested that the

General Assembly hear a report on the situation of theatre for youth in South Africa. Apparently this was never acted upon!

The meeting was adjourned at 5:00 PM.

New EXCOM Meeting/19 June 1981

President: Ilse Rodenberg (GDR); **Vice-Presidents:** Ann Shaw (USA) as 1st Vice-President, Maria Sunyer (Spain) as 2nd Vice-President, and Eddy Socorro (Cuba) as 3rd Vice-President; **Secretary General:** Rose-Marie Moudoués (France); and **Treasurer:** Ion Lucian (Romania). **Permanent Financial Consultant (non-voting):** Shaun Hennessey (Great Britain).

Members of the EXCOM: Geoffrey Brown (Australia), Sara Lee Lewis (Canada), Vladimir Adamek for Ladislav Knižátko (Czechoslovakia), Kathrin Türks (FGR), Shaun Hennessey (Great Britain), Ottorino Negri (Italy), Elisabeth Cozona (Switzerland), Natalya Satz (USSR), Zvjezdana Ladika (Yugoslavia).[56] [Only the countries are named in the French Minutes, but these would be the individuals voted in by the 1981 elections.]

Members absent: Victor Georgiev (Bulgaria), João Luiz Brites (Portugal).

Invitee: Nat Eek (USA) to present the Danish Problem Report and suggested solution.

President Rodenberg proposed the appointment of two permanent counselors for administrative questions: Vladimir Adamek and Shaun Hennessey. They were appointed, and Hennessey was specifically designated as Financial Counselor, without vote.

Next she said they needed to make decisions about the future work of the Commissions, and they were designated as follows:

Statutes: Moudoués (Chair), responsible for all amendments and clarification of the statutes in legal form, as well as their translation into the three official languages. Included are all Minutes, Reports, etc., and they need three people appointed who know the three languages. Sara Lewis (Canada) will be responsible for the French/English translations and the USSR delegate for the Russian.

Creative Activity & Themes: Lucian (Chair) with Cozona, Knižátko. They will recommend themes for the EXCOM and the Congresses, such as "Repertory for Adolescents".

Publications: Sunyer (Chair).

Promotion & Publicity: Rodenberg (Chair), Kathrin Türks.

Third World: Eddy Socorro (Chair).

Projects & Fund Raising: Shaw (Chair).

Liaison w/ IATA/UNIMA & UNESCO: Negri (Chair), Ladika.

Danish Report: Eek presented a written Report from the Committee of four who investigated the Danish problem. A letter from Inga Juul was submitted dated 16 June 1981 withdrawing from the General Assembly in protest of the "illegal Danish group" displaying and distributing their materials.

Eek had given Juul a copy of the Committee's Report and asked her if she found any errors in it. She was to meet with him that morning, but did not, and submitted a written document instead withdrawing from the Congress.
- Juul's withdrawal did not solve the problem. However, the Committee's Report recommended the following solution as two of seven conditions:
- That Juul must accept the Danish applications for membership, and
- Then call a General Assembly of the Danish Center before the end of 1981. [57]

As a result, about 20 companies applied for membership, and Juul called a General Assembly for 27 December 1981 in the little village of Birk, a four hour drive from Copenhagen! All the new members showed up, either personally or by proxy. "There were no reports from the [Danish] Board, no accounts, no working plan, no budget—no nothing!"[58]

According to the Danish Center's Statutes, a General Assembly was to be held every year, but the President of their Center was elected for a 3-year term in accord with the ASSITEJ Statutes. Juul was elected their President in 1980. Despite many requests for a General Assembly by the membership, none was called for in 1982 and 1983. Juul continued as President until 1983 representing an almost non-existent Center.[59]

Meanwhile the EXCOM appointed a new Committee to study the Danish problem: Ann Shaw (USA)—Chair; Ottorino Negri (Italy); Zvjezdana Ladika (Yugoslavia); Sara Lee Lewis (Canada), and Kathrin Türks (FGR). The Committee was to meet at the Cuban EXCOM Meeting and present their report to the EXCOM hopefully with a final solution.

Next EXCOM Meeting: The EXCOM accepted the invitation of Eddy Socorro to hold their next EXCOM Meeting in Havana, Cuba in the first week in April in 1982. Socorro announced that all hotel accommodations and food would be paid for by the Cuban Center.

Lastly, Rodenberg requested that all the members send her their comments on the strengths and problems at the Lyon Congress.

The meeting was adjourned.

During the Congress the US Center hosted a reception for all the international delegates at the home of the USA Consul in Lyon.

Performances[60] "A total of 14 plays were presented—8 from France and one each from Czechoslovakia, GDR, Italy, Sweden, USA, and USSR. The quality was high, and represented a wide-ranging variety of styles, from opera to mixed media to agitprop to Commedia del'Arte. The major impression, no doubt weighted by the greater number of French plays, was of abstraction, of experimentation in form and idea which predominated over plot or character. There were few heroes, few well-told tales, and even fewer happy resolutions.

"When the Czech play *Charlie* (a homage to Charlie Chaplin) became the most popular at the Congress with its combination of brilliant slapstick along with tender romance, there was almost an audible sigh of relief from the audience. 'Thank God, the happy ending isn't dead.' was one comment.

"The most traditional offerings were the USSR's *Little Red Riding Hood* and the USA's *Sleeping Beauty*, although the latter was criticized as not being "American", since it used Japanese Kabuki as its style.

"Among the plays death was a recurrent theme, as was violence and sex. Political polarities were not softened, and in the critiques the spirit of competition was stronger than the spirit of international cooperation. But the avant-garde had its down-side. One spectator commented 'What I wouldn't give for a good *Pinocchio* right now!'

"The transformations of settings and ideas and people—at their best in *The Pastimes of A Stone*, an exploration of the mental life of Einstein— were often brilliant. [To Whitton] the most provocative play was *Enter and Close the Page*, in which two actors shared the stage with two large screens, one horizontal, one vertical, upon which beautiful art work was projected at a slow crawl, complementing and illuminating the dialogue, becoming a third actor in the play."

In many ways the excellent variety of quality productions shattered the traditional view of theatre for children. Surprisingly, the many children from Lyon who were in the audience, sitting in un-air-conditioned theatres, sometimes through long, wordy performances, showed every appearance of appreciation and absorption.

But the successes of the performances accomplished what the General Assembly may not have—a complete exchange of a variety of intellectual ideas and artistic ideas, while giving excitement and pleasure.

1981

At the end of the Lyon Congress in its Report the Czech Bulletin listed the following ASSITEJ Centers:[61]

Algeria	Italy
Argentina	Japan
Australia	Netherlands
Belgium	Peru
Brazil	Poland
Bulgaria	Portugal
Canada	Romania
Cuba	Spain
Czecholslovakia	Sri Lanka
Denmark	Sweden
Finland	Switzerland
FGR	Turkey
France	Uruguay
GDR	USA
Great Britain	USSR
Hungary	Venezuela
Iran	Yugoslavia
Iraq	Norway (corresponding center)
Israel	

A grand total of 36 National Centers, with one Corresponding Center.

PART IV:

THE OPEN CLASH OF POLITICS

THE WORLD OF 1981-1990

The decade of the '80s was one of a revitalization of capitalism and a demand for democracy. It was also a decade of remarkable changes in the failing of old governments and the creation of new governments. All these world events had considerable impact on the growth, development, and the implementation of the goals of ASSITEJ, although sometimes imperceptible at the time.

In the Soviet Union from 1980 to 1985 the communist government became increasingly harsher in the treatment of dissent, in the restriction of emigration, and had begun the invasion of Afghanistan in 1979. Each of the three successive Premiers who died in office, Leonid Brezhnev (1982), Yuri Andropov (1984), and Konstantin Chernenko (1985) had ruled with an iron hand, but with the ascension of Mikhail Gorbachev in 1985 things changed radically. He promoted *glasnost* and *perestroika*, economic and social reform as of 1987, cut the military budget and withdrew troops from Afghanistan in 1989. He did not interfere with the democratization of Poland and Hungary, and allowed the Soviet people a voice in choosing new Congressional candidates. He is widely credited with the 1989 ending of the Cold War.

In Poland Solidarity, the labor union founded by Lech Walesa was legalized in 1988, and free elections brought a Solidarity victory. One year later Marxist economies failed in Hungary, GDR, Czechoslovakia, Bulgaria, and Romania ending the communist domination with an accompanying demand for democracy. The Berlin Wall was hauled down in November 1989, thus uniting East and West Germany after 40 years of separation.

During the first eight years Ronald Reagan was President of the USA. This brought the longest economic boom in US history through tax cuts, deregulation, "junk bond" financing, mergers and takeovers, and a strong anti-communist stance enhanced by increased defense spending and increased missile systems. It also brought a large trade imbalance and an increased national debt, reaching a low-point with the Iran-contra scandals.

The Middle East remained militarily unstable with sharp divisions on economic, political, racial, and religious lines. Drought and starvation affected virtually all of the African nations during the first five years, and AIDS took a heavy toll. Wars erupted in Ethiopia and the Sudan.

In 1983 South Africa gave "Coloreds" a voice in the government for the first time, but still excluded the blacks who comprised 70% of the population. In 1989 F.W. de Klerk was elected on a platform of "evolutionary" change via negotiation with the black community.

At first under Chairman Deng Xiaoping, China pursued far-reaching changes in political and economic institutions, expanding commercial and technical ties to the industrial world. But in 1989 by demanding more changes, riots occurred in Tiananmen Square with a death toll of up to 7,000, 10,000 injured, and up to 10,000 arrested. The conciliatory government was ousted.

Japan which was prospering as a result of international trade imbalances in her favor was forced to adhere to "fair trade" practices or face trade restrictions.

Greece, Portugal, and Spain joined the European Common Market, raising its serving population to over 300 million, the West's largest trading entity. Margaret Thatcher became the first Prime Minister of Great Britain to serve three terms; France elected its first socialist president, François Mitterrand, and Italy elected its first socialist Premier, Bettino Craxi.

With the overthrow of the Shah of Iran, terrorism became a prominent political tactic, increasing through the '80s but decreasing in high-profile attacks after 1985.[62]

ASSITEJ/USA-1981

Under the leadership of Ann Shaw, President of the US Center for ASSITEJ, the US Center was incorporated as ASSITEJ/USA in 1981, and separated its ties with the American Theatre Association (ATA), which had been the parent group of the US Center since 1965. This separation allowed the US National Center to speak directly to the international association with one voice as the official USA voice for professional theatre for young audiences.

1981
BUREAU MEETING
Lille, France/11–13 October 1981

The Bureau of ASSITEJ met in Lille, France from 11–13 October 1981. President Ilse Rodenberg presided, with Ann Shaw (USA) as 1st Vice-President, Maria Sunyer (Spain) as 2nd Vice-President, Eddy Socorro (Cuba) as 3rd Vice-President, Rose-Marie Moudoués (France) as Secretary General, Ion Lucian (Romania) as Treasurer, and Shaun Hennessey (Great Britain) as Counselor.[63]

The Agenda was approved as follows:
- The National Centers
- Listing of the Centers to be invited to EXCOM Meetings in 1982, 1983, and 1984
- Commissions
- Theatres of the World
- Requests from the General Assembly of the Lyon Congress (1981)
- Relations with UNESCO
- Meeting of the EXCOM in Cuba
- Miscellaneous

The National Centers:
- **Mexico:** In a letter dated 17 September the Mexican Center sent their Statutes and requested to become a member of ASSITEJ. The Center had been formed with the approval of the Mexican Minister of Culture. Moudoués stated that the statutes were in conformity with the International ones, and it included both professional and amateur companies. Its President, Sra. Socorro Merlin, indicated they had special activities for the handicapped. The Mexican Center was admitted unanimously.
- **Denmark:** In accord with the Committee report of Nat Eek at the Lyon Congress, Inga Juul (Demark) announced that in mid-August 8 new groups had joined the center.
- **Panama:** A center is in the process of organizing, as a result of the meeting in Madrid, Spain in 1978.
- **USA:** At Shaw's urging ASSITEJ/USA had initiated the Pacific Rim Exchange with both the Australian and the Japanese Centers joining in the organizing of their activities of mutual interest. Included were Australia, China, Japan, Korea, the Philippines, and the USA. The Honolulu Theatre for Youth hosted their first conference (3

days in May 1982) to develop relations among the countries in that geographic area.

A major Festival was being organized in New Orleans, Louisiana in 1984 as part of their World Exposition. Orlin Corey (ASSITEJ/USA) was in charge of an international festival of theatres for children and young people for two weeks as part of the Exposition. There would be a total of 12 theatres performing, 6 from foreign countries and 6 from the USA. The Exposition would run from June to October 1984. The children's theatre Festival was scheduled for June at the same time that there would be an international conference with the theme. International authorities and specialists would participate in this colloquy.

Moudoués then stated that this Festival poses a major problem since it will take place at approximately the same time as another Festival in Moscow. The President of ASSITEJ/USA [Shaw] must correspond with the USSR Center to harmonize these dates, and for example move the ASSITEJ Congress to May 1984.

Centers to be invited to EXCOM Meetings in 1982, 1983, and 1984

- 1982: Argentina, Peru, Uruguay, Venezuela, Brazil, and Mexico.
- 1983: Algeria, Finland, Turkey, Belgium, Denmark, Netherlands, and Sweden.
- 1984: Hungary, Poland, Israel, Japan, and newly admitted centers

Commissions: There were the following reports from the commissions:

- **Statutes:** Rose-Marie Moudoués (Chair). No report.
- **Themes and Repertory:** Ion Lucian (Chair). He proposed to create a permanent seminar for dramaturges, and had asked Maurice Yendt to assist in its creation.

   Lucian proposed the following themes for consideration: "Plays without Literary Texts", "The Collective Creation", and "The Work of Amateurs in ASSITEJ". A fourth theme "A Comparative Analysis of work between permanent groups and free groups" was discussed at length but tabled for lack of an internationally common name because of the differences in organization from one country to the next.

   Lucian then proposed to find a theme for the Moscow Congress in 1984 by correspondence which would be presented at the Cuban EXCOM.
- **Terminology and Publications:** Maria Sunyer (Chair). Sunyer proposed to establish a new publication and asked for articles from

each center. Its purpose would be to include new pieces, lists of festivals, etc. Rodenberg will confer with Adamek about this.

- **Publicity:** Ilse Rodenberg (Chair). A brochure explaining ASSITEJ is indispensable to this commission. Adamek will write the historical background, Lucian the introduction, and ASSITEJ/USA will design the format.
- **Liaison with the Third World:** Eddy Socorro (Chair). This commission hoped to interest UNESCO in its project, by submitting their program for Statute B status, along with a plan to finance it.
- **Liaison with international organizations:** Ottorino Negri (Chair). The meeting with IATA at the Lyon Congress was disappointing. In the future their critics must be invited to be present at the performances and to participate in the critiques the next day rather than hold their regular congress.

    A project for an Encyclopedia of Theatre of the 20th Century is being studied by ITI, but it will be necessary to establish a listing of theatre personalities in theatre for children in all countries in order to be included.
- **Projects and Finances:** Ann Shaw (Chair). Shaw is working with people in the USA to begin to circulate new plays. At first the plays will be in English.

Theatres of the World: Victor Georgiev (Bulgaria) proposed the creation of a Theatres of the World for children. For the sake of discussion this title was used, but it really properly belongs to ITI, and Maurice Yendt has been able to use it for his theatre festival in Lyon for the past six years with a Festival every two years which features performances, workshops, seminars, etc.

A general discussion followed concerning criteria for choosing performances, restrictions on choices, the financial control of the operation, that the European base would be at Lyon, but all continents would have the right to establish their own Theatres of the World. However, it would be necessary for groups to obtain financial support from their governments.

An example: Cuba has obtained their government's support for an international festival in the fall of 1982. If it is a success, they will be able to repeat it two years later. Moudoués stated that the Bulgarian proposal was not contradictory, since Lyon could hold their festival on even years and Bulgaria the odd years.

Recommendations from the Previous Congress: The Secretary General reiterated that it was not a proper function of the Bureau to interfere in internal problems of any of the centers. ASSITEJ can only make recommendations.

An ASSITEJ brochure can let countries know that the Association is able to help with the creation of an organizational structure, performance companies, and national centers in countries where none exist. The best means of distributing information to these countries seem to be through calendars and bibliographies.

Relations with UNESCO: The Secretary General and the Secretary of the Belgian Center met with M. de Malompré of UNESCO. They were informed that ASSITEJ has sufficient representation to request Class B status in UNESCO, but the application will take a long time. An absolute precondition is that South Africa cannot be a member of ASSITEJ, because of its country's *apartheid*.

EXCOM Meeting in Cuba: The dates of the EXCOM meeting in Cuba were set as 5–12 April 1982.

Hotel costs would be courtesy of the Cuban center. Delegates would be responsible for any personal costs.

On the program one day will be assigned for discussion on the artistic theme chosen in accord with the Commission on Themes. The various centers will be able to distribute their written Reports before the Meeting. The Commissions with have a half-day for meetings, the Bureau will have 2 sessions of 2 hours each, and the EXCOM will have 4 sessions.

Miscellaneous: Peter Hale of Baker, Rooke, and Amsdons of London, Great Britain, was named as the second Auditor of the ASSITEJ financial accounts.

For the Theatres of the World project, in addition to Ion Lucian and Maurice Yendt, the Commission would be able to co-opt a representative from Canada and one from Australia.

This concluded the Minutes of the meetings.

1982
EXECUTIVE COMMITTEE MEETING
Havana, Cuba/5–11 April 1982

The Executive Committee of ASSITEJ met in Havana, Cuba from 5–11 April 1982. Ilse Rodenberg (GDR) presided as President, Ann Shaw (USA) as 1st Vice President, Maria Sunyer (Spain) as 2nd Vice-President, Eddy Socorro (Cuba) as 3rd Vice President, and Rose-Marie Moudoués (France) as Secretary General. Shaun Hennessey (Great Britain) as Financial Counselor. Ion Lucian (Romania) as Treasurer was absent.[64]

Members of the EXCOM in attendance were: Andrew Bleby (Australia), Sara Lee Lewis (Canada), Kathrin Türks (FGR), Ottorino Negri (Italy), João Brites (Portugal), Jean Gradel for Elisabeth Cozona (Switzerland), and Vladimir Borodin for Natalya Satz (USSR), and Zvjezdana Ladika (Yugoslavia).

Members absent: Victor Georgiev (Bulgaria) and Ladislav Knižátko (Czechoslovakia).

Observers: Garcia Clovis (Brazil), Maurice Yendt (France), Wolfgang Wöhlert (GDR), and Socorro Merlin and Javier Rojas (Mexico).

The Bureau and the EXCOM were the guests of the Ministry of Culture of Cuba and ASSITEJ/Cuba. Room and board were provided for the entire meeting. All delegates were housed at the Capri Hotel, a tourist facility in suburban Havana. Meetings were held at the nearby Casa de las Americas, a small public building. A vintage minibus was placed at the disposal of the EXCOM by the Ministry of Culture, as well as translators who worked in English, French, Russian and Spanish.

The Minister of Culture of Cuba hosted a party for the delegates which included the opportunity to dance to the music of a small combo. The Minister invited Shaw to dance, and to the astonishment of many, she accepted. They danced together to the music and the applause of all attending, providing an unusual example of the bonds of international friendship breaking national political barriers.

Later, on the mini-bus to the hotel Rodenberg asked Shaw to sit with her in the front seats. She complimented Shaw for accepting the Minister's invitation to dance saying "You are good woman of great courage to accept the Minister's invitation in these times. I think I made good choice of you as my First Vice-President."

Havana, Cuba.

The EXCOM Meeting/7-9 April 1982

The following Agenda was set in place:
- Approval of Minutes of the 1981 Lyon Congress
- New Members
- Financial Statement
- National Centers
- The Danish Center Problem
- Peruvian Center
- UNESCO Relations
- Commissions
- Theatres of the World
- 1984 Moscow Congress
- Future Meetings
- Reports from Cuba, Brazil, and Mexico

The Minutes of the 1981 Lyon Congress were approved. Brazil and Mexico were accepted as new members of ASSITEJ, and were welcomed to the sessions. Since the Treasurer was absent, an interim Financial Report was tabled.

National Centers: There was considerable discussion about retaining centers that had not paid their dues. Often these Centers were victims of political or economic conflicts, rendering them incapable of meeting their financial obligations. Cited were Algeria, Iraq, Iran, Peru, Poland, Sri Lanka, and Turkey. In most cases these centers had an active potential membership, but communication was difficult. Canada proposed that a concerted effort be made to establish a realistic membership roster, especially in consideration of the ASSITEJ application to UNESCO for Status B recognition.

The Danish Center Problem: The Ad Hoc Committee chaired by Shaw with Negri, Ladika, Lewis, and Türks presented the following recommendations:

1. The two disputing groups [Juul's and Melskens'] must agree upon a legal mediator in Denmark, and engage this person to meet with them to discover the current facts in the dispute, and to reach a solution.
2. The engagement of this legal mediator and the beginning of mediation must have taken place by the time of the meeting of the ASSITEJ Bureau in early October of 1982. Both parties must have notified the Secretary General that this has been done. Such written notice must arrive at the Secretary General's office in Paris no later than September 15th.
3. That a national General Assembly must be held in Denmark by October of 1982, its purpose to create a new and all-inclusive Danish Center.
4. Once the two groups agree upon a legal mediator, at the last session of mediation, an official representative of ASSITEJ (Shaun Hennessey) was to be present. All this was to be resolved by the next meeting of the EXCOM.
5. The Committee felt that the integrity of ASSITEJ must be defended, but that they must not interfere in national affairs.

The EXCOM reviewed all the documents related to the Danish problem. Essentially some thirty "non-institutional" theaters were seeking membership and leadership in the Danish Center as opposed to three to four large long-established theaters. Part of the concern of the current Center under Juul was undoubtedly based on a shift of political philosophy from conservative to liberal, as well as the possible loss of its government subsidy.

An Ad Hoc committee of four, appointed at the Lyon Congress, had turned in a report, but it became moot when Juul, one of the litigants resigned from the Congress. A new Ad Hoc Committee was appointed from Canada, FGR, Italy, USA, and Yugoslavia. This Committee recommended the appointment of a Danish Mediator to study the problem and all the documents, and to attend all the national Center's meetings. They also recommended that Shaun Hennessey (Great Britain) be appointed as Observer for ASSITEJ. The EXCOM approved these recommendations requesting that they be acted upon prior to the next Bureau meeting in October 1982.

The Peruvian Center: Because of the Center's internal difficulties as well as non-payment of dues, the EXCOM moved that the situation must be clarified by the end of the year, or the incumbent head of the Center must withdraw from the office.

UNESCO Relations: The Secretary General reported serious efforts to obtain Status B recognition from UNESCO. Work on the necessary dossier had begun towards a major submission by September 1982.

Commissions:

- **Creative Activity & Themes:** It was felt that attention should be focused on specialized groups, such as: directors, authors, researchers, etc. citing the success of the annual Director's Seminars in East Berlin. The EXCOM felt continuity once started was important in seminars of distinction. The Format should be established as soon as possible and limited to no more than twenty participants.
- **Terminology:** Its booklet on Terminology had been distributed at the Lyon Congress. It provides a cross-cultural glossary of terms and definitions. Moudoués asked for changes and additions to be put in place in a new edition in time for the Moscow Congress in 1984.
- **Third World:** The Commission consisting of Portugal and Cuba had written a Report calling for specific projects under UNESCO, and artistic and technical exchanges to raise standards and educate audiences.
- **Liaison w/IATA, UNIMA & UNESCO:** An exchange of Board members had begun. Also, first attempts to coordinate dates of national and international festivals had already begun.
- **Promotion & Publicity:** *Promotional Brochure:* A brochure has been designed to promote the work of International ASSITEJ which the EXCOM approved. *New Play Exchanges:* Canada and the USA proposed an annual or semi-annual newsletter giving synopses of new plays for young audiences in French and English. Its object was to promote the exchange of new work on the international level. The EXCOM approved the project.

Theatres of the World: The concept of Theatres of the World involved the creation of a regular international festival and symposia dedicated to professional theatre for young audiences. The working Title properly belongs to ASSITEJ. Maurice Yendt submitted a request that ASSITEJ designate his bi-annual Rencontres Internationales du Théâtre pour L'Enfance et La Jeunesse (RITEJ) at Lyon, France as the "ASSITEJ Theatres of the World." It already had a record of success, gave financial support to visiting artists, and distributed publications which resulted from the symposia.

Bulgaria submitted a modifying proposal that their trial international festival in 1982 be so designated should it prove successful.

The Secretary General proposed that the two theatres be granted the title on alternating years.

Prior to this very active discussion Canada, USA, Great Britain, Australia, and Yugoslavia had informal discussions promoting the merits of a rotating site. Lewis (Canada) passed out information about the Vancouver-Edmonton-Toronto international children's theatre festival as a major focus for world-class theatre for young people.

Shaw (USA) pointed out that while ASSITEJ was not strong financially, it possessed considerable status, and its endorsements should not be given lightly. She proposed the establishment of criteria and guidelines, a shared focus among continents, and the demonstrated ability of the host country to assume financial responsibility.

Canada, Yugoslavia, Portugal, and the USA favored a rotating site, with Canada and Australia proposing specific years. Consensus stated that all centers must be made aware of the proposals before the EXCOM could decide on a permanent designation.

Accordingly the following was agreed upon:
- The Theatres of the World festival would be in Lyon in 1983
- It would be in Bulgaria in 1984, provided it was successful in 1982
- It would be again in Lyon in 1985
- Beyond these dates, the title would be open, with Canada a possibility for 1986
- A multi-continent Commission was established to draw up criteria and guidelines: Ann Shaw (USA), Victor Georgiev and Maurice Yendt (Europe), Andrew Bleby (Australia), and Eddy Socorro (Cuba)

Artistic Discussions/10 April 1982

These discussions[65] were held in a small and attractive children's theatre, located in the basement of a high-rise apartment building. The morning session featured a panel of Cuban writers, directors, and performers working in the field of youth theatre.

The discussions focused primarily on the plays seen by the EXCOM members, especially those for young children drawn from fable and folktales, and the collective-creation "docudrama" for senior students. Adult classic theatre was available also to younger audiences.

The discussions revealed that the status of those working in theatre in Cuba was high. There were 23 groups in Cuba, with a Youth Theatre in every province. Directors were schooled in pedagogy and psychology, so their plays while entertaining were also didactic. Unfortunately their isolation made them unaware of world trends in theatre.

Classic adult theatre featured a very good production of *Twelfth Night*, strongly influenced by the GDR production in staging and design. It was felt that children should be exposed to tales of morality, to fairy stories, to simple bright colors and costumes. Only at the high school level was the young audience exposed to situations of conflict or realistic plots.

Great focus was placed on "collective creation" companies working in the Isle of Youth, a former prison colony which has become the home of some 40,000 teenagers who work in citrus groves while attending secondary school. While drawn from real-life situations, these plays would be defined as "sociodrama" rather than a creative endeavor. However, such a play "The Wooden Compass" was well received by the young audience, and generated a good discussion.

Afterwards, the Cuban hosts were surprised to learn of similar collective companies in Mexico, Great Britain, France, USA, and Canada, to name a few. Also, they were astounded to hear that Canadian children might attend plays which touched on immigration, culture clash, death and divorce, political issues, and the changing nature of families. In addition, they hadn't realized that other countries used puppets and live actors as they did. Obviously they lived in a creative vacuum, and hosting the ASSITEJ EXCOM was a distinct step towards broadening their theatrical vision.

Performances: 6 April: *The Wooden Compass* presented by the New Pines Youth Theatre, outdoors in the evening in Lenin Park before secondary school students. A sociodrama, the play dealt with the problems faced by young bright students when they had to study with young unskilled professors, trained hastily after the Revolution. In this case a young, intelligent, well motivated student arrives at a boarding school to face a teacher who resents his talent. He is persecuted, and transferred to another school. While the play was interesting in its theme and offered an honest portrayal of family and school life, it lacked theatrical values.

7 April: *The Circus Is Here* performed by the Children's Theatre Group, was produced in a small theatre in the daytime to several classes of elementary school children. The audience warmly responded to a simple morality tale about a dog and a cat who wanted to join the circus. They were refused, so they switch roles of barking and meowing and were hired as "freaks". They learned that holding a job was hard work, so they learned real skills to earn acceptance. While the staging was simple, the actors patronized the audience in their vocal skills.

The playwright, who proved to be quite charming, had been trained in Cuba's Superior Institute of Art, majoring in playacting for children in the Revolution. He pointedly expressed his view that young audiences should be protected, and not disturbed by discordant images or ideas.

9 April: *Little Cockroach Martena* was performed by the Theatre Guignol-National Puppet Theatre and presented in a small theatre in the daytime for elementary school children. The play dealt with a cockroach that finds a coin, buys makeup to make herself more attractive, and then must respond to the suitors who responded to her looks. Finally the shy mouse wins her. Imaginative mesh masks were used for some of the characters, along with puppets and actors. A simple story with unimaginative directing.

In discussion the company was amused that the delegates felt that teachers and students in their countries would be outraged by the cockroach's mindless preoccupation with her looks to attract "males". "Machismo" was still a strong part of Cuban culture.

11 April: *Ballet for Children—National Ballet of Cuba* was performed in the Garcia Lorca Theatre on Sunday morning, before an audience of 3,000 uniformed school children.

Preceding the performance, the children watched a 15-minute explanatory TV presentation by Calabacita (meaning: a small squash), a well-known story-teller in Cuba. The curtain raiser focused on a toy box filled with costly, elegant playthings, but the little girl chooses her old black rag doll. The major ballet told of a young rich girl discovering the poor side of the beach. She discovers a dying child, and gives her rich things, even her pink toe shoes, but the child dies. The ballet ended with a chorus singing "These things must end!"

The three-hour program was performed by Alicia Alonso's celebrated company, which was proud of their efforts. The children were quiet and generally responsive. It was danced on a bare stage in tutus and on point, but would have been better in leotards and tights, and bare-footed. The choreography seemed traditional and dated. A singer and a guitar provided the musical accompaniment. When asked whether any of Cuba's folk themes and rhythms had been incorporated into the work of the company, they replied that they were beginning to think about it.

Lewis[66] closed her comments saying how instructive the productions and their discussions afterwards were. "They gave a rare opportunity to see the Cubans at work and at play, the casual manner of the teachers, the use of grandmothers as childcare workers, and the open, confident manner of the teenagers."

The official conclusion of the meeting was held at "El Patio" Restaurant on the evening of 10 April.

1982
BUREAU MEETING
Paris, France/12–13 October 1982

Ilse Rodenberg (GDR) presided as President, Ann Shaw (USA) as 1st Vice-President, Maria Sunyer (Spain) as 2nd Vice-President, Eddy Socorro (Cuba) as 3rd Vice President, and Rose-Marie Moudoués (France) as Secretary General, and Ion Lucian (Romania) as Treasurer. Shaun Hennessey (Great Britain) as Financial Counselor was absent.[67]

The Agenda included the following items:
- Agenda for the EXCOM Meeting in Havana, Cuba in April 1982
- Resolution re: the existence of children's theater (Rodenberg)
- Information on Šibenik trip in September 1982 and its results
- Establishing contact with potential new member countries
- Current situation in some existing centers
- Current UNESCO status of ASSITEJ
- Update on "ASSITEJ—Theatres of the World"
- Planning for the VIIIth International Congress in Moscow in June 1984

The discussions covered the following items:
1. Minutes were approved with one correction
2. A draft resolution by the GDR expressed concern over the reduction or removal of financial support in the socialist countries for many youth theatres was approved
3. The President reported in favor of accepting an invitation for the EXCOM to meeting in Šibenik, Yugoslavia on the occasion of the 25th Anniversary of their Festival of the Child, and in connection with the "ASSITEJ 1985—Theater of the World" celebrating the 20-year existence of ASSITEJ. The two Festivals, Lyon and Šibenik should arrange their schedules so that Lyon theater groups could also appear in Šibenik. The EXCOM would be happy to provide a list of recommended performance companies and their plays.
4. **Vietnam and Austria** had inquired about membership. Moudoués was charged with following up both contacts. In **Panama** a preparation committee had been organized for possible membership to ASSITEJ. **Greece** would soon unify its working theatres for youth and apply for membership, assuming it could pay its dues.

There was no current contact with the **Danish Center**. The **Cuban Center** has contact with the new leadership in **Peru**.

Venezuela has paid its dues, but the check was returned for insufficient funds. The **Uruguay Center** in Montevideo has given no response to current correspondence. **Mexico** held a large festival with many companies performing. The performances were reported as very good.

5. The Secretary-General continued her efforts to achieve UNESCO Status. President Rodenberg had a discussion with the GDR Deputy Ambassador Thun to UNESCO to acquaint him with Moudoués and give his support.
6. At the insistence of Maurice Yendt the EXCOM approved the title "ASSITEJ 1985—Theatre of the World" for the Lyon Festival, as approved at the Cuban EXCOM Meeting in 1983. The Festival planned for guest performances from Mexico, Cuba, Australia, Spain, Italy, Japan, India, and Romania. There was also an oral invitation for a performance from the GDR.

    All financial arrangements were in place so the Festival could continue every two years, and hopefully one of the socialist countries would host the Festival on the off-years.
7. The President was requested to establish contact with the Soviet Center so the EXCOM could get information about the USSR hosting of the Congress in 1984. An appointment on 6 December was arranged.

During the meeting, Rodenberg kept constant contact with Ambassador Thun who showed great interest in the activities of ASSITEJ.

The meeting was then adjourned.

INTERIM/ASSITEJ/USA—1983

The US Center for ASSITEJ (now ASSITEJ/USA) wanted their Wingspread Conference of 1983 in Wisconsin to bring focus on professional theatre for young audiences to the attention of the entire country: USA leaders of the adult regional theatre, the National Endowment for the Arts, foundations, educators, community leaders, parents and children, everyone! They wanted people to see good professional theatre for young audiences from the USA and as many foreign countries as the Center could afford.

To achieve these goals, Shaw enlisted her colleagues in the adult theatre as friends and influential allies. They began to speak of "One Theatre World" of artists, managers, educators relating to the adult theatre *and* the theatre for young audiences. They needed a plan of action by a "think tank" of theatre leaders. Shaw (President of ASSITEJ/USA) contacted Henry Halstead, an advocate of theatre for young people and Director of the Johnson Foundation's Wingspread Center in Racine, Wisconsin, who in turn invited the forming group to be guests at the Wingspread Conference Center. Moses Goldberg agreed to design the program for the event and persuaded Tom Bailey, a General Electric corporate leader from Louisville, Kentucky, to act as program facilitator. Jessica Andrews (Foundation for the Extension and Development of the American Theatre) gave support, and a cross section of the theatre world gathered, professional and educational, and hammered out a list of five-year goals to unite and advance the worlds of theatre. Socorro Merlin (President, ASSITEJ/Mexico) was invited to attend. This special group ultimately succeeded in achieving all of their 5-year goals.

At the Wingspread Conference heated discussions prevailed. It was agreed that too much of the theatre currently offered to young audiences was substandard, often embarrassing. Greg Falls, Artistic Director of American Conservatory Theatre, Seattle shouted, "We must get theatre for young audiences out of the station wagon and into the theatre!" Someone suggested people producing substandard theatre for children should either "shape up or shut down", a suggestion which attracted a number of "amens". At which point Susan Zeder suggested, "How do we bring this about? Should someone just stand up and say 'O.K. All of you who are doing shit, just stand up and leave the room.'" Everyone laughed, but no one left the room. General complaints of being mistreated by people in the adult theatre were frequent. Finally Martha Coigney, Director of the International Theatre Institute (ITI) for the USA, threw down the knitting she had attacked with increasing fervor and said, "My advice to you children's theatre people is 'GET OUT OF YOUR

GHETTOS!' Stop feeling sorry for yourselves! Devise a plan and pursue it." The creation of a long-range plan was the major accomplishment of that 1983 conference.

Hugh Southern, Deputy Director of the National Endowment for the Arts in the USA, described the Conference as "one of the most spirited, honest debates I've heard in the theatre world." The ASSITEJ/USA Wingspread Conference was born, and the group began to speak of "One Theatre World" with theatre artists crossing from adult theatre to theatre for young audiences and back.

The results of this Conference, the New Orleans, Louisiana Festival and Colloquium, and the creative "One Theatre World" Festival at the John F. Kennedy Center for the Performing Arts have greatly changed the nature and quality of theatre for young audiences in the USA for the better, as well as confirming the importance of ASSITEJ/USA's participation in ASSITEJ International. It's considered mandatory!

1983
EXECUTIVE MEETING
Lisbon, Portugal/28–30 June 1983

The Executive Committee of ASSITEJ met in Lisbon, Portugal from 28–30 June 1983. Ilse Rodenberg (GDR) presided as President, Ann Shaw (USA) as 1st Vice President, Maria Sunyer (Spain) as 2nd Vice-President, Eddy Socorro (Cuba) as 3rd Vice President, Rose-Marie Moudoués (France) as Secretary General, and Ion Lucian (Romania) as Treasurer.[68]

Members of the EXCOM in attendance were: Andrew Bleby (Australia), Victor Georgiev (Bulgaria), Diane Bouchard (Canada), Ladislav Knižátko (Czechoslovakia), Wolfgang Anraths deputized for Kathrin Türks (FGR), Maurice Yendt (France), Ottorino Negri (Italy), João Luiz Brites (Portugal), Elisabeth Cozona (Switzerland), Alexei Borodin deputized for Natalya Satz (USSR), Berislav Frkič deputized for Zvjezdana Ladika (Yugoslavia).

Absent were: Ion Lucian (Romania) as Treasurer, Nena Stenius (Finland) as observer.

Financial Advisor: Shaun Hennessey (Great Britain).

Observers: Inga Juul, Michael Ramløse (Denmark), Dirke Fröse (FGR), Maurice Yendt (France), Else Mazure (Netherlands), Maria Navarro (Spain) who would replace Maria Sunyer at the Moscow Congress in 1984, Mårten Harrie (Sweden), and Irina Miheeva (USSR).

Invitees: Dieter Wöll (FGR) re: the Munich EXCOM Meeting in 1984, Mozambique, Guinea-Bissau, and San Tomé, all invited by the Portuguese Center.

Meeting of the Bureau/27 June 1983

President Ilse Rodenberg presided, with Socorro, Sunyer, Shaw, Moudoués and Hennessey present. Lucian and Satz were absent.

The following Agenda was approved by the Bureau:
- Verbal Presentation of the Minutes from the Cuban Meeting
- New Centers
- Financial Report
- News of National Centers
    1. Denmark
    2. Spain, Uruguay, Paraguay
    3. Japan
    4. Possible New Centers: Egypt and China
- Report of the Commissions
- 1983 Report of *Theatres of the World*
- 1984 Congress in Moscow, USSR and Festival
- Date and place of the 1984 EXCOM
- ASSITEJ Brochure (USA)

- Collaboration with ITI for the organization of World Theatre Day, 27 March, at the Spanish ITI Meeting
- Letter to governments
- 20th Anniversary of ASSITEJ (Italy)
- New Members of Honor (Spain)
- UNESCO
- Miscellaneous discussion

Moudoués distributed the Agenda for the EXCOM Meetings along with the Financial Report.

The Commissions:

As Shaw was on the committee to prepare the commission guidelines, she suggested she chair the **"Theatres of the World" Commission** since Lucian was absent. The Bureau agreed and that Commission was established with the following membership: Ann Shaw (USA)—Chair, Andrew Bleby (Australia), Victor Georgiev (Bulgaria), Diane Bouchard (Canada), Maurice Yendt (France), and Berislav Frkiç (Yugoslavia).

Commission on Liaisons: Shaun Hennessey (Great Britain)—Chair, Dirke Fröse (FGR), Ladislav Knižátko (Czechoslovakia), and Else Mazure (Netherlands).

Commission on Artistic Activity & Themes: (Related to the 1984 Moscow Congress) Ilse Rodenberg (GDR)—Chair, Rose-Marie Moudoués (France), Alexei Borodin (USSR), Elisabeth Cozona (Switzerland), and Ottorino Negri (Italy).

Commission on the 3rd World: Eddy Socorro (Cuba)—Chair, João Luiz Brites (Portugal), and Maria Navarro (Spain).

The Danish Center:

The EXCOM recommendations re: the Danish Center which had been approved in Cuba had been sent to both the Danish Center and the group of theatres protesting the "exclusivity" of the Danish Center. Inga Juul attended the EXCOM Meeting as one of the "observer" countries. Michael Ramløse, a member from the other group, also attended the Portuguese Festival. Shaun Hennessey was again asked to serve as arbitrator in an attempt to solve the problem. Members of the Havana, Cuba Committee were asked to meet with Hennessey and Juul: Shaw, Negri, and Anraths, the deputized representative from the FGR.

Ramløse[69] remembers meeting with Juul in their hotel in Lisbon, and their agreeing to call a new Danish General Assembly to dissolve the old Center, start a new Center, and then apply for membership in ASSITEJ. Apparently Juul reported their meeting and agreement to the EXCOM after Ramløse had left.

This General Assembly was then held in September 1983 in Denmark, the old Center dissolved, a new one started, and a Board elected to which neither Juul nor Melskens were elected. There was no President of the Center but a "collective" Board which applied for membership and was accepted. This finally solved the long "unsolved" Danish problem.

The Moscow Congress in 1984:

The report was presented by Rodenberg. She had gone to Moscow and met with both Natalya Satz and representatives of the Ministry of Culture. September was set as the date of the Congress, since the summer months were out of the question because of vacations, and school being out.

Rodenberg recommended a national Festival with perhaps 2 or so foreign groups with whom the USSR had cultural relations and which are often not seen in ASSITEJ Congresses: for example: Japan and Vietnam.

Rodenberg had stressed the need to have hotels available at three different price ranges because of various economic difficulties. Also, she stressed the need for a Hospitality Center where people could gather and meet in the evenings.

Theatres of the World Festival:

Rodenberg was in Lyon, France for 2 weeks, and reported it a good beginning. She was disappointed that no one from Great Britain or the USA was present. She felt the host [Maurice Yendt] needed to invite the President of the Center, and if that person could not come then they should appoint an alternate. She also suggested that the Festival run only for one week, not two.

Moudoués commented that the Festival will take place in 1985 and 1987, and the City of Lyon will support it every other year. Shaw pointed out that after 1985, the opportunity for other countries to apply for the title had been guaranteed by the EXCOM Meeting in Havana, Cuba. Rodenberg expressed the opinion that ASSITEJ would have to make some adjustments because of financial difficulties faced by many countries.[70]

Future Bureau Meeting:

Great Britain through Hennessey extended an invitation for the Bureau to meet in London, arriving on 31 October and continuing through 3 November 1983. He stressed the need to set the tentative agenda in order to meet the demands of the British Council. The following Agenda was agreed upon:

Tuesday:
- 1984 Moscow Congress
- Statute changes
- Theatres of the World

- Other items as they arise
  Wednesday:
- Theatre in Education in Great Britain
  Thursday:
- Other groups in Great Britain
- Seminars on these companies
- Related issues
- The meeting was then adjourned.

Lisbon, Portugal

1st EXCOM Meeting/28 June 1983

President Ilse Rodenberg opened the meeting. The Agenda approved by the Bureau was followed:

Minutes of the 1982 Havana, Cuba EXCOM Meeting: After a brief discussion and corrections by the Secretary General and Switzerland, the Minutes were approved.

New Centers: The Secretary General requested that the following new centers be admitted to ASSITEJ:

1. **Norway** had a correspondent who was a university teacher. She had

assembled as members people working in the area of theatre for children.
2. **Greece** had about 50 groups playing for children. Both the Minister of Culture and the Minister of Education supported their Center's application.
3. **Vietnam**—their activity had been verified.
4. **South Korea**—their activity had been verified.

Borodin (USSR) protested the admission of South Korea unless North Korea was also admitted. Moudoués pointed out that North Korea had not applied, so it could not be considered at this time. She indicated that each of the others had submitted their statutes, the list of their members, the names and addresses of their correspondents in writing. After a brief discussion the four centers were approved unanimously.

Finances: In the absence of the Treasurer because of professional commitments, the Secretary General presented to each member of the EXCOM financial documents for them to examine, and questions could then be asked at the next meeting of the EXCOM.

Report on the 1983 *Theatres of the World* Festival: First Rodenberg reported on her attendance at the entire Festival held just recently, stating that was an excellent Festival, a bit too long, and there was not enough translation into English. She reported that the participants gave very positive opinions. She felt that the next Festival in Lyon promises to be excellent for the meeting of the EXCOM in 1985.

Maurice Yendt (France) was called upon to give a complete report. He stated that financially the city of Lyon assumed 60% of the budget, and the State 40%.

At their recent Festival 11 companies had performed: 6 foreign and 5 French. Those from foreign countries were: Australia, Canada, Belgium, Spain, USSR, and Yugoslavia. They gave 75 performances in 7 theatres for a total of 15,000 spectators. At this recent Festival 700 people participated in the meetings (plus members of the performing companies), and 19 countries were in attendance.

Yendt pointed out the need for performances to have a high artistic quality and the difficulties of knowing about the plays. He insisted on the importance of helping the national centers send the information about the performances on the highest level in their countries.

A heated discussion followed on the role of the playwright, and on formalism versus more provocative forms. All agreed that children's theatre is dealing with more social questions of the world than the adult theatre.

Cozona (Switzerland) brought up the conflict between the Swiss

Festival which precedes the Lyon Festival, with Lyon demanding that performance groups appear in Lyon first. It was agreed that this was not an ASSITEJ problem, and it needed to be resolved between Lyon and Geneva.

Commissions: Shaw presented the necessary guidelines and criteria. They agreed to the document with slight modifications. After this brief discussion, it was decided to distribute it to all EXCOM members, and discuss it with the modifications at their next meeting.

News of National Centers:
- **Denmark:** Juul had reported in Lisbon that there would be a reorganization of the current center in October with new members, and it was agreed that Juul, Melskens, and Birte Loksa would not be officers. Currently Juul was representing Denmark as an Observer, since "the Danish Center does not now exist." Juul stated that ASSITEJ was of great importance to her, and she had founded in Copenhagen a permanent theatre for children that produced four plays last season. She asked ASSITEJ to continue sending her all correspondence, and Melskens, Loksa, and she would act as a working group.

    The Sub-Committee on the Danish Problem went into executive session, accepted Juul's report, and moved to "dissolve" the current Danish Center so that it could be reformed and then apply for membership as a new center. They also agreed to return one-half of the 1983 dues paid by the previous Center.
- **Uruguay:** It was stated that the Uruguay Center continues to undertake projects, but its address keeps changing, and its checks for dues are not good. Sunyer (Spain) will report on its activities at a later date.

2nd EXCOM Meeting/29 June 1983

At the beginning of the meeting the EXCOM welcomed João Luiz Brites (Portugal), and complemented him and his theatre O Bando for their excellent performance. Rodenberg then presented Maria Navarro (Spain) who was currently an Observer, but in the future would be the Spanish representative, and Dirke Fröse (FGR) who would be one of the hosts of the EXCOM in Munich in 1984.

Finances: Shaw raised the issue of those centers who had not paid their dues, and were far in arrears. This had been brought up in Cuba, and it was decided that if centers had not paid for 5 years with any satisfactory explanation for their failure to pay, they were to be dissolved.

Moudoués responded that she had written those centers, and the results were as follows:
- **Venezuela and Turkey**—no reply

- **Algeria**—is in the process of restructuring its Center and is expanding, but they cannot export their currency. They understand they have no vote, but want continued information.
- **Poland**—Cannot export currency at the moment. They hope to pay their dues soon.
- **Sri Lanka**—In the same position as Poland.

SHAW: What do we do about Venezuela and Turkey who do not pay, do not respond to letters, and fail to file reports?

SUNYER: Eddy Socorro is trying to set up contact with Venezuela.

RODENBERG & MOUDOUÉS: Because of ASSITEJ's application for UNESCO status, it is best to wait on excluding centers.

Moudoués then presented to the EXCOM, the decision on Denmark. Juul questioned the word "dissolved", and asked again for ASSITEJ to pass information on to her and her library. She also said for them to keep the other half of the dues. Rodenberg said that information can only go to an official center, but that other centers are free to send her information.

1984 EXCOM Meeting: The Federal Republic of Germany (FGR) would like to host the EXCOM Meeting from Saturday 9 June to Sunday 17 June, with the EXCOM Meeting from Monday 11 June through Friday 15 June. They planned to have 12 productions for children and youth with a guest production from Italy. Observing Centers would be: Poland, Hungary, Israel, Japan, and Paraguay.

After a short meeting with Dirke Fröse (FGR), it was decided that the EXCOM would meet in Munich, FGR, from 9-17 June 1984. This meeting would coincide with their national Festival of Theatre for Children and Youth. The Bureau of Rodenberg, Shaw, and Moudoués agreed that the EXCOM Meetings should begin on Sunday 10 June, and be over by 12th or 13th of June.

VIIIth International Congress in Moscow, USSR: Alexei Borodin (USSR) presented the following report:
- **Dates:** The Bureau Meeting—18 September. The EXCOM—19 September. The General Assembly—20-27 September 1984.
- **Theme:** Theatre for children and young people and education of the younger generation in the spirit of peace, humanism, and progress.
- Sub-Themes:
  1. The modern world in playwriting for children
  2. The Director in the theatre for children and young people: Creator of performance and Director of theatre company.
  3. Prestige of theatre for children and young people, and means to popularize it.

4. Problems of theatre for children and young people to be suggested by participants in open forum.
- **The Festival:** Will be national, showing theatres from various republics and major cities. Will show the wide variety of style and forms in the Soviet Union.
- **Invitations:** Will be sent in September 1983.
- **Hotels:** Will try to have 2 or 3 categories of hotel prices. Asked the Centers to respond quickly in terms of how many would plan to attend.

They will provide precise synopses and summaries of the performances. They hope to have simultaneous translation of many of them. There will be professional critiques of the performances.

In the discussion which followed Bleby (Australia) was concerned that no foreign companies would perform. Moudoués countered that the decision was up to the host country, and the USSR had a multiplicity of cultures. Shaw commented that plans were underway, and the delegates would see good theatre and receive excellent hospitality.

Report from the Spanish Center: Maria Navarro (Spain) reported that the Ministry of Culture was giving the Spanish Center further financial assistance and support. The Center was in the process of organizing a library, a video center, and a festival, which would be held in 1984.

Maria Sunyer (Spain) reported on Paraguay and Uruguay and their desire to form a permanent commission for the development of theatre in Latin American with headquarters in Montevideo, Uruguay.

Sunyer again pointed out the need for Spanish as a fourth language. However, the Secretary General pointed out that the EXCOM at the Cuban Congress felt that having another multi-national center would be like an ASSITEJ within ASSITEJ. She had written a letter accordingly but had received no response. She would send another letter, and they would study the document from Sunyer at the Munich or Moscow Meeting. Also, this question had been posed to the General Assembly, and it was rejected because of the extra costs to both the Secretariat and the country hosting the Congress. She continued that with the many centers in ASSITEJ, it was important to have only two official languages.[71]

New Centers: Shaw presented a report after her visit to three countries. She had established very good contacts with the Japanese Center, and in the future there will be good contacts between the Japanese and the USA Center. Their first collaboration will be at the New Orleans World's Exposition in 1984. Also, the Australian Center proposed to establish cultural relations between theirs and the Japanese Center.

During her trip to Egypt, Shaw reported an interest of their Minister of Culture for Drama—Ahmed Zakhi—on the possible development of a Center. However, Moudoués reported a visiting journalist from Egypt expressed doubts about the establishment of an Egyptian Center.

While in China Shaw reported an approach to the Chinese Theatre Association, and Moudoués added she had accompanied a French theatre group to China and had given documentation to people there.

ASSITEJ Brochure: Shaw in her report stated that the printing of the brochure in three languages would cost more money than that available from the poster project. Either more money must be put into the brochure fund, or they should pursue another project. The EXCOM seemed to agree that they should pursue a different project. Brites (Portugal) commented that he might be able to get it printed in Portugal at much less cost. It was decided to have the Bureau review the project at their next meeting.

UNESCO: Shaw asked for a report on the status of the application to UNESCO for Class B status. Moudoués reported that their dossier had been presented and the Secretariat was awaiting their reply. She felt that the new President of ITI would be supportive, but that UNESCO is not too eager to award such status since there were a number of groups applying for it.

3rd EXCOM Meeting/30 June 1983

Letter to Governments: Rodenberg stated that it would be very helpful for the national centers to have an official letter from ASSITEJ about theatre for young audiences in the world, which in turn could be used in any circumstance where one deemed it would be useful. Hennessey (Great Britain) added the suggestion of the Commissions that ASSITEJ draft this letter to send to cultural ministries, government leaders, etc. regarding the importance of theatre for young audiences in a national cultural program.

Rodenberg had prepared a written draft of such a letter. The EXCOM decided to use this original draft with an insert of 1-2 paragraphs from the Commissions. Rodenberg said that a new draft would be sent to the centers.

Swiss Video Center: The Swiss Center for ASSITEJ asked each national center to gather information which would help them to assess the usefulness of their establishing an ASSITEJ Video Library for the purposes of information sharing and promotion. The key questions to be answered would be distributed by questionnaire.

3rd World Commission: The purpose of this Commission was to put 3rd World countries in contact with ASSITEJ. Negri (Italy) pointed out that such an undertaking needs money. Shaw proposed that the Commission, the Secretary General, and she project a budget and recommend that this become a line item in the ASSITEJ annual budget. This sub-committee was to meet before the Munich EXCOM to establish a concrete proposal, even though the Secretariat had little money for such a project. Moudoués appointed Hennessey as the new Head of this committee.

Miscellaneous Discussions:
- **Invitation from Australia:** Andrew Bleby proposed a meeting of the EXCOM in Australia in 1985. Moudoués stated that the EXCOM was already scheduled to meet in Lyon and Šibonek that same year. Lyon would mark the 20th anniversary of the founding of ASSITEJ in Paris, and Šibonek would be presenting their annual Festival of the Child. Moudoués requested that Bleby consider that 1986 would be a better year, since 1987 was also the year of the next Congress. Bleby said he would consider this.[72]
- **Center Addresses:** Moudoués requested that all centers inform her immediately of any change in their addresses for correspondence.
- **Bibliography:** Shaw asked about the status of the Bibliography, and Moudoués replied that she had given all the materials to Adamek, and had followed up on this during a recent visit to Prague. She also requested that Centers continue to send materials to him.
- **Play Script Exchange:** Shaw reported on the development of the International Playscript Exchange and said a Special Edition of ASSITEJ/USA's Bulletin would be printed in August. She named the countries that had sent in information, and others agreed to do so. Several Centers at the meeting gave Shaw materials. Others promised to send it. She also reported on the 1984 USA World Theatre Festival in New Orleans, Louisiana, USA.
- **GDR Book:** Rodenberg reported that the 2nd Edition of *Theatre for Children and Young People* would be ready by the 1984 Moscow meeting or earlier.
- **Future of ASSITEJ:** Negri expressed concern that time was needed for a discussion of the future of ASSITEJ which had been discussed at the Prague meeting, but time had not been set aside for such discussions. Shaw commented in her notes that this would take place if enough members pushed for it.
- **Canada:** Diane Bouchard reported on the activities of the Canadian Center which had published a book on the theatre activities for children in the schools. The Center was preparing a special edition of their revue *Theatre/Children and Youth*.
- **USSR:** Irina Miheeva requested that all changes of address be sent to them immediately so that their invitations to the Moscow Congress would be sent to the correct addresses.

- **Yugoslavia:** Bereslav Frkič informed the EXCOM that this year a Glossary of over 1400 terms in 6 languages would be published in Zagreb.

Reports from the Observing Centers

- **Netherlands:** There is virtually no center in the Netherlands. Two years ago Else Mazure (Netherlands) was asked to be its President, but no one knew about ASSITEJ. She felt that ASSITEJ lacked efficiency, since there were about 100 professional theatres and many amateur groups in the Netherlands.
- **Sweden:** The delegate reported that there are about 100 professional companies performing, about 50 are independent groups for children, and about 50 perform part-time for children. There are about 30 members of ASSITEJ/Sweden. Next year they want to have a Scandinavian Festival.
- **Guinea:** Very little has been happening since independence was sought. Their standards are very low. The first grammar schools opened in 1957. They must depend on the goodwill of individuals. They are very interested in "the creation of a new man", and feel theatre must play an important role in that.
- **San Tomé:** Reported things were very similar to Guinea. There were a few amateur groups on the island, and the possibilities of creating professional groups. They need ASSITEJ to help in their development.

President Rodenberg concluded the meeting by thanking those of the EXCOM for their attendance, along with thanks to the interpreters and the members of the Portuguese Center for the use of all their facilities for their work, making it comfortable in a very warm climate!

Performances:

During the time of the EXCOM Meeting in Lisbon, the Portuguese Association of Theatre for Children and Young People held their annual Festival. Some ten productions were scheduled, and Shaw saw five of them and part of a sixth, and attended two of their discussions.

She reported[72] that the work of João Brites' theatre Bando was excellent ". . . performing their own script of *Alfonso Henrique*. The others ranged from 'weak' to 'good possibilities'."

Dramatic material in these collectives remains a real problem, since they lack the creative guidance of a good playwright. The directors spoke of looking for an "authentic Portuguese voice", but failed to define it. The groups did not have much formal training in the theatre, or any on-going work in movement and voice.

Such a great amount of improvisation occurs during the performance that one senses their real concern is that of impressing themselves and each other, rather than a concern for the audience. Arrogance comes through in some of the work, a kind of confidence that they know what children need and will present it to them.

The Portuguese Center also arranged a half-day excursion to the Port of Sinter and the Coast of Estoril, as well as a tour in a vintage trolley car. Both trips were a pleasure to all.

1983
BUREAU MEETING OF ASSITEJ[73]
London, Great Britain/31 October to 3 November 1983

The Bureau of ASSITEJ met in London, Great Britain from 31 October to 3 November 1983. Ilse Rodenberg (GDR) presided as President, with Ann Shaw (USA) as 1st Vice President, Maria Sunyer (Spain) as 2nd Vice-President, Natalia Satz (USSR) as 3rd Vice President, with Galya Kolosova as interpreter, and Rose-Marie Moudoués (France) as Secretary General. Shaun Hennessey (Great Britain) was Financial Advisor.

Absent: Eddy Socorro (Cuba) and Ion Lucian (Romania) as Treasurer.[74]

Great Britain through Hennessey had extended on invitation for the Bureau to meet in London, arriving on 31 October 1983 and continuing through 3 November. He stressed the need to set their tentative agenda in order to meet the demands of the British Council. The following Agenda had been agreed upon in 1982.

Ilse Rodenberg presided as President. She opened the meeting with a Tribute to Kathrin Türks followed by a moment of silence, for she had recently died. On a positive note, this was followed by congratulating Natalya Satz on her 80th birthday!

London, England.

Tuesday, 1 November 1983:

1984 Moscow Congress[75] Natalya Satz and Galya Kolosova made the Congress presentation. The invitations are ready, and were to be mailed as soon as they returned to Moscow. Hotel arrangements in a variety of prices were to be handled by Intourist. The Congress Committee is to meet on November 10 in Moscow.

Satz wanted the Opening to be a unification between theatre artists who work for children and those who work in adult theatre. Performances will be shown at the Bolshoi and the Maly theatres. She wants to show how ASSITEJ has helped broaden the theatre in the USSR. Productions will be chosen to showcase the best of Soviet theatre. There will be no foreign companies. The Theme will essentially be "Theatre for Children in the USSR."

One evening will be devoted to young talent in performance. Hopefully the government would award prizes for longevity of work in the field to Klaus Urban (GDR) and Karl Richter (Czechoslovakia).

Rodenberg requested a shorter opening program, and Sats indicated it would only be one-half hour.

On the Agenda they indicated the following:
- Report by the President
- Reports on the Theme: USSR, Mexico, France
- Group Reports: 1) Modern world in playwriting for children (Great Britain); 2) The Director (Spain); 3) Prestige (USA); Problems of theatre suggested by participants—Wolfgang Wöhlert (GDR)
- Moudoués asked to discuss the general theme: 1) USSR—30 minutes; 2) France—Responsibilities of directors and playwrights—20 minutes; 3) Mexico—Relationship to audience and education—20 minutes. Reports were to be sent in by 1 July.
- All groups will have simultaneous translation; the Chair of each group will make the final report.
- Observers could come to the elections
- There would be no limit on numbers who could come from one country
- The USSR would invite 3 people from other countries as a delegation. However, they would only pay for the EXCOM
- A suggested attendance of 1,000
- Centers are to send the names of the 3 official delegates. These names will go through the USSR Embassy; others will go to Intourist for visas.

News from the Centers:
- **Senegal:** In a letter from the Ministry for Young People & Popular Theatre, wanted to become a member of ASSITEJ. Moudoués has sent them the information, and requested their documentation. She felt the Liaison Committee should handle this, and make a recommendation.
- **Denmark:** A new center has been established as of the Lisbon EXCOM.
- **Algeria:** The center is restructuring, changing its address, its responsibilities, and perhaps even it Statutes.
- **Netherlands:** After the comment made by Else Mazure at the Lisbon EXCOM, its situation must be clarified.
- **Lain America:** The Spanish Center plans to organize a meeting in Spain before the Moscow Congress in 1984. The Center will pay the travel costs to Madrid. A similar reunion was held in Lyon, prior to the Congress in 1981 with great success.
- **Third World:** A financial grant will need to be made to this Commission to pay the costs of documentation. The approval of ITI will be necessary in order to make such an investigation.

Miscellaneous: Rodenberg was recently in Switzerland and found many groups performing, but their quality was poor. Thinks this is a problem for many countries. Shaw asked about the Netherlands, and Rodenberg said she would contact them.

Sunyer reported that Spain had attempted to have a meeting of South American members, and to pay their way to Spain, and they would be able to obtain Visas in Madrid. However, it was only in the project stage. No promise of money yet.

Shaw wanted more information of "Theatres of the World" and Moudoués, and she projected a correspondence for the information. To be resolved at the Munich 1984 meeting.

Rodenberg reported that UNESCO had received their Resolution Letter to Governments. Moudoués had met with Mme. Gobai of UNESCO and realized that all the ASSITEJ documentation which had been sent in was lost. She now was in the stages of a second application.

Hennessey inquired on the status of Negri's letter requesting ASSITEJ to begin to update its current long range program, and Moudoués suggested that Hennessey underline the most important aspects of his proposal and write to the members of the Commission: Rodenberg, Negri, Shaw, Knižátko, and Ruiz.

At this point the notes ended.

Wednesday, 2 November 1983:
- Theatre in Education in Great Britain

The Bureau also attended the Theatre Center which was the home of the Unicorn Theatre, and then attended a performance there. A reception was held for them by the Greater London Council in the County Hall.

Thursday, 3 November 1983:
- Other groups in Great Britain
- 2 performances were seen by the Bureau at the Fulham Library with a luncheon hosted by the Theatre Centre
- Seminars on these companies
- Related issues

This was also Rodenberg's birthday, which was properly celebrated. The meetings were then adjourned.

INTERIM /June 1984

The second major project of ASSITEJ/USA was the Louisiana World Exposition and an agreement for them to co-sponsor the WORLD FESTIVAL OF THEATRE FOR YOUNG AUDIENCES in June 1984. In turn ASSITEJ/USA undertook sponsorship of a World Theatre Symposium entitled "Theatre and Children in Tomorrow's World" in cooperation with the Exposition. Their goal was to bring professional theatre for young audiences to the attention of the entire country. Following the Festival/Symposium, ASSITEJ/USA hosted the Pacific Rim Conference of theatre for young audiences. Representatives from Japan, Korea, New Zealand, and Australia came.

Jackson Square, New Orleans, Louisiana, USA.

Since the title "Theatres of the World" with an ASSITEJ imprimatur was pre-empted by the Bulgarian Festival in 1982 and 1984, it was doubtful if the current EXCOM would approve the title being given to the USA Festival. Although there had been much discussion in the EXCOM, and a clearly defined series of requirements listed before the title was granted, and strong interest from Canada, Australia, Switzerland, and the USA, the title was granted to Lyon in 1981 and 1983, and to Sophia in 1982 and 1984. To the best of these writers' knowledge it was never granted to any other Festival.

In the meantime, the USSR had been accepted as the host country for the 1984 ASSITEJ International Congress. Natalya Satz, the USSR Representative, attempted to get the USA to change the date of their World Festival, an impossible feat since the dates had been set by the administration of the Exposition.

As host for the 1984 Congress, Satz was asked by the EXCOM what countries would be performing at the Congress? Satz explained because the Soviet Union had such a huge number of outstanding theatres performing for children, they would not be bringing productions from other countries to the Congress. Several representatives expressed considerable disappointment since this supposedly was an "international" Congress. ASSITEJ President Rodenberg (GDR) attempted to smooth over these tensions by saying "Well, they will come from many of the republics of the Soviet Union so it will seem like other countries." Orna Porat (Israel) in a low but audible voice commented "Once they were other countries!"

Satz was furious that any other country would offer a children's theatre festival the same year as their Congress, and consequently none of the eastern countries were able to accept the USA invitation to perform at the Exposition. However, Czechoslovakia was scheduled to bring its remarkable performance of *Charlie* to the Exposition, but under Soviet pressure they ended up canceling their tour to Canada and the USA just one week before the performances were to begin.

Despite gargantuan obstacles, the USA Festival showcased eleven theatre companies, four from the USA and seven from other countries: Mexico, France, Great Britain, Japan, Italy, Canada, and Brazil. The World Theatre Symposium attracted national and international theatre artists who represented 62 theatres in 16 nations, 29 colleges and universities, 22 arts agencies and presenting organizations, and 6 state arts councils. 17 student interns from 12 colleges and university theatre programs in the USA and two foreign countries were coordinated by Harold Oaks (USA), and Bruce Halverson (USA) facilitated Festival and Symposium events.

Financial support for the Festival, Symposium, and Pacific Rim Conference was secured by Orlin Corey (Producer of the Festival), Shaw (Director of the Festival), and Wendy Perks (Associate Director of the Festival) from 28 corporations and foundations as well as many individuals. Arts leaders in New Orleans hosted parties and provided transportation.

Jim Henson, the world famous creator of the Muppets, agreed to introduce the Classical Puppets of Sicily for an Exposition Pass and dormitory lodging and food for himself and his child. The puppet plaza was packed with youngsters and oldsters more eager to see Jim than to enjoy the group from Sicily. Shouts for "Kermit" and "Miss Piggy" greeted him. Somehow he managed to enchant them and transform them into an attentive audience for the Puppets of Sicily. This conference thoroughly convinced the Symposium participants from the USA National Endowment of the Arts of the importance of professional theatre for young audiences.

A major contribution to the Symposium, held in a nearby University laboratory, was Swedish Director Suzanne Osten describing the gripping play, *Hitler's Childhood*. The play, written by Niklas Rådströöm, was based on the inspired work of the Swiss psychologist Alice Miller's *Am Anfang was die Erziehung* (In the Beginning was the Upbringing). Osten followed her description by presenting the remarkable soliloquy from that play as performed by Etienne Glaser, a famous Swedish director/actor who, because there was no stage available, leaped onto a high laboratory table and brought the abused/disturbed child Hitler to life before the eyes of the audience.

In the first week of June Shaw as Vice-President of ASSITEJ had to leave the Festival to attend the EXCOM meeting in Munich, hosted by the FGR.

1984
EXECUTIVE COMMITTEE MEETING
Munich, FGR/9–17 June 1984

The Executive Committee of ASSITEJ met in Munich, FGR from 9–17 June 1984.

Ilse Rodenberg (GDR) presided as President, Ann Shaw (USA) as 1st Vice President, Maria Sunyer (Spain) as 2nd Vice-President, Eddy Socorro (Cuba) as 3rd Vice President, Rose-Marie Moudoués (France) as Secretary General, and Ion Lucian (Romania) as Treasurer.[76]

Members of the EXCOM in attendance were: Andrew Bleby (Australia), Victor Georgiev (Bulgaria), Diane Bouchard (Canada), Ladislav Knižátko (Czechoslovakia), Wolfgang Anraths deputized for Kathrin Türks (FGR), Ottorino Negri (Italy), João Luiz Brites (Portugal), Elisabeth Cozona (Switzerland), Natalya Satz (USSR), and Zvjezdana Ladika (Yugoslavia).

Advisor: Shaun Hennessey (Great Britain)

Present according to Shaw's Notes: Wolfgang Wöhlert, Hildegard Bergfeld, and Greg Hollands.

Saturday, 9 June 1984

There was an official reception in the evening and a performance. Shaw commented that the play seen involved an 18th Century horse trader who had been a victim of injustice and became a rebel. He believed in Christ and Martin Luther, and was executed. The next day there was a tour of Munich for the delegates.

Bureau Meeting/Sunday, 10 June

The Bureau approved the following Agenda for the EXCOM Meeting:
- Approve the Minutes of the Lisbon EXCOM
- Discuss the 1984 Moscow Congress: Candidates, delegates, organization, etc.
- Commission Reports
- Finance: Financial Report & projected budget
- Questions of Centers
- Meeting of EXCOM
- Meeting of General Assembly
- The 20th Anniversary
- Report of the FGR Center
- Report of the Centers
- Miscellaneous

Danish Center: Moudoués informed the Bureau that she had no news of the Danish Center, but that she had heard from the Swedish Center than in January they had received news of a new center in Denmark.

South America: The South American Centers all say it is very difficult to attend meetings in far countries, and they want to organize regional meetings (not a separate ASSITEJ), but to organize some things with the help and agreement of ASSITEJ. Peru says they can be helped by such an alliance to organize a Festival of South America with the help of ASSITEJ.

RODENBERG: It is possible but it must be clear that it is part of ASSITEJ, and it must be possible for all to take part if they wish to do so.

MOUDOUÉS: It will be possible to do this with Spain and Cuba.

Everyone agreed to this concept of a regional association as long as it was inclusive, not exclusive.

SOCORRO: Cuba will organize a seminar for all countries of Latin America in December 1984.

Future Meetings: In 1985 the EXCOM had been invited to meet in France and Šibenik, Yugoslavia. There were two proposals to host the 1987 Congress: 1) Belgium from the French part (the Flemish part was not interested), and 2) Australia.

Negri Paper: Hennessey reported there had been no responses from the other Centers.

Then it was announced that this would be the last EXCOM before the Moscow Congress in September.

Munich, Germany

EXCOM Meeting/Monday, 11 June/9:15 PM

1984 Moscow Congress: Satz presented the following report:

Intourist has prepared a hotel for the EXCOM. The price would be 32 rubles for one room—it was the lowest price they could get.

The following countries had not yet responded: Greece, Argentina, Hungary, Iraq, Peru, Poland, Portugal, Algeria, FGR, Romania, and Finland plus 2 more for a total of 15.

The following countries had replied: Romania, Australia, Turkey, Bulgaria, Uruguay, Cuba, USA, France, Venezuela, Great Britain, Italy, Mexico, Japan, South Korea, and Norway.

Brites raised the point that no invitation had come, only information on hotels and trips. Satz replied that she had been ill. At the beginning of July everyone will receive complete information. Moudoués responded that July would be too late, since everyone would be on vacation. They must have the information before that. She also said that a certain number of the EXCOM members had been invited by the Soviet Center for ASSITEJ. These people must have an invitation to get a Visa and an airplane ticket. Rodenberg demanded "Did you bring these invitations with you?"

Satz said that they had already sent invitations to the members of the EXCOM, but mail takes a long time to come from Moscow. She would send them again when she returns to the USSR. Apparently no Center had received invitations. Only some people had! Rodenberg commented that all the information should be together—the invitation, prices, program, etc.

Satz continued that there had been problems in printing, the switching of the logo, name cards, the selection of the hotel. Now they have been told that everyone will be housed in the Hotel Rossia in the center of Moscow. Someone asked if it could it be written down, and given to them at this conference?

Satz promised to provide it as soon as possible. Rodenberg then interjected that everyone will be in the Hotel Rossia, and will pay 31 rubles per night for a single room, 20 rubles per person per night for a double. No meals would be provided. Shaw mentioned the USA problems of visas and flight arrangements, and Satz replied that Canada had the same problems.

Satz and Kolosova said they had already received three lists of people coming from the USA, and when Shaw asked if they were all the same or different, they replied they didn't know! Satz apologized, but said she could do no more.

Brites said his country wanted to send a delegation, but they could only come with complete information—hotel, prices, plays, schedule, etc. Satz replied that they already had too many applications, but she would give them general information:

- There would be 12 theatres from many of the Soviet Republics performing: Moscow, Leningrad, Gorky, Armenia, Kazakhstan, Latvia (Riga), Kirov, Siberia, Ukraine, Tbilisi, and Alma Ata. The performances would be for small children, middle school, and adolescents. The plays would be by new Soviet authors as well as classics, and foreign dramatists, as well as those of national minorities in the USSR. Some will perform in their own languages, others in Russian. Outlines and synopses will be handed out.
- A visit to the School of Choreography at the Bolshoi, and a concert
- The opening would be at the Satz Theatre with a ballet
- September 18: Arrival; 6 PM Bureau Meeting; 7 PM—Performance
- September 19: More arrivals and visit to exhibition
- September 20: 10 AM: Opening of Congress at the State Musical Theatre; Speech by Rodenberg; Greetings from the Minister of Culture; Presentation of papers from France, Mexico, and USSR.

Lucian asked Satz to set the priorities in the sending of invitations. She replied: 1st—the official invitations to all the Centers along with information; 2nd—personal invitations to all members of the EXCOM; 3rd—to send to everyone the rest of the program materials, schedules, performances, the theme, etc. They would like to have Reports in advance to translate them into Russian.

Brites asked what are the conditions for participants who are not part of an official delegation? Satz replied that they would be able to see everything on the official program. She continued that there would be 800 attendees, so tickets will be hard to get, but there is no charge. She also said there is a large group coming from the USA as tourists, who are interested in seeing Soviet children's theatre. Shaw is working with Intourist to handle those details.

The General Assembly: Moudoués announced each center can have 3 official delegates who will vote in the Assembly. Others can observe but may not vote. Some centers have confirmed their participation, but others have not sent in the names of their official delegates.

She will prepare a packet of information for the delegates that will include the Financial Report, the EXCOM Report, the Committee Reports, etc.

On the coming elections Moudoués stated that the Secretary General and the Treasurer are nominated by the EXCOM, and they are then elected by the Assembly. Then the rest of the EXCOM is elected. The next day they elect the President and the Vice-Presidents. She wanted to be sure that all the delegates understood the official procedure.

She then announced that the following countries had proposed themselves for possible election: Bulgaria, Canada, Cuba, Czechoslovakia, Finland, France, FGR, GDR, Great Britain, Israel, Italy, Japan, Portugal, Romania, Spain, Switzerland, USA, USSR, and Yugoslavia—for a total of 19 nominations. There was no nomination from Australia.

She commented that she had received a nomination from French-speaking Belgium, but she informed them that both groups (French and Flemish) must sign on together. The problem is that there can be only one person representing the country. She added that some countries had not named their representative, and they must do so by July 15! Cozona asked since each center had 2-3 votes, what if a center had only one representative. Moudoués replied that that person would have three votes. However, that representative must be willing and able to work continuously for ASSITEJ during the next three years after the country's election to the EXCOM.

In the discussion which followed Brites said that the Centers needed to be sent short biographies on the various representatives, so that they would know for whom best to vote. Also, for their center's continuity they wished to change their representative every three years, but their information and responsibilities could be easily passed on.

Satz replied that she disagreed. The representative should be continuous and permanent to provide continuity.

Corzona (Switzerland) felt it would be desirable to have all nominations made by the General Assembly but it would require a change in the Statutes

Moudoués concluded the meeting by requesting that everyone get the names of their delegates, with short biographies, sent in to her before July 20.

EXCOM Meeting/Tuesday, 12 June 1984

Theatres of the World: The EXCOM approved unanimously the recommended revisions in the requirements. The next official ASSITEJ Theatre of the World Festival would be held in Lyon, France in 1985. Canada would be a possibility for 1986, and Lyon and Australia would be possibilities for 1987.

Maurice Yendt (France) stated that they would continue their Festival as previously done. For this second Festival they have better financing from the City of Lyon, because of the success of the first Festival along with the Congress. The City had decided to fund a biennial festival of theatre for both children and adults. Yendt and his Co-chairman Michel Dieuaide would be the Directors.

As a result of this support they proposed to have a variety of performances on a high artistic level. They planned to invite several companies from each country to prepare two plays for comparison. This would include forms of theatre not presented before, for example: street theatre. They also wanted to have premieres, so they could work with playwrights on the text. The struggle for better texts would be their goal for the next few years. He figured about 80% of the performances will be for children and 20% for adults.

In response to questions he added that the texts would be new, and musical theatre would be included. A committee will select some French and some foreign texts, and the French texts will be translated. 5-10 texts will have public readings.

Finances: A budget for ASSITEJ was projected for the next three years. In Lyon in 1984 they had proposed to raise the dues to 175 US$. This led to an animated discussion. These points were made:
- Payment would be very difficult for some.
- The cost is very cheap.
- Costs of administration are steadily increasing with no new funds.
- The French Center finances the costs of the Bureau and publications.
- Canada pays the expense of translation of the French Minutes to English, and cannot do this anymore. It has appealed for government help, but none has come forth.
- A way to raise money beyond dues must be found.
- Portugal proposed to raise dues to 200 US$, with the proviso that a Finance Commission be appointed to find new sources of income.
- The USA proposed adding a $10 fee to the Registration for the Theatres of the World Festival and have it designated for ASSITEJ, but this was opposed as the public would object and this would lead to misunderstandings.
- Could there be different fees depending on the wealth of a country? This was turned down as dividing the world deliberately into rich and poor.

Finally it was agreed that it would have to be up to each country to find the necessary money to pay their dues, and they approved raising the dues to 175 US$ for the next three years. The General Assembly in Moscow would have to approve this decision.

Lucian as Treasurer announced that in October 1984 they will receive the interest for their 3 years deposit made in a Paris bank—30,000 French Francs in the account at 11.4% interest, and was now equal to 45,498 French Francs; the capital had increased by 51%. Lucian would ask the General Assembly whether to repeat this investment for the next three years or not. However, Moudoués said that the EXCOM is responsible for financial decisions.

The discussion turned to centers which had or had not paid their dues, and whether they would have the right to vote in the General Assembly or not.

Lucian stated that his country was deeply in debt, and was not allowed to export their currency. However, he was assured by their Minister of Culture that their dues would be paid by the time of the General Assembly.

He then raised the question of payment for Paraguay. They have indicated they had paid for 1982, but that bank no longer exists, and the Secretariat has received no money. Moudoués added that she had received a letter from them saying that they were trying to re-collect money to pay this debt.

Brites then asked about those other countries that have not paid? Moudoués replied that Poland could not export any money, and Rodenberg said either a country pays its dues, or they cannot vote. Brites complained that we are an organization of countries not individuals, and the non-payment question comes up again and again.

Rodenberg added that payment is a problem of all international organizations. ITI doesn't put them out for non-payment. Moudoués continued that Argentina and Peru had not paid, but have sent reports of their activities.

Future Meetings: Moudoués announced that they had two invitations for the next EXCOM: June 1985 in Šibonek, Yugoslavia, or 1986 in Venice, Italy during the Biennale.

Negri spoke in support of the Italian proposal saying that they had a new President in the Italian Center for ASSITEJ, and he had been elected to the Biennale Theatre Commission. It would be possible now to have an International Festival for Children in Venice. They would have a date to propose by that afternoon; it would probably be in September or October.

Ladika stated that Yugoslavia wanted to celebrate the 30th Anniversary of their Festival as well as the 20th anniversary of ASSITEJ at the same time, and she had been in communication with Rodenberg, Moudoués, and Drago Putnikovič, the Director of their Festival. They would plan to host 5 foreign companies, and they would present their plan at the Moscow Congress. Rodenberg commented that Putnikovič, had promised a full week of professional theatre for ASSITEJ.[77]

Ladika added that there would be two exhibitions, one of Yugoslav theatre and one of the 20th Anniversary of ASSITEJ. The Festival would begin in the second half of June in Šibonek, and the EXCOM Meeting would be in the third week in June.

This discussion closed the meeting.

1984
VIIITH INTERNATIONAL CONGRESS OF ASSITEJ
Moscow, USSR/19–27 September 1984

Background: Many of the leftist governments by mid-decade were under severe questioning and both philosophic and physical attacks. In the eastern European countries the years of 1980 to 1985 were ones of astonishing change. However, in the Soviet Union General-Secretary Yuri Andropov was "old regime", and severe in his handling of dissent. The major political shift under Mikhail Gorbachev who would promote *glasnost, perestroika*, and economic and social reform in the USSR would not take over until 1985.[78]

Consequently, the VIIIth International Congress of ASSITEJ was held with these enormous world changes as a current and future background. This Congress was tightly controlled, and all the delegates stayed at the Hotel Rossia in Moscow.

The VIIIth International Congress of ASSITEJ met in Moscow, USSR on 19–27 September 1984. Ilse Rodenberg (GDR) presided as President, Ann Shaw (USA) as 1st Vice President, Eddy Socorro (Cuba) as 2nd Vice President, Nena Stenius (Finland) as 3rd Vice President[79], Rose-Marie Moudoués (France) as Secretary General, and Ion Lucian (Romania) as Treasurer.

Members of the EXCOM in attendance were: Andrew Bleby (Australia), Victor Georgiev (Bulgaria), Peter J. Gallagher (Canada), Ladislav Knižátko (Czechoslovakia), Hildegard Bergfeld (FGR), Ottorino Negri (Italy), Kazuto Kurihara (Japan), João Luiz Brites (Portugal), Natalya Satz (USSR), and Zvjezdana Ladika (Yugoslavia).

Special Financial Advisor: Shaun Hennessey (Great Britain).

Absent was Elisabeth Cozona (Switzerland).

The following 35 countries were represented: Argentina, Australia, Bulgaria, Canada, Cambodia, Cuba, Czechoslovakia, Denmark, Finland, France, GDR, Great Britain, Hungary, India, Israel, Italy, Japan, Madagascar, Mexico, Netherlands, Nicaragua, Norway, Paraguay, Peru, Philippines, Poland, Portugal, Romania, South Korea, Spain, Sweden, Vietnam, USA, USSR, and Yugoslavia.[80]

The large delegation from the USA, led by Shaw and Nicholas Wandmacher (Tour Director—USA), was in the waiting room in Helsinki when they were told that their flight to Moscow on Finair had been cancelled, but they could take a flight the next morning. Upon inquiry, no explanation was given, and Shaw surmised that it was a political move to prevent her from attending the Bureau meeting in Moscow the next morning at 8:15 AM. Shaw protested to the Finair authorities citing her Vice-Presidency and her need to be at that meeting, and miraculously a space was found for her. She also asked Finair to notify Galya Kolosova in the USSR to have her met at the flight, which undoubtedly prompted Finair into action. However, the rest of the delegation had to wait until the next morning. As Shaw boarded the plane, she noticed that there were a number of empty seats on the plane. Shaw was met at the airport by Sabina Molevskaya, the interpreter who had helped her in Moscow several years prior when she had visited the Soviet Union, and a young administrator from the Natalya Satz Musical Theatre.

St. Basil Cathedral, Soviet Square, Moscow, USSR. Photo courtesy of Jane Campbell.

Nellie McCaslin, Laura Salazar, and Jane Campbell, USA delegates to the VIIIth International Congress in Moscow, USSR, September 1984. Photo courtesy of Jane Campbell.

Wednesday 19 September 1984
Bureau Meeting at 8:30 AM[81]
Secretary General Moudoués made the following report to the Bureau:
- Currently those in the Danish Center were in the process of writing a new Constitution
- The Secretariat had recently heard from the Iranian Center since their revolution, and they would like to attend the Congress
- Ecuador had appealed their dismissal

The EXCOM Meeting at 2 PM
Ilse Rodenberg (GDR) presided as President. Present: Shaw, Socorro, Moudoués, Lucian, Bleby, Georgiev, Gallagher, Knižátko, Bergfeld, Negri, Satz, Hennessey, and Ladika. Absent: Spain, Switzerland, and Portugal.

The following was listed as the Agenda for the EXCOM:
- Approval of the Munich Minutes
- New Centers—Denmark and Ecuador
- Iranian Center
- General Assembly Agenda
- Miscellaneous

Danish Center: New materials had been received by the Secretariat in November 1983. They would be applying for membership as of 1 August 1984. Moudoués said this date would be impossible since the EXCOM would have to accept the new Center officially. After a lengthy discussion, on motion of Shaw, seconded by Hennessey, the new Danish Center was admitted unanimously. Moudoués commented that now they can be seated in the current General Assembly in Moscow assuming they would pay their dues.

Since the Danish Board governed the Center as a collective, much of the administrative work was being handled by TEATERCENTRUM (formerly Samarbejdsudvalget) where Melskens had been replaced by Biba Schwoon.[82] Juul, as a self-appointed representative of Denmark, had been attending ASSITEJ since its inception in 1965, but was now no longer on the Board. At this Congress the Danish Center was represented for the first time by Biba Schwoon and Anette Nissen.

Ecuador Center: They were founded in June and had applied for membership in August 1984. They had sent in a list of directors, actors who were active members of the theatre, a program of a festival which occurred in May, but they had no professional theatres. They can be admitted with only one vote for amateur members. Approved.

Iran Center: Wrote asking for information on the Soviet Congress with the same address as the previous center. This was for information only.

General Assembly Agenda: Negri raised the question of a change in the Statutes, thinking that they had approved it at the Munich Meeting. This had not been done. The intent had been to require each country in their nomination to return the same representative for the three year term. No action was taken.

Voting Commission: The following four countries were appointed as Tellers for the election: Mexico, Sweden, Poland, and Hungary.

Theatre of the World: This appellation remained the same as previously defined and selected, setting the Rencontres Internationales du Théâtre pour L'Enfance et La Jeunesse (RITEJ) at Lyon, France, under the direction of Maurice Yendt its only recipient.

Secretary General and Treasurer: On a unanimous vote the EXCOM recommended the re-appointment of Moudoués as Secretary General and Lucian as Treasurer for the next three years (1984–1987).

1987 Congress: Ladika announced that in Zagreb they were building a new theatre which would be ready in three years, which would coincide with the next Congress. While she did not have an official invitation, she hoped that there would be one forthcoming for the next EXCOM meeting.

Moudoués announced that invitations had been received from Belgium and Australia. While the Belgian delegate was not there to make a presentation, their Minister of Culture favored it, but it would be only French speaking. Also, there could always be another change in government.

Andrew Bloby presented the Australian proposal, stating that their Center was growing, they hosted the very large "Come Out Festival" every two years, and it would be important for ASSITEJ to see what is happening in that part of the world. In addition it would occur one year before Australia celebrated its 200th Anniversary as a country.

After a spirited discussion the EXCOM accepted the Australian invitation for the Congress in 1987.

Brochure: Romania announced that it would print the new ASSITEJ Brochure, and it would be partially financed by the sales of the posters sponsored by the USA Center.

Report of the Commission on New Projects: Shaw (Chair)[83] reported Vol. 2 of the Playwright Exchange was to be published by 1987. Funding was being provided by the Mobil Foundation. She recommended that the Brochure Project be abandoned for lack of funds, and that the poster sale earnings be applied elsewhere. She also recommended a New Project on Artistic Issues to be discussed in Moscow. The Commission also recommended that criteria for awarding the "ASSITEJ Theatres of the World" title be established. Finally, Hennessey had begun a survey of possible financial support sources for ASSITEJ.

Eve—Performance of *Les Miserables* at Moscow Central Children's Theatre

Exterior of the Natalya Satz Musical Theatre for Children in Moscow, USSR, September 1984. Courtesy of Dr. Harold Oaks, Archives, ASU, AZ, USA.

10 AM—Official opening session

President Ilse Rodenberg presided, with Shaw, Socorro, Stenius, Moudoués, and Lucian on the platform.

In her welcoming speech Rodenberg commented that ASSITEJ was returning to the country (USSR) which created the first professional children's theatre (1917), and which was involved in the creation of the professional association of ASSITEJ in Paris in 1965, almost 20 years ago. She also complemented the early hard work of Alexander A. Bryantsev and Natalya Satz as Soviet pioneers in youth theatre.

She further stated on a historic note that "Our work can only flourish in peace. It seems to me to be no coincidence that at this critical and troubled time our Congress is taking place in the country whose first message to the world in 1917 was the call for peace."[84] (See Appendix I).

She acknowledged the recent illness and resignation in October 1983 of Kathrin Türks, Past President of the FGR Center, recognized the budgetary and financial needs of ASSITEJ, and stated that the strength of ASSITEJ rested on the membership of the many centers and their volunteer efforts.

She proceeded to list the following future activities for ASSITEJ to achieve:
- The continued organization of all congresses, meetings, and assemblies
- The importance of the continued publication of the *Boletino Ibero-americano* by the Spanish Center
- The continued publication of the International Bibliography, published by the Czech Center
- The International Information Center, called *Hotline!*, published by the USA Center
- The GDR publication of "Children's and Youth Theatre of the World"
- The bi-annual Youth Theatre Festival of the World in Lyon, France
- The annual Bryantsev Seminar sponsored by the Soviet ASSITEJ Center
- The annual Seminar for Theatre Directors by the GDR ASSITEJ Center

She re-stated the main goal of ASSITEJ, not just as to educate, but "to facilitate the development of theatre for children and young people on the highest artistic level."[85] This will require good literature as well as performance. We must bring discussions of artistic values back into our work, rather than concentrating on organizational details.

    3 PM—Ballet performance: *The Blue Bird*, **directed by Natalya Satz**

    7 PM—Drama performance: *Bambi*, **directed by Zinovy Korogodski**

Friday, 21 September 1984/10 AM—1st General Assembly

President Ilse Rodenberg presided, with Shaw, Socorro, Stenius, Moudoués, and Lucian on the platform. The Agenda covered the following items:
- The Assembly approved the Minutes from the 1981 Lyon Congress
- Appointed the Voting Commission for the elections—Sweden, Poland, and Hungary

Secretary General's Report: Secretary General Moudoués gave her Report on the past three years of activities since the Lyon Congress in 1981. Her report included the following: [86]
- **EXCOM & Bureau Meetings:** With the changes in Statutes at the Lyon Congress, the EXCOM now had a total of 17 members. They did not co-opt any members, but continued to invite representatives of various unelected centers.

- Bureau Meetings were held prior to all EXCOM Meetings in Lyon (1981), Havana (1982), Lisbon (1983), and Munich (1984). There were additional Bureau Meetings at Lille, France (1981), Paris (1982), and London (1983).
- **New Centers** had been accepted from **Greece, Mexico, Norway, Uruguay, South Korea,** and **Vietnam**. The old **Danish Center** had been dissolved, and a new one admitted to ASSITEJ, which brought the total number of national centers to 41.
- **Commissions:** Moudoués indicated that there were now a total of 8 Commissions: 7 were created in 1981 in Lyon, and 1 more in Havana in 1982.
    1. **Statutes: Moudoués (Chair)** Published changes in the Statutes, Minutes, and Centers Address List;
    2. **Publications: Sunyer (Chair)** Supervised ASSITEJ official publications: the Review, the Czech Bulletin (cancelled as of 1982), Bibliography, and the *Boletino Ibero-americano*;
    3. **Liaison w/Other Int'l Organizations: Negri (Chair)** IATA, UNIMA, UNESCO, other theatre organizations;
    4. **Agendas & Repertory: Lucian (Chair)** Organized artistic agenda;
    5. **Information & Coordination: Rodenberg (Chair)** Essentially promotion and publicity;
    6. **Project Planning & Financing: Shaw (Chair)** Essentially fund raising;
    7. **3rd World Liaison: Socorro (Chair)** Establishing contact with 3rd world countries; and
    8. **"Theatres of the World": Shaw (Chair)** Establishing guidelines for appointing such a "named" theatre.[87]

Moudoués briefly covered the activities and accomplishments of each of the Commissions, and the Assembly accepted the Report of the Secretary General unanimously.

Other Reports:
- The Treasurer presented the Financial Report which recommended that the annual dues per Center be increased to 175 US$. This request was passed with Spain and Czechoslovakia abstaining.
- The Assembly accepted the concept for the "Theatres of the World" Festival for Lyon.

The Assembly was then adjourned.

Evening performance

<u>Saturday, 22 September 1984/10 AM—Meeting of the Commissions</u>

Delegates met with the Commissions of their choice to use these sessions for discussion of their concerns.

Afternoon—2 performances

Sunday, 23 September 1984/10 AM—2nd Plenary Session/ Continuation of the established Agenda

Report from Peru: Their Center needed help to become more dynamic, wanted to set up workshops, do more work in the schools and rural areas, etc. They needed economic aid to fulfill these plans. Could ASSITEJ assist them? Rodenberg commented that ASSITEJ had no such monies.

They announced their Festival for 23-30 September 1985 was to be held in Lima. They would perform in two halls, one seating 200-300 and the other seating 1,000-1,500. Performers will receive room, board, and travel within Peru. After the Moscow Congress the delegate was going to some other European countries to seek participants in the Festival.

Report from Uruguay: Maria Navarro asked for a postponement until the representative could be there. Meanwhile Paraguay will speak for them.

Function of the EXCOM: Prompted by Portugal and Italy there was considerable discussion about the duties and responsibilities of the EXCOM. The major points of the discussion were:
- EXCOM has nothing to do
- Strong national centers are best leaders
- Best representatives are elected by their countries
- EXCOM needs to be more dynamic, have more thrust
- A national representative must be aware of all the work going on in his country
- Personal relationships must not interfere
- No room for career seating and nepotism
- Individuals must represent creative activity as well as administrative activity
- Activities are coming only from centers; EXCOM needs its own activities
- EXCOM must have a central plan and assign activities
- Must learn how to raise money
- Friendship is the most potent force

Hennessey then commented that ASSITEJ was past the point of just doing administrative details. It must change radically in the next 3-5 years in order to survive. There must be further concepts of interchange; there must be new traditions, not just those of Europe. There are 167 countries in the world; all ASSITEJ's future potential is away from Europe. ITI began breaking with its European image ten years ago. We should be prepared to have 50% of the EXCOM non-European.

The discussion was lively, and ultimately called for more and better communication, energy, getting away from traditional points of view, and getting out into "the world" to see what theatre for youth was doing. In many cases children's theatre was new to many countries of the world.

Rodenberg closed the discussion saying "It is normal to have different opinions!"

Nominations of Secretary General & Treasurer: On the recommendations of the Bureau and the EXCOM, the General Assembly accepted the nominations of Moudoués as Secretary General and Lucian as Treasurer.

Monday 24 September 1984

A major event that evening was a performance at the Satz' State Musical Theatre for Children by a young Soviet pianist followed by a large reception for all the official delegates. At the end of the reception, Satz thanked all for their attendance, and asked that everyone leave except Ann Shaw and Patricia Snyder, and Shaw's interpreter. Satz then took them to her personal office in the theatre where they met with an official from the Ministry of Culture and from the Ministry for Foreign Exchange, and a few members of the theatre staff.

The purpose of this meeting was to pressure Shaw to decline if any center nominated her for President of ASSITEJ. The elections were to be held the next day.

If Shaw would withdraw her name, then Rodenberg could be assured of election as positively as possible. Shaw had also heard it said that no American could possibly be elected President at a meeting held in Moscow, USSR (Cf. 1984 Munich EXCOM Meeting). Despite these pressures, plus Pat Snyder's comment in this meeting that "I too would like someone with more charisma!", and the fact that she was kept a virtual prisoner in that office until 1:30 AM, Shaw refused to agree to withdraw her name and said "Let democracy and a free election take its toll!" After her many refusals, she was finally driven by limousine back to her room at the Rossia Hotel.

Meeting of the General Assembly, Bolshoi Theatre, VIIIth International
Congress of ASSITEJ, Moscow, USSR, September 1984.
Courtesy of Dr. Harold Oaks, Archives, ASU, AZ, USA.

Son Finn Juul, Mrs. Inga Juul (Denmark), Zinovy Korogodski, Director of the Leningrad
Theatre for Young Spectators (USSR), and Orna Porat (Israel)
at the VIIIth International Congress in Moscow, USSR in September 1984.
Courtesy of Dr. Harold Oaks, Archives, ASU, AZ, USA.

Performance of *Bambi*, the much acclaimed production directed by Zinovy Korogodski of the Leningrad Theatre for Young Spectators, in Moscow, USSR, September 1984. Courtesy of Jane Campbell.

Unidentified performance for the VIIIth International Congress of ASSITEJ, Moscow, USSR, September 1984. Photo courtesy of Carol Korty, Archives, ASU, AZ, USA.

Tuesday 25 September 1984/
10 AM—1 PM—The Elections

The elections were held in the new Moscow Art Theatre, a handsome stone and wood building about 10 years old or less, with paneled walls and 3 balconies, altogether seating 1200-1400 people. While not an intimate theatre, the walls were stained a light brown with padded seats in an olive tweed with brown and black accents. The dark burgundy curtain hid a full stage with an orchestra lift. The feeling of the house was warm and welcoming.[88]

Galya Kolosova was the head Teller and supervised the ballot counting. There was no indication in the Minutes or the notes of the total number of ballots nor what constituted the majority for election.

The Secretary General announced that the following 19 countries had nominated themselves to run for election to the EXCOM: Australia, Bulgaria, Canada, Cuba, Czechoslovakia, FGR, Finland, France, GDR, Great Britain, Italy, Japan, Portugal, Romania, Spain, Switzerland, USA, USSR, and Yugoslavia.

Each center had 3 votes, and some split their votes.[89][90] Shaw also noted that several countries had 2-3 proxies each from other countries, which could be used to affect the election process. Apparently a minimum of 47 votes were required for election.

The Secretary General & the Treasurer: First the Assembly approved the re-election of both Moudoués and Lucian to another 3-year term as Secretary General and Treasurer respectively. This placed France and Romania on the 17-person EXCOM automatically.

The Executive Committee: The following countries were elected to the new EXCOM: Australia (Andrew Bleby)—78, Bulgaria (Victor Georgiev)—47, Canada (Peter J. Gallagher)—73, Cuba (Eddy Socorro)—75, Czechoslovakia (Ladislav Knížátko)—78, FGR (Hildegard Bergfeld)—75, Finland (Nena Stenius)—70, France (Rose-Marie Moudoués), GDR (Ilse Rodenberg)—71, Great Britain (Shaun Hennessey)—53, Japan (Kazuto Kurihara)—75, Portugal (João Luiz Brites)—66, Romania (Ion Lucian), Spain (Maria Navarro)—47, USA (Ann Shaw)—55, USSR (Natalya Satz)—69, and Yugoslavia (Zvjezdana Ladika)—74 for a total EXCOM of 17.

Italy and Switzerland of those self-nominated were not elected. According to the notes taken by Oaks (USA), the following countries received votes but not enough to be elected: Israel—37; Italy—31; Denmark—29; and Switzerland—21.[91]

Election of the President and Vice-Presidents: Following the election of the EXCOM, the new EXCOM met to recommend a slate of officers. For President they recommended Ilse Rodenberg (GDR), and Ann Shaw (USA) was nominated from the floor by Italy (Ottorino Negri), and seconded by Great

Britain (Shaun Hennessey). Rodenberg was re-elected to a third term by 7 votes.

While the votes for the president were being counted, Rodenberg had exited the auditorium. Shaw went out to find her; they walked together; and then at Shaw's urging returned to the Auditorium to sit together. When the results were announced, Shaw escorted Rodenberg to the podium to take her proper place to preside over the election of the Vice-Presidents. As she returned to her seat, Shaw received a standing ovation by the General Assembly.

The New EXCOM had recommended that the Assembly elect Shaw, Socorro, and Stenius. They were elected accordingly as 1st, 2nd, and 3rd Vice-President.

Thus the Bureau for 1984–1987 became: Ilse Rodenberg as President (GDR) for her 3rd term; Ann Shaw (USA) as 1st Vice-President, Eddy Socorro (Cuba) as 2nd Vice-President, and Nena Stenius (Finland) as 3rd Vice-President; Rose-Marie Moudoués (France) as Secretary General; and Ion Lucian (Romania) as Treasurer.

Shaw later found out that also during the Congress before the elections, all the delegates from the Eastern bloc were called into an office of the Soviet Office of Cultural Affairs, and an official, not connected with ASSITEJ but with the government, informed all those present that it was expected that each of them would cast their vote for Ilse Rodenberg (GDR) for President. If not he said ". . . we won't be able to help you with money for your theatres." Zvjezdana Ladika (Yugoslavia) walked out of the meeting, but the others stayed.[92] Later, Ion Lucian (Romania) told this to Shaw while openly weeping and asking for her forgiveness.

Eve—Performance
Wednesday 26 September 1984
10 AM—Final Plenary Session

The Secretary General officially announced the results of the elections to the entire Assembly the next day. The delegates filled most of the Orchestra Section in the Moscow Art Theatre, and Observers sat in the area behind them. President Rodenberg concluded the Congress by thanking the assemblage for their confidence in her as well as the new people on the EXCOM.

4 PM—Reception
Thursday 27 September 1984
Departure

ADDENDUM

Both before and after the 1984 Moscow Congress, there was considerable correspondence between Shaw and various members of the EXCOM. Below are excerpted some of their comments, grouped by topic and date, which focused on the politics of the upcoming Congress.[93] The following exchanges occurred before the Congress convened.

15 December 1982 Rodenberg wrote Shaw about the details of the 1984 Moscow Congress, having just returned from a visit in Moscow. The date had been set for 17 September for the first Bureau Meeting which resolved its conflict with the World's Exposition in New Orleans, Louisiana in June.

23 April 1983 Shaw wrote Negri re: the future of ASSITEJ responding to his letter of December 1982 urging her to run for President. She would be willing if there was enough support. She did not feel that Rodenberg should run for a 3rd term. Others to consider were Sunyer (not strong enough), Shaun Hennessey (good possibility but the British Center would not support him), and Kathrin Türks "who has as much independence of mind as a piece of over-cooked pasta." As possible President she did feel she had a "world view," liked to get things done, and make things grow, which would definitely benefit ASSITEJ. She closed her comments by urging him to get the Italian Center more involved.

16 May 2003 Negri wrote Shaw in response to her letter of 23 April about possible support for her Presidency. He stated that what he wanted was a strong Bureau that looked to the future, and that was willing to move ASSITEJ forward rather than maintain the status quo. These questions needed to be discussed with diplomacy at the next Meeting in Lisbon, Portugal.

13 June 1983 the Japanese Center wrote to Shaw asking for help and advice re: their nomination to the EXCOM.

25 October 1983 Satz wrote Shaw that she and 3 official representatives from the USA were invited to attend the VIIIth International Congress of ASSITEJ from 17-27 September 1984. Shaw's expenses would be paid by the Soviet center, and she would be given an interpreter to help her with all the events and meetings related to the Congress. She requested a response by 1 March 1984.

3 December 1983 Satz wrote Shaw acknowledging Shaw's acceptance of the Soviet invitation.

3 February 1984 Negri wrote Shaw urging her to make a decision re: the Presidency and about the future of ASSITEJ. "We must stop managing ASSITEJ like a group of house-keepers. . . ." The level of the meetings must be raised artistically and culturally, and ASSITEJ has a responsibility for the future. The EXCOM seems to be responsible for nothing, and there are no plans for projects to advance the association; it only manages little things. It essentially was a letter of complaint, and a request to start working towards the future.

9 March 1984 the Korean Center wrote Satz that they were sending 6 delegates (3 official and 3 others) to the Moscow Congress and they would need visas issued in Tokyo.

16 April 1984 Sunyer cabled Shaw stating that she and Hennessey would be absent in Munich, and she requested Moudoués to announce her nomination of Shaw as President.

22 May 1984 Shaw wrote Kolosova (USSR) asking the Soviet Center to issue an invitation to Mrs. Ofira Navon, wife of the former President of Israel and an official of the Israeli Ministry of Culture, and Dr. Baruch Levy of Israel to come to the Moscow Congress. They were very interested in helping the development of children's theatre in Israel. [Apparently none of the theatre artists involved in theatre for young people in Israel knew anything about ASSITEJ or that there was an ASSITEJ Center in Israel headed by Orna Porat.] Shaw's request to the Soviet Center was refused.

15 June 1984 Shaw cabled Bleby to be sure to nominate Australia for the EXCOM. The deadline was 20 June.

26 June 1984 Rodenberg wrote Shaw after the Munich EXCOM (which Shaw had to leave early for the Louisiana Festival) that 1) Negri would request that 19 instead of 17 EXCOM Members be nominated; 2) Bergfeld reported attempts to prevent closure of children's theatres in FGR; and Ecuador was applying for membership in ASSITEJ but will have trouble paying its dues.

17 July 1984 Shaw wrote to Rodenberg following the Munich Meeting: While she felt she would make a good President, she was only available for 1984-87 because of her career commitments. Meanwhile, she did not want to create conflict within ASSITEJ, and suggested that the two of them should keep the elections on a professional level. She wrote that other possibilities could be Maria Sunyer (Spain), Shaun Hennessey (Great Britain), Maria Navarro (Spain), and João Brites (Portugal).

28 July 1984 In reply to Negri's letter of 3 February 2004 Shaw wrote that ASSITEJ needed both a new Secretary General as well as a President. In a moment of candor she wrote "Moudoués is a very bright, clever woman. She must have been an excellent Secretary General in the early years when ASSITEJ was young and her enthusiasm and energy for work was strong. Now she neglects her responsibilities and discourages those who try to make the organization operate more efficiently and effectively. As is the case with most people who become entrenched in an office, [she] has become comfortable with the old patterns which she knows so well."

In response to Negri's inquiry about Shaw's intentions she listed four things she was willing to do: 1) be nominated; 2) stand for re-shaping ASSITEJ; 3) withdraw at any time in the best interest of ASSITEJ; and 4) help search for a good compromise candidate. The forward motion of ASSITEJ was her greatest concern. Copies were sent to Sunyer and Hennessey.

1 August 1984 Rodenberg wrote to Shaw, in response to Shaw's letter of 17 July 1984, expressing a misunderstanding about her wanting Shaw to become President. She felt it would be impossible for the USA to be elected since they were wanting to withdraw from UNESCO, especially while ASSITEJ was petitioning for Class B Status; separate nominations were not necessary—the Assembly could vote as it wished [thus no loss of face for anyone], she proposed two new Statutes: a limitation on the Presidency to 2-3 terms and the 1st Vice-President should come from a different continent than the President; Moudoués should not become President since she and her Paris office were more valuable to ASSITEJ as a Secretariat. Rodenberg sent copies to all involved.

9 August 1984 Shaw wrote to Navarro (Spain) asking her opinions about the future of ASSITEJ, whether Moudoués could be President, whether Navarro might be an alternative candidate, how to avoid a political conflict.

10 August 1984 Shaw wrote to Hennessey re: the results of the Munich Meeting in June. She was concerned that the fight over the Presidency was beginning to turn "ugly". Rodenberg in Munich met with Shaw informing her she could not support Shaw's candidacy, and had been told by her government to run again for a third term. She hoped that Shaw would be her 1st Vice-President if she could not finish her term. Moudoués had openly criticized Shaw for failing her duties as a Vice-President. Satz openly stated that the USA should not be President. Shaw had stated to all that she felt ASSITEJ needed a fresh perspective, that Moudoués should move to the Presidency, and that Hennessey should run for the Secretary General. There were great internal tensions by the time the Munich Meeting ended. Ultimately she was concerned that Satz, Rodenberg, and Moudoués were the real powers behind ASSITEJ at the moment, and there were no changes in sight.

20 August 1984 Brites (Portugal) wrote Shaw saying he felt that the east-west conflicts had no place in ASSITEJ, and that while he recognized the value of Rodenberg and her experience, he felt that her only possible replacement was Moudoués but could the Secretariat be moved? He also indicated that he would no longer be able to serve on the EXCOM.

24 August 1984 Shaw cabled the Soviet Center that visas in Tokyo were absolutely essential for the Korean delegation to get to Moscow. Please help immediately.

24 August 1984 Eek wrote Shaw that Rodenberg would probably be elected, ASSITEJ would elect Moudoués for another 3 years, and then Spain could possibly take over. Once more the sacred name of UNESCO is invoked, but ASSITEJ had yet to receive much recognition, any support, and no money. ASSITEJ should recognize that it is primarily a political organization, rather than an artistic one

performing good works for the sake of youth theatre.

5 September 1984 Moudoués wrote Shaw (Shaw received it 13 September 1984—just 4 days before she left for Moscow) regretting the east-west conflicts, and denying that she ever wished to serve ASSITEJ for only 3 years. She was willing to continue until 1987, where she felt she was more useful to ASSITEJ as its Secretary General. She felt that Maria Navarro would make a good President.

10 September 1984 Shaw cabled the Soviet Center stating that at considerable expense she had changed her flight accommodations to the new dates on her visa, and would they hold off the Bureau meeting until she got to Moscow. [Apparently there had been deliberate manipulation to prevent Shaw from attending the meeting.]

11 September 1984 Ladika wrote to Shaw supporting her view of supporting Moudoués for President, possibly moving the Secretariat to the USA, and that she was grieving over the recent death of her husband. Much to talk over in Moscow.

11 September 1984 Shaw wrote the Soviet Embassy to re-issue her visa since she needed an exit date of 30 September in order to visit Israel.

The following correspondence occurred after the Moscow Congress:

22 October 1984 ASSITEJ/Korea wrote Shaw thanking her for helping get them their visas on time.

26 October 1984 Shaw wrote Navarro expressing her admiration for Navarro's presentations. In the fallout from the Congress Shaw suggested that Yendt was being setup to succeed Moudoués as Secretary General, and both Spain and Great Britain were returned to the EXCOM by a deliberately maneuvered low vote to express dissatisfaction. Also Canada was nominated for Vice-President to divide a vote for Shaw with Canada in representing the Americas. Yendt had also asked Bergfeld to nominate herself for Vice President to oppose Navarro, but Socorro (Cuba) was re-elected which gave the Spanish-speaking countries a voice. Since Shaw was re-elected as 1st Vice-President, she stated that they must elect a new Secretary General in the Congress in 1987 in Adelaide. While Navarro had lost, Shaw suggested that she hoped they would nominate her as a Counselor.

29 October 1984 Wendy Perks of ASSITEJ/USA sent a letter to the USA delegates to the Moscow Congress advising them if they wished to thank any of their Soviet hosts, they could do so but make their notes short, *do not* send any gifts, and do not mention politics or foreign policy.

A SUMMARY OF 1978–1984

1978

There was a sense of euphoria and accomplishment after the Madrid conference. Spain was on the economic and political mend with the death of Franco and the ascension of Juan Carlos to the throne. With the elections at the Congress of ASSITEJ, the EXCOM now was complete with the 15 authorized members: Bulgaria, Canada, Czechoslovakia, FGR, France, GDR, Great Britain, Israel, Italy, Romania, Spain, Switzerland, USA, USSR, and Yugoslavia. In addition, there seemed to be a good balance in number between east and west on both the EXCOM (6 east and 9 west) and among the Bureau (3 east and 2 west). Since France's sympathies were primarily with the east, this made the east-west division almost equal (7 to 8 in the EXCOM).

In Madrid besides the open elections, Lyon had been selected for the 1981 Congress, the next EXCOM would again be in Šibenik in 1979, and then in Washington, D.C. in 1980, the first return to the USA since the Congress of 1972. A good balance seemed to be working, although the organization was still heavily Eurocentric. However, the publishing and distribution of the *Boletino Ibernoamericano* by Spain which listed the activities of ASSITEJ seemed to be opening the Spanish-speaking countries to the international association, especially in South America. However, for some strange reason the Secretary General still considered North and South America as one continent since they were linked by a land bridge!

Although Vladimir Adamek served only one term as President, he had set several policies in action which benefited the organization tremendously. The most important was his creation of the Commissions which would become the working groups of the association. They started as five in number: Statute and Official Documents—Moudoués (Chair); Publications and Terminology—Sunyer (Chair); Themes—Lucian (Chair); Publicity and Coordination—Rodenberg (Chair); and Co-operation with AITA/IATA and UNIMA—Doolittle (Chair).

His second policy was that of scheduling more Bureau meetings to create policy and action. This took power away from the EXCOM while speeding up the decision making process. President Tyler had originally created the concept of the Bureau merely to produce the agenda for the EXCOM Meeting which would immediately follow the Bureau meeting. Adamek now used it as an entirely separate meeting of deliberation.

Although all decisions had to be ratified by the EXCOM at its next scheduled meeting, in practice the EXCOM never reversed any of the Bureau's recommendations. Also, since Adamek and Moudoués had formed a smooth working alliance, the Bureau's recommendations tended to favor the eastern centers.

The first Bureau Meeting after the Madrid Congress was held in October 1978 in Paris, and all were in attendance: Rodenberg, Doolittle, Sunyer, Satz, Moudoués, and Lucian. Their main achievements were to confirm Šibenik for their June 1979 EXCOM Meeting and their inviting representatives from Denmark, Finland, Sri Lanka, Turkey, and Japan to attend; to confirm the 2nd International Meeting of the "Theatres of the World" in Lyon in June 1979; and to accept the Polish Center in membership.

1979

The first EXCOM Meeting of the new term was held in Šibenik, Yugoslavia in June 1979, and noted several major changes in personnel. Doolittle had resigned leaving her Vice-Presidency vacant and Susan Rubes became the Canadian representative, and Ann Shaw had replaced Patricia Snyder as the USA representative, although Snyder attended the meetings and the Festival as an invited guest.

The 19th Yugoslav Child's Festival in Šibenik had become a major annual international event as a showcase for youth theatre which involved professional performers as well as amateurs and children. It was sponsored by UNESCO, a membership that ASSITEJ as an organization had yet to achieve.

A true international festival, this particular summer featured 61 performances from Yugoslavia, 2 from Belgium, 18 from Bulgaria, 24 from Czechoslovakia, 5 from Great Britain, 3 from Finland, 17 from France, 3 from Israel, 1 from Korea, 3 from Madagascar, 1 from the Netherlands, 7 from GDR, 5 from FGR, 5 from the USA, 46 from Poland, 18 from Romania, 18 from the USSR, 11 from Spain, and 6 from Sweden. In addition there was an international exhibition of posters and children's drawings, an arts conference, and many marionette and film showings.

Of particular interest were the puppet productions. The Zagreb Puppet Theatre presented a fairy tale entitled *Bas-Celik* ("Bad-Iron"), a black metal bullet-headed monster with copper teeth and two bull horns, black drapery body, no hands, and riding a 7-foot horse with a shiny black head. The horse stomped him to death at the end of the puppet play.

The company used rod-puppets—a carefully crafted head on a metal rod with shoulders attached. The body was draped fabric with the hands at the end of the fabric supported by two rods, one for each hand. The actor speaking the lines moved the head, while another manipulated the two hands.

The Drak Puppet Theatre of Czechoslovakia presented a very adult and highly political *Circus Unicum* ("The Greatest Circus on Earth") featuring an evil Ringmaster (Premier Brezhnev?), his dwarf son (a puppet country?), a dancing bear (Russia?), a blond magician (corrupt youth?). The company's cry for freedom and simple honesty was almost audible.

Of note is the fact that this year the Australian Center had finally begun to be active, and it would ultimately host the ASSITEJ Congress eight years later in 1987.

A Bureau Meeting was held in June of 1979 at the time of the opening of the State Children's Theatre of Music in Moscow. This building was later named in honor of Natalya Satz. The undated Czech Minutes stated that all the members of the Bureau attended: Rodenberg, Adamek, Sunyer, Moudoués, and Lucian. Doolittle having resigned was not present, and Shaw was not invited.

When Shaw took over as President of the US Center for ASSITEJ in 1978, Snyder requested that she continue as the international representative and Shaw be the national representative. Shaw replied that the President of the Center really needed to do both.

Snyder was interested in keeping her ASSITEJ contacts for the benefit of her touring program for the Empire State Youth Theatre, and had developed strong ties with the Soviet Union. However, with her step-down from the Presidency of the US Center so she could devote more time to her theatre, she now was on her own. Regardless, she had been appointed as an Advisor to the EXCOM, and had maintained her Soviet contacts. Because of this conflict, Satz told Shaw that Satz could only invite one representative from the USA, and because of their friendship and the theatre exchange program, she preferred to invite Snyder.

The main items of discussion were the upcoming EXCOM in the USA in 1980, the Lyon Congress in 1981, and the possibility of the 1984 Congress being held in Moscow.

1980

The next EXCOM Meeting was held in Washington, D.C., USA in April. Since the meeting was being sponsored by the US Center, it had invited all its members, at their own expense, to attend the annual conference held by the Kennedy Center in conjunction with their Imagination Celebration. That conference focused on issues and approaches involved in management, directing, and pedagogy related to theatres for young audiences. The attendees were also hosted at the reception being held for the EXCOM during their meeting. Most of the 60 members of the US Center accepted the invitation, and they were treated to a special buffet at a Washington home, with dishes named for the various states of the union featuring Maryland shrimp, New

Mexico nachos, Virginia pumpkin soup, Georgia baked ham, Wyoming lemon chicken, Florida key lime tarts, and a red-white-and-blue cordial to complete it, all prepared by Nat Eek, Patricia Snyder, and Bill Gleason of the US Center. Michael Ramløse held sway at the piano for entertainment, and many crowded the dance floor.

In their meetings the EXCOM accepted new centers from Sweden, Turkey, and Argentina, set the dates and locations of the next Bureau and EXCOM meetings, and accepted the USSR invitation to hold the VIIIth Congress in Moscow in 1984. Of particular interest was scheduling the first ever meeting of ASSITEJ in Havana, Cuba in 1982, thanks to the efforts and activities of Eddy Socorro (Cuba). While this obviously created embarrassing problems for some of the western delegates because of their embargo on Cuba, more importantly it indicated that ASSITEJ was open to membership of centers of all political persuasions. Also, the reports of activities presented by the various centers at the meeting indicated a renewed international vitality in youth theatre.

The Bureau Meeting in Dortmund (FGR) in November concentrated on codifying the preparations for the 1981 Lyon Congress, and reinforced the requirement that only dues-paying centers would be allowed to vote in the elections.

1981

The EXCOM met in Prague in March 1981 primarily to approve the final preparations for the upcoming Congress in Lyon, France. Maurice Yendt and Michel Dieuaide presented the details of the Lyon Congress. 6 foreign companies (USSR, GDR, USA, Czechoslovakia, Italy, and Sweden) and 7 French companies would present 14 productions for a total of 76 performances. The repetition of performances would allow all those at the Congress to see every play presented. The productions had been chosen to fit into the theme of the Congress, and would serve as a basis for discussion, while showing-off companies which operated under very different material circumstances. All the municipal theatres of Lyon would participate.

The EXCOM would be housed at a hotel only a few yards away from the Congress location. Simultaneous translation would be available for the Plenary Sessions, the General Assemblies, and the Commissions. Performances would be in various venues in the afternoons and evenings. There would be four receptions and A Celebration on the last evening.

As of 10 March 267 persons from 27 countries had registered. These included: South Africa, Great Britain, Argentina, Australia, Belgium, Brazil, Mexico, Portugal, GDR, FGR, Sweden, Sri Lanka, Czechoslovakia, Bulgaria,

Canada, Denmark, Spain, France, Finland, Guatemala, Israel, Italy, Japan, USSR, USA, and Yugoslavia. There was concern that fewer had registered than expected; they had hoped for 400 participants. This estimate was probably based on the success of the Madrid Congress in 1978, and it should be noted that Japan was the only Pacific Rim country registered at this time.

There were no new centers to be admitted, and there was continued discussion on the unwillingness of the current Danish Center under Inga Juul to admit new applicants. There would not be a newly constituted Danish Center until the Moscow Congress in 1984.

Shaw in her Minutes felt extremely positive about this Prague meeting. "The EXCOM began to assume the responsibilities for leadership for which it is elected and individuals 'spoke up' and 'spoke out' in a direct and thoughtful manner on issues of importance to the organization and to the world wide movement in theatre for children and young people . . . for the first time in my three year experience on this committee—we took some time to explore 'possible projects' for ASSITEJ"[94]

The VIIth International Congress in Lyon, France proved to be a high water mark for the decade of the '80s. While not as large in attendance as hoped for, it was given total support by the City of Lyon, the weather was perfect, the accommodations excellent, and the planning thorough and concise.

Yendt had originally hoped for an attendance of 400 or more which had been at the 1978 Madrid Congress, but his estimate probably did not take into account that Spain had just become a constitutional monarchy, had not been frequented by tourists, people were now curious about the "new" Spain, and costs were considerably lower.

The first problem that the EXCOM had to deal with was the seating of the Danish delegation, the presence of the two factions, one of their illegal exhibits, and the walking out of the official delegate. Another investigating committee was appointed, but no solution was yet in sight.

At the EXCOM Meeting prior to the beginning of the Lyon Congress, Dieuaide had announced that the General Assembly Meetings would only be open to the three official voting delegates, and appointed advisors and counselors.

This was a decision that had no basis in the Statutes. That only the three official delegates could attend the General Assemblies, and participate in the discussions and the voting was appallingly restrictive and controlling. In the past members at the Congress were allowed to attend all the Assemblies, but only the official delegates could speak and vote. While the excuse was given that the meeting hall was too small to seat everyone, this decision seemed to be another obvious attempt to control the organization and eliminate observation and possible confrontation. There should have been a strong protest against this decision, but there was none.

The Secretary General announced that since the Madrid Congress in 1978 six new countries had joined ASSITEJ: Japan, Ecuador, Iraq, Sweden, Argentina, and Poland, which brought the total affiliate centers to 36. Norway was trying to establish a Center, and negotiations were underway with Austria, Egypt, Mexico, Zaïre, Panama, and China.

Thanks to the efforts of Shaun Hennessey (Great Britain) as Financial Advisor, a complete Financial Report was distributed and accepted. As a result an increase in dues to 150 US$ was approved by 59 votes with 21 abstentions. There were six minor additions to the Statutes, the most important being the increase of the EXCOM to a total of 17, so that the centers of the Secretary General and the Treasurer would be included automatically in the total authorized by the Statutes.

Honorary titles were granted to Hans Snoek (Netherlands)—Honorary Member, Sozaburo Ochiai (Japan)—Honorary Member (posthumously), and Vladimir Adamek (Czechoslovakia)—Honorary President.

Moscow, USSR was approved as the site of the VIIIth ASSITEJ Congress in 1984.

Prior to the elections Portugal had applied for status and nomination to the EXCOM in a document written in Portuguese. At first it was not admitted as a voting delegate, but after discussion and explanation in the EXCOM Meeting prior to the Assembly, Portugal was admitted to full status. Portugal, which was leftist in its political sympathies, had not been active in ASSITEJ at this point. Its nomination and possible election was perhaps a ploy for a more leftist EXCOM.

In the elections Moudoués for Secretary General and Lucian for Treasurer were nominated and then re-elected. The following national centers were elected to the EXCOM for 1981-1984: FGR (Kathrin Türks); Czechoslovakia (Ladislav Knižátko); Australia (Geoffrey Brown); Canada (Sara Lee Lewis); GDR (Ilse Rodenberg); Yugoslavia (Zvjezdana Ladika); Cuba (Eddy Socorro); Great Britain (Shaun Hennessey); USA (Ann Shaw); Portugal (João Luis Brites); Spain (Maria Sunyer); Bulgaria (Victor Georgiev); Switzerland (Elisabeth Cozona); USSR (Natalya Satz); and Italy (Ottorino Negri) to complete the total of 17.

Following this election with Israel being voted off the EXCOM, its representative, Orna Porat, who had had a personal history of erratic behavior, was seen exiting in anguish walking up the aisle of the General Assembly after the announcement of the vote. Apparently she tried to eat the paper ballots as she exited. Whatever the cause of her anguish, the Secretary General wisely called for a temporary adjournment of the meeting, and Porat was hurried from the hall. Kathrin Türks (FDR), as a friend, was called to be with her. A psychiatrist was called in immediately, but reported that Porat seemed normal. Porat's husband was summoned from Israel, and he and her daughter arrived the next day and took Mrs. Porat home.

After the recess, the Assembly elected Rodenberg as President, and Shaw, Sunyer, and Socorro as the 1st, 2nd, and 3rd Vice Presidents respectively. Later, after Shaw was elected as 1st Vice-President of ASSITEJ, President Ilse Rodenberg told Shaw she hoped that Shaw would succeed her as President when she completed her second term in 1984, a comment that she repeated several times at other meetings. The 1984 Congress proved otherwise.

Among the many performances the quality was high, and represented a wide-ranging variety of styles, from opera to mixed media to agitprop to Commedia del'Arte. The major impression, no doubt weighted by the greater number of French plays, was of abstraction, of experimentation in form and idea which predominated over plot or character. There were few heroes, few well-told tales, and even fewer happy resolutions.

When the Czech play *Charlie* (in homage to Charlie Chaplin) became the most popular at the Congress with its combination of brilliant slapstick along with tender romance, there was almost an audible sigh of relief from the audience. One person commented, "Thank God, the happy ending isn't dead."

In many ways the excellent variety of quality productions shattered the traditional view of theatre for children. Surprisingly, the many children from Lyon who were in the audience, sitting in un-air-conditioned theatres, sometimes through long, wordy performances, appeared to be absorbed, responsive, and appreciative.

The successes of the performances accomplished what the General Assembly may not have—a complete exchange of a variety of intellectual ideas and artistic concepts, while giving excitement, entertainment, and pleasure.

Of particular interest following the Lyon Congress, the Czech Bulletin listed a total of 36 National Centers of ASSITEJ with Norway as a Corresponding Center.[95]

After the Lyon Congress, the Bureau met for the first time in Lille, France in October. The major items of discussion were the Festival at the New Orleans, Louisiana World's Exposition in the USA; the setting of the dates of the Cuban EXCOM Meeting in Havana as 5-12 April 1982; a codification of the criteria for naming a Theatre of the World Festival; and the UNESCO application of ASSITEJ.

In 1981 the US Center had negotiated a contract with the New Orleans World's Exposition which included a World Festival of Theatre for Young People in conjunction with an International Colloquium of scholars and practitioners, as well as a meeting of the Pacific Rim countries. With the selection of the Congress site in Moscow in 1984, the two international dates were in possible conflict. The US Center was asked to harmonize the dates with the USSR, possibly moving the ASSITEJ Congress in Moscow to May. Already in contract, the US Center could not change its dates, and the USSR selected September for their Congress. However, there was bad blood in the negotiations, and ultimately the Soviets prevented some of the "eastern" countries from appearing in New Orleans.

In the discussion over the title "Theatres of the World", it was decided that only countries which had obtained government subsidy could use this appellation, such as Cuba and Bulgaria as well as Lyon, and that every two years Lyon could use the title one year and Bulgaria the next without conflict.

Moudoués reported that she had met with UNESCO officials and was informed that ASSITEJ had sufficient representation to request Class B status in UNESCO, but their application would take a long time. An absolute precondition was that South Africa could not be a member of ASSITEJ, because of its "apartheid" practices. ASSITEJ had now been trying for Class B Status for 16 years.

In 1981 the US Center for ASSITEJ became a professional theatre organization, and by separating itself from the American Theatre Association, it became the country's direct contact with ASSITEJ International, and renamed itself ASSITEJ/USA, a titling pattern that many other centers followed. During the next three years it spent a great deal of time solidifying its organizational structure and optimizing its finances through foundation grants and individual donations.

Over the past fifteen years the Czech Center for ASSITEJ had issued a total of 41 issues of the "International Information Bulletin" between 1966 and 1981 which it distributed to National Centers for ASSITEJ all over the world. It carried information on all the meetings of ASSITEJ as well as news of the National Centers. It was accurate, fairly complete, and issued on time, but it was only as good as the information sent to the Czech Theatre Center by the other Centers.

In 1981 on the recommendation of the ASSITEJ EXCOM it was supplanted by the "Bibliographical Bulletin", whose first issue was in the three official languages (French, English, and Russian) listing abbreviations for names of countries and the addresses of the national centers. The notice was signed by Vladimir Adamek, and to the best of these writers' knowledge, no other issue appeared.

Adamek had done a remarkable job as Editor, as well as keeping the Bulletin alive in his lifetime. He died in 1990.

1982

For the first time the Cuban Center for ASSITEJ hosted the EXCOM Meeting in Havana in April. Despite the difficulties for some of the western delegates to get there, the meeting was regarded as a great success and its discussions very productive. All the delegates were hosted by the country at the Capri Hotel in suburban Havana, and translation was provided in the three official languages as well as Spanish.

The Cuban Ministry of Culture hosted a party for the delegates which included the opportunity to dance to the music of a small combo. The Minister of Culture invited Shaw to dance, and to the astonishment of many, she accepted. They danced together to the music and the applause of all attending, providing an unusual example of the bonds of international friendship breaking national political barriers.

The major items of discussion were the Danish Center Problem; the new ASSITEJ publications; and the Theatres of the World concept.

Despite multiple reports and several committees, the Danish Center problems remained unresolved. Part of the concern of the current Center under Juul was undoubtedly based on a shift of political philosophy from conservative to liberal, as well as the possible loss of its government subsidy. The EXCOM appointed Shaun Hennessey (Great Britain) as a mediator for ASSITEJ, and requested that a resolution be presented to the Bureau at their October meeting.

New publications for promoting ASSITEJ were commended, as well as recent broader international communication.

The consensus of a lengthy discussion on granting the title "Theatres of the World" to various festivals stated that all centers must be made aware of the various proposals before the EXCOM could decide on a permanent designation. Meanwhile Lyon would use the title in 1983 and 1985, and Bulgaria in 1984. In fact only one other country was ever given the title (FGR in Munich in 1984 as a thank-you to Kathrin Türks), and it eventually became the exclusive property of the Festival in Lyon every two years.

Excellent artistic discussions focused around the productions seen by the delegates, and these closed the meetings.

This was a time of great tension between Cuba and the USA (and within the Western Hemisphere). Hennessey (Great Britain), Ladika (Yugoslavia), and Lewis (Canada) flew to Cuba via Miami, Florida, USA, where Shaw joined them. Upon arrival in Havana loud speakers boomed the speeches of President Fidel Castro throughout the city, and even into their hotel rooms. Demonstrations were held rallying people to the cause. On the fifth or sixth day of the Meeting, it was clear that trouble was brewing. Ladika paid a courtesy visit to her embassy, and was warned that the tension between Cuba and the USA was mounting rapidly, and she should be prepared to stay at the embassy in Cuba. Ladika explained that she was concerned for her friends in the USA, Canada, and Great Britain. The Embassy officials said they would provide for those people also.

Later Lewis, returning from her walk near the hotel, said she had read headlines in the local newspaper that President Reagan had announced that all flights to Cuba from the USA had been cancelled, and that the last flight from Havana to Miami would be the next day. Socorro arrived at their hotel at 6 AM to get them to the airport when it opened so that they would be first in line for that last flight. Socorro got them their boarding passes, quickly said *adios*, and left immediately. As the four boarded the plane the door was closed on Shaw with the other three inside. By her pounding on the door outside and them on the inside demanding it be opened, they were able to get Shaw on board.

1983

The June EXCOM Meeting in Lisbon, Portugal was thorough and extensive, and brought several personnel changes to the group. While the Bureau remained stable, new delegates were deputized for Canada, FGR, USSR, and Yugoslavia. In addition observers had been invited by Portugal from Mozambique, Guinea-Bissau, and San Tomé.

The major accomplishment of the meetings was the resolution of the Danish Center problem. The members of the Committee appointed in Cuba, along with Mediator Shaun Hennessey, met representatives of both factions (Inga Juul and Michael Ramløse, who then met together), and they agreed to dissolve the old Center, start a new Center, and then apply for membership in ASSITEJ.

The Danish General Assembly was then held in September 1983, the old Center dissolved, a new one started, and a Board elected to which neither Juul nor Melskens were elected. There was no President of the Center but a "collective" Board which applied for membership and was accepted. This ended the long "unresolved" Danish problem.

The VIIIth Congress in Moscow was set for September 1984, ending that controversy; the program was approved for the Moscow Congress; the Agenda set for the London Bureau Meeting in October 1983; and Australia proposed to host the EXCOM in 1986, but ultimately agreed to host the 1987 Congress.

Many Portuguese plays for young people were seen, and Shaw reported that ". . . a great amount of improvisation occurs during the performance and one senses their real concern is that of impressing themselves and each other, rather than a concern for the audience. Arrogance comes through in some of the work, a kind of confidence that they know what children need and they will present it to them."

Obviously the meeting had proved to be productive.

The October London Meeting of the Bureau was primarily a one day meeting, followed by visiting Theatre in Educations Centers and viewing performing companies. The major item of business was the Moscow 1984 Congress. The program was standard, except that all performances were to be from the Soviet Union, even though it was an international Congress.

The recent death of Kathrin Türks was duly noted, and Satz presented the program. The Bureau was primarily concerned on the lateness of the invitations as well as information on accomodations. Observers would be allowed to witness the elections, and there was no restriction on the number of delegates from one country.

However, by the end of the presentation and the meeting it was obvious that there were severe financial restraints, and pre-planning was still going on.

1984

From the USA Center's standpoint, June 1984 was the time of their World Festival of Theatre for Young Audiences in New Orleans, Louisiana, which proved to be a huge success. It succeeded in showcasing seven foreign companies along with four from the USA. The Symposium had attracted artists representing 62 theatres in 16 nations. However, in the first week of June Shaw as Vice-President of ASSITEJ had to leave the Festival to attend the EXCOM meeting in Munich, hosted by the FGR, a date which may have been chosen in part to conflict with the opening of the Festival.

The June Munich EXCOM meeting held three months before the Moscow Congress finalized the Agenda for that meeting, solidified Lyon as the designated ASSITEJ *Theatre of the World* Festival, increased the dues to 200 US$, and set the next EXCOM meeting in June 1985 in Šibenik, Yugoslavia. The choice of meeting locations was many times considered for a vacation, and with the soft currency situation and travel difficulties it was easier to select a location in the east rather than the west.

Of particular interest was an invitation for Shaw to have tea with Rodenberg at the end of the EXCOM meeting. Shaw was told that for political reasons Rodenberg could not support Shaw for the Presidency, as she had promised to do. Rodenberg would have to run for a third term herself. The Minster of Culture of the Soviet Union had spoken to the Minister of Culture of the GDR saying that it was impossible for an American to be elected President of ASSITEJ at the Congress in the Soviet Union.

Shaw asked her "Must you do everything that your Minister of Culture says?" Rodenberg replied that 'Yes, I must! But I am an old woman, and I will have served two terms. I don't think my doctor will allow me . . . !' And then she added that they had even gone with her to her doctor to get approval for her to run a third term. Shaw replied "You must do what you must do!" The meeting in Munich ended, and on the next day Shaw returned to the World Festival in New Orleans, Louisiana, USA.

In many ways the Moscow Congress signaled the beginning of the decline of the east-west split with the destruction of the Berlin Wall in 1989 symbolizing its ending. However, during 1983 to 1985 the Soviet government dealt harshly with dissent, restricted emigration, and was still at war with Afghanistan. This made their control of the 1984 Congress obligatory, which made for pointless and unforgivable incidents in the world of the arts.

It was important to see that every detail in 1984 was closely supervised. No foreign companies were to be presented, all delegates were to be carefully screened, and in some cases deliberately inconvenienced. It was a last ditch defensive; *glasnost* was only a year away in 1985.

An impressive 35 countries were represented at the VIIIth International Congress of ASSITEJ in Moscow, USSR: 18 from Europe, 4 from North America, 3 from South America, 1 from Africa, 2 from the Mideast, and 6 from the Far East.

New centers were announced for Ecuador and Denmark, and there had been correspondence with a possible new center in Iran. The General Assembly accepted the invitation to hold the IXth ASSITEJ Congress in Adelaide, Australia in 1987. The dues were raised to 175 US$.

At this time the problem of "soft currency" created a problem for the Secretariat in the payment of a country's annual dues. This meant that some countries, especially those in the Eastern Bloc, could not transfer the necessary monies from their countries in payment of their dues. This is turn could deprive them of the all important votes at the Congresses. In most cases it was out of their hands, but in one case previously Romania had reassured the EXCOM that his Minister of Culture had assured him that the necessary transfer of funds would be made in time for the election.

The reports of the Commissions codified their existence as a working concept, even though some of their duties were realigned. Over the years they continued to function well although modified in both terminology and usage.

However, there were signs of considerable unrest in the discussions. Prompted by Portugal and Italy, they centered on the needs for change. Hennessey (Great Britain) commented that ASSITEJ was past the point of just handling administrative details. It must change radically in the next 3-5 years in order to survive. There must be further concepts of interchange; there must be new traditions, not just European. There are 167 countries in the world; all future potential of ASSITEJ is away from Europe. ITI had begun breaking with its European image ten years ago. ASSITEJ should be prepared to have 50% of the EXCOM non-European.

The discussion was lively and ultimately called for more and better communication, energy, getting away from traditional points of view, and getting out into "the world" to see what theatre for youth was doing. In many cases children's theatre was new to many countries of the world.

Although President Rodenberg closed the discussion by saying "It is normal to have different opinions!,", the gates for radical change had been opened.

The incarceration of Shaw in Satz' office the night before the election along with official members of several Ministries of the USSR was appalling, especially when a party was being held at the Actors' Club for all the delegates. The discussion revolved around the need for Shaw to withdraw her name if nominated from the floor, in order that Rodenberg could be assured of election as positively as possible. Shaw had also heard it said that no American could possibly be elected President at a meeting held in Moscow, USSR (Cf: 1984 Munich EXCOM Meeting).

Despite this pressure and the fact that she was kept a virtual prisoner in Satz' office until 1:30 AM, Shaw refused to agree to withdraw her name. "Let democracy and a free election take its toll!" After her many refusals, she was finally driven by limousine back to her room at the Rossia Hotel.

Unfortunately the elections expressed business as usual. Both Moudoués as Secretary General and Lucian as Treasurer were re-elected, only Australia and Japan represented the Far East, and Europe continued to dominate the EXCOM. In tight control Rodenberg was returned for a third term as President against her personal wishes, and Stenius (Finland) was the only new face on the Bureau, a woman who had studied in Moscow and had been active with the Cuban theatre program.

Elected to the new EXCOM were Australia, Bulgaria, Canada, Cuba, Czechoslovakia, FGR, Finland, France, GDR , Great Britain, Japan, Portugal, Romania, USA, USSR, and Yugoslavia for a total of 16.

While the votes for the president were being counted, Rodenberg had exited the auditorium. Shaw went out to find her; they walked together; and then at Shaw's urging returned to the Auditorium to sit together. When the results were announced, Shaw escorted Rodenberg to the podium to take her proper place to preside over the election of the Vice-Presidents. As she returned to her seat, Shaw received a standing ovation.

Elected to the Bureau were Ilse Rodenberg as President (for her 3rd term); Ann Shaw as 1st Vice-President, Eddy Socorro as 2nd Vice-President, and Nena Stenius as 3rd Vice-President.

Shaw later found out that also during the Congress before the elections, all the delegates from the eastern bloc were called into an office of the Soviet Office of Cultural Affairs, and an official, not connected with ASSITEJ but with the government, informed all those present that it was expected that each of them would cast their vote for Rodenberg for President. If not, he said ". . . we won't be able to help you with money for your theatres." Zvjezdana Ladika (Yugoslavia) walked out of the meeting, but the others stayed.[96] Later Ion Lucian (Romania) told this to Shaw while openly weeping and asking for her forgiveness.

The tragedy of all this political maneuvering is that it had nothing to do with the individuals involved as well as the art of youth theatre, but was instigated by officials outside the association who were being forced to support and promote national policy. Unfortunately all countries can be guilty of this non-productive behavior.

Despite the heavy political manipulation, the pressure on Shaw not to run for President, and the continued Eurocentric EXCOM, the seeds of dissent had been planted, which would grow into an open revolt in Stockholm by 1990. It was also disturbing to note that Moudoués seemed to be setting Maurice Yendt up to succeed her as Secretary General in 1987, thus keeping the Secretariat in France and under her control.

After the Congress, on leaving Leningrad by plane, the USA delegation passed through security, went to the waiting room, and boarded the plane without any problem. Shaw was singled out, held, questioned, searched, and released as the doors to the gate were closing. Governor Jerry Brown (California), who was himself a visitor to the Soviet Union, and who was flying on to a meeting in Germany, realized there was a problem. He consulted Nick Wandmacher (Tour Director) and joined him in waiting at the plane's doors until Shaw was safely on board.

1985
BUREAU MEETING /Paris, France/2–3 February 1985[97]

The Bureau met in 98 Boulevard Kellerman, Paris, France on 2–3 February 1985. Ilse Rodenberg (GDR) presided as President, Eddy Socorro (Cuba) as 2nd Vice President, Nena Stenius (Finland) as 3rd Vice-President, and Rose-Marie Moudoués (France) as Secretary General.
Invitee: Zvjezdana Ladika (Yugoslavia), host of the upcoming EXCOM Meeting in Šibenik, Yugoslavia.
Excused: Ann Shaw (1st Vice-President) for reasons of health, and Ian Lucian for professional reasons.

This was the first Meeting since the Moscow Congress in September 1984, and there was a great deal of business to be conducted by the Bureau.
Prague Invitation: Moudoués informed the Bureau that they had been invited to meet in Prague, Czechoslovakia during the 50th Anniversary of the founding of the Jiří Wolker theatre, which would take place from 30 September to 7 October 1985. Seven theatres would participate, and the week would be dedicated to the theme "The current status and perspectives of theatre for children and young people." The opening ceremony would be on 2 October, and the Bureau Meeting would be 4-5 October 1985.
RITEJ and "Theatres of the World" 1985: RITEJ has had considerable difficulty in establishing its program for the "Theatre of the World" Festival, especially with those countries in the East. However, a troupe from Czechoslovakia will perform. RITEJ has also invited each national center of ASSITEJ to send two people to the Festival.
To celebrate the 20th Anniversary of the founding of ASSITEJ, President Rodenberg has proposed an official informal reception under such a sign, and that they organize an informal meeting of the delegates from the centers. The Secretary General will write a general paper on ASSITEJ and the Theatres of the World Festivals.
News of the Centers:
- **Switzerland:** The Swiss delegate Elisabeth Cozona was not able to attend the 1984 Moscow Congress because of ill health. The Center has not yet been able to agree on an appropriate replacement.
- **FRG:** The center has established the Kathrin Türks Prize to be given to a woman working in theatre for young people.
- **Italy:** The Secretary General after an exchange of correspondence met in Venice with representatives of the Association of Theatre and

Radio Artists and the Italian Center for ASSITEJ in hopes of finding a solution to unify the two organizations.
- **Argentina:** The new center is definitely established under Sra. Maria Teresa Corral and the Minister of Education and Culture in Buenos Aires.
- **Portugal:** Their theatre groups have many difficulties: only two companies receive a subsidy; for lack of money, there is no longer a Secretariat, and all correspondence should be addressed to José Caldas. The Center requested that the Secretary General write the Minister of Culture a letter requesting financial support. This has been done.
- **Viet Nam:** The first theatre building dedicated to youth theatre is being constructed. The Viet Nam Center requests that people send them stage equipment if possible.
- **Peru:** They will have a Festival from 30 October to 7 November. The Secretary General has received an invitation, but cannot attend. Eddy Socorro will represent ASSITEJ. Zvjezdana Ladika observed that it was important that ASSITEJ have an official presence there for the Festival.

AITA: AITA will have a Congress in Canada. Their invitation has been forwarded to ASSITEJ/Canada for representation.

Commissions: Some Commissions must absolutely have a meeting between EXCOM Meetings. In particular the Commissions on Liaison with Africa, Asia, and Latin America, as well as the Commission on Themes. They must prepare for the 1987 Congress. The Moscow Congress in 1984 was not satisfactory as to themes. Also, Nena Stenius has requested to be appointed to the Commission on Themes.

Seminars: With the assistance of the GDR, a seminar for actors has been organized in Cuba. Also, a seminar will be held in November 1985 with the French Center.

EXCOM Meeting in Šibenik: Their Festival of the Child will be held from 22 June to 6 July 1985. The EXCOM will meet from 22-28 June, leaving on 29 June. The Festival will celebrate two anniversaries: the 25th Anniversary of the Yugoslav Festival, and the 20th Anniversary of the founding of ASSITEJ. The official program will be published on 12 April. Official invitations will be sent 16 April.

The program will feature many forms depending on the choices to be made by the Director of the Festival. The Secretary General has written and requested that Drago Putnikovič concentrate presentation of the foreign and Yugoslav plays during the time that the EXCOM is meeting.

There will also be an exhibit, a symposium, a presentation of Yugoslav theatre, and a brief official discussion on the theme: Youth in the contemporary world, led by President Rodenberg. There will also be a Press Conference, and critiques of the performances.

6 centers have been invited as Observers for 1985: Greece, Hungary, Italy, Switzerland, Poland, and Argentina. The following seven have been selected if the meeting is held in Stockholm: Sweden, Denmark, Norway, Israel, Netherlands, Peru, and Mexico. This 1986 meeting was actually held in Odense, Denmark and Stockholm, Sweden.

ASSITEJ Brochure: Ian Lucian reported that the Brochure would be ready for the Šibenik Meeting if the cost of printing would be sent to the Romanian Center in time.

Bank Account: The Bureau decided to renew their savings account with the Bank of Spain. However, they decided to transfer their Account to Crêdit Agricole, and the Secretariat will let all the centers know the new Account Number.

Payment of Dues: In a Financial Report distributed by the Secretariat, a total of 43 National Centers were listed. Of those the following were listed as not having paid their dues: Algeria, Argentina, Brazil, Iraq, Paraguay, Peru, Sri Lanka, Turkey, Uruguay, Venezuela, Denmark, Ecuador, and Iran. Since the new Danish Center had just been accepted at the Moscow Congress, there was undoubtedly a delay in their remittance of dues.

The Statement of Account for 1984 revealed a total income of 56,113.19 FrF, total expenditures of 25,455.24 FrF, leaving a positive balance of 30,657.95 FrF.

This completed the Minutes.

1985
EXECUTIVE COMMITTEE MEETING
Šibenik, Yugoslavia/22–29 June 1985

The Executive Committee of ASSITEJ met in Šibenik, Yugoslavia from 22–29 June 1985 during the 25th Anniversary of their annual Festival of the Child.[98]

Ilse Rodenberg (GDR) presided as President, Ann Shaw (USA) as 1st Vice President, Eddy Socorro (Cuba) as 2nd Vice President, Nena Stenius (Finland) as 3rd Vice-President, Rose-Marie Moudoués (France) as Secretary General, and Ion Lucian (Romania) as Treasurer.

Members of the EXCOM in attendance were: Michael FitzGerald (Australia), Victor Georgiev (Bulgaria), June Fawkner replacing Diane Bouchard (Canada)[99], Vladimir Adamek (Czechoslovakia), Kasuto Kurihara (Japan) w/ Fusako Kurahara as interpreter, Halina Machulska (Poland), Maria Navarro (Spain), Natalya Satz (USSR) w/Galya Kolosova as interpreter, Zvjezdana Ladika and Berislav Frkič (Yugoslavia).

Advisor: Shaun Hennessey (Great Britain)

Themes Commission: Franco Passatore for Ottorino Negri (Italy).

Observer: Mårten Harrie (Sweden), and Wendy Perks (USA) for the Themes Commission.

Absent: Hildegard Bergfeld (FGR).

Meeting of the Bureau—23 June 1985

President Ilse Rodenberg presided, with Socorro, Shaw, Moudoués, Lucian, Satz, and Hennessey present.

New Center: Argentina had applied for membership, and the Bureau recommended acceptance. EXCOM approved.

Finances: Presented by Lucian. There were no major problems at the moment. The Treasurer recommended putting funds in a time Savings account which would earn 12% interest, and can be drawn on at any time without penalty. Approved.

Report of the Commission on Themes/Artistic Issues Commission: Ion Lucian, Chair: Wendy Perks, Maurice Yendt, Nena Stenius, José Caldas, Hildegard Bergfeld, and Michael FitzGerald.

The Commission stated that ". . . we are at the end of an era in the work of ASSITEJ. The world of 1965, when ASSITEJ began, no longer exists. The child has become a constant spectator, bombarded with audio-visual effects. Perhaps deformed, but well informed. The child sees and participates in all kinds of media spectaculars, often of questionable quality. To appeal to the child of 1985, theatre cannot be a passive art. It must show the range of emotions and events of today. Our theatre must be defended in the purely artistic sense, not for pedagogical or political reasons."

The Commission recommended themes for two meetings: 1) New ways of theatrical creation in connection with cultural evaluation of young audiences (for Helsinki 1986), and 2) Artistic approach of the director as the basis of theatre of high quality (for the Meeting of EXCOM before the Berlin 1987 meeting); and then after a long discussion 3) asked Australia to find an adequate theme for their work for the Congress in 1987, to be accepted in Helsinki at the EXCOM Meeting in 1986. The Commission also wanted the Working Groups to function better. They must be able to discuss productions seen as part of each Congress.

Members of the EXCOM of ASSITEJ: (Left to right) June Fawkner (Canada), Galya Kolosova (USSR), Nina Stenius (Finland), Kasuto Kurihara (Japan), (unidentified), Vladimir Adamek (Czechoslovakia), Victor Georgiev (Bulgaria), Eddy Socorro (Cuba), Ilse Rodenberg (GDR), Ann Shaw (USA), Maria Navarro (Spain), (unidentified), Fusako Kurahara (Japan), Michael FitzGerald (Australia), Rose-Marie Moudoués (France), Natalya Satz (USSR), Shawn Hennessey (Great Britain), (Kneeling—unidentified), Ion Lucian (Romania), Zvjezdana Ladika (Yugoslavia), (lying down) Halina Machulska (Poland). Šibenik, Yugoslavia, June 1985. Photo courtesy of Michael FitzGerald.

Report of the Liaison Commission: Members; Japan, Portugal, Cuba, and Spain. **José Caldas** reported with the impending Symposium in 1990, the Commission's duty was to persuade these countries to participate in the ASSITEJ activities, to be observers, and to create new ASSITEJ Centers.

- **Brazil:** In Sao Paulo most groups belong to the Association of Artists of the Theatre for Children. They have forwarded ASSITEJ information to the Association. The various Brazilian states are preparing information for the Commission. Most of them did not know of ASSITEJ.
- **Algeria:** There is no special organization for children and youth. All are amateur performing organizations for all ages. They know nothing about ASSITEJ.
- **Mozambique:** No answer to their letters.
- **Morocco:** Many groups are working for children. In July there was a Festival in Safid. There is no Association. They know nothing of ASSITEJ. Caldas is preparing information on the groups. Not allowed to form an organization.
- **Tunisia:** There were no specialized troupes. Information will be prepared.

Ultimately he said that it would be necessary to go to Africa to talk about ASSITEJ.

Socorro (Cuba) reported as follows on Latin America:

- **Spain:** through ASSITEJ/Spain distributes a Bulletin to all Latin American countries. In Cuba there is an ASSITEJ Center and a national Festival every 2 years. They hold an annual director's Seminar, most recently helped by the GDR.
- **Mexico:** presented a paper on their activities.
- **Venezuela:** There are problems with the Center, and Cuba will send a representative to assist them with a solution, and then will report to the Commission.
- **Uruguay:** The old center has disappeared, and a new one has been created, and is currently seeking approval from their national government, and then will ask to be approved as a new Center.
- **Paraguay:** There has been no answer.
- **Peru:** Things are better now. It will have an international festival in 26 October—2 November. Socorro will report officially to ASSITEJ on the results.
- **Argentina:** There is much activity. ASSITEJ/Spain has contacted their new President, and we are waiting for information on their troupes, activities, etc.

- **Nicaragua:** Cuba had contacted their General Director of Theatre, sent information, and is trying to create a new Center.
- **Ecuador:** Have contacted their Director of Culture in their capitol. Very interested in ASSITEJ, and working to create a new Center for ASSITEJ.
- **Spain:** Sends all these countries information on ASSITEJ as well as translations of plays.

This report was to assist the EXCOM in choosing delegates to the 1990 Symposium. Soft currency is a real problem in Latin America. They proposed to have Festivals of Solidarity in every country, and the proceeds would go to theatres in Latin America.

ASSITEJ should send technical assistance to these countries in the form of directors, playwrights, etc. to help and to educate them in theatre. The countries sending this assistance should pay for the travel, and the countries receiving the assistance should pay for meals and lodging of the visiting artists.

The Commission promised in the future to keep contact with each other, and to try to aid Centers in Latin America, Africa, and Asia, and requested the EXCOM to schedule meetings of the Commission two days in advance of their meetings.

Moudoués thanked the Commission for their careful work. She added the caveat that before they encourage the formation of new centers, they must make sure that there are enough "professional" participants to form the center properly. She continued that Africa did not have the same concept of theatre as ASSITEJ. Since they have such varieties of performance, it will be difficult to define "theatre for children". We must not force them into a form of neo-colonial theatre. They first should come to an EXCOM Meeting as observers for artistic discussions, and we have much to learn from them. We must enlarge our views by looking at new cultures.

Caldas commented further that he had been to Angola, and the theatre he saw was quite different from what Moudoués had said. There are amateur troupes who want to imitate what our countries do in performance. To Caldas it would be most important, if someone should go to these African countries, for those persons to ask to be shown the "real" African theatre.

Report on Lyon *Theatres of the World* Festival/2-19 June 1983: Reported by Maurice Yendt: 17 plays presented, 14 groups (101 performers), 8 different countries, France, Brazil, Netherlands, Italy, Japan, Portugal, Switzerland, and Czechoslovakia—3 continents. 9 theatre venues plus on the streets, 23,900 spectators, colloquium, 880 theatre artists (including companies), 33 countries represented by invited delegates, 50 people sent by ASSITEJ Centers.

The major problem was how to maintain high quality in such a large venue. They needed constant input re: the best companies from the Centers. Costs: 4 million French Francs [800,000 US$] which comes from the Ministries of Culture, Foreign Affairs, Education, and Youth, and 20% from ticket sales.

Membership: In 1985 the following national centers of ASSITEJ were listed: Algeria, Argentina, Australia, Belgium, Brazil, Bulgaria, Canada, Czechoslovakia, Cuba, Denmark, Ecuador, Finland, France, FGR, GDR, Great Britain, Greece, Hungary, Iran, Iraq, Israel, Italy, Japan, Korea, Mexico, Netherlands, Norway, Paraguay, Peru, Poland, Portugal, Romania, Spain, Sri Lanka, Sweden, Switzerland, Turkey, Uruguay, USA, USSR, Venezuela, Vietnam, and Yugoslavia making a total of 43.[100]

Meeting of the EXCOM/24 June 1985

The delegates were welcomed by Drago Putnikovič, President of the Yugoslav Child Festival. As part of the Festival was the opening of a special exhibit entitled "20 Years of ASSITEJ", and while at this Festival the delegates were able to see a total of 10 different performances.

There were EXCOM meetings scheduled during the next four days, inter-mixed with performances. The Asian Center Report was part of those days.

Asian Centers: Yasuo Fukushima, ASSITEJ/Japan, as an invited Observer, reported the following information to the EXCOM:[101]

At the moment in Asia there are only four ASSITEJ Centers: Sri Lanka, South Korea, Vietnam, and Japan. ASSITEJ/Japan sent letters of inquiry to 18 embassies hoping to determine the extent of activity in youth theatre in their countries. Those it contacted were: Afghanistan, India, Malaysia, Pakistan, Thailand, Papua New Guinea, Bangladesh, Indonesia, Mongolia, Philippines, Fiji, Western Samoa, Burma, Laos, Nepal, Singapore, and Nauru.

It received responses from the Philippines and Thailand, and additional information about China, Indonesia, Malaysia, and Singapore.

The Cultural Center of the Philippines gave them names of ten groups, and seven sent information about their programs. There were 3 theatre groups, 3 puppet theatres, and 1 TV production.

This ended the report.

Polish Center: Machulska handed out a printed Report, and stated that they now had an exchange going with Greenwich, Great Britain and Lyon, France. In the future Poland hoped to participate in workshops and meetings with them.

Italian Center: Passatore handed out a printed Report, and commented that Italy had two theatre organizations—ASTRA for the professional theatres and ASSITEJ for the amateur theatres. They are now joining together. Moudoués met with both in a good, fair meeting, and the problems are expected to be solved by September.

Lucian asked about their large membership of educators and professors, and Moudoués replied that these are professionally trained people working with children in the schools, and that the Statutes give membership to such different theatre groups, persons, organizations, etc.

Greek Center: The slow mail delivered their Šibenik invitation on June 10. They have sent a short report: The Center has 18 members; 2 of 5 professional companies belong. The rest are individual members—3 playwrights, a theoretician, 1 psychologist, 1 actress, a teacher, 2 sociologists, and 3 pedagogues. The Center was formed in 1983 with no money. Now they are working better. They published Greek Plays for Young Audiences in Greek and have had them translated. The Ministry of Young People is sponsoring it.

Switzerland: Elisabeth Cozona, who was quite ill, wrote that the Center is reorganizing. There is a new committee of 8 people (3 former members and 5 new members) which meets on principle every month. Their former library went to the theatrical library in Berne. They hope to publish a pamphlet 6 times a year. They feel they do not have enough educators involved.

Yugoslavia: Their Center has prepared a special issue of their Bulletin on "New Theatre Since the 2nd World War".

New Business: Between the EXCOM Meeting in Munich and the Moscow Congress in 1984, the British Center (Hennessey) spent time among themselves discussing the papers of Portugal (Brites) and Italy (Negri) regarding the future of ASSITEJ. The EXCOM supported the Portuguese paper in Moscow. The British Center feels 1) the EXCOM can do much to improve the quality of representation in its own Committee, and 2) the Agenda and major papers should be circulated before the Meeting, which would allow the EXCOM Members to discuss the papers with their own country's membership. These papers must be sent in advance, and the Bureau should make a Timetable accordingly. Moudoués agreed to this, but commented that it depends entirely on the Centers.

Hennessey continued that in 1977 the artistic level of work was of a high standard in Great Britain, but the ASSITEJ Center was somnolent. It needed to wake up, and Hennessey was elected to do it. The 1978 Madrid Congress brought in new excitement. The need now is different. ASSITEJ is strong, and now it needs to be represented by the artistic directors. While Hennessey would still remain a Financial Counselor, a new person will come to Helsinki to represent Great Britain. He then thanked everyone for their support and their friendship.

The meeting closed with concerns about the approval of the Moscow Minutes. According to some, large sections were left out. Moudoués responded that she would give the French text to new translators, and pay for the translation.

Apparently, this concluded the meeting.

Meeting of the EXCOM/27 June 1985/9:00 AM

Miscellaneous Discussion: Moudoués stated that the changes in the Statutes would be considered at the next meeting. These changes will be presented in the three official languages. Shaw asked for a full day of artistic discussions at the next meeting.

José Caldas, who was a member of the Commission on Themes and not on the EXCOM, commented that some of those on the EXCOM were not the best people to represent their countries. Only theatre artists should be allowed. Navarro responded that selection of representatives is the business of each center only, and while having artists is important, so are producers, representatives of their culture, etc. Usually this problem is a result of being a one-person center without a constituency in the national center. ASSITEJ can insist that there be a proper membership.

Stenius commented that the EXCOM is chosen by the General Assembly, but if we are to have true artistic discussions, this question needs to be addressed. Rodenberg responded by looking at the group present, and saying ". . . most of the people here are theatre artists!"

Caldas continued his concern that despite the reports citing the need for change ". . . we still work in the old way!" He felt that ASSITEJ should be stimulating activity in the national centers, and artistically the EXCOM had yet to discuss the productions being seen at Šibenik. Ladika commented that there would be a Critics Round Table on the program tomorrow, and perhaps one of them could come to the EXCOM meeting for a discussion. No one responded!

Bergfeld stated that it is a question of what kind of theatre do we want—professional, theatre in education, or ballet? Moudoués responded with citing the Statutes which stated ASSITEJ was for professional/adult theatre for young people, which is why the Association was founded. Socorro added that it was a question that interested all of them. This must be put on the Agenda. Moudoués said she will try to put it in the schedule. Ladika added that the Sibenik Festival was not under the control of the Yugoslavia Center, but they wished they had more control.

Czechoslovakia announced that the Jiří Wolker Theatre would be celebrating their 50th Anniversary having been founded in 1935 on the Soviet model of Natalya Satz' theatre. The Celebration will be from 29 September through 4 October, with a Bureau Meeting on 4-5 October 1985.

In response to Caldas before giving some details about the 1987 Congress, FitzGerald commented that in his observation representatives of the national centers were chosen with the respect and support of their members to hold that position to serve their best interests. This was regardless of whether they were artists, administrators, or other theatre personnel. Members around the table were cases in point.

He then announced the dates proposed for the Congress as Wednesday 8 April to Thursday 16 April 1987. He drew attention to the fact that the following day would be Good Friday. He suggested people come a day earlier to rest for a day because of the jet lag they would experience as a result of the long flight to Australia. Malaysia Airlines, the Congress' official carrier, had direct flights from Los Angeles, Amsterdam, Frankfort, and Paris.

Mårten Harrie, the observer from Sweden, had three questions: 1) while international exchanges are most desirable, they have tried to establish contact with the USSR, but their mail is not answered. Satz answered that the mail has been very slow because they had been celebrating their 40th Anniversary of freedom. She got the letter only one month ago, and while they would like to accept the invitation, they need to know the terms of the contract, etc. Also the chosen director Zinovy Korogodski was currently in Peru; 2) what are the general principles of ASSITEJ for proving their non-alignment with any racism, fascism, etc? Moudoués pointed out that this has been made clear in the Statutes from the very beginning of ASSITEJ; and 3) when will be the next meeting of the EXCOM? Moudoués responded that it was scheduled for Berlin (GDR) on 6-11 January 1987.

This concluded the meetings.

(Top and Bottom) "A Treasure Pickax", performance of the celebrated Kazinoko Company of Japan at the All Japan Performing Arts Festival for Young Audiences on Sado Island, Japan, August 1985. Photos courtesy of Jane Campbell.

Delegates and their hosts at the All Japan Performing Arts Festival for Young Audiences on Sado Island, Japan, August 1985. (1st row center) Dr. Ilse Rodenberg (GDR, President of ASSITEJ); (1st row, second from left) Frances Sey (Ghana); (1st row, third from right) Fusako Kurahara (Japan) (second from right) Luo Ying (China); (immediately behind Kurahara) Michael FitzGerald (Australia); (top row, far left) Harold Oaks (USA); (behind Oaks and right) Jane Campbell (USA); (to her right) Shannon Edwards (USA). Photo courtesy of Jane Campbell.

(Left to right), Harold Oaks (USA) at microphone, and Yuriko Kobayashi (interpreter/Japan) during the Question and Answer Session at the First All Japan Performing Arts Festival for Young Audiences on Sado Island, Japan, August 1985. Photo courtesy of Jane Campbell.

1985
Background on the Israeli Center

In 1985 the USA White House through Nancy Reagan, wife of the President, contacted Shaw in New York City asking if Shaw would meet with Ofira Navon, wife of the former President of Israel, who was visiting Washington D.C. Mrs. Navon wanted information about "theatre for the disabled" which was one of Shaw's specialties. Shaw agreed and the two struck up a friendship.

Later in June 1985 Navon invited Shaw to come to Israel to help them with their program on theatre for the disabled. Shaw was 1st Vice-President of ASSITEJ at the time, and prior to this visit Shaw wrote Porat that she would be visiting Israel, and then while there left a phone call for Porat. Neither the letter nor the phone call was answered. Shaw also copied Porat on her letters to Navon.

In the conversations with Navon about ASSITEJ, Navon said that Israel should establish a center. When Shaw informed her that they already had one headed by Orna Porat, Navon said she knew nothing of it, even though her husband worked for the Ministry of Culture. Shaw then left Israel for the Šibenik Meeting of the EXCOM that June in 1985.

On further investigation after Shaw had left, Navon found that Porat was indeed the only member of the center, and any of the other Israeli groups performing theatre for youth were not allowed to belong, even though the actors and directors were professional.

In 1986 Shaw visited Israel again to further Israel's work regarding theatre with the disabled, and then traveled to Helsinki for the next EXCOM Meeting in May. The EXCOM first attended part of the 2nd Nordic Festival, then boarded a boat to ride to Stockholm, and then held their EXCOM Meeting in Stockholm. All through the voyage there was considerable tension among the members which was inexplicable to Shaw the time.

1985
BUREAU MEETING /Prague, Czechoslovakia/4–5 October 1985

There were no Minutes available related to this Bureau Meeting in any of the sources consulted in the Archives in Arizona. Based on the elections in Moscow in 1984, the attendees would have been: Ilse Rodenberg (GDR) as President, Ann Shaw (USA) as 1st Vice President, Eddy Socorro (Cuba) as 2nd Vice President, Nena Stenius (Finland) as 3rd Vice-President, Rose-Marie Moudoués (France) as Secretary General, and Ion Lucian (Romania) as Treasurer.

1986
BUREAU & EXECUTIVE COMMITTEE MEETINGS
Helsinki, Finland and Stockholm, Sweden/3–10 May 1986[102]

Ilse Rodenberg (GDR) presided as President, Ann Shaw (USA) as 1st Vice President, Maria Sunyer (Spain) as 2nd Vice-President, Eddy Socorro (Cuba) as 3rd Vice President, Rose-Marie Moudoués (France) as Secretary General, and David Johnston (Great Britain) as Acting Treasurer.

Absent: Ion Lucian (Romania) as Treasurer who was in Japan.

Members of the EXCOM in attendance were: Michael FitzGerald (Australia), Ladislav Knižátko (Czechoslovakia), Nena Stenius (Finland), Orna Porat (Israel), João Luiz Brites (Portugal), Maria Navarro (Spain), and Zvjezdana Ladika (Yugoslavia). Invited was Maurice Yendt (France)—Commission on Themes.

Observers: Mårten Harrie (Sweden) and Penina M'Lama (Tanzania).

Absent: Victor Georgiev (Bulgaria), Hildegard Bergfeld (FGR).

Other representatives of the Commissions had been invited to participate.

Helsinki, Finland

These meetings were held in conjunction with the 2nd Nordic ASSITEJ-Festival and Symposium, which was the first time that it had been hosted by Finland, who had become a member of ASSITEJ in 1975. Stenius provides an excellent description of the perils of international planning entitled "A MEMORY" in the Summary. *(See A Summary of 1985–1990)/p.280).*

Officially from 3–7 May they would see performances and meet with colloquium members. There were 2-3 performances each from Sweden, Finland, Denmark, and Norway in the first days, and there were 10-12 performing companies and 100-150 attendees.

On 7 May they would take the boat to Stockholm in the afternoon and have a 2-hour meeting in the evening. They would arrive in Stockholm the next morning and have 3 more days of meetings and Swedish performances.

Apparently there was a mix-up in scheduling caused in part by the irregular arrival of the participants because of the various strikes, so most of the meetings of the EXCOM were held on the boat trip and in Stockholm.

Wednesday, 7 April 1986/On shipboard/6 PM

President Rodenberg appointed Nena Stenius (3rd Vice-President) to preside, deliberately ignoring Shaw and Socorro who had precedence. Rodenberg had remained in Helsinki to fly to Stockholm.

Stenius thanked those responsible for their hospitality, and briefly remembered Elisabeth Cozona (Switzerland) who had died.   Moudoués announced that Canada had resigned from the EXCOM in order to reorganize their Center.

There was considerable discussion on appointment of Observers. Moudoués stated there was only one Observer. Johnston asked permission for Stuart Bennett and Ramon Stefansky who were coming to sit as observers. M'Lama was already seated as an Official Observer.

Harrie (Sweden), apparently as an Observer, commented that his country was interested in helping poorer countries, particularly Africa, reach children outside the urban areas. FitzGerald declared his interest on the part of the Asian and Pacific countries asking how can he get them invited? Moudoués said only non-member countries can be chosen as observers. There was another long discussion on how to become a full-time center. Moudoués said FitzGerald should refer these questions to the Commission on Themes. When FitzGerald asked how Observers were chosen, Moudoués replied from centers who were not members of ASSITEJ! FitzGerald obviously wanted to understand the rules and regulations.

They approved the Šibenik Meeting Minutes with slight amendments. Porat asked that they be amended to show she had invited ASSITEJ to have their Congress in Israel in 1989, as well as being designated for a Theatre of the World Festival. Moudoués said she would check the correspondence.

Translation: Moudoués stated that they had approved having translations of the Minutes at the Šibenik Meeting—the cost would be 10,000 FrFs (approx. 2,000 US$). Another source estimated costs at 3,500 FrFs (700 US$). Navarro suggested using someone from Spain, which would be less expensive. Spain would do it in exchange for their dues. The USSR Center volunteered to do it gratis. This offer was accepted.

New Centers: Moudoués had received in March a request from **Senegal** asking permission to let a children's group from Senegal apply. She told them to follow the usual procedures.

One from **Mauritania** was given the same information.

Madagascar says they now have a Constitution, and would talk to Moudoués in Paris, but they never arrived. Mails were a continuing problem.

China hasn't applied, but Moudoués would try to renew contacts with them. FitzGerald stated that it was Hong Kong not China that was interested in membership.

Knižátko noted that **Uruguay** was missing from the list. Why? He was told that the old center was dissolved, and the new one was not yet formed.

There followed a long and involved discussion on high standards, professional versus amateur, how active were the performing groups, etc. Clarification was referred to the Commission on Themes. Caldas commented that it was not so much a question of professional versus amateur, but they needed to know what it is they do in theatre in these centers! Moudoués continued that a center to be admitted must: 1) be active; 2) have several groups in the proposed Center; but 3) the final decision would be up to the EXCOM on a case by case basis. Shaw added that this should be clarified in order to maintain high standards, and then encourage others to join as Corresponding Centers.

Stockholm Meetings/8–10 May 1986

President Rodenberg presided.

Future Meetings: Rodenberg invited the EXCOM to meet early in January 1987 in Berlin. The dates were later set as 6-11 January 1987. She also announced that Denmark had invited the EXCOM to meet in Odense in 1988, and they hoped to have an international festival.

Publications: Satz was asked if the Soviet Center planned to publish the results of the 1984 Moscow Congress. Yes, she replied, by the end of the year in the three official languages. Moudoués reported on *The Review's* continuing policy of reporting on centers not so well known. April 1985's issue was on Canada with two international Congresses. The Bureau is recommending Scandinavia for the next issue. Stenius responded that they would have the materials by the end of the year. Moudoués asked that Australia send materials for 1987 by October 1986, and they would devote 65 pages to it. Cuba and Portugal would be featured in the 2nd Issue in 1986.

Report of the Liaison Commission: There was a meeting in April 1986 of the Commission, and they have decided to start on themes of interest to all associations. Their meeting in October will liaison with ASSITEJ, Amateurs, and Critics associations. They will need a representative, a writer and co-editor. It will be a 10-year project. The Editor-in-Chief is Don Ruben, the University of Toronto President, who lives in Canada. Rodenberg recommended Wolfgang Wöhlert to work with the project.

Liaison w/Chile: Rodenberg reported that the President of the ITI in Chile had been put in prison, and his son was killed. ASSITEJ should stay out of it, but individual centers may write as they wish as long as it does not create additional problems.

Saturday, 10 May 1986/Riksteatern/1:30 PM

Vice-President Nena Stenius presided.

Report and Discussion from the Commission on Liaison: There was a follow-up discussion re: the delegates to the proposed Symposium and Congress in 1990.

M'Lama thanked the group for accepting her report the previous night. ASSITEJ/Japan was to print an informational leaflet to send to all the countries who attended the Sado Island Seminar.

ASSITEJ/Portugal would contact Mozambique and others. They were to go to Morocco in August for vacation, and they will try to organize meetings while there. Their Minister of Culture has organized a Bureau for Children and Youth.

There was a center in Brazil, but they have combined with the Portuguese Center to work together to solve their economic problems. Socorro gave information about a Festival in Havana sponsored by ASSITEJ/Cuba. They have made contact with Columbia, Nicaragua, and Argentina. ASSITEJ/Argentina has been restructured under Miguel Montano, Vice-President. Spain continues to publish its Bulletin, which contains special information, photographs, and plays.

As a new project, the Commission had accepted ASSITEJ/Japan's offer of printing special greeting cards to be sold by the Centers with the profits to go to ASSITEJ. The Commission also wished to print a special calendar listing workshops, seminars, etc. to be held in Asia, Africa, and Latin America to be distributed to Centers to help them make contacts within these countries.

The Commission had a budget of 5,000 FrF, and asked for another 5,000 FrF to allow them to travel to meet people at various seminars.

ASSITEJ/Cuba would hold a seminar in cooperation with the Union of Scenic Artists, and would like to work with the Swedish Center. This year Maurice Yendt would participate with them for 10 days, and they would like to invite others to participate. They would like Centers to propose possible directors for the future. However, they can no longer pay for travel to the seminar. Also, the ITI International Congress will meet in Havana in June 1987.

Moudoués stated that it was reasonable to give the Commission an additional 15,000 FrF until January 1987. Navarro suggested that the calendar be prepared, and in January make decisions on who will travel where. The suggestion was accepted.

Publications: *The Review* won't be out in June because of the Postal strike in Scandinavia, but will appear in the autumn. She had received copy for the Cuban issue, and needs copy for the Australia issue by the autumn.

Report from Finland: A report was handed out. Their Center had decided that their creation of International Festivals was the most important to the work of ASSITEJ. Accordingly, they were hosting a Festival in the autumn of 1985 and now one in the spring of 1986. They have already had two festivals for theatre which featured 14 groups (1 from Denmark and 1 from Italy) as well as some theatres with young people in them. About 3,000 young people saw the performances.

Report from Mexico: Socorro reported that ASSITEJ/Mexico was developing contacts with other centers in order to strengthen their Center, despite their grave economic problems. They would like to have playwrights and directors come to their workshops, and if they would pay their travel, the Center would pay their expenses in the country. Already there are 5 producing groups working, and they are adding 5 others. They may try to send performances out into the country. The purpose of the workshops is to contribute to pedagogic development in Mexico which would create pedagogic and theatrical techniques. The results would be published and sold, with the profits going to ASSITEJ. Visiting experts could work in Spanish, or in their own language.

Report from the Netherlands: Anja Yansen Schnilling, an Invitee, gave her report orally. She apologized that her Report had been sent to France, but apparently was lost in the Post. As a Center they are re-emerging. They have national contacts but few international ones. A new person has undertaken to resurrect the ASSITEJ Center. She requested all other national Centers to send them information on festivals, workshops, etc. Their financial situation was good. There are about 25 professional groups, and there are two new centers for children in Amsterdam and Rotterdam. In September 1987 a children's theatre festival will be held in Amsterdam.

Report from Israel: Orna Porat asked the EXCOM to excuse the form of her Report, since she was having severe difficulties in her private life. Her additional purpose was to raise funds abroad, so her Report was sometimes incorrect, and ". . . it looks a bit like an ego trip of Orna Porat." She then said there will be time to answer questions after it is read.

Report from Norway: Marit Jerstad reported their having 74 theatre groups and individuals, 44 of whom were members of ASSITEJ/Norway. Though Norway is rich, their authorities do not think culture is very important. They operate with a broad definition of culture, and a football player can be awarded a cultural prize. Norway is still a developing country in children's theatre.

Most theatres do a Christmas play for young people, and a few "leftist" theatres make a conscious effort to reach children. Free groups get very little money. Norway gets 4.3 million kroner for 32 groups, not all of whom play to children, in contrast to Denmark's 55 million krone! ASSITEJ/Norway continues to sponsor conferences, seminars, and to invite foreign performing groups to appear. This fall a Swiss company will perform *The Snow Queen*, and teach a course, and Cleo, a story-telling group from Chartres, France will appear. Money continues to be their most important problem.

Report from Denmark: Ramløse reported that Danish theatre for children has always been well organized. They plan to have an International Festival in 1988 which will combine the Inter-Nordic Festival with an International Festival. They are developing an international model for the festival, and the plays will be performed publicly.

This concluded Shaw's notes, and apparently the meetings. The Porat denunciation followed that meeting.

The Israeli Center, Concluded

At the last EXCOM Meeting in Stockholm, Porat requested the floor and accused Shaw of destroying the Israeli Center. Shaw quietly denied this categorically, saying she was invited to Israel as an expert to help them with the theatre for the disabled. What had happened to the Israeli Center was an internal affair that she had nothing to do with, and it could only have been a result of Porat's unwillingness to open the center to other theatres.

That night after the final meeting Porat demanded that she and Shaw meet together. When Shaw refused, several times that night Porat went to Shaw's hotel room, and pounded on the door demanding a meeting. The next day when the group was in the Stockholm subway station waiting for the train to that evening's performance, Mårtin Harrie quietly advised Shaw not to stand too close to the edge of the platform for fear of being pushed off onto the tracks.

It was an appallingly ugly situation, which according to Ramløse created a tension throughout all the meetings.

Six months later in January 1987 at the EXCOM Meeting of ASSITEJ in Berlin, GDR Shaw personally distributed her letter of explanation of the Porat debacle to the Members of the EXCOM and the Observers at the meeting in Stockholm.[103] Shaw's letter was in answer to Porat's written statement published in a theatre brochure and distributed in the 10 May 1986 meeting in Stockholm. Porat had stated:

"The Vice-President of ASSITEJ Mrs. Ann Shaw has become involved in organizing a meeting in Israel with various representatives of the Israeli theatrical scene with regards to the activities of the Israeli Center of ASSITEJ without having the courtesy of informing me of her intentions."

Shaw's letter countered the accusations as follows:
- She was invited to visit Israel by Mrs. Ofira Navon, wife of the former President of Israel to give lectures and talk about "theatre for the disabled."
- At a luncheon where Porat was present, Shaw was asked to present information about ASSITEJ. After she had done so, the audience formed two groups: those who didn't know there was an Israeli Center, and those who had tried to join the Center and had been refused.
- Having given them the facts of ASSITEJ, Shaw referred them to Porat.
- Porat admitted to knowing of both visits in advance but she was too occupied to take calls.
- The accusation of "interference" was preposterous,

The truth of the situation was that the Israeli Center was a "ghost" center, consisting primarily of Porat, and had been so from the very beginning of ASSITEJ in 1965. Within the next few years (1987-1989) after this denunciation of Shaw, Orna Porat was made Honorary President and Gila Almagor became head of the real Center, and other theatre groups were allowed to join. The Center has continued to this day to be active in ASSITEJ, instead of being a one person center for the traveling and participatory convenience of one individual.

PART V:

HIGH CONFLICT AND INTERNATIONAL EXPANSION/ AUSTRALIA 1987/ SWEDEN 1990

1987
EXECUTIVE COMMITTEE MEETING
Berlin, GDR/6–11 January 1987[104]

President Ilse Rodenberg (GDR), Ann Shaw (USA) as 1st Vice-President, Eddy Socorro (Cuba) as 2nd Vice-President, and Nena Stenius (Finland) as 3rd Vice-President, Rose-Marie Moudoués (France) as Secretary General, and Ion Lucian (Romania) as Treasurer.

Members present: Australia (Michael FitzGerald), Bulgaria (Victor Georgiev), Czechoslovakia (Ladislav Knížátko), FGR (Hildegard Bergfeld), Great Britain (Shaun Hennessey), Japan (Kazuto Kurihara), Portugal (João Luiz Brites), USSR (Natalya Satz), and Yugoslavia (Zvjezdana Ladika).

Counselor: Maria Navarro (Spain).

Member absent: Canada had resigned as of 1986.

According to Shaw the group stayed at the well known hotel—Unter den Linden.

The delegates arrived in Berlin on 6 January. In many ways this meeting was a "farewell" to Rodenberg, according to Shaw.[105] The officers were hosted at supper at Rodenberg's home in suburban Berlin, and were able to see remarkable memorabilia of the joint careers of Rodenberg and her husband Hans who had died in March 1978, and who had been Minister of Culture for the GDR. They had dedicated both their lives to serving their country well.

In response to questions about her spacious and elegant home, she said "Why not? Hans and I work always for GDR. I am twice political prisoner. I make success for my country. I deserve it." [106] They also visited the Red House—the palace where "the party officially gathered . . . a kind of capital."

1st EXCOM Meeting/7 January 1987

The EXCOM convened at 9 AM at the Zentrum für kulturelle Auslandsarbeit. President Ilse Rodenberg presided. Members present were the entire EXCOM.

Brandenburg Gate, Berlin, Germany.

There was dinner with the Minister of Culture, and an evening performance.
8 January 1987
Meeting of the Commissions
Dinner with the Secretary of the Ministry of Culture and an evening performance
2nd Meeting of the EXCOM/9 January 1987
9 AM—Shaw, as outgoing 1st Vice-President [she would step down at the Australian Congress], noted that many of her proposals were now treated with respect, rather than being dismissed outright. Moses Goldberg (USA), Vice-President of ASSITEJ/USA, told her that this was probably because she was no longer the "official" USA representative, which normally required automatic rejection by the East. Also, excellent simultaneous translation sped the discussions and resulting decisions. In addition, *glasnost* in the Soviet Union was ongoing, and the world was changing!

Changes to the Statutes which would be voted upon in Australia evinced some discussion. Of particular interest was recognition of the need in centers for the expansion of the "amateur" category, since many of the newer countries did not have professional companies. It was felt that one member centers were destructive to the goals of ASSITEJ.

6 PM—Evening performance

3rd Meeting of the EXCOM/10 January 1987

9 AM—**The Commission on Artistic Themes** selected a theme to guide work in ASSITEJ for the 1987 Congress: "The role of theatre for children and young people in searching for ethnic and cultural identity." This theme was also to determine the working groups for the next three-year term.

Soft Currency: There was considerable discussion of the problems of dues, and the attendant problems of receiving and sending soft currency. They felt that attendance in Australia would not only be expensive but might restrict attendance. Shaw felt that delegates would find a way to get there, especially since it was "new" territory and in some ways an "exotic".

Scandinavia: Finland, Sweden, Norway, and Denmark had been meeting together for several years to support their mutual work. They now designated themselves as the "Nordic" Centers.

In a paper Australia again underlined the dangers of "euro-centricity", indicating that ASSITEJ was a "world" organization and needed to commit itself to a "world" view. Obviously, the Membership was getting very restless. Shaw felt it was time for a full-time Secretary General, rather than an unpaid volunteer.

The Secretary General informed the EXCOM that 20 countries had nominated themselves for election to the 17 positions on the EXCOM. Re-nominated from the current EXCOM were:

        Australia (Michael FitzGerald)
        Bulgaria (Zdravko Mitkov)
        Cuba (Eddy Socorro)
        Czechoslovakia (Ladislav Knižátko)
        FGR (Hildegard Bergfeld)
        Finland (Nena Stenius)
        France (Rose-Marie Moudoués)
        GDR (Ilse Rodenberg)
        Great Britain (David Johnston)
        Japan (Kazuto Kurihara)
        Portugal (Luiz Pisco)
        Romania (Ion Lucian)
        Spain (Maria Navarro)
        USA (Nancy Staub)
        USSR (Natalya Satz)
        Yugoslavia (Zvjezdana Ladika)

Nominated for the first time were:
    Denmark (Michael Ramløse)
    Poland (Halina Machulska)
    Sweden (Mårten Harrie)
    Vietnam (Ha Nhan)
    At the closing meeting, President Rodenberg referred to "final" times. The EXCOM gave her flowers, and she graciously accepted many verbal tributes. She finally said to Shaw ". . . we have the ones we love who have gone and we cannot keep them waiting too long."

    At 3 PM there was a reception by the Lord Mayor of Berlin for the EXCOM, and the next day 11 January they departed. It was the end of an era.

1987
IXth WORLD CONGRESS OF ASSITEJ
Adelaide, Australia/8–16 April 1987

The IXth World Congress of ASSITEJ met in Adelaide, Australia from 8–16 April 1987. President Ilse Rodenberg presided, Ann Shaw (USA) as 1st Vice-President would step down at the end of the Congress, Eddy Socorro (Cuba) as 2nd Vice-President, Nena Stenius (Finland) as 3rd Vice-President, Rose-Marie Moudoués (France) as Secretary General, and Ion Lucien (Romania) as Treasurer in name only since he had had trouble attending the meetings over the past three years. Paul Harman (Great Britain) as Acting Treasurer (replacing both Lucian and Hennessey as an appointed Financial Counselor).

Financial Advisor: Shaun Hennessey was ill and would die in 1989, so the British Center decided David Johnston and Paul Harman would alternate giving the Financial Reports, since the funds had been transferred to banks in Great Britain.

Counselor to the Bureau: Maria Navarro (Spain).

Members present: Michael FitzGerald (Australia) replacing Andrew Bleby, Zdravko Mitkov (Bulgaria) replacing Victor Georgiev, Marjorie MacLean (Canada) see Summary (1987), Ladislav Knižátko (Czechoslovakia), Hildegard Bergfeld, (FGR), Franco Passatore (Italy), Kazuto Kurihara (Japan), Halina Machulska (Poland), Luiz Pisco (Portugal) replacing João Brites, Natalya Satz (USSR), Nancy Staub (USA) replacing Ann Shaw, and Zvjezdana Ladika (Yugoslavia).

Members absent: Romania (Lucian) had been elected in Moscow in 1984, but with the appointment of Harman as Treasurer, he would have lost his place on the EXCOM. Poland had apparently taken the place of Romania. Harrie (Sweden) had replaced Shaw as Vice-President. These appointments made the total of 17 elected centers.

There were now a total of six replacements of heads of the national centers and one new center (Romania replaced by Poland) on the EXCOM since Moscow in 1984.

The IXth World Congress of ASSITEJ was organized by Michael FitzGerald, Director, and Penny Ramsay, Co-coordinator. In the words of David Johnston (Great Britain) "The Congress was extremely well organized and ASSITEJ/Australia showed itself to be efficient, caring and above all else, very flexible."[107] [108]

City Hall, Adelaide, Australia

The following Agenda was approved by the EXCOM and the General Assembly:
- Approval of the Minutes of the 1984 Congress in Moscow
- Nomination of the voting commission
- Report of the Secretary General
- Financial Report, which included setting the dues for 1988-1990
- Statute Amendments
- Plan of Activities for 1987-1990
- Honorary Titles
- Approval of the location of the 1990 Congress
- Nomination of the Secretary General and the Treasurer
- Nomination of the Auditors

- Election of the Executive Committee
- Meeting of the New Executive Committee to name a slate of Officers
- Election of the President and the Vice-Presidents
- Miscellaneous Business

Wednesday, 8 April 1987
Both the Bureau and the EXCOM met on this day.

The Congress was opened at 4 PM with an address by the Hon. John Bannon, Premier of South Australia, and the state in which Adelaide was located. In his speech he stated "Our overriding belief was that through this international forum, ASSITEJ countries would gather together and exchange views and ideas, and be able, through healthy discussion and argument, to shape the nature and the future of the arts for young people."[109]

This was the first time that an ASSITEJ Congress was held in the Southern Hemisphere, and only the second time that a Congress was being held outside Europe since the Paris Constitution Conference in 1965. Previously Canada and the USA had hosted a joint-Congress in 1972.

A total of 426 delegates, representing 30 countries, participated. There were 228 delegates from Australia, and 198 from the other 29 countries. Represented were: Bulgaria, Canada, China, Czechoslovakia, Denmark, FGR, Finland, France, GDR, Great Britain, Hong Kong, India, Italy, Japan, Korea, Malaysia, Mexico, Netherlands, New Zealand, Norway, Poland, Portugal, Spain, Sweden, Thailand, USA, USSR, Vietnam, and Yugoslavia. Of these countries represented, 17 were in Europe, 3 in the Americas, and 9 in Asia and the Pacific.

The Congress coincided with the "Come Out 87 Festival" of Australian plays, plus performances by the Dong Rang Theatre from Seoul, Korea, and the Honolulu Theatre for Youth from Hawaii, USA.

The theme of the Congress was "Staging the Future: new influences and artistic processes in theatre for children and young people."

Each day began with three keynote speakers, then a brief question and answer session, followed by small group discussions for the remainder of the day on that day's topic.

There were eleven discussion groups led by Australian group leaders. The Congress was conducted in the three official languages of ASSITEJ— English, French, and Russian, plus Japanese to accommodate their 18-person delegation. The leaders then summarized the discussions of their group, which were compiled, translated, and distributed to all delegates together with copies of all the keynote addresses by the end of the final Plenary Session.

Meals were provided for all the delegates in a dining marquee in the Pioneer Women's Memorial Gardens opposite the Festival Center, which proved to be an excellent venue for meetings and conversations among all the delegates.

(Left to right) Dr. Nat Eek (USA), Honorary President of ASSITEJ; Dr. Ilse Rodenberg (GDR), President of ASSITEJ, and Patricia F. Eek (USA), wife of Dr. Eek at the IXth International Congress in Adelaide, Australia, May 1987. Photo courtesy of Harold Oaks, Archives, ASU, AZ, USA.

Zvjezdana Ladika (Yugoslavia) holding a Koala Bear at the Cleland Conservation Park at the IXth International Congress at Adelaide, Australia, May 1987. Courtesy of the Archives, ASU, AZ, USA.

Song for the Navigator by Michael Cowell, with actors (right) Tremaine Tamayose as the Navigator with (left) Lino Olopai of Saipan and Satawai Island, the Honolulu Theatre for Youth's Micronesian advisor for the production. A performance by the Honolulu Theatre for Youth, Hawaii, USA at the IXth World Congress of ASSITEJ in Adelaide, Australia, April 1987. Photo courtesy of Jane Campbell.

Friday, 10 April 1987
1st Plenary Session:

In her Report the Secretary General first named the members of the Bureau and the EXCOM, and listed their various meetings. She stated that attendance had been excellent, and representatives of the following countries had accepted the invitations of the EXCOM to attend: Italy and Poland in Šibonek; Israel, Mexico, Netherlands, and Norway in Helsinki/Stockholm; and Poland and Vietnam in Berlin.

Of particular interest was the EXCOM's attendance at Helsinki/Stockholm in 1986 which featured a Seminar with Third World delegates put together by the Nordic Centers. This would spawn the incredible growth of new ASSITEJ centers from 1987 to 1990. The EXCOM's Prague meeting was on more familiar territory.

Under News of the National Centers Moudoués announced that the EXCOM had accepted Argentina's application for membership, bringing their total to 42. Also, Mauritania, Malagasy Republic, China, and Senegal had inquired about possible membership. However, she warned that while it was vital to continue to spread ASSITEJ's influence throughout the world ". . . it also remains vital to be very strict about membership conditions and to ensure that the candidate center truly exists and operates effectively in the field of children's theatre practices by adult actors, and as such to exclude theatre activity practiced by children themselves since this falls outside the scope of ASSITEJ."[110]

Moudoués reported on the work of the Commissions as "working groups":

- **Commission on Statutes and Official Texts:** Rose-Marie Moudoués, Chair, with members representing each of the three official languages, updating the Statutes for changes to be approved by the General Assembly.
- **Commission on Theatres of the World:** Ann Shaw, Chair, examined the rules for designating a theatre with this ASSITEJ Seal of Approval. The Seal had been awarded to RITEJ in Lyons, France for 1985, 1987, and 1989; and the Munich Schauspiele in Munich, FGR for 1988. The Commission also recognized that it could not give official approval from ASSITEJ to the many Festivals presented by its centers around the world.
- **Commission on Artistic Themes & Activities:** Ion Lucian, Chair, particularly in examining the new trends in artistic performance being presented in Adelaide, recommended professional training programs, and the publication of a Liaison Bulletin to keep centers posted on new artistic developments.
- **Commission on Liaison with Third World Countries:** This Commission had primarily been striving to obtain a general view of the status of youth theatre in these countries. It acknowledged reports from the Spanish Center, the Japanese Center's contacts with central Asia, the Australian Center, the Stockholm Report of Penina M'Lama (Tanzania), and the Portuguese Center's report on central Africa.
- **Commission on Publications:** The French Center continues to publish its *Review*, which is available free to each national center. *The Bibliographic Bulletin* had been published in time for the 1984 Moscow Congress. Spain continues its publication of the *Boletino Iberoamericano* and distributes it to Spanish-speaking countries. The Soviet Center distributed its Report of the 1984 Moscow Congress. Wolfgang Wöhlert continues to edit *The Contemporary Theatre Encyclopedia*.

The Secretary General also indicated that their UNESCO application would have to be resubmitted. She concluded her Report that the Xth Congress in Stockholm, Sweden would be the 25th Anniversary of the existence of

ASSITEJ. "Theatre for children and young people must be ambitious so as to attain the highest level of artistic quality in the context of an international exchange of ongoing experience and the intertwining of cultures based on respect for individual identity."[111]

There was a total of 3 Plenary Sessions: Saturday 11 April 1987, Sunday 12 April 1987, and Tuesday 14 April 1987. During these sessions various resolutions were approved.

1987-1989 Artistic Theme: Can the contemporary theatre for children and young people promote the development of individual identity through the search for a better ethnic and cultural awareness? This would be used to establish the agendas for the Working Groups.

Other resolutions:
- ASSITEJ will continue to promote special festivals and international activity
- The EXCOM will determine the Budget for the next three years and how to raise additional monies
- The EXCOM will clarify the qualifications for membership
- The EXCOM will try to improve the circulation of information
- The EXCOM will try to raise funds for the 1993 Congress in Cuba
- The EXCOM will encourage countries to organize training sessions, workshops, and exchanges with other countries

Miscellaneous: The Congress approved the following:
- Elected Maria Sunyer y Roig (Spain) as a Member of Honor
- Approved having the Xth World Congress in Sweden in 1990
- Increased the annual dues to 200 US$ and corresponding centers dues to 50 US$
- Approved minor statute changes to clarify membership requirements
- Requested all centers to nominate a permanent deputy to replace their delegate at any meeting which they cannot attend

All these were passed unanimously

Wednesday 15 April 1987

The Elections: Oaks noted that there was a total of 84 votes, making a majority of 43 required for election to the EXCOM. The following countries and delegates were elected to the EXCOM and the Bureau for 1987-1990:

Twenty centers had nominated themselves for election to the EXCOM, sixteen were already on the old EXCOM and four nominations were from new centers.

A total of seventeen (17) countries were elected to the EXCOM: Australia (Michael FitzGerald); Bulgaria (Zdravko Mitkov); Cuba (Eddy Socorro); Czechoslovakia (Ladislav Knižátko); FGR (Hildegard Bergfeld); Finland (Nena

Stenius); France (Rose-Marie Moudoués); GDR (Ilse Rodenberg); Great Britain (Paul Harman); Italy (Franco Passatore); Poland (Halina Machulska); Portugal (Luiz Pisco); Spain (Maria Navarro); Sweden (Mårten Harrie); USA (Nancy Staub); USSR (Natalya Satz); and Yugoslavia (Zvjezdana Ladika).

From these centers the following were elected to the Bureau: Hildegard Bergfeld (FGR) as President; Mårten Harrie (Sweden) as 1st Vice-President, Maria Navarro (Spain) as 2nd Vice-President, Eddy Socorro (Cuba) as 3rd Vice-President, Rose-Marie Moudoués as Secretary General, and Paul Harman as Treasurer.

Five of the six Bureau members now came from Europe! The three centers not elected were Japan, Poland, and Vietnam. The entire EXCOM of 17 was now 14 Europeans, 2 North Americans, and Australia representing all of Asia.

"Other activities included a Lord Mayor's reception, a day excursion and picnic barbecue in Cleland Conservation Park where delegates could see native animals in their habitat (and first hand experiences holding koalas!), and a final night dinner and party at Carclew with an Australian bush band."[112]

Thursday 16 April 1987
Final Plenary Session
Farewell dinner and party

Many delegates were upset as a result of the manipulated elections the day before. The fact that five (5) proxies were held by France and the GDR between them gave considerable heft to the European landslide. At the final Plenary Session Rodenberg saw that Shaw gave the final address to the Assembly. With fire in her eye Shaw (USA) burned into the consciences of the delegates the following words:

"ASSITEJ has just committed a grave error. It failed to re-elect Japan to the EXCOM—Japan—one of the most active progressive dedicated Centers of ASSITEJ. A Center which has extended its hand in friendship to all ASSITEJ Centers. A Center which has strained its own resources to assist other ASSITEJ Centers to develop communication, which has led ASSITEJ into the Pacific and Asia.

"The outgoing EXCOM alone holds 45 votes. The outgoing EXCOM knows *very well* the outstanding contribution of the Japanese Center. Other members outside the EXCOM know the excellence of Japan's work.

"What were we thinking? Why was Japan removed? Let us each examine our reasoning and our actions.

"ASSITEJ speaks of the world, of the importance of developing communication and exchange with Africa, South America, and countries of the

Pacific and Asia. We speak fine words, but our *actions* speak much more clearly and directly.

"Last night in this room we gathered—the night before last—Tuesday evening—in this very room over 200 people from 12 Pacific Rim countries met.

"Yesterday in this same room where the Pacific Rim countries were on the ballot to be elected to the EXCOM, only Australia received the required number of votes—and with few to spare. The new candidate Vietnam was refused and to the expressed dismay of all to whom I have spoken—Japan was refused a second term on the Executive [Committee].

"We speak of our interest in the countries of Asia and the Pacific, but our actions are different.

"The theme proposed to guide the work of ASSITEJ over the next three years is of the highest importance.

"We must be sincere in our desire to bring the art of theatre for children and young people and use the potential of the theatre to unite people in the spirit of appreciation for others and peace. "But as we debate the question we must simultaneously examine and make every effort to develop ASSITEJ itself, and that is all of us asking how each of *us* might develop a better ethnic and cultural awareness." [113]

Shaw concluded her comments as follows: "It is a mystery to me when I asked individuals if their center had voted for Japan, not a single center would admit that they had not! The mystery deepens when we recognize that Japan had been one of the hardest working centers on the EXCOM. How the hell could this have happened since most centers tell me they voted for Japan?"

At the closing night party Michael Ramløse (Denmark) came to Shaw and said he was embarrassed to admit that his Center had not voted for Japan, but had voted for the new man from Portugal, who had never been to ASSITEJ before!

Performances: A total of thirteen productions were listed as available to the delegates during the Festival and Congress. "Director FitzGerald attempted to make it clear that the selection of the shows for the Youth Festival's program was intended as a 'warts and all' cross-section to show delegates what is happening in young people's theatre here and now . . . It was definitely not intended as a showcase of the best work available, Michael stressed." [114]

The Congress opened with a premiere performance of *Frankie*, an opera for young people, music by Alan John, libretto by David Holman, directed by Neil Armfield, "one of Australia's most highly regarded main stage directors," with sets designed by Ken Wilby and Mark Thompson. Professional in every aspect, with its cast of over 80 young people, the delegates saw "a sympathetic tragedy of rare sensitivity." However the fact that young people were in the roles added fuel to the fire of ASSITEJ discussions of "professional" versus "amateur".

Zvjezdana Ladika (Yugoslavia) and Michael FitzGerald (Australia) at the IXth International Congress at Adelaide, Australia, May 1987. Courtesy of Dr. Harold Oaks, Archives, ASU, AZ, USA.

Several delegates found the following productions of particular interest: [115] *Song of the Navigator* by the Honolulu Theatre for Youth, a tale of bonding between a Micronesian grandfather and grandson while recognizing the awesome influence of the ocean; *Wandering Star* by the Dong Rang Theatre for Young People company of Seoul, Korea, directed by Kim Woo Ok, a musical look at high school delinquency and parental neglect; *The Women There* by the Arena Theatre of Melbourne, Australia, dealing with the experiences of women during the settling of Australia; and *Dreaming of Tomorrow* by the Troupe Theatre of Adelaide, featuring four short plays written by teenagers, performed with humor, whimsy, energy, and total assurance.

In addition audiences responded to "the much acclaimed production of Magpie Theatre's *No Worries*, written by David Holman, dealing with misplacement and identity in a changing multicultural society." Australian Aboriginal artists performed at the Congress Club and at the final night party.

There was also an outstanding foyer exhibition of Aboriginal Arts and Crafts, including rare bark paintings.

"A major achievement of the Congress was the significant Asian and Pacific representation from 12 countries within the region on a scale unprecedented in any previous Congress. This culminated in The Pacific Exchange whereby representatives and observers met to exchange information and discuss future developments within the region.

"Other activities included a Lord Mayor's reception, a day excursion and picnic barbecue in Cleland Conservation Park where delegates could see native animals in their habitat (and experience first-hand holding koalas!) and a final night dinner and party at Carclew with an Australian Bush band."[116]

At the end of the Congress there was great praise for its organization, administration, and management. Sweden indicated that it would use it as a model for their Congress in 1990. Australia was immediately recognized as a center of energy and creativity in youth theatre. On the down side there was the rejection by the European theatre community of the beliefs and practices of the plurality and diversity in youth theatre in many other countries. This issue would continue to be contentious.

Lastly, the chaos of the election left Europe in charge, dropped Japan, lost Vietnam, and raised serious questions of ballot stuffing which when cast couldn't help but influence the outcome.[117]

The Program of the Adelaide Congress in 1987 listed the following 43 countries as centers of ASSITEJ. The Secretariat issued an address list of these centers as of September 1987:

Algeria	Great Britain	Romania
Argentina	Greece	Spain
Australia	Hungary	South Korea
Belgium	Iran	Sri Lanka
Brazil	Iraq	Sweden
Bulgaria	Israel	Switzerland
Canada	Italy	Turkey
Cuba	Japan	USA
Czechoslovakia	Mexico	Uruguay
Denmark	Netherlands	USSR
Ecuador	Norway	Venezuela
FGR	Paraguay	Vietnam
Finland	Peru	Yugoslavia
France	Poland	
GDR	Portugal	

INTERIM / 1987

The East-West split between countries and centers had cast a pall on all the meetings from 1984 until 1987 at the Australian World Congress. After the elections in Adelaide many of the delegates realized that all the Asian nations had been deliberately excluded from the EXCOM by manipulated voting.

The Adelaide Congress was a watershed, because Australia with the assistance of Japan and Korea had invited representatives of the Pacific Rim countries, as well as many Asian countries, to attend the ASSITEJ World Congress, and to consider establishing centers. But only Australia was elected to carry the Asia-Pacific banner and the rest of that world!

From this point on many members of ASSITEJ began to realize that in order to be a true "world" organization, ASSITEJ absolutely had to develop a more open organization—open to all countries who had and fostered some form of theatre for young people. The Nordic Centers led the way by beginning to organize an invitational Symposium for non-member countries before the next Congress in 1990, and to open the Congress itself to include established centers, those newly forming, and those still to be formed as centers of ASSITEJ.

1987
ASSITEJ COMMISSION ON THEMES & ARTISTIC ACTIVITIES MEETING
Modena, Italy/3–8 November 1987[118]

Maurice Yendt (France) as Chair of the Commission presided. Members of the Commission who attended were Zdravko Mitkov (Bulgaria), Ladislav Knižátko, (Czechoslovakia), David Johnston for Paul Harman (Great Britain), Franco Passatore (Italy) and Luiz Pisco (Portugal). Ion Lucian (Romania) as Technical Consultant was absent but excused.

Invitees Present: Benvenuto Cuminetti (Italy) and Mårten Harrie (Sweden).

The approved Agenda included four items:
- The Summary of the ASSITEJ Congress in Adelaide, Australia
- The Working Program for the next three years
- Preparations for the 1990 Stockholm Congress of ASSITEJ
- Project for a News Report

In opening the meeting Yendt thanked the representatives of ASSITEJ/Italy for hosting this exceptional meeting, and for the very favorable conditions provided for their working group. He welcomed Harrie, who from this time forward would participate as the organizer of the 1990 Stockholm Congress.

4 November 1987

Summary of the ASSITEJ Congress in Adelaide, Australia:
The Commission assigned its first session on 4 November to a long discussion on the Australian Congress in 1987. They were particularly concerned about the printed comments of John Emery and Ian Chance which had appeared in the Australian Review *Lowdown* in May 1987.

They unanimously deplored the "conditions of confrontation" in which some of the sessions were held, felt a huge discrepancy between the original program as proposed by the Commission at their meeting in Berlin (GDR) in January 1987 as "The role of theatre for children and young people in searching for ethnic and cultural identity."

Many participants felt frustrated by a program essentially composed of "student and amateur works", and discussions were dominated by advocates of "theatre *by* children".

The lengthy discussion resulted in the Commission proposing to write a text specifying objectives and methods to be used at the next congress in 1990; specifically:

- The purpose of ASSITEJ is theatre, not pedagogy
- It deals with theatre *for* children, not theatre *by* children
- The ASSITEJ Congress every three years is for the participation of "confirmed professional representatives", and to inform the general public of major artistic developments in theatre designed for young audiences
- The ASSITEJ Congress demands a close collaboration, without ambiguity, between the Commission on Themes and the local organizers of the event.

5 November 1987

Working Program for the Commission: In this session all participants agreed that the aim of the Commission was NOT to impose an "official" concept of theatre for young audiences, but should acknowledge and summarize the different modes of dramatic approach. The Commission must support the plurality of conceptions as well as encourage discussion of them for mutual enrichment. Their work must be conceived on the highest artistic level. Cuminetti recommended that ASSITEJ support seminars for invited researchers and university members known for their work in this field.

6-7 November 1987

Preparation for the Stockholm Congress: The next two days concentrated on the upcoming Congress in Stockholm. The Commission proposed that the EXCOM encourage all national centers from now until the Congress to concentrate on the proposed theme through their various activities, and then report the results to the Secretariat for transmission to the Commission on Themes.

Lastly, the Commission proposed to establish some sub-themes related to the main theme, and these should be specified at the upcoming meeting in Odense, Denmark.

Miscellaneous: The Commission discussed the desirability of holding two meetings per year, but realized the difficulties of scheduling and financial support. Also, the publication of a Commission News Report, which had been planned for several years, was still unrealized. The French ASSITEJ Center was studying the problem.

This concluded the meetings of the Commission on Themes & Artistic Activities.

1988
EXECUTIVE COMMITTEE MEETING
Odense, Denmark/15–22 May 1988[119]

President Hildegard Bergfeld (FGR), presided as President, Mårten Harrie (Sweden) as 1st Vice-President, Maria Navarro (Spain) as 2nd Vice-President, Eddy Socorro (Cuba) as 3rd Vice-President, Rose-Marie Moudoués (France) as Secretary General, and Paul Harmon (Great Britain) as Treasurer.

Counselor to the Bureau: Ilse Rodenberg (GDR).

Members present: Michael FitzGerald (Australia), Marian Lucky replacing Ladislav Knížátko (Czechoslovakia), Nena Stenius (Finland), Benvenuto Cuminetti replacing Franco Passatore (Italy), Kazuto Kurihara (Japan), Halina Machulska (Poland), Luiz Pisco (Portugal), Alexei Borodin w/ Galya Kolosova as Interpreter (USSR), Harold Oaks (USA) replacing Nancy Staub, and Zvjezdana Ladika (Yugoslavia).

Counselor from the Commission on Themes: Maurice Yendt (France).

Counselors from the Commission on Liaisons: Penina M'Lama (Tanzania) and Tony Gouveia (Great Britain).

Invitees: Christian Girard, Catherine O'Grady (Canada) and Thérèse Lowtagie (Belgium).

Absent: Zdravko Mitkov (Bulgaria). Co-opted Kazuto Kurihara (Japan) and Ion Lucian on the Commission on Themes were invited but excused.

Background

*I*n the early 1980s the four Nordic countries of Denmark, Norway, Sweden, and Finland joined forces to hold meetings for the discussion of items of mutual interest and concern as well as to sponsor Festivals of Theatre for Young People featuring performances from their countries. The 1st Nordic Festival was held in Oslo, Norway in 1984; the 2nd in Helsinki, Finland in 1986; the 3rd in Odense, Denmark (which was also international) in 1988 celebrating the 1,000 year's establishment of the city; and the 4th in Stockholm, Sweden which would coincide with the ASSITEJ Congress of 1990.

While originally established to promote the plans and plays of the four Nordic countries, they soon adopted the title the Nordic Centers, and began to focus on their concerns for the growth and the future of ASSITEJ. Denmark was the primary leader. They had formed a new Center, which was present for the first time at the 1984 Moscow Congress of ASSITEJ.

Finland had formed their Center in 1975, Sweden in 1980, Norway in 1983, Denmark in 1984, and Iceland in 1990. It was a formidable group.

The leadership at that time was Michael Ramløse (Denmark), Helge Andersen (Norway), Nena Stenius (Finland), and Mårtin Harrie (Sweden).

Their first major international activity for ASSITEJ was to support the attendance of many of the Third World delegates to the Adelaide, Australia Congress of 1987. The individual countries also supported meetings of the EXCOM in Denmark, Finland, and Sweden.

In 1986 concerned over the lack of growth in ASSITEJ and the immobility of its leadership, they conceived of a plan uniting a Symposium for non-member countries of ASSITEJ with one of their international Congresses, which hopefully would promote the creation of new centers and the promulgation of new forward-thinking ideas about theatre for young people. This planning culminated in the Symposium for delegates from Africa, Asia, and Latin America one week prior to the Stockholm Congress in May, 1990, and concluding with their attendance at the Congress.

The 4th International Nordic Festival which would coincide with the Stockholm Congress featured two productions from each of the Nordic countries, as well as those from Great Britain, France, Germany, and several other countries. In addition, there was the week-long Symposium before the Congress for non-member countries from Africa, Latin America, and the Asian-Pacific countries. It was a mammoth undertaking, and the planning allowed the members of ASSITEJ to attend all performances, the Symposium, as well as the Congress.[120]

The majority leadership in ASSITEJ fought this proposal by offering constant alternatives to the suggested planning, as well as requiring that the Commission on Themes and the Commission on Liaison be consulted for approval of all their plans. However, the Nordic Centers as members of the ASSITEJ leadership and sponsors of the Stockholm Congress went ahead with their plans, and found the funding which culminated in a remarkable double event—the Symposium and the Congress. ASSITEJ would never be the same again.

Bureau Meeting/15 May 1988/1 PM to 7:30 PM

Present were: President Bergfeld, Vice-Presidents: Harrie, Navarro, Socorro, Secretary General Moudoués, and Rodenberg as Advisor.

According to the Minutes, this was a brief session which 1) rearranged the Agenda to fit with the arrivals and departures of the members; 2) posed questions from the Centers as very important and discussed them on the session of the Commission on Themes, and which might be reserved for the Symposium, rather than during the EXCOM Meetings. The concerns expressed at the Adelaide Congress were added to the Agenda.

Hildegard Bergfeld (FGR), President of ASSITEJ (1987–1990). Photo by Horst Krompke. Courtesy of Meike Fechner, Archives, ASSITEJ/Germany.

Meeting of the EXCOM on Wednesday, 18 May 1988

Report of the Canadian Center: Christian Girard stated that there are currently two Canadian Centers—an English one and a French one. He distributed Reports from both centers. The current official address is in Montreal. Their government helps subsidize their international costs, but not those of administration.

Minutes of the Australian Congress: The EXCOM approved the Minutes of both the EXCOM and the General Assembly of the IXth Congress in Adelaide, Australia in 1987 with one abstention. At the Bureau Meeting in Modena, Italy apparently Hijikata (Japan) had requested some corrections in the Adelaide Minutes. The EXCOM gave preliminary approval in Odense.[121]

Points Raised at the Australian Congress: While the results of the entire Congress were regarded as very satisfactory, FitzGerald raised two points for consideration:
1. If ASSITEJ is to become a "world" organization, the EXCOM must include non-European members. If ASSITEJ continues to be European dominated, it will lose the participation of the other continents.

This is obvious from the failure to elect any of the non-European candidates present at the Australian Congress.
2. ASSITEJ must harmonize ideology and practice between the theatre *for* and *by* children. We must not be exclusive; it is a problem of organization in the Congresses to guarantee a balance.

Navarro (Spain) pointed out that the voting in the General Assembly was completely independent of the EXCOM recommendations. As a result of this discussion, FitzGerald moved that Japan be co-opted to the EXCOM, which was seconded by Oaks. The motion was passed with 16 for and 1 against. Accordingly, Japan was co-opted until the next Congress in 1990.

New Centers: The Secretary General recommended that **Austria** and **Ireland** be accepted as new Centers. Both were accepted unanimously. She recommended that because of internal problems **Sri Lanka** be accepted only as a Corresponding Center, which was approved.

Greece was not accepted, although they have 24 troupes, since the Secretariat had had no further contact with the Greek Center for ASSITEJ. Letters were not answered.

Wednesday, 18 May 1988 *Cont'd.*

Finances: In Paris Monique Rodocanachi had prepared the financial documents for compatibility, sent them to London to Shaun Hennessey who was to mail out the request for dues. In turn he had asked David Johnston to present the Financial Report. However, there was a delay in the mails. Meanwhile they clarified Japan's payments, ". . . which will allow Japan to vote, and this will be discussed at the next meeting."

Dated 31 December 1987, seven months after the Adelaide Congress, the EXCOM was given a complete Balance Sheet in French francs of the financial Credits and Debits of ASSITEJ over the most recent years. It was attached to the Minutes of the Odense Meeting, and it was an impressive document.

It balanced at 154,446.15 FrF with assets of 6,076.28 in cash, and the balance in savings and bank deposits in 3 different French banks. On the Debit side under Previous Years (not indicated) was listed 127,159.25 FrF in expenses. 20,265.31 FrF were listed as paid support of the Liaison Commission, leaving a Balance of 7,021.59 FrF.

More importantly the Balance Sheet for 1987 showed an Income of 46,896.49 FrF (from dues and interest on deposits), with Expenditures of 39,874.90 FrF (Travel, office expenses, postage, telegram, telephone, and translation), leaving a positive Balance of $7,021.59 FrF. As it had graciously done from the beginning, the French Center had donated the cost of Rent (2,600 FrF) each year.[122]

Oaks commented that problems came from the non-payment of dues, and the fact that the US$ had been devalued over the past two years. However, the accounts looked good, and there was a surplus.

Reports of the Commissions:
- **Commission on Themes: Maurice Yendt, Chair** reported that the Committee had met in Modena, Italy and now in Odense to prepare the Themes for the 1990 Stockholm Congress. At Modena Benvenuto Cuminetti (Italy) had proposed "Theatre and Cultural Identity" as the main theme. Three sub-themes had been proposed:
    1. New theatrical forms in relation to diverse traditions—cultural, aesthetic, and ethnic.
    2. Theatre for young audiences as a place of resistance for cultural minorities.
    3. What are the specific effects of the contemporary theatre on young audiences?

This raised once more concerns about performing companies using child actors!

Thursday, 19 May 1988
- **Commission on Statutes:** Moudoués stated the Commission was preparing a document on functions and responsibilities for the next EXCOM in Sophia.
- **Commission on Publications:** In the Commission's discussion they proposed that Cuminetti's article from the *ASSITEJ Review* be published to help prepare the 1990 Stockholm Congress. Then in future years it would be possible to make the *ASSITEJ Review* a working instrument of the Commission.

    The Commission also studied a New Project—a general distribution of copies of important texts. There was then serious discussion of theatre *for* children and theatre *by* children. While the Statutes are clear that ASSITEJ is composed of adult theatre organizations producing plays *for* children, Stenius pointed out that the organization must not exclude their consideration of theatre *by* children. Ladika pointed out that many centers have members that work with young people, training them as future professionals, as well as working with the schools and children, but Moudoués pointed out these are supplementary activities which are appropriate to ASSITEJ. ASSITEJ as a professional association cannot embrace all forms of children's theatre. Bergfeld concluded the discussion stating that the discussions of the sub-themes at the next Congress would deal with these problems.

- **Commission on Liaison:** Navarro essentially presented the program proposed by the Nordic Centers, and reported that the Commission primarily was concerned with the upcoming Symposium being held just before the Stockholm Meeting. They had divided the areas of responsibilities as follows: Asia—Michael FitzGerald; Africa—Mårten Harrie; and Latin America—Maria Navarro and Eddy Socorro.
- She also suggested a program of two weeks, instead of the one week proposed by the Nordic Centers, for Africa, Latin America, and Asia just prior to the 1990 Congress in Stockholm. The Nordic Centers were expected to raise this extra money. The Symposium would seek special grants from UNESCO, and 1) would give the participating countries information on ASSITEJ, 2) would draw the attention of UNESCO to these countries and ASSITEJ, and 3) finally would create inter-activity between these countries and ASSITEJ.[123]

Particulars of this proposed program included:
- A duration of two (2) weeks followed by their attending the Congress
- Each country would present a detailed report of what is happening in their country in children's theatre
- This meeting will take place in Europe, possibly Sweden
- 8 nations per continent with 1 delegate per country would be invited to attend
- The meetings would be conducted in 3 languages—English, French, and Spanish

The Commission would also set the calendar and the budget in order to submit it to the Secretariat. A list of participants must be ready for the EXCOM at their meeting in Sophia, and they listed the following countries as desirable participants:
- Asia-Oceania: China, Malaysia, India, Thailand, New Zealand, Philippines, Indonesia, and New Guinea—FitzGerald in charge
- Africa: Ghana, Burkina Faso, Egypt, Ethiopia, Uganda, and Zimbabwe—Harrie in charge
- Latin America: Guatemala, Nicaragua, Uruguay, Paraguay, San Domingo, Chile, Bolivia, and Brazil—Socorro in charge

Moudoués regrettably noted the absence of many French-speaking African countries in the list, and insisted that the seriousness of this project not do any harm in search of new funds. Hopefully the project would result in the creation of new centers for ASSITEJ, and suggested a possible division among the countries, but Harrie ended the discussion with the statement that the African countries would decide that for themselves.

The Symposium was planned for two weeks; the first part by

continents in 3 places (e.g. Copenhagen, Oslo, and Helsinki); the second in Stockholm for the participants to share information and experiences; and the third at the ASSITEJ Congress in Stockholm. The Nordic countries felt they would be able to find the necessary financial support.

Johnston and Yendt were to be in charge of establishing the criteria for the selection of the delegates who have experience in the field of theatre for children. Rodenberg suggested they offer special privileges to those countries that had already started the movement toward a national center, and this would help them develop it. M'Lama commented that Africa had a great variety of forms in children's theatre that differ from country to country, some of them unknown in Europe, and to impose special privileges that would exclude such delegates would be wrong.

FitzGerald added that it might be more reasonable to concentrate on one region at a time. If not, they would need a plan for each region that would consider the culture, its development, its forms of representation, etc. Stenius stated that it was necessary to clarify the motivations of ASSITEJ. What is really important is to find out what is the essence of theatre in a region, and what access children have to it. Moudoués commented that there is no universal model. Bergfeld added that we cannot trust neo-colonialism, but we must develop theatre for the young as an art form without pretending that European Theatre is a model.

After lengthy discussion it was decided that Navarro would collect all the proposals, the Bureau would discuss them, and they would prepare a final financial proposal at the Moscow Meeting in 1988. Both the Themes and Liaison Commissions would have to work closely together to prepare this document.

FitzGerald then reported on the Asia Region as follows:
- China—The Ministry of Culture had authorized the founding of an ASSITEJ Center, but they had to find how to finance it; however, they were interested in hosting an EXCOM Meeting or a Congress;
- Japan—Their regional festival was considered mediocre, and their ASSITEJ Center was not satisfied; while their Center had offered help, it had no responsibility for the choice of presentations; however, the Center had organized an international Symposium of Playwrights; a meeting of Asian countries has been held, and the Japanese Center is very active on contacting other Asian countries; their 2nd Festival will take place in 1991.

M'Lama reported on the African Region: All the members of the Union of African Performing Arts (UAPA) were interested in the proposed Symposium. They wished to join ASSITEJ, and UAPA would help countries gather the necessary information to join. UAPA would facilitate inter-African and international exchanges, and would finance study tours of ASSITEJ members to start the exchanges. Dr. Hansel Eyoh (Cameroon) was the Secretary General of UAPA.

Commission on Festivals: The Munich Festival, given the seal of "ASSITEJ -Theatres of the World", had run into conflicts with the ITI "Theatres of the World" Festival, and had to modify its promotional printings. Also, the question of responsibility had come up, so now all correspondence and applicants for the Festival title must write to Ladika in Zagreb, Yugoslavia for appointments and clarification.

The Commission had also decided to create three separate lists: a) International Festivals; b) Regional or National Festivals; and c) Irregular Festivals for the year 1989-1990. In their information Bulletin, each Festival would list its place, dates, and general theme. The Commission had divided up their work among its members as follows:

- Oaks (USA)—North America, Australia, China, and Japan (who in turn would make a list for Asia)
- Socorro (Cuba)—Latin America
- Bergfeld (FGR)—Western Europe, Israel
- Machulska (Poland)—Eastern Europe, Vietnam, Korea
- Stenius (Finland)—Northern Europe

The Vlaamstheater Institut in Brussels, Belgium will publish such a calendar.

There was a lengthy discussion over the definition of a Festival, amid the concern that the same companies appeared again and again in the same places. ASSITEJ could help by granting its label to two or three Festivals of a completely different variety.

Bergfeld announced the change of the Munich Festival from June to May 1988. The EXCOM Meeting in Sophia would be followed by a Festival in Berlin. RITEJ (the Festival in Lyon) would follow the Berlin Festival, and would have 20 countries represented, with 35 companies giving 49 performances.

A complete discussion followed on the concerns expressed at the Adelaide Congress, and the responsibility for solutions was distributed among the various Commissions and the Treasurer.

Thursday, 19 May 1988

There was a long discussion on the details of the coming Symposium. There would be a total of 50 participants. These would include 8 from each of the three continents: Africa, Latin American, and Asia. Applications must be received by 15 September and be given to UNESCO. This way they could be reviewed at the upcoming Bulgarian Bureau meeting in November. The three (3) separate Symposia would be held in Helsinki, Oslo, and Copenhagen.

At the request of Moudoués, Navarro would clear things with Yendt on Themes and Festivals. Johnston was to set up a budget from the information he would then receive, and help seek sponsors after the Bureau Meeting.

Friday, 20 May 1988
Reports of the Centers:
- **Belgium:** After reactivation and reorganization, it now consists of two centers, one French with 35 companies having a tradition of touring internationally, and one Flemish with 10 companies, and which produces an annual international festival.
- **Denmark:** There are three separate organizations: 1) ASSITEJ National Center with 25 members, which primarily has an international role; 2) the Danish Children's Theatre Association which unites companies on the national level, 46 of whom are members of ASSITEJ; and 3) The Theatre Center as a semi-official organization. All three organizations have work in common, and support an annual festival (the last one in Aarhus featured 400 performances by 70 companies).

ASSITEJ/Denmark cooperates with the Nordic Centers in four meetings a year, and has two major projects: the Festival in Odense and the Soviet-Scandinavian project.

It is also active in preparing the Stockholm Congress, and supported the sessions of the Commissions on Themes and that on Liaison.

Future Meetings: The EXCOM approved the following meetings for 1989-1990: a Bureau Meeting in Moscow on four days in November 1988; the EXCOM Meeting in Sophia, Bulgaria 8-15 May 1989; and a Bureau Meeting in Havana, Cuba in February 1990. A colloquium was planned in Cuba following the meeting to discuss the present work of ASSITEJ. Six representatives from Europe, Asia, Africa, and Latin America, along with theatre workers from Cuba would be invited to join the colloquium.

Since the Havana meeting was only three months away from the Stockholm meeting, Socorro was asked to host an EXCOM Meeting instead of a Bureau Meeting at that time.

Questions of the Centers: Several national centers had sent in the following questions for ASSITEJ to consider: From Poland—What kind of theatre can we offer children in this age of computers?; Bulgaria—What is the influence of modern literature on modern theatre for young audiences? (Later withdrawn for consideration by the Commission on Themes); Iran—Can theatre for young people remain indifferent to injustice and oppression of the society? Stenius suggested all these must be studied by the Themes Commission.

Commission Appointments:
- **Commission on Themes:** Yendt (Chair), Cuminetti, Johnston, Lucien, Lucky, Rodenberg, Mitkov, and Pisco.
- **Commission on Liaison:** Navarro (Chair), FitzGerald, Harrie, and Socorro. Advisors: Gouveia, and M'Lama.
- **Commission on Statutes:** Moudoués (Chair), FitzGerald, Johnston, Ludiski, and Kolosova.
- **Commission on Festivals:** Ladika (Chair), Machulska, Oaks, Stenius, and Satz

This concluded the meetings of the EXCOM.

Saturday, 21 May 1988

Penina M'Lama (Tanzania) gave an extensive report on the problems that youth theatre faces in Africa. Highlights were as follows: [124]
- We cannot control as individuals or as communities the cultural effect of the media
- There is no need for human contact in the current industrial society
- There are currently 15 to 20 countries at war in Africa
- There is no chance to live a normal life, much less participate in the theatre
- In central Africa theatre is used to boost the morale of the soldiers
- Theatre is always political, always takes sides
- In a divided country, focusing on ethnic issues can divide the country even further
- In Tanzania the wealthy can get outside videos, and consequently are national and international in outlook; while the poor get no videos, and their cultural outlook is local only.
- Working with a group of 10-12 year olds, the teachers used rhythmic play, response with dance, and song and drums
- They feel Michael Jackson is more fashionable than native culture
- Tanzania is in a cultural crisis
- There are no theatre buildings, and no money for tickets, which means: open-air theatres, children performing for children, theatre is tied to the schools, there are many different forms—drama, dance, mime—not just theatre and puppets
- Theatre is professional in the towns; in the villages, they rely on story tellers, theatre clubs, school theatre, and church theatre
- Adults attend with the children, making an audience half and half
- School theatre is performed by children, in French and English, and is used to teach French and English culture and language

- After independence (since 1967) school theatre has fought against foreign culture and colonial power
- Tanzanian Theatre must be different; it should instill pride in being of that nation, and knowing its culture

Her presentation was followed by a question and answer period: What theatre do you have? Schools go to the community to learn traditional dances coming from their culture. By 6-10 years the children can do good dance performances. Swahili poems are compressed, and children dramatize the words. There are semi-professional dance groups, who also improvise drama as a cast, not a dance group. Families go to performances together.

M'Lama went to Missionary School, and dancing was a sin. Now there are 123 different ethnic groups in Africa, and each country has 2-10. Theatre can teach and help make life better. The Culture Clubs seem to do the best job of integrating culture and drama for young people.

This presentation concluded the meetings.

In the name of the EXCOM, President Bergfeld gave her warm thanks to the Danish Center, to Michael Ramløse and his staff and their interpreters for their excellent hospitality in support of a very productive meeting.

Since this was the first EXCOM Meeting since the Adelaide Congress, it should be noted that the discussions were more serious, various plans for bringing more new centers aboard had been activated, and new blood was beginning to flow in old veins.

1988
BUREAU MEETING OF ASSITEJ
Moscow, USSR/16–18 November 1988[125]

President Hildegard Bergfeld (FGR), presided as President, Eddy Socorro (Cuba) as 3rd Vice-President, Rose-Marie Moudoués (France) as Secretary General, and Chris Wallis for David Johnston (Great Britain) as Treasurer.

Counselor to the Bureau: Ilse Rodenberg (GDR).

Counselor from the Commission on Themes: Maurice Yendt (France).

Excused: Maria Navarro (Spain) for family reasons and Mårten Harrie (Sweden) as 1st Vice-President because of lack of a Visa and a plane reservation, but arrived as of November 18.

The meeting had originally been scheduled to be held in Bulgaria, but instead they met in Moscow.

The Agenda was changed to accommodate the absences and late arrivals. Bergfeld reminded Wallis that nominations to the Bureau were individual and personal, and normally replacements were not admitted. However, she welcomed Wallis and his willingness to assume temporarily the duties of Johnston, who was in Australia. Also, via telephone Bergfeld had persuaded Mårtin Harrie to attend later on 18 November since his counsel was needed.

The Minutes of the Odense EXCOM in 1988 were approved tentatively with the proviso that the names of the Advisors to the Commissions be added.

News of the Centers:
- **Zaïre:** The Company "Theatre of Indigents" which belongs to Club UNESKO works on a regular basis creating performances for young audiences, and performing theatre with them. Katanga Mupey in Kinshasa, Zaïre is the contact.
- **India:** Has applied as a Corresponding Center, and the Bureau admitted them for three years in the hopes that at the end of that time they would have formed a permanent center.
- **Japan:** The Secretary General has informed the Japanese Center that the EXCOM has co-opted Japan, and they have appointed Kazuto Kurihara (President of ASSITEJ/JAPAN) to be its representative. The Bureau was very pleased at his acceptance.
- **Greece:** There has been no correspondence or contact. The Secretariat will continue to try to establish contact.

Centers to be Invited to Attend Future EXCOMS: Greece and Brazil, since they have internal difficulties, and Austria and Ireland, since they are new Centers.

Festival in Peru: A second international festival will be held in Lima, Peru. The contact is Myriam Reategui who was in Havana in 1988, and who has been working with Eddy Socorro and the Minister of Culture to establish a Latin American School for young people. So far there has been no further response.

Miscellaneous:
- A Festival in Berlin sponsored by the Theater der Freundschaft has invited 50 countries. Each performing company will give two performances, one of a small production and one of a large production. There will be workshops and seminars, and visits to schools.
- RITEJ in Lyon, France will take place 31 May-7 June 1989. Productions have been invited to come from Australia, Mexico, Italy, Canada, Sweden, GDR (Dresden), and the Netherlands. Musical theatre and street theatre will be presented. The City of Lyon has guaranteed financial support for 1989, 1991, and 1993. The French section will present a rock opera, and *Les Enfants et La Sortilege* of Ravel. The activities will be concentrated at the Bellcour Square in the International Theatre Plaza, a space constructed especially for the Festival. Bergfeld praised the fact that the performances chosen had not been seen at other festivals, and an important place was being given to musical theatre and rock music.
- Cuba will host an international colloquium 1-11 February 1990. The theme will be discussed at the Sophia Meeting. 10-12 productions will be shown, and it will provide ample opportunity for ASSITEJ members to meet their Latin American counterparts.
- Great Britain's Center is concentrating on international activities, and assisting other festivals to find foreign productions. There will be performances for young people in Sheffield (1989), Glasgow (1990), and Edinburgh (1991). Ladika (Yugoslavia) has requested festival information for their calendar.

Symposium 1990: Harrie presented the Report. The purpose of the Symposium was to gather representatives of countries throughout the world that did not yet have ASSITEJ Centers. By partially subsidizing their attendance, they would discover ASSITEJ and want to form a center in their own country.

Mårten Harrie was the official coordinator of the African countries, and he could ask for assistance from Penina M'Lama (Tanzania), but Moudoués stated a member of the EXCOM should take charge of any outcomes.

Michael FitzGerald could ask for assistance from Japan as a co-opted center if he wished for help in Asia.

Eddie Socorro and Maria Navarro would coordinate Latin America.

The Bureau would modify the questionnaire required of all the candidates for attendance.

Symposium Organization: Three weeks were deemed to be too long. It was recommended that the Symposium last one week only, and then that the Symposium and the Congress in Stockholm last only one week. The Symposium sessions could take place during the meetings of the General Assembly which were ". . . for ASSITEJ Members only . . . which are of no interest for the participants of the symposium."[126]

In the discussion that followed it was felt that the Scandinavian countries were too expensive for the week of the Symposium, and the Secretary General was to write Maria Navarro if it could be held in Spain instead, and to make a budget accordingly. Then the next week the Symposium delegates would move to Sweden and attend the ASSITEJ Congress.

To help with finances it was suggested to contact: UNESCO's National Commissions; Great Britain's Action Aid and Oxfem; Portugal's Gulbenkian Foundation interested in the former Portuguese colonies; Norway's foundation interested in Bangladesh, Sri Lanka, and India; Finland's FINIDA: aid for Nicaragua and Peru in cultural exchanges; Denmark's aid for Tanzania in cultural exchanges; and Sweden's SIDA with a budget for cultural exchanges, and a meeting of them will be held in January.[127]

Wallis estimated it would cost £100 per day to support one participant. Each invited center must make out a budget. The general budget would include: transportation from and return to the delegate's country, as well as the costs in the Symposium's country; hotel, meals, registration, theater tickets, rental of space for the Symposium; and costs of interpreters.

Symposium Program: Each group will plan its own use of the time. The general theme was set at the Odense meeting as "Theatre and Cultural Identity". The work will be done in three stages: 1) Separate; 2) Mutual with high level speakers; and 3) the Congress. Speakers have yet to be chosen. The Commission on Themes is already addressing the first two stages. A final report will be presented to all the groups assembled at the end of the first week in Stockholm.

Names of potential speakers familiar with international theatre and new directions included: Directors: Peter Brook or Benno Witz; Playwriting: Wole Soyinka or Sony Labou Tansi; Production Economics: Yohei Hijikata

(Japan); Actors' Art: Santiago Garcia (Columbia); Actors' Position: consult the International Federation of Actors (FIA).

Harrie stated that the Nordic Centers would meet in January 1989, set a budget, and discuss possibilities of where to get the money. The Congress budget will come to 350,000 krone with the dates of 19-27 May 1990 in Stockholm, and would be in conjunction with the International Nordic Festival and in cooperation with ITI.[128]

The Festival would present only professional companies with one exception: there would be a musical performance with the participation of children from four Nordic countries directed by professionals from these countries with a special budget.

This ended the Report by Harrie, as well as the Minutes of the Bureau Meeting. Ultimately the Symposium and the Congress were held back to back at the 1990 Congress in Stockholm, Sweden.

1989
EXECUTIVE COMMITTEE MEETING
Lyon, France/3–6 June 1989

The EXCOM Meeting originally scheduled for Sophia, Bulgaria on 8–15 May 1989 was postponed, and rescheduled for Lyon, France where the EXCOM was invited to attend the RITEJ Festival.[129]

President Hildegard Bergfeld (FGR), presided as President, Mårten Harrie (Sweden) as 1st Vice-President, Maria Navarro (Spain) as 2nd Vice-President, Eddy Socorro (Cuba) as 3rd Vice-President, Rose-Marie Moudoués (France) as Secretary General, and Deborah Bestwick representing David Johnston (Great Britain) as Treasurer.[130]

Counselor to the Bureau: Ilse Rodenberg (GDR).

Members present: Michael FitzGerald (Australia), Marian Lucky (Czechoslovakia), Kaija Siivala representing Nena Stenius (Finland), Franco Passatore (Italy), Yoshishiga Kagawa representing Kazuto Kurihara (Japan), Halina Machulska (Poland), and Harold Oaks (USA).

Advisors to the Commissions: Maurice Yendt (France), Tony Gouveia (Great Britain), Benvenuto Cuminetti (Italy), and Ion Lucian (Romania).

Invitees: Peter Back Vega (Austria) and Emelie Fitzgibbon (Ireland).

Absent: Zdravko Mitkov (Bulgaria), Luiz Pisco (Portugal), Natalia Satz (USSR), and Penina M'Lama (Tanzania)—Advisor to the Commissions.

Saturday, 3 June 1989

President Bergfeld opened the first session, and turned the meeting over to Maurice Yendt (France), who welcomed the EXCOM on behalf of TJA, RITEJ, and ASSITEJ/France, and stated that they were happy to take over for the Bulgarian Center.

The EXCOM approved the following Agenda:
- Approve the Minutes from Odense, Denmark Meeting in 1988
- Applications for membership
- Reports from Israel and the Netherlands
- Finances
- Commissions
- Symposia—Asia, Africa, Latin America: place, organization, program, candidates
- Organization and Program of the Stockholm Congress
- Questions from the Centers
    1. Zaïre—Sponsorship
    2. Finland—Voting Procedure
    3. Japan—Greeting Cards

4. 1989—Meeting of the Theme Commission in Poland
   5. October 1989—2nd Meeting of the Secretary Generals in Poland
- Reports of the invited Centers
- Miscellaneous

Minutes from Odense: In approving the Minutes from the Odense, Denmark 1988 Meeting, FitzGerald commented that the Minutes were accurate but poorly written. Moudoués commented that the USSR Center was doing it as a favor, and she would write asking for better translation. He also commented that there had been correspondence among the Statutes Committee, but Moudoués stated that there was a document ready for discussion at this meeting.

Applications for Membership:
- **Zaïre:** Since the theatre company that was applying for membership shared the offices of UNESCO, on their behalf UNESCO asked them to be admitted as a Corresponding Member of ASSITEJ.
- **India:** A new Corresponding Center for 3 years, with the understanding that it would become a full member within those 3 years.
- **Madagascar:** Was approved as a Corresponding Member for 3 years. Their Center is a large organization group and individual members. The University of Madagascar has representatives who want to develop a new theatre for the young.
- **People's Republic of Mongolia:** A Corresponding Center for the next 3 years. Letter came from their Ministry of Culture. They have 2 professional theaters and 1 amateur theater. There is only one theatre in the Capitol. Its Theatre for Children and Youth has existed since 1924. Does classics, national drama, and has performed in the USSR, the GDR, and Bulgaria.
- **Egypt:** They are interested in joining. Talked with people in Berlin at their Festival. Requested more information.
- **Jordon:** Requested information.
- **Luxemburg:** Requested information and an application.
- **Thailand:** Requested information and have heard nothing further.
- **Tunisia:** Requested information on setting up a Center.

Reports from the Centers:
- **Israel:** Now in the process of restructuring. New person in charge. New Constitution. Will comply with ASSITEJ Statutes. New committee and President. Orna Porat has become Honorary President and has remained on the Board of Directors.

- **Netherlands:** Has restructured. Has a new office and is supported by the Government.
- **Iran:** Talked with a man at the Berlin Center indicating they are starting again. Doing some work for children's theatre again.
- **Japan:** Reported on the conditions of theatre for youth in Japan. Japan is hosting a Conference with 11 countries invited on "Social Mutations in the Far East & Theatre for the Young". This conference grew out of the 1987 Adelaide Congress. 7 countries met later in Japan to discuss Theatre for Young Audiences in the Far East. 3 countries have been added this year. Japan is paying their return transportation and hotel costs for each representative to come to this Conference. Countries invited are: Thailand, Malaysia, Indonesia, People's Republic of China, South Korea, India, Philippines, Singapore, Sri Lanka, Viet Nam, and Japan. The dates are 18-23 October 1989.

Finances: Great Britain: There was considerable criticism of the Center's lack of a permanent Treasurer. The Center had nominated Paul Harman to substitute for David Johnston, who was not present at the Moscow meeting in 1988, but Chris Wallis came instead, and now Deborah Bestwick. Bestwick was to ask Wallis to fax the necessary documents. They arrived the last day.

Moudoués reminded the EXCOM that members who had not paid their fees were retained as members, but they would not be allowed to vote at the next Congress until all fees had been paid.

Following the meetings, there was a Cocktail Party sponsored by the Secretariat and RITEJ, followed by a Performance.

<u>**Sunday, 4 June 1989/Agenda** *Cont'd.*</u>

Themes: FitzGerald announced that it would be necessary to define the Themes for the next three years, as decided at the Symposium and the Congress in 1990.

Statutes: Finland had asked how to propose a change in the Statutes. Moudoués stated that it must be proposed by letter. The Adelaide General Assembly had asked for a guide about the different Commissions. A document was handed out to be discussed at the next EXCOM meeting.

Festivals: Information from the various centers had come too late to create a calendar for 1989; this information is essential to prevent Festival dates conflicting with each other.

Theatres of the World: Italy made a pitch for the Turin Festival to be endorsed as an ASSITEJ "Theatres of the World" Festival the week prior to the Stockholm Congress—9-17 May 1990. Turin had been presenting this Festival since 1972, with support both from the City of Turin but also the

Cultural Organizations of All Italy. It is held every year for 9-12 days with 17-20 groups from Italy, plus foreign countries. Last year companies came from Europe, China, Canada, Japan, and Africa. They plan to concentrate on a different country each year. Next year—Russia.

Apparently no decision was made re: giving the title to the 1989 Turin Festival. However, it was usually granted to the Lyon Festival on odd-numbered years, so it was probably not available.

The Czech proposal for a "strolling Festival" was too difficult to be realized in Stockholm, but seemed to be an excellent artistic idea.

The title was given to Lyon for 1991. There were no other applications.

Liaison: There will be an international seminar in conjunction with the EXCOM Meeting in Cuba in 1990. The EXCOM will meet from 4-11 of February, and the seminar from 9-10 of February.

Symposium: Maria Navarro (Spain) gave the following Report on the proposed Symposium. The Scandinavian foundations of DANIDA, NORAD, FINNIDA, and SIDA had granted money to support the Symposium.

Participants from South America could come to Madrid for the Symposium, and Spain would pay their travel expenses and arrange a seminar for them. The dates would be one week before the Congress, and then they would proceed to the Congress. Harrie responded that he wasn't sure that Finland would accept this, since at the moment Finland was to host the Latin American delegates, and had been funded by the FINNIDA Foundation. He would have to inquire.

Delegate selection from Africa will be carried out by Penina M'Lama, and FitzGerald will be responsible for the Aslan contacts.

In response to several questions, FitzGerald stated that coordinators and representatives are from the Nordic Centers. The invited delegates would have their own special sessions at the Congress, and they would meet their sponsors.

Navarro pointedly stated that the final choices must be made by the EXCOM. If they do not make the selections by the deadlines, the Nordic Centers will make the decisions. Countries may send observers at their own expense.

Stockholm Congress in 1990: The following information was presented by Mårtin Harrie to the EXCOM:
- They would see theatre in the schools.
- There would be many performances, both *for* and *with* children.
- All theatres in the area (both adults' and children's) will be doing performances.
- There will be many production companies.

- It is being financed by the Nordic Centers, and Sweden, both state and local.
- The Registration Fee will include the performances—100 to 500 krona.
- There will be performances all days, and all the times, plus directions on how to get there.
- Any number of delegates are welcome, but they will have to pay their own expenses as well as the Registration Fee.
- There will be three (3) Opening Speeches (Europe, Asia, and Latin America) taking a Psychological and Socialized approach.

In the discussions which followed, and the Minutes are not too clear in their translation, there was considerable conflict about who was to be responsible for the decisions on delegates and program, the EXCOM or the Nordic Centers and Sweden. This meeting did not resolve these differences.

Monday, 5 June 1989

The EXCOM met in the morning, and then there were performances in the afternoon and evening.

Tuesday, 6 June 1989

1990 Congress: President Bergfeld proposed that she and Harrie make the final decisions regarding speakers for the Congress. Harrie commented that there are too many important people who must have a say *on* the program that the EXCOM would not know about. It was decided that Bergfeld, Moudoués, and Harrie would meet in Sweden and make the Decisions. Oaks commented that he felt it was important to include speakers outside of Europe. FitzGerald added that it was important to hear ". . . new voices and not just listen to ourselves."

In the discussion which followed Moudoués underlined the fact that the EXCOM and the Themes Commission at Odense had requested that both the Themes and Sub-Themes be addressed by the ASSITEJ delegates, rather than by people outside the Association. Socorro also asked that the term "Third World" be dropped from discussion since it was too derogatory a term to the countries involved. Rodenberg asked that they be informed of the Registration Fees as soon as possible.

Miscellaneous: Zaïre requested to be "adopted" by one of the more prosperous Centers so that they could develop resources and facilities. They needed support both in time and money. EXCOM welcomed the idea but there was no move to accept it.

ASSITEJ/Japan said they would absorb the 700 US$ cost of the Christmas cards, but that the ASSITEJ budget should transfer this cost to the

Liaison Committee. Unfortunately the cards had not sold well. The transfer was approved.

The Polish Center offered to host the Themes Commission in conjunction with a Bureau Meeting in October or November 1989.

News from the Centers: The Australian Center was now in need of governmental assistance to continue its outreach program. FitzGerald also inquired if their magazine *Lowdown* was reaching the other centers on a regular basis, and the magazine would like to publish articles and pictures from other centers.

The Israel Center is being reorganized. They sent a telegram of apology for not attending the Lyon Meeting.

The Romanian Center is in a deep financial crisis, since they had lost all governmental support and were forbidden to export their currency to pay their ASSITEJ dues. Lucien said it was not his lack of commitment, but there was nothing he could do.

Socorro of the Cuban Center presented an enthusiastic pitch for the EXCOM Meeting in Cuba on 4-11 February 1990. There would be a Festival on 10-11 of February. He could be contacted on their new Telex machine, whose number will be given to all Centers.

Rodenberg reported that the May 1989 Berlin Festival had been a great success with 38 countries present, with delegates from Iran, Iraq, and Turkey present.

Passatore presented information on the Festival in Turin, which had existed for 11 years. This year they were only inviting productions from one country—the USSR. In the future they would only concentrate on one country in order to cement relations between the two countries. He publicly thanked Galya Kolosova for her assistance with the selection of the five USSR companies. He commented that with our current concentration on Africa, Asia, and Latin America, we must not lose sight of European artistic contacts.

This concluded the meetings, and the EXCOM thanked Maurice Yendt, RITEJ, TJA, and the French Center for their taking over the organization of the meeting, after the default of Bulgaria.

Wednesday, 7 June
Departure

1989
BUREAU MEETING OF ASSITEJ[131]
Warsaw, Poland, 4–10 November 1989

**President Hildegard Bergfeld (FGR), presided as President, Mårten Harrie (Sweden) as 1st Vice-President, Maria Navarro (Spain) as 2nd Vice-President, Eddy Socorro (Cuba) as 3rd Vice-President, Rose-Marie Moudoués (France) as Secretary General, and Paul Harman (Great Britain) as Treasurer.
Counselor to the Bureau: Ilse Rodenberg (GDR).**

City center, Warsaw, Poland

Minutes: The Bureau tentatively approved the Minutes of the EXCOM Meeting in Lyon, France in June 1989, since the English Minutes from Russia had not yet arrived. Moudoués expressed her dissatisfaction, and Harman volunteered to do the English translations. His offer was accepted.

New Members: Taiwan was accepted in full membership for the next three years. The Kenya Center was accepted as a Corresponding Center for the next three years, with the hope that it would become a full member at the end of that time. The political situation there was of great concern.

Dues: Harman stated that he was sending letters to those Centers in arrears informing them that all past dues must be paid in order for them to vote at the Stockholm Congress. New members must also pay their dues immediately. There was some discussion about the difficulty of transferring funds for some of the Latin American countries, and Harman urged expulsion, but the Bureau felt that moderate tolerance was preferable.

Statute Changes: The proposed changes in the Statutes were presented, and there was no further comment.

Halina Machulska (Poland), Member of the EXCOM, and her husband, Xth International Congress of ASSITEJ, May 1990.
Photo courtesy of Dr. Harold Oaks, Archives, ASU, AZ, USA.

Miscellaneous: José Caldas would be traveling to Brazil seeking information about MOTIN, their organization of theatrical companies. Approved unanimously.

The Portuguese Center was experiencing great difficulties in survival, and asked that the Secretary General write the Ministry of Culture requesting its support. The letter was sent.

Oaks (USA) had sent a written request that all centers send in the detailed forms asking for new play information as soon as possible in order to make the publication dates of the Bibliography.

EXCOM Meeting in Havana, Cuba in February 1990: Socorro gave members of the Bureau their Letters of Invitation, and indicated that the economic situation was difficult, but the Minister of Culture had given his support. There would be a Seminar with four presentations, two from Cuba and two from abroad. The Cuban speakers had fought a great deal for a Cuban cultural identity in relation to Africa and Spain. Maurice Yendt and Christel Hoffman would be the speakers from abroad.

Harman asked if the papers could be distributed before hand, and Socorro said he would try. However, the discussions following the papers were more important. Invited Centers were: Argentina, Brazil, and Venezuela.

Stockholm Congress: Harrie presented an up to date report. Financial problems had been solved. Working parties were preparing the Symposia. Individuals and countries had been selected.

1) Finland in Helsinki and Kuusankoski would host Argentina, Brazil, Chile, Columbia, Nicaragua, and Peru. There would be a Peruvian performing company, and possibly one from Nicaragua.

2) Denmark in Odense would host the African countries (yet to be chosen), and one African performing company.

3) Norway in Oslo and Trondheim would host India, Sri Lanka, Bangladesh, Thailand, and the Philippines (two people per country), and one performing company from the Philippines.

All three companies will perform in Stockholm during the Congress, all will be accommodated in the same hotel, all will have a similar program, and all will attend the Congress.

Bergfeld reminded the Bureau that the purpose of the Symposium was to gather information about youth theatre in these countries, and to inform them abut ASSITEJ. She expressed concern that the choices of delegates had been dictated by the funding agencies, which may not have had sufficient information to make proper choices.

Navarro felt that the Commissions had done a thorough job of recommending people who were directly involved with youth theatre, but their list arrived too late and was incomplete in Lyon. Harrie suggested that the names would be considered if there were any cancellations.

Joint Meeting with Commission on Themes: Yendt reiterated the main Theme and the Sub-Themes:
- Main Theme—Can contemporary theater help in the development of individual identity through a search for a better ethnic and cultural awareness?
- Sub-Theme 1—New theatrical forms in relation to diverse cultural, aesthetic, and ethnic conditions.

- Sub-Theme 2—Theatre for young people as a place of resistance for cultural minorities.
- Sub-Theme 3—What specific effects does contemporary theatre have on young audiences?

There was considerable discussion from this point on over the details of presentation. The Bureau was concerned that there was too much emphasis on the Symposia delegates' presentations than on ASSITEJ informing them about the Association. Bergfeld kept insisting that all should be ASSITEJ presentations, since the Symposia delegates were not members. These delegates would be primarily "observers".

Moudoués proposed that each Symposium be organized in the following way: 1) a presentation re: ASSITEJ by one of members of the Commission on Themes; 2) an overview of world theatre for children and young people; 3) work on the general theme of the Congress; 4) meetings, exchanges, and reports; 5) a summary of the work of each Symposium for presentation to the Congress by one of the participants. This was to be prepared for approval at the Havana EXCOM Meeting in February 1990. Harrie agreed to the proposal.

Bergfeld again expressed concern that the Congress must be one of "clarification", placing ASSITEJ and its aims first and foremost. While Harman pointed out that the Symposia and the Congress are on different dates, and the Symposia should "improve our knowledge of the theatre of Asia, Africa, and Latin America." Harrie subsequently mentioned that the funding agencies had dictated certain organizational aspects of the Symposia, and that must be respected.

The Bureau and the Commission on Themes then recommended the following speakers for presentations on the Theme and Sub-Themes: Cuminetti (Italy), M'Lama (Tanzania), Lucian (Romania), Merlin (Mexico), Souza (Portugal), Roger Deldime (Belgium), and Lucky (Czechoslovakia).

Since some members of ASSITEJ would not be able to observe the Symposia, it was finally decided that a paper be prepared outlining the world movement of theatre for young people. Yendt, Harman, and Souza were so appointed.

Bergfeld adjourned this final meeting with thanks to all who attended, and to their Polish hosts for their hospitality.

On a historic note, the Berlin Wall was in the process of being torn down while the EXCOM was meeting in Warsaw!

1990
BUREAU & EXECUTIVE COMMITTEE MEETING
Havana, Cuba/4–11 February 1990[132]

President Hildegard Bergfeld (FGR), presided as President, Mårten Harrie (Sweden) as 1st Vice-President, Maria Navarro (Spain) as 2nd Vice-President, Eddy Socorro (Cuba) as 3rd Vice-President, Rose-Marie Moudoués (France) as Secretary General, and Paul Harman (Great Britain) as Treasurer.
Counselor to the Bureau: Ilse Rodenberg (GDR).
Members present: Michael FitzGerald (Australia), Zdravko Mitkov (Bulgaria), Marian Lucky (Czechoslovakia), Nena Stenius (Finland), Franco Passatore (Italy), Halina Machulska (Poland), João Luiz Souza replacing Luiz Pisco (Portugal), and Yervand Kazanchyan (USSR).
Invitees: Maurice Yendt (France) and Benvenuto Cuminetti (Italy)—Themes Commission; Penina M'Lama (Tanzania)—Liaison Commission.
Excused: Kazuto Kurihara (Japan), Ion Lucian (Romania), Harold Oaks (USA), and Zvjezdana Ladika (Yugoslavia).

Sunday/4 February 1990
Arrival
Monday/5 February 1990
Minutes: The EXCOM first approved the Minutes of the Lyon Meeting in June 1989 as amended.
New Centers: The Bureau recommended the acceptance of Taiwan and Kenya as Corresponding Centers, which was approved. Turkey was in the process of reorganizing, and her status must be clarified before the Stockholm Congress.
Finances: The cancellation of the Sophia, Bulgaria meeting had caused translation expenses, which the Secretariat had to pay. Also the costs of the trip to Stockholm by the Secretary General had yet to be paid.
In view of increased costs for 1990-1993, the EXCOM recommended that the dues be increased to 250 US$. This was approved.
Symposium: FitzGerald reported on the Symposium initiated by Japan in 1988 in Sado Island, and reported it as excellent. Japan hoped to continue with the Seminars in Asia, with one planned in Korea in 1992, and another possibly in Australia in 1991 and 1993. Currently there are large scale exchanges going on among Japan, China, Korea, Thailand, and Vietnam.
A Newsletter was declared very useful, and Harman agreed to publish it.
2 performances

Tuesday/6 February 1990
Meetings and Report of the Commissions:
- **Statutes Commission:** Approved the recommended changes from the Nordic Centers, and they would be presented to the General Assembly for approval in Stockholm. One stated that ASSITEJ was against any form of intolerance, and the other limited one proxy to a country.
- There was considerable discussion of the proposals of Great Britain, which would set up a structure for regional meetings of ASSITEJ. The proposal was returned to the British Center and Paul Harman for rewriting, and members of the EXCOM were to give their comments to him in writing. The resultant changes in Statutes would be mailed to the centers for consideration at the Stockholm Meeting as of March 20.
- **Festivals Commission:** The Commission had prepared a provisional calendar. Also the "Theatres of the World" title had been awarded to Lyon for 1991. Leeds was a possible future candidate. The Commission had not received an application for a candidate for 1990.
- **Themes Commission:** The Commission was concentrating on: 1) preparation of the Stockholm Congress; 2) an Introductory Paper about ASSITEJ; 3) a proposal of working themes for the next three years; and 4) a study of the recent paper by Franco Passatore.

They approved the following speakers on the 3 sub-themes for the Stockholm Congress:

> Sub-Theme 1—Penina M'Lama (Tanzania) and Ion Lucian (Romania);
> Sub-Theme 2—Socorro Merlin (Mexico) and João Luiz Souza (Portugal); and
> Sub-Theme 3—Roger Deldime (Belgium) and Marian Lucky (Czechoslovakia).
>
> There was considerable discussion on the costs and advisability of using an expert outside of ASSITEJ, in this case Roger Deldime, a sociologist. They ended up recommending paying his expenses, to avoid having ASSITEJ listening only to themselves. The Commission would continue work on the Themes for 1990–1993

The Passatore Paper proposed the development of an annual forum, which would concentrate on artistic themes. After considerable discussion, it was decided to wait until the results of the Stockholm Symposium and Congress were in.

2 performances

Wednesday/7 February 1990
The Stockholm Congress: Harrie (Sweden) presented the plans for the meeting:
- 19 May—Meeting of the EXCOM
- 20 May—General Assembly. Play attendance would be available
- 21 May—Themes and Sub-Themes. Seminar: Finding the Child Within Yourself
- 22 May—Speeches and discussion from the regional seminars
- 23 May—Excursion to Goteborg Festival and performances
- 24 May—Nordic Theatre Day in collaboration with ITI
- 25 May—Discussions: Myths as Dramatic Sources, Shakespeare for Young Audiences, and Critiques of plays seen
- 26 May—General Assembly—the Elections
- 27 May—Meeting of New EXCOM and departure

Of the plays to be seen, 8 were from the Nordic Countries, 1-2 from Latin America, 1 from Africa, 1 from Asia, 1 from the USSR, 1 from the USA, and possibly 2 from Europe. On the Fringe would be mime, puppet performances, and dance groups. There would be a place for the performers to hold their meetings.

There was considerable discussion on details: 1) an outside speaker was too costly, 2) only 2 of the speakers are non-European, 3) the extra cost of speakers was approved despite serious concerns, and noted that 4) the EXCOM costs of registration and stay would be complementary.

Oaks (USA) asked the Secretary General to convey an offer to the General Assembly to hold the 1996 Congress in the USA. It was also possible that Canada would make a similar proposal for 1993.

International Symposium: Navarro (Spain) and Stenius (Finland) reported as follows:
- **Africa**—M'Lama has distributed information in 26 countries, and 14 replies have been received. Only 6 countries would eventually participate. The program will include an exchange of information among the participants, theatre work with both Danes and Africans, visits to Danish schools, and an exchange between a Tanzanian group and a Danish group.
- **Latin America**—the Symposium is to be held in Finland with six countries participating: Chile, Columbia, Nicaragua, Argentine, Brazil, and Peru. It will begin with the Finish Festival, and conclude at the Stockholm Congress. There will be 3 days of exchanges, and 2 Latin American groups will perform at the Congress.
- **Asia**—Norway will host the following countries: Sri Lanka, Thailand,

India, Philippines, and Bangladesh. In Oslo there will be three days of discussion on Art, Mythology, and Religion. If successful, the results will be presented to the Congress.

There will be Observers from the USA, USSR, Asian countries, and Australia (FitzGerald). Mongolia and Taiwan plan to attend.

In the ensuing discussion FitzGerald pointed out that 1) what ASSITEJ is must be clearly explained; 2) it is important for more and more parts of the world for young audiences to interact with each other and ASSITEJ; and 3) themes for 1990-1993 should not be chosen until after the Stockholm Congress.

It was noted most positively that the Stockholm Congress was the result of three years hard work by the Nordic Centers and the Themes and Liaison Commissions working together.

2 performances
Thursday/ 8 February 1990

Miscellaneous: Topics covered the training of actors to perform in theatre for young people, especially to make sure that they perform for both adults and young people; the need for more and better playwrights; and the fact that the exchanges among centers helped promote higher artistic quality.

2 Performances
Friday/9 February 1990

The next two days were given over to presentations by the Cuban Center, showing how things had changed since their last EXCOM meeting in Cuba in 1982.

AM—International Colloquium on Theatre & National and Cultural Identity

> Key Speeches by Inés Maria Maritiatus (Cuba), Gerardo Fulleda León (Cuba), Christel Hoffman (GDR), and Maurice Yendt (France)

PM—Theatre performance and meeting with the members of "El Papalote" Theatre Group

Saturday/10 February 1990

AM—Discussion on Key Speeches
PM—Continuation of Colloquium
Eve—Farewell dinner, Final Performance, & Closing Activity

Sunday/11 February 1990

Departure

1990
Xth WORLD CONGRESS OF ASSITEJ
Stockholm, Sweden/19–27 May 1990

<u>The Executive Committee of ASSITEJ Meeting/Stockholm, Sweden/ 20–26 May 1990</u>[133]
President Hildegard Bergfeld (FGR), presided as President, Mårten Harrie (Sweden) as 1st Vice-President, Maria Navarro (Spain) as 2nd Vice-President, Eddy Socorro (Cuba) as 3rd Vice-President, Rose-Marie Moudoués (France) as Secretary General, and Paul Harman (Great Britain) as Treasurer.
Counselor to the Bureau: Ilse Rodenberg (GDR).
Members present: Michael FitzGerald (Australia), Zdravko Mitkov (Bulgaria), Marian Lucky replacing Ladislav Knižátko (Czechoslovakia), Nena Stenius (Finland), Franco Passatore (Italy), Halina Machulska (Poland), João Luiz Souza replacing Luiz Pisco (Portugal), Galya Kolosova replacing Natalya Satz (USSR), Harold Oaks replacing Nancy Staub (USA), and Zvjezdana Ladika (Yugoslavia).
Co-opted: Kazuto Kurihara (Japan).
Invitees: Maurice Yendt (France) and Benvenuto Cuminetti (Italy) representing the Commission on Artistic Activities.
The following 33 countries were present at the Congress: Australia, Austria, Belgium, Bulgaria, (Catherine O'Grady) Canada, Cuba, Czechoslovakia, Denmark, FGR, Finland, France, GDR, Great Britain, Hungary, Iraq, Israel, Italy, Japan, Korea, Mexico, Norway, Netherlands, Poland, Portugal, Romania, Spain, Sweden, Switzerland, USA, USSR, Vietnam, Yugoslavia, and Ireland (by Proxy/Australia). Corresponding Centers present were Madagascar, Mongolia, and Zaïre. Attending was Gila Almagor (Israel) replacing Orna Porat.

Flora B. Atkin congratulating Swedish director/actor/television star Stephan Westerberg whose play *Rune Kapsyl of 11 Pancake Street* was the opening production of the Xth World Congress in Stockholm, Sweden, May 1990.
Photo courtesy of Flora B. Atkin.

View of Stockholm, Sweden in May 1990.
Courtesy of Dr. Harold Oaks, Archives, ASU, AZ, USA.

The Xth World Congress in Stockholm, Sweden opened with the delegates attending a performance of *Rune Kapsyl of Plattvagun II*, written, directed, and performed by Steffan Westerberg, famous Swedish actor/puppeteer, and television star. The plot concerned environment and pollution through the eyes of Charlie (Westerberg) who focuses on little things, such as banana skins, band aids, soda bottles, in other words discarded trash. This gentle comedy also featured Turilda (Tured Lundquist) who wrote the music and lyrics, and along with Charlie's magic, it was perfect for young children.[134]

1st Meeting of the EXCOM/Saturday, 19 May 1990

The EXCOM presented the following Agenda for approval:
- Approval of the Adelaide Congress (1987) Minutes
- Nomination of the Voting Commission
- Report of the activities (1987-1990)—Secretary General
- Financial Report
- Amendments to the Statutes—both the Nordic Centers and the British Center
- Activities program for 1990-1993

- Approval of the site for the 1993 Congress
- Nomination of the Secretary General and the Treasurer
- Nomination of the ballot Auditors
- Election of the EXCOM
- Meeting of the EXCOM for a slate for the Bureau
- Election of the Bureau
- Miscellaneous
    1. Motion re: the actual situation of theatre for young audiences in Portugal
    2. Annual meeting of ASSITEJ/Australia
    3. Can we as theatre for children influence the personality of 21st Century men? (Proposed by Poland)
    4. The world and ASSITEJ in evolution for a constant theatrical movement (Proposed by Italy)

Following this EXCOM Meeting, there was a special reception for all the 3rd World delegates who were attending the Seminar and the Congress.

The Congress was officially opened that night with a performance, a welcoming speech, and a buffet.

Members of the USA delegation: (front row) Moses Goldberg, Flora B. Atkin, Pat Whitton, Linda Hartzell, Holly Johnson, Marilyn Raichle, Ann Shaw; (second row) Gayle Cornelison, Harold Oaks, David Saar, Shannon Edwards; (third row) Nat Eek, Nicholas Wandmacher. Xth World Congress of ASSITEJ in Stockholm, Sweden, May 1990.
Courtesy of Dr. Harold Oaks, Archives, ASU, AZ, USA.

Sunday, 20 May 1990

The General Assembly: President Bergfeld presided, welcoming the General Assembly, and paid respect to Vladimir Adamek, Honorary President from Czechoslovakia, who had died recently. A minute of silence in his memory was observed.

During this day's session, the General Assembly confirmed the Agenda first, and then the Candidates for election to the EXCOM were presented, two performances were interspersed, and finally an evening meeting of the Chairs of the various Working Groups of the Congress.

Monday, 21 May 1990—Friday, 25 May 1990

The next five days were given over to the three Discussion Groups of the Congress. Each of the three topics was assigned to a different day: 1) Theme: Can the contemporary theatre for children and young people promote the development of individual identity through the search for a better ethnic and cultural awareness?; 2) Theatre for children and young people in professional training, and Drama in Education; and 3) Children's theatre in the Nordic countries.

Half a day was dedicated to Reports by the non-member delegates who had attended the Symposia. These Reports covered theatre for youth in their individual countries, as well as impressions of the performances seen. Many performances were available throughout every day.

Saturday, 26 May 1990/The General Assembly[135]

Approval of the 1987 Minutes: The Minutes of the General Assembly at the Adelaide Congress in 1987 were approved as distributed.

Voting Commission: The General Assembly elected the following Voting Commission: John Prior (Great Britain), Galya Kolosova (USSR), and Soccoro Merlin (Mexico).

Report of Activities (1987–1990): A report written by the Secretary General of the ASSITEJ Activities for 1987-1990 was distributed with time to have it read by the delegates on the spot. There was some complaint that it should have been included with the materials sent to the Centers before hand. However, it was accepted.

Of particular interest was the Secretary General's statement that ASSITEJ currently had 44 full member Centers and 6 Corresponding Member Centers. Since ASSITEJ was celebrating its 25th Anniversary of existence, 25 years ago only 23 countries established Centers to form ASSITEJ as an Association.[136]

Financial Report: The Financial Report presented the Accounts for 1987-1990 and had been sent out in advance. Recognizing that ASSITEJ existed on a very low budget, it was obvious that funds must be found from other sources. Moudoués commented that it was the responsibility of the Secretariat to find the necessary funds for projects. The Treasurer also projected a budgeted income of 45,000 FrF for 1990, with expenditures utilizing the entire amount. He also reported that if all Centers paid their dues in a timely fashion, their annual income would be 50,000 US$.

FitzGerald (Australia) reported that the EXCOM had recommended yesterday an increase of dues to 250 US$ per year per Center, and one of 50 US$ per year for Corresponding Members. The EXCOM had also recommended the creation of a Financial Committee within the EXCOM to investigate the handling of finances.

This was approved for the years 1991-1993 with one abstention. (The Report can be found in Enclosure A of the Minutes.)

Amendments to the Statutes: The Assembly approved the two amendments proposed by the Nordic Centers;

Chapter III, Article IV, to be added to the article:
No theatre, organization, or individual can be refused admittance to the national center of ASSITEJ on grounds of race, religion or political conviction.

Chapter IV, Article IX, to be added to the Article:
A national delegation can hold proxy for only one other National Center.

The proposal by Deborah Bestwick (Great Britain) involved having Regional Meetings of ASSITEJ in order to save transportation costs and to move their programs forward faster. There was considerable discussion, but ultimately the Assembly accepted Flüge's (FGR) recommendation that the EXCOM handle this proposal for the next 3 years and then draw up the necessary Statutes. President Bergfeld suggested that this proposal be considered a Working Paper. It was approved as such.

Activities for 1990–1993: Since the proposals were just read aloud by Bergfeld, the Assembly found it difficult to discuss them intelligently without their being in written form. They appointed Stenius (Finland) as Chair of a Sub-Committee to create a Working Program for the next three years. There were so many interested volunteers that Stenius had to limit the number on the Committee. (Their report was included with the Minutes as Enclosure B.) The proposed working Program was accepted. In essence it proposed:

- Improvement of Information: Must be continuous. Must establish a regular Newsletter. Secretary General must collect information from all member centers and forward it through the Newsletter.
- Improvement of Artistic Exchange: Need to analyze artistic work in order to improve its quality.
- ASSITEJ shall encourage Regional activities.

- ASSITEJ shall establish and work out the details for major artistic projects. Projects can be world-wide, regional, or just between two countries.
- The EXCOM shall work out a new subscription system to benefit economically weak countries to establish centers with the right to vote.
- The EXCOM will review the Statutes to ensure that all countries will have the possibility of membership in ASSITEJ.

1993 Congress: Three invitations to host the 1993 Congress had been received. They were from Canada, Cuba, and the USA. LeBlanc (Canada) withdrew the Canadian invitation until 1996 in order to support the Cuban invitation. Oaks (USA) stated that the USA would defer to Cuba so that the Congress would be held in the Western Hemisphere. He also said the USA would give all possible help to Cuba in arranging the Congress. His remarks were greeted with extended applause. Socorro (Cuba) stated that hosting the Congress would be a great responsibility. The performances would be mainly by Latin American theatres, and they would consider February 1993 as an appropriate time for the Congress.

The Cuban invitation was accepted by general consensus.

The General Assembly/The Elections/Saturday, 26 May 1990

Proposal for the Voting Commission: The EXCOM recommended to the General Assembly that the following tellers be appointed for the elections: John Prior (Great Britain), Socorro Merlin (Mexico), and Galya Kolosova (USSR). They were approved.

Verification of the Centers' Right to Vote: Thirty-one (31) Centers were verified according to the payments of their dues for the past three (3) years.[137] All those verified had both professional and amateur members which gave each center a total of three votes. The total was stated as 93 votes, making 47 as a majority needed for election. In the discussion Uruguay was surprised that they were not listed, but Moudoués stated that their center had been dissolved, and had been informed that it would have to reconstitute itself for admission.

FitzGerald requested that before the 1993 Congress, a brief written statement should be requested from each center. Moudoués stated that a precise questionnaire was established in 1987, and perhaps it should be taken up again in 1993.

Meeting of the EXCOM/Friday, 25 May 1990/Prior to the General Assembly Elections

Nomination of the Secretary General: A circular letter dated 14 May 1990 had been sent to all centers for candidates for office to be prepared to present their credentials to the General Assembly. A circular letter from the Danish Center addressed to all centers announced that the Nordic Centers would propose Michael Ramløse for nomination and possible election as Secretary General. This letter was also circulated to all official delegates on the first day of the Congress.

In the EXCOM meeting prior to this General Assembly Session, the following discussions occurred related to the nomination of the Secretary General.

Moudoués stated that she would have preferred a personal letter rather than one addressed to the President of the French Center. She also stated that since her initial appointment as Secretary General in 1965, she had always served in a voluntary capacity.

However, she added that in order to organize her succession, she should have been asked about her future intentions. She further stated that she would continue as Secretary General until 1993 when she would retire. A new Secretary General could prepare himself or herself during those three years.

Lastly, Moudoués declined to answer any questions in competition with Ramløse, as she was known by the quality of her work in the past, working on a voluntary basis. The EXCOM must make its decision accordingly.

Mårten Harrie (Sweden) then had nominated Michael Ramløse (Denmark) also for Secretary General, and handed out a letter from the Nordic Centers stating that Ramløse's candidature would be supported financially by them. Ramløse was known by the majority of the EXCOM. He spoke several languages, and was a good administrator.

In the discussion which followed Navarro said Ramløse had not been on the EXCOM previously, and was not familiar with the ways of ASSITEJ. Passatore commented that the position had been voluntary, and now he would be paid, which raises judicial problems which the centers should discuss. Also, he would have his office in a *semi-official* center (Cf: the Danish problem).[138] Navarro added that the EXCOM should not be impressed by the proposed sum of 40,000 US$, since little would be left once salaries were paid.

Souza (Portugal) added that the problem was really changing the position from a voluntary one to a paid one. It would be best to have this proposition discussed at an extra-ordinary session of the General Assembly.

Stenius stated that Ramløse would take over the position as a member of the EXCOM representing Denmark, and that he had already organized the EXCOM meeting in Odense. Then Navarro proposed that the EXCOM nominate Rose-Marie Moudoués to the General Assembly. Passatore supported this proposal based on the fact that Moudoués would provide continuity with her theatrical, judicial, and administrative knowledge. Harman proposed that the two candidates should present themselves to the EXCOM before any decision is taken.

President Bergfeld called for a vote, but Harman requested that it be postponed to the next meeting. However, Bergfeld ignored his request and asked for a vote. The result was; 7 for, 7 against, with 2 abstentions. To break the tie, Bergfeld cast a second vote and then the two abstentions changed their vote *For*, and the EXCOM proposed Moudoués be continued as Secretary General with a vote of 10 for Moudoués and 7 for Ramløse.

Nomination of Treasurer: Harman was nominated for re-election to the position of Treasurer by Stenius, seconded by Oaks, and the vote was 15 for, 2 against.

Bergfeld had estimated that the EXCOM would need to meet to define the Agenda more precisely, and also the position of the EXCOM after the elections in the General Assembly. Both these recommending votes were then to be presented to the General Assembly.

At this point Stenius and Mitkov said goodbye to the EXCOM, since they were not candidates for election. Bergfeld stated that she would be stepping down as of this Congress, so she thanked everyone for their goodwill and support. This concluded the meeting.

Saturday, 26 May 1990/The General Assembly/The Elections

Vote for Secretary General and Treasurer: President Bergfeld announced that two names had been forwarded from the EXCOM—Moudoués (France) and Ramløse (Denmark), with the EXCOM proposing Moudoués. FitzGerald asked what the Danish Center offered in support of the Secretariat.

Ramløse proposed a professional General Secretariat, subsidized by the Nordic Ministries of Culture—Denmark, Sweden, Norway, Finland, and Iceland—in the amount of 40,000 US$ per year for the next three years.[139] He said the proposal did not express dissatisfaction with Moudoués, but was aimed to meet the increasing needs of efficiency and professionalism for ASSITEJ.

Netherlands[140] asked why did the EXCOM recommend Moudoués? Yendt (France) explained how ASSITEJ should remain independent of any single country's control. Ramløse responded that the Center would certainly be independent of Danish control. Navarro (Spain) stated that the EXCOM felt that Moudoués should run again. She expressed astonishment at the huge amount of money which Denmark would provide. She understood that this primarily would pay the salary of the Secretary General rather than be used for ASSITEJ. Oaks stated that the recommendation of the EXCOM to present the name of Moudoués was not unanimous [The vote was ten (10) "yes", and seven (7) "no"]. Consequently the Danish Center could be considered. Tony Gouveia (Great Britain) stated that the subsidy would certainly not interfere with the business of ASSITEJ. Moudoués explained what the Secretary General does: the first servant of ASSITEJ, correspondence, communication with all Centers, communication with other theatre and artistic organizations, does what the EXCOM instructs, involves much time, provides services free of charge.

The vote was called for. Thirty-one (31) Centers were eligible to vote with three votes each, making a total of ninety-three (93) votes. A majority would be forty-seven (47). The result of the vote was thirty-three (33) votes "yes", and fifty-five (55) votes "no", five (5) blank. The vote indicated that Moudoués was not approved to continue as Secretary General, and that the old Executive Committee would need to go into session to recommend another name.

Moudoués expressed her thanks to all those that she had had the privilege of working with during the past twenty-five years. She reminded the Assembly of the excellent work of the Past Presidents who have since died: Gerald Tyler (Great Britain), Konstantin Shakh-Azizov (USSR), and Vladimir Adamek (Czechoslovakia). In the future she said she would still stand for the ideals of ASSITEJ, and hoped that new centers will continue to be formed and serve the children's theatre well. She was given a standing ovation as she left the dais.

After an intermission, the EXCOM returned with the following recommendation: that Michael Ramløse of the Danish Center be approved as the new Secretary General. The Executive Committee vote was ten (10) "yes" and seven (7) "no" recommending him.[141][142]

A new vote of the Centers of the General Assembly was held. A total of ninety-three (93) votes was cast. The result was sixty-five (65) "yes", twenty-six (26) "no", and two (2) abstentions. Accordingly, Michael Ramløse of Denmark was elected as Secretary General for the next three years.

Ramløse spoke to the General Assembly indicating that he would do his very best, but would need Moudoués' help and counsel for the next three years, especially with her 25 years of knowledge. He also acknowledged that there were now two opposing camps, but he would need everyone's help in order to serve all the needs of ASSITEJ.

Bergfeld then announced the vote for Treasurer (Paul Harman) as recommended by the EXCOM. Ninety-three votes were cast: sixty-six (66) "yes", twenty-six (26) "no" and one (1) abstention. Harman was accepted as Treasurer for the next three years.

The meeting was adjourned until the afternoon. Following her defeat as Secretary General, Eek presented Moudoués with a large bouquet of red, white, and blue-dyed carnations—the colors of the French flag.

Saturday, 26 May 1990/Afternoon/Continuation of the Morning Session

Nomination of Centers: After the approval of the Auditors, the General Assembly turned to the election of the new EXCOM.

Rodenberg (GDR) withdrew her name from consideration in favor of Christel Hoffman, and stated that once the Germanys were unified, they would be able to agree on a single representative. Since this would be the last Congress she would attend, Rodenberg thanked all for their good work and support in the past. She was given a standing ovation.

31 countries were represented with voting privileges, making a total of 93 votes. A majority of 47 was needed for election. A total of nineteen 19 countries stood for election. Since only countries are elected to the EXCOM, Secretary General Michael Ramløse instructed the Assembly to strike Denmark and Great Britain from their ballots, since those two countries had already been elected as Secretary General and Treasurer. Another 15 countries could be elected, but each would have to receive a majority.

Election of Executive Committee: The following eleven (11) centers were elected to the new EXCOM in order of the highest votes: Japan (Hijikata)—87; Cuba (Socorro)—84; USA (Oaks)—81; USSR (Shapiro)—75; FGR (Flügge)—72; France (Moudoués)—69; Australia (FitzGerald)—64; Sweden (Harrie)—64; Italy (Passatore)—63; Czechoslovakia (Lucky)—54; and Portugal (Souza)—50.

The following six (6) Centers were not elected: GDR (Hoffman)—46; Poland (Machulska)—41; Yugoslavia (Ladika)—41; Romania (Lucian)—38; Spain (Navarro)—34; and Switzerland (Oberholzer)—32.

With the addition of Denmark and Great Britain the EXCOM for the next three years consisted of 13 members. Lucky, Hijikata, Souza, and Shapiro were the only new faces on the EXCOM, and it numbered only 13 instead of the total of 17.

Election of the Bureau: The new EXCOM went into executive session to select a slate of officers for the Bureau, and returned with three names for President. Their names and the result of the balloting were as follows: Michael Fitzgerald (42 votes), Jurgen Flügge (18 votes), and Adolf Shapiro (33 votes). On this first ballot no one had a majority. Since Flügge had the least votes of the three, his name was dropped from the ballot. On the second ballot Shapiro was elected by an exact majority of 47, winning by one vote over FitzGerald for the majority.

The new EXCOM then presented five names for Vice-President: FitzGerald (60 votes), Flügge (48 votes), Harrie (36 votes), Oaks (61 votes), and Socorro (55 votes). Elected were FitzGerald, Oaks, and Socorro.

2nd Meeting of the EXCOM/Friday, 25 May 1990

Recommendations for the activities 1990-93: In the discussion of Activities for 1990–93, Bergfeld summed up the different points for the General Assembly:

- The role of the ASSITEJ Centers and an analysis of the work of ASSITEJ
- The formation of Regional Assemblies
- The Commission of Liaison
- The Commission of Themes
- The Cuban Third World Project in connection with UNESCO in Havana, Cuba
- The Establishment of a Newsletter
- The Establishing of "ASSITEJ Festivals" of a lighter character with "Theatres of the World"

Discussion of Activities for 1990-1993: While the various ballots were being counted, Nena Stenius (Finland) presented the Report of the 3-Year Planning Committee with its three major goals: 1) Establish a regular Newsletter, making sure it got to all members and centers; 2) Improve artistic exchange, including funding for special artistic projects; and 3) Improve the subscription system so that emerging countries could become full-fledged members of ASSITEJ. Her Report was accepted with commendation.

Miscellaneous Discussion: While the balloting continued, there was discussion on regionalization (the Report needed to be in all three languages), funds should be sought from UNESCO, there should be special incentives for playwrights to write for children, the theme for the 1993 Congress would be discussed later, Oaks reported on the Bibliography of new plays put out by ASSITEJ/USA, and President Shapiro commented that ASSITEJ had an excellent program of projects, and should try to accomplish as many of them as possible.

Honorary Presidents Award: Honorary President of ASSITEJ Nat Eek announced his creation and funding of the Honorary Presidents Award of 1,000 US$ which would be given to a person or theatrical group for "artistic excellence" during the past three years. The Award would be given for the first time at the 1993 World Congress in Havana, Cuba. The Award had been created in memory of his wife, Patricia Fulton Eek, who had been a major advocate of children's theatre and ASSITEJ. Eek pledged a minimum of 10,000 US$ for the continuation of the Award. He also mentioned that the winner would receive a silver goblet and a bottle of champagne for celebration. Complete details would be presented to the EXCOM within the next six months.

President Shapiro closed the meeting noting that "champagne and dollars" were a wonderful way to begin his Presidency.

(Left to right) Jürgen Flügge (Germany—Vice-President), Eddy Socorro (Cuba—Vice-President), Michael Ramløse (Denmark—Secretary General of ASSITEJ), Adolph Shapiro (Russia—President of ASSITEJ), and Michael FitzGerald (Australia—Vice-President), members of the new Bureau at the Xth World Congress of ASSITEJ, Stockholm, Sweden, May 1990. Photo courtesy of Dr. Harold Oaks, Archives, ASU, AZ, USA.

Meeting of the New EXCOM/27 May 1990/Stockholm[142]

Adolf Shapiro (USSR) presided as President; with Michael FitzGerald (Australia), Harold Oaks (USA), and Eddie Socorro (Cuba) as Vice-Presidents; Michael Ramløse (Denmark) as Secretary General; and Paul Harman (Great Britain) as Treasurer.

Present were: Marián Lucky (Czechoslovakia); Rose-Marie Moudoués (France); Jürgen Flügge (Germany); Franco Passatore (Italy); Yohei Hijikata (Japan); João Souza (Portugal); and Mårten Harrie (Sweden).

The EXCOM approved the following Agenda: 1) Co-options; 2) Commissions; 3) Next meeting of the EXCOM; and 4) Any other business.

Co-options: FitzGerald proposed co-opting Christel Hoffmann (GDR) and Annie van Otterloo (Netherlands), but Moudoués stated it was not a good idea to co-opt members from Europe at this time, despite their qualifications.

FitzGerald felt that more women should be represented on the EXCOM. Passatore proposed Halina Machulska (Poland).

Flügge felt it was more important to find out how and with what the EXCOM should work. They decided to postpone the question until their next meeting.

Commissions: The EXCOM agreed on the following three Commissions: 1) Themes Commission (Commission on Artistic Problems); 2) Commission on Liaison with Countries in Africa, Asia, & Latin America; and 3) Financial Commission. They also agreed on the need for a Statutes Commission, but that could wait.

There was considerable discussion, and Harman stated that they should consider these three major issues: 1) the need to support the activity of member centers; 2) the financial problems of ASSITEJ; and 3) contact with non-ASSITEJ member countries.

Finally they recommended postponing the final decision on membership until the next meeting. In the meantime members of the EXCOM would staff the Commissions as follows:

Themes Commission: Marián Lucky, João Souza, and Franco Passatore.

Commission on Liaison with Africa, Asia, and Latin America: Michael FitzGerald, Mårten Harrie, Yohei Hijikata, and Eddy Socorro.

Financial Commission: Jürgen Flügge, Paul Harman, and Harold Oaks.

Next Meeting: Moudoués said that the Hungarian Center had offered to host their next meeting in Budapest, and if selected wanted to know about numbers and costs. She said there was also the possibility of a Bureau Meeting in Vienna prior to an EXCOM Meeting in Budapest. The EXCOM decided to let Ramløse as the new Secretary General and Harman as Treasurer discuss this with the two involved Centers.

Miscellaneous: In connection with moving the Archives from Paris to Copenhagen, Flügge recommended that the Archives go to the German Center under the leadership of Wolfgang Schneider, who was already registering materials from the children's theatres in Germany. He would see that the database would be available to ASSITEJ Centers.

The EXCOM instructed Ramløse to contact Schneider about the proper procedures of moving the archives from Paris to Frankfort.

This concluded the meeting, as well as an Era of 25 years.

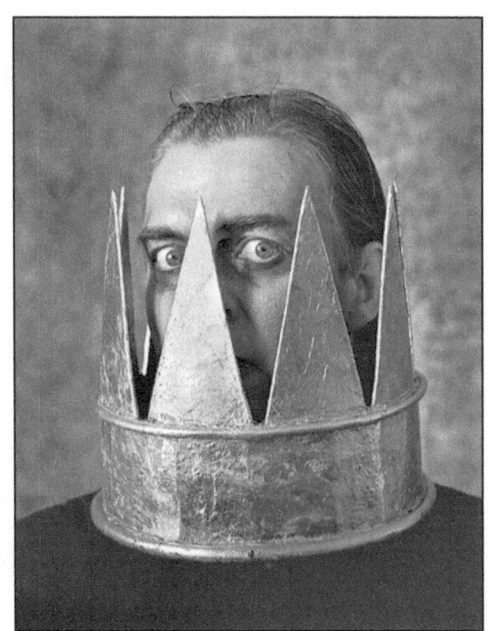

Peer Gynt by Henrik Ibsen. (Cited on the Front Cover.) Performed by Byteatern at the Xth World Congress of ASSITEJ in Stockholm, Sweden, 19–27 May 1990. Photo by Bertil Herzberg. Courtesy of Niclas Malmcrona, ASSITEJ/Sweden.

Peer Gynt by Henrik Ibsen. (Cited on the Front Cover.) Performed by Byteatern at the Xth World Congress of ASSITEJ in Stockholm, Sweden, 19–27 May 1990. Photo by Bertil Herzberg. Courtesy of Niclas Malmcrona, ASSITEJ/Sweden.

Performance in the Drottningholm Theatre, Xth World Congress of ASSITEJ, Stockholm, Sweden, May 1990. Photo courtesy of Gary W. Sweetman. Archives, ASU, AZ, USA.

Delegate Flora B. Atkin (USA) surrounded by an international improvisation group. Xth World Congress, Stockholm, Sweden, May 1990. Courtesy of Flora B. Atkin.

Ogre Tales, directed by Thorhallur Sigurdsson, performed at the Xth World Congress of ASSITEJ in Stockholm, Sweden, 19–27 May 1990. Photo courtesy of Gary B. Sweetman. Archives, Harold Oaks, ASU, AZ, USA.

Performances: The Stockholm Theatre Festival held in conjunction with the ASSITEJ Congress featured Nordic plays from Sweden, Denmark, Finland, Iceland, and Norway. In addition, there were plays from Bangladesh, Netherlands, USA, Lithuania, and Peru. Performance times were at 11 AM, 3 PM, and 7 PM each day in 15 different venues.[143]

Of special interest for 25-plus delegates was a trip to Göteborg to see the Backa Theatre's production of *The Hunchback of Notre Dame*, directed by Eva Bergman. Presented in a huge reconstructed factory building, the audience was moved to four different locations within the space for the telling of the familiar story.

The Unga Klara Company presented a "sexually charged" production of Shakespeare's *The Tempest*, directed by Etienne Glaser. Several productions used puppets, in particular *The Adventures of Peer Gynt* presented by Byteatern. The Wederzijds Theatre from the Netherlands astounded viewers with *Swans Always Look So New* ". . . because during the performance two scene designers painted pictures on the walls which alternately mocked and supported the story."

Mohammed, performed by Baggårdteatret from Denmark, featured two refugees from Iran, dealing with the universal problems of refugees in any country, and in this case their son who was being mobbed and teased by his Danish classmates.

McKerrow (an official USA delegate) had written in her report that you needed to be two people in order to see all the plays and attend the Congress at the same time.

In a letter to Mårten Harrie thanking him and his staff for a remarkable World Congress, Eek commented regrettably that several members of the EXCOM were highly critical of the Congress, primarily because some productions were "not professional" since they used children in their casts, and the dispute during the elections had been divisive, and disrespectful of the organization and its leadership. The fact that Europe and the EXCOM in a sense had lost their control was never mentioned. However, Eek closed his letter by saying "It was a magnificent week. Most importantly you brought new blood, new ideas, and new energy to ASSITEJ."[144]

A SUMMARY OF 1985-1990

1985

It was clear from the Moscow Meeting that the organization was firmly Euro-centric again. The total of 16 elected to the EXCOM was: Australia, Bulgaria, Canada, Cuba, Czechoslovakia, FGR, Finland, France, GDR, Great Britain, Japan, Portugal, Romania, USA, USSR, and Yugoslavia. 11 were from Europe, 3 from North America, and 2 from the Pacific.

Of these 16 member countries elected, Finland was the only new center. 9 were from the "eastern bloc", and 7 from the West—but 3 usually voted East. This gave the East a majority of 12 to 4 West.

The Šibenik EXCOM Meeting in June, 1985 brought no major changes. Argentina was accepted as a new center. The Commission on Themes under the leadership of Lucian pointed out that it was now 20 years since the founding of ASSITEJ, and the organization needed to change its themes with the new times, especially asking Australia to choose a new theme reflecting this change.

The Commission on Liaison felt that they must concentrate on the impending Symposium in 1990, and their major function was to convince the non-member countries to participate. Countries listed and contacted included: Brazil, Mozambique, Morocco, Tunisia, Venezuela, Uruguay, Paraguay, Peru, Nicaragua, and Ecuador.

The Japanese Center had done a thorough job of surveying the Asian possibilities in a full report. Of the 18 contacts, only six had responded, two positively. Obviously much more needed to be done.

Yendt's Report on the ASSITEJ "Theatres of the World" Festival in 1983 showed positive growth and funding, but demonstrated a real concern for how to maintain high quality in such a large venue. This Festival obviously had a lock on the ASSITEJ title, thanks to its close liaison with the Paris Secretariat.

There were now 43 National Centers belonging to ASSITEJ, but unrest was beginning to emerge. The British Center requested sharply that the Agendas and the major papers must be circulated well before each meeting, rather than being handed out and probably left unread and never discussed. They also pointed out that it was time that the EXCOM primarily should consist of artistic directors rather than theatre managers and bureaucrats. At the same time Hennessey announced his retirement from the EXCOM.

Mårtin Harrie (Sweden) asked probing questions about ASSITEJ as a relatively new center (1980), but undoubtedly signaling the Nordic Centers' concerns which would be expressed concretely at the next official meeting in Helsinki in 1986.

1986

The Bureau and EXCOM Meetings were held in conjunction with the 2nd Nordic ASSITEJ-Festival and Symposium, which was the first time that it had been hosted by Finland, who had become a member of ASSITEJ in 1975.

The best description of the perils of international planning of meetings comes from "A MEMORY" written by Nena Stenius (Finland) who was responsible for the organization of the meetings. Her descriptions are so remarkable and personal that they are quoted in their entirety.[145]

"The third Nordic ASSITEJ-Festival and Symposium was to be held in Helsinki, Finland on 3- 7 May 1986. It required an enormous amount of work raising money, making contacts, finding partners for cooperation, etc. It was the biggest festival of theatre for children and young people ever organized in Finland up to that time. The international Executive Committee of ASSITEJ was invited to attend the festival in Helsinki, and afterwards to make a short visit to Stockholm. The annual meeting of the EXCOM was to be held mainly on the boat between Helsinki and Stockholm, since these boats were equipped with excellent conference facilities. In addition, this was the first time the ASSITEJ EXCOM was going to meet in a Nordic country.

"In retrospect 24 years later, it is hard to understand how we actually managed to make the contacts at that time—totally without internet and e-mail. All contacts had to be normal international mail letters, sometimes telegrams, and telephone calls. It was not always easy to find people by phoning in those days, long before the mobile cellular phone. Automatic answering machines were used in many places, but they gave you messages in whatever languages were used where you were calling. Some new means of contact were possible: During these preparations I sent the first telefax in my life! But I had to go to the main post office in Helsinki, and ask them to fax my letter to Japan.

"However, all contacts were made, all performing groups were contracted, and the committee members and other international observers were invited. Theatres, members of the delegations from different Nordic countries, and invited international guests were sent registration forms to fill out and return by mail in order to confirm all the details of their arrivals in Helsinki, which meant 180 persons from 22 countries.

"About two or three weeks before the Festival a strike of the Postal Service of Finland was announced. It was expected to last for some time. However, most of the participants had returned their forms by then, but many were still missing. Several members of the ASSITEJ EXCOM had invited observers coming from far away who had not yet confirmed their attendance.

I went to the post office and sent lots of telegrams: Asking them to please confirm immediately by telegram how and when they were going to arrive, since very soon no messages would reach us because of the Postal strike which was to start in three days. Some telegrams and phone calls arrived, but many people never responded.

"On 26 April the Nuclear Power Plant in Chernobyl, USSR blew up. Though not in the immediate vicinity of Finland, it was not so far away either, and it was difficult to get accurate information on the situation. Several people from the Nordic countries started to telephone and cancel their reservations, fearing nuclear pollution.

"One week before the Festival the Postal strike was still going on. After a few days, at least the performing groups decided to come, in spite of the nuclear risk. Most of the other Nordic people did too. But the international guests! When the hell would some of them arrive and how? Then four days before the Festival, the staff at the airport in Helsinki decided to go on strike immediately.

"We were told that all flights to Helsinki would arrive either in Turku or Tampere, both 120 kilometers from Helsinki. Travelers were to be taken by bus to Helsinki. Suddenly everyone, who was not coming by boat from Stockholm, became an unknown! How, when, and WHERE would they arrive?

"I knew that guests would start to come on the first of May, perhaps even earlier. So we mobilized all the volunteers we could get to go to different places of arrival, depending on the times we knew from the registration forms when they might come. But for those who had never responded, there was nothing we could do about them, just wait and see.

"30 April happened to be the day of Spring Carnival in Finland, and that evening everyone is supposed to party, and the streets are crowded with drunken people dressed in funny hats. That would continue until 1 May. Then the streets are filled with marching workers, drunken people, and those with terrible hangovers, balloons and rubbish everywhere. Some of the guests who arrived during those days got a very peculiar first impression of Finland, a country that was supposed to be peaceful, neat, and tidy. 30 April also happened to be my wedding day. I had gotten married exactly ten years earlier, so my husband expected me home for the anniversary.

"In spite of that, and in spite of the Carnival evening, I was working until eight o'clock in the evening. I still had to ensure that the interpreters got their materials in time. Then I took a taxi home, fixed some dinner, opened a bottle of wine, dressed in my old wedding dress, and sat down to the table in front of my husband. Two minutes later the telephone rang: 'Hello, Nena—I found some Portuguese guy lost in the center of Helsinki asking for you.'

"Our Portuguese friend had been really lucky. The woman he asked happened to work at the French Cultural Center in Helsinki, she spoke many languages, and we had been slightly acquainted some 15 years earlier. But I really hope he was led to think that I was tremendously well known in my country!

"Another guest out of those who never confirmed, arrived, and was annoyed by not being met, so he took a suite at the most expensive hotel in Helsinki, expecting Finish ASSITEJ to pay the bill.

"Everything turned out all right at last, everyone found their hotels at last and their way to the Festival Headquarters, all 16 different performances were seen and discussed, and the boat trip to Stockholm through the spring green archipelago was very much appreciated by all the international guests. And as far as I know, nobody was affected by nuclear pollution."

The Helsinki/Stockholm Bureau and EXCOM Meetings of May 1986 ushered in some fresh air both literally and figuratively. It started in Helsinki but as a result of many different personnel strikes, there were no meetings in Helsinki. They only met on the boat trip and after they had arrived in Stockholm, following a very pleasant boat trip.

In order to keep proper control of the meetings, Rodenberg had skipped precedence, and appointed Stenius to preside at the shipboard meeting and in Stockholm when Rodenberg was absent, thus by-passing Shaw as 1st Vice-President and Socorro as 2nd Vice-President.

On the shipboard meeting there was considerable discussion over the appointment of Observers to their meetings, which seemed arbitrary and exclusive. The situation was never clarified, but it seemed obvious that such appointments were really on the recommendation of the Secretary General, not the EXCOM, even to the point of Moudoués saying, without precedence or substantiation, that there could be only one Observer.

The Nordic Centers had succeeded in getting many of the Third World countries together to consider creating ASSITEJ Centers, but more importantly to talk youth theatre among themselves, and among the members of ASSITEJ. The stage was being set for the Symposium.

The remainder of the meetings consisted primarily of reports from the Centers, with Finland commenting that they were going to concentrate on holding international Festivals as being the most helpful to the growth of ASSITEJ.

In their discussion on possible guest speakers it should be noted that 5 came from Europe, 1 from Africa, and 1 from North America. With the exception of Roger Deldime (a Belgian non-member) all were heads of national centers, and five had spoken more than once at various Congresses and EXCOM Meetings. So much for informing the members of ASSITEJ about the wide, wide world out there!

Probably the most startling and unpleasant event came at the end of the last meeting of the EXCOM when Orna Porat (Israel) accused Shaw of sabotaging the Israeli Center by visiting her country twice to talk about ASSITEJ. The reality was that Shaw had been invited to visit to talk about "theatre for the disabled", but in the course of their meetings the Israeli Center and Porat's name came up. The fat was in the fire when the Israelis discovered there was an Israel Center that in fact was a "ghost" center since Porat would allow no one else to join. They had now called her to account, which ended in her angry denunciation of Shaw. Rodenberg commented privately to FitzGerald, "When we go at home we are a little wiser more!"

In the January 1987 Berlin EXCOM Meeting Shaw personally distributed a "white paper" listing all the charges and her refutations hoping to end the controversy. The result of this entire debacle was that Porat was named Honorary President and the Israeli Center came under the new leadership of Gila Almagor, and took its rightful place as an active all-encompassing ASSITEJ Center.

Also, in 1986, ASSITEJ lost the gracious and determined leadership of Maria Sunyer. Always beautifully groomed, she had first appeared in 1966 at the Ist International Congress in Prague, Czechoslovakia. She headed the Spanish Center for 20 years, turning its leadership over to Maria Navarro soon after the 1984 Moscow Congress. During her tenure she fought strongly for Spanish as a 4th ASSITEJ language. But when that could not happen, she established the *Boletino Ibero-americano*, printed in Spanish, which featured articles, schedules, news of other centers, Festival Schedules, and information about ASSITEJ, and saw that it was sent to all Spanish-speaking countries, especially in South America. She was solely responsible for getting governmental funding, and for supporting the 1974 EXCOM Meeting in Madrid/Seville, and the International Congress in Madrid in 1978. She worked tirelessly for ASSITEJ, for her Center, for her Spanish-speaking compatriots, and for children and young people. She was named an Honorary Member of ASSITEJ in 1987.

1987

Beginning in the mid-1980s the GDR had come face to face with serious problems. The Soviet Union, one of its major supporters, in 1987 had embarked on *glasnost* which the GDR strongly resisted. However, the GDR's faltering economy was crippled by shortages of natural resources and labor plus a huge debt to Western lenders, and the young people were leaving in droves seeing a richer life style in the West. By October 1989 the entire country was faced with demonstrations and demands for reform. Then Erich Honecker, their President since 1976, was forced to resign, the Czech border was opened to the West for emigration, and as a final symbol the Berlin Wall was torn down on 8 November 1989. In October 1990 the two Germanys were reunited.

In 1987 these world events had begun to take a surprising turn, which affected everything that ASSITEJ was trying to do about expanding beyond its narrow European borders.

The January EXCOM Meeting in Berlin was a farewell to Ilse Rodenberg. She would step down as President at the Australia Congress in May, after 9 years of strong leadership. She had been a vigorous and responsible leader, and had visited many of the centers personally, attended many Festivals, and devoted herself to the needs of ASSITEJ. While she was constrained politically and rigidly by her government, wherever possible she proved to be welcoming, fair, and decisive. She had become one of ASSITEJ's major leaders with a strong love of theatre for young people.

The Bureau was treated to a dinner at her home, and a tour of her many mementos, but the two Germanys were close to being united, and a clear solution was to have its delegate come from the FGR, and to retain Rodenberg on the EXCOM as an Advisor. Soon there would be one Germany, and one head of the delegation.

Meanwhile, twenty countries had nominated themselves for election to the EXCOM in 1987, and of them four were new: Denmark, Poland, Sweden, and Vietnam.

The Adelaide, Australia Congress was a phenomenal success. First of all, as predicted, it had a huge turnout—198 foreign delegates, and 228 Australian delegates for a total of 426.

Of particular interest was the appearance of Marjorie MacClean (Canada), although Canada had resigned from the EXCOM in 1986. She later told FitzGerald "I was in Adelaide, assuming the role for Canada. Canada was in such disarray [that] there was no real "board". Quebec threatening to separate meant there could be no elections or cooperation from Quebec. I tried to get ASSITEJ/Canada [which] had folded as an organization to start from scratch, but that was actually impossible because I was not an elected board member, but the 'once upon a time' elected board had scattered to the wind with Quebec refusing to cooperate. Quebec wanted their own ASSITEJ/ Quebec but as the International only recognizes countries, stalemate. So I took over."[146] FitzGerald commented further that ". . . take over she did!" As Canada's representative she was elected to the EXCOM, became a Vice-

President, and proved to be a strong, effective member of ASSITEJ.

The Adelaide Congress was extremely well organized: 3 Plenary Sessions of papers, discussions, and reports with simultaneous translation in the three official languages, plus Japanese; a festive dining tent where everyone met, ate, and conversed; and a plethora of plays which showcased the incredible variety of productions in the Pacific area, as FitzGerald put it—"warts and all". Unfortunately, to some of the Europeans, this was "amateur" theatre at its worst, which in turn made them very protective of the "professional theatre only" concept. And it should be remembered that the Secretary General personally was totally opposed to any productions featuring child actors as being definitely "non-professional".

From the very beginning of ASSITEJ at that first Constitution Conference in 1965, the Association was dominated by the European Centers. Most of them had excellent professional theatres performing for young audiences; their companies consisted of professional adult actors with technical support systems and managements operating on a high artistic level of achievement. Creative drama, and the children who were involved in it, were regarded as "amateur" in the worst way, and in the late 1970s creative drama was eliminated from consideration as a part of ASSITEJ's provenance.

More importantly the European dogged adherence to "professional theatre only" helped raise performance standards world-wide, and while many of their actors were in their late teens and twenties, they were professional in their training, their talents, and their believability.

But in the real world of theatre for young audiences, many countries used children and teens in their performances, usually to excellent effect. This was what concerned FitzGerald as well as many of the new and younger members of ASSITEJ. If ASSITEJ was to be a true "world organization", it must include these countries, many of whose leaders had had professional training, but who used young people in their companies. The only alternative was to have two separate organizations, which would destroy any "world association" of theatre for young audiences.

Unfortunately, the elections at Adelaide had decidedly been rigged in Europe's favor. Of the 16 centers elected to the new EXCOM: 12 came from Europe, 3 from North America, 1 from Asia (Australia), and "none" from Africa and South America. The fact that five (5) proxies were held between France and GDR gave considerable heft to the European landslide. Perhaps it should be called a last ditch defensive with Australia kept on since the recent Congress had been hosted there. On a positive note, such a one-sided manipulated election gave a huge impetus to the cataclysmic changes about to be brought in at the Stockholm Congress.

Elected to the EXCOM for the next three years were: Australia (Michael FitzGerald); Bulgaria (Zdravko Mitkov); Cuba (Eddy Socorro); Czechoslovakia (Ladislav Knižátko); FGR (Hildegard Bergfeld); Finland (Nena Stenius); France (Rose-Marie Moudoués); GDR (Ilse Rodenberg); Great Britain (Paul Harman); Italy (Franco Passatore); Poland (Halina Machulska); Portugal (Luiz Pisco); Spain (Maria Navarro); Sweden (Mårten Harrie); USA (Nancy Staub); USSR (Natalya Satz); and Yugoslavia (Zvjezdana Ladika).

Elected to the Bureau were Hildegard Bergfeld (FGR) as President; Mårten Harrie (Sweden) as 1st Vice-President, Maria Navarro (Spain) as 2nd Vice-President, Eddy Socorro (Cuba) as 3rd Vice-President, Rose-Marie Moudoués (France) as Secretary General, and Paul Harman (Great Britain) as Treasurer.

As a result of the embarrassment over Japan not being returned to the EXCOM in the election, the EXCOM co-opted Japan at its Odense, Denmark meeting in 1988, and Kazuto Kurihara took his rightful place of deliberation for the next two years.

The fact that Denmark was not elected to the EXCOM led to some criticism of Ramløse in 1990 in Stockholm. He should not stand for Secretary General since he had never been on the EXCOM.

That November in the Commission on Themes Meeting in Modena, Italy, serious consideration was given to the points of "European exclusivity" that had been raised in Adelaide. It would be essential that these concerns be directly addressed at the 1990 Stockholm Meeting. While lip-service would be given to an all-inclusive world organization, the real agenda was to confirm "high artistic standards" and "adult theatre" which excluded young people as performers, even with the leadership of adult professionals, and to deny admission to many centers outside Europe. A world view was desperately needed, not another iteration of the European "old guard".

In many ways the next three years following the Adelaide Congress were years of grudging change for the Bureau and the EXCOM. The 1984 Moscow Congress was tightly controlled, and all seemed right with the world. However, younger members were joining the Association, even though the older members had control. Correspondence was slow, and not always accurate. Regular postal mail was relied on, while the world was rapidly shifting to electronic mail. In addition, the Bureau which was mostly "old guard" wanted to keep things running as they always had, which was no longer acceptable to the membership. New and non-European Centers needed to be created, moneys needed to be found to support the Association, and most importantly younger people needed to be at the helm.

The French Secretariat had begun to try to deal with these needs after the Moscow Congress, by moving in new faces to the old jobs, but who shared the same views of "the old regular way". Moudoués had created strong ASSITEJ support for Maurice Yendt of Lyon and his RITEJ Festival every two years. Lyon proved to be host to an excellent and valuable international festival, and one with the imprimatur of ASSITEJ behind it. Only Bulgaria every other year was able to get the same stamp of approval. Others attempted to apply, but somehow they were never approved, except for Munich in 1988, which was in Bergfeld's territory!

Part of the political plan seemed to be to maneuver Yendt into position to take over the Secretary General's position when and if Moudoués decided to retire. In addition, Maria Navarro had replaced Maria Sunyer in the Spanish Center, and seemed a likely young candidate for the Presidency, who was endorsed by the old guard. However, world events derailed such plans.

While the EXCOM had expressed great concern that it would be too expensive for members to attend a Congress in Australia, the reverse was true. The Australian Congress had the largest attendance of any Congress since the joint Congress of 1972 in Canada and the USA—a total of 426 delegates were in Adelaide!

On top of this the Nordic Centers were getting restless over the lack of change and the absence of new memberships from the Third World. While the Australian Congress made it evident that change was wanted, the politically manipulated elections prevented it.

Immediately following that Congress, the next several meetings had to deal with the demanded changes. In addition, the Nordic Centers boldly proposed a Symposium for Third World non-member delegates for one week just before the Stockholm Congress in 1990, which would also allow them to attend the Congress.

The Bureau continued to drag its feet, trying to select and restrict the delegates, and sending the plans to the Commission on Themes and the Commission on Liaison for recommendations and editing. However, by the end of 1989, the Nordic Centers had the Symposium and Congress well in hand, as originally planned by them, and fully funded also by them. The leadership of ASSITEJ had roughly accomplished nothing but delay and obstruction.

1988

This year in many ways was one of trying to keep the "wolf" of reform away from the door. At the Meeting in Odense, Denmark in May 1988, the EXCOM seriously considered points raised at the Adelaide Congress regarding the future of ASSITEJ. FitzGerald pointed out strongly that ASSITEJ would only grow by becoming a "world" organization, which meant more "non-

European" members in its leadership. Secondly, it must harmonize the concept of theatre *for* and *by* children, since many of the world's countries used young people as performers in their theatres. ASSITEJ could not be just for "adults", and still claim to be a world organization while eliminating half of its possible membership.

New centers in Austria and Ireland were added, with Sri Lanka as a Corresponding Center. Greece was not accepted for lack of correspondence.

A major financial achievement was made with the transfer of the ASSITEJ accounts to Great Britain under the leadership of Shaun Hennessey and David Johnston, and with Paul Harman elected as Treasurer. The accounts were in good shape, and there was a positive balance. From this point on the Association's financial accountability was more transparent.

Perhaps the most important achievement was the presentation of plans by the Nordic Centers for a Symposium of Third World Countries to be held prior to the Stockholm Congress in 1990. It was being designed to assist these countries in creating viable national centers, and in turn making ASSITEJ a true world organization.

As a corollary Penina M'Lama (Tanzania) gave a remarkable Report on her country and what African theatre was doing. Highlights indicated that the lack of money prevented much if any but the most rudimentary theatre. Theatre was usually in the form of drumming, song, and dance. While colonialism had introduced some of Western theatre to the people, the African parishioners were taking the Western form and transforming it through African culture, customs, and folklore. Dance was the dominate performing arts form. The major question would be whether such elementary theatre, in the name of theatre for children, would mesh with the sophistication of the European style. But the seed had been planted.

The Bureau met in Moscow in November of 1988 and received Harrie's report from Sweden. The Nordic Centers (Sweden, Norway, Finland, Iceland, and Denmark) proposed to hold the Symposium for one week just prior to the Stockholm Congress which would bring non-affiliated countries producing theatre for young people together. They recommended the week before the Congress, which would allow these new delegates to attend the week of the Stockholm Congress immediately following.

It was clear that the Nordic Centers had given considerable thought to the preparing of the entire plan. All the continents were included (with the exception of Antarctica), and for the first time an enormous attempt had been made to be a "world" organization.

There was much discussion, and many of the details of the Symposium were supposedly codified at the Moscow Meeting. In many ways the Symposium was the answer to FitzGerald's expressed concerns, and Harrie stated that the Nordic Centers would meet in January 1989 to set the budget, find the money for the Congress and the Symposium, and set the organizational details. This was an extremely bold step, but one which allowed ASSITEJ to become a world organization in absolute fact. While the EXCOM insisted that the Commission on Themes and the Commission on Liaison be involved in the planning, none of their alternate recommendations were ever accepted. It was the plan of the Nordic Centers all the way, conceived, outlined, organized, and most importantly funded entirely by them. It was a magnificent achievement, attained while the elected leadership of ASSITEJ primarily dragged their feet.

Starting in 1988 ASSITEJ lost the leadership of three very strong women—Ann Shaw (USA) in 1988, Ilse Rodenberg (GDR) in 1989, and Rose-Marie Moudoués (France) in 1990. Each had given full measure in her devotion to ASSITEJ and its programs; each had been outspoken in her belief in youth theatre; and each had committed her own personal time and resources to the Association when other support was unavailable. Moudoués served 25 years, Rodenberg 24 years, and Shaw 16 years, for a combined total of 66 years of service to ASSITEJ. Rodenberg has been named an Honorary President of ASSITEJ, and Moudoués and Shaw have been named as Honorary Members of ASSITEJ.

1989

In June 1989 the EXCOM met in Lyon, France with Hildegard Bergfeld (FGR) presiding as President. Rodenberg had stepped down officially, and with the anticipated uniting of the two Germanys, it was appropriate that Bergfeld take over with Rodenberg retained as an Advisor. However, Bergfeld had been almost hand-picked by the GDR for this position.

The Secretariat reported nine new national centers in the process of forming. Again a token effort to indicate growth and change, but in reality it was more "smoke and mirrors!" Only two of these became Corresponding Centers.

There was considerable discussion of the plans as they were shaping for the Stockholm Congress the next year. The EXCOM agreed to meet in Cuba in February 1990 to finalize the details, but this was another token effort, since the plans were already completed.

"During the Meeting, the Tiananmen Incident occurred in China. Members of the EXCOM watched in horror as events were shown on television. To many it brought home the fact that change from an older order to a new, whether at home or abroad, is never easy."[147]

Ultimately ASSITEJ was overtaken by all these world events. The Berlin Wall crashed to the ground in November 1989, and suddenly the "Eastern bloc" was crumbling and the rubble disappearing. This could not help but auger well for the Stockholm Congress.

1990

The Bureau and EXCOM met in Havana, Cuba in February 1990 to set the final details of the Swedish Congress. Bergfeld presided with Harrie presenting the program.

Harrie outlined the program of the Stockholm Congress concisely, which concentrated on the informational interaction of all the delegates and those non-ASSITEJ members who would be attending the Symposia. Only one day was given over to the elections, and the rest were a generous mix of speeches, presentations, discussions, and performances. It would be a World Congress not dominated by Europe.

Undoubtedly the most important achievement in this meeting was the presentation by Stenius and Navarro of the Program of the 3 Symposia which would meet prior to the Stockholm Congress, the result of three years of hard work led by the Nordic Centers with advice from the Commissions on Themes and Liaisons, which were mostly ignored. There would be representatives from 6 different African countries in Denmark, 6 Latin American countries in Finland, and 5 Asian countries in Norway. It was an impressive total.

However, when the Nordic Centers met for their annual meeting in March 1990, they were incensed that the EXCOM ". . . rather than support the symposia and the work we [the Nordic Centers] did in this connection was—if not directly hostile—then at least very reluctant to listen to our arguments and plans for the event."[148]

This feeling was further supported by both Harrie and Stenius that despite the turbulence in the Adelaide Congress in 1987, nothing had happened to change the pattern and leadership in the organization.

The Nordic Centers first decided to submit two changes in the Statutes: 1) disavowed any form of discrimination in its membership, especially racial and cultural, and 2) would allow only one (1) proxy to be held by any country. Both changes were later approved by the General Assembly in Stockholm.

In January 1990 Ramløse and Anette Nissen (Denmark) over a bottle of whiskey discussed all the election possibilities as well as the Secretary Generalship. Ramløse had an office and four expert employees. "Why not?" What about money? "Let's go to the Minister of Culture!" which Ramløse did on his return to Denmark. The next day they explained their plan to the Nordic Centers, and there was immediate total agreement. They worked on their plan from January to May, which accounts for the delay on their announcement via a circular.

The Nordic Centers next met in Stockholm the end of March, and at that time President Hildegard Bergfeld on invitation met with them, and they informed her that the Nordic Centers would be proposing Michael Ramløse for the office of Secretary General. However, she startled and angered them by urging them not to proceed, and to show respect for the work of Moudoués. Since Bergfeld had worked in Sweden as Artistic Director of the Kronoberg Teatern for many years, spoke excellent Swedish, and was considered politically progressive, her word carried considerable weight. However, Bergfeld had been handpicked, lobbied for, and supported by Rodenberg and the GDR to succeed Rodenberg as President of ASSITEJ in 1987.

In anger at this betrayal, Harrie responded to her: "We have heard what you said. There is nothing more to discuss. You can tell your friends in the E.C. that we will go ahead with this plan. Thank you for coming." Interesting enough, even though Bergfeld now knew two months ahead of time of Ramløse's decision to run for Secretary General as well as the plans of the Nordic Centers to continue their project as planned, it has been assumed that she never revealed that information to Moudoués or to Rodenberg,

Later upon meeting with the Danish Minister of Culture, Ramløse found not only did he agree, but wisely the Minister suggested that he approach the other ministers so that all five nations would support the concept, while also helping him bear the financial burden. It was done, but it wasn't a *fait accompli* until just 10 days or so before the opening of the Congress in Stockholm.

At the Stockholm Congress in May 1990 major changes were voted in. One week prior to this Congress the Symposia with 17 countries from around the world met, exchanged information, and were encouraged to form potential new centers. Attending the three Symposia were delegates from: Malawi, Tanzania, Zimbabwe, Uganda, Madagascar, and Zaïre in Africa; Chile, Columbia, Nicaragua, Argentine, Brazil, and Peru from Latin America; Sri Lanka, Thailand, India, Philippines, and Bangladesh from Asia, exclusive of Japan and Korea.

In the elections after 25 years of devoted volunteer service Rose-Marie Moudoués (France) was defeated as Secretary General, and Michael Ramløse (Denmark) was elected to succeed her. At the same time Paul Harman (Great Britain) was re-elected to continue as Treasurer for the next three years.

On a humorous note: the most popular mineral water in Sweden is labeled "Ramlösa". On the day before the elections an American noting the water bottles on every table in the Congress approached Ramløse saying "Michael—I just want to tell you that you are running a fantastic campaign." 149

At this Congress, three countries offered to host the 1993 Congress—Canada, Cuba, and the United States. It was felt by most delegates that it was time to return to North America. However, since Canada and the USA had co-hosted the Congress in 1972, both countries withdrew their invitations in deference to Cuba. The USA delegate (Oaks) received an ovation for supporting the Cuban Congress, particularly since the USA was currently boycotting Cuba, and such support was a contradiction of official USA foreign policy.

In the elections in Stockholm only eleven (11) countries were voted into the EXCOM: Australia (Michael FitzGerald), Czechoslovakia (Marian Lucky), Cuba (Eddy Socorro), FGR (Jurgen Flügge), France (Rose-Marie Moudoués), Italy (Franco Passatore), Japan (Yohei Hijikata), Portugal (João Luiz), Sweden (Mårtin Harrie), USA (Harold Oaks), and USSR (Adolf Shapiro), which made a total EXCOM of thirteen (13) with Denmark and Great Britain added.

Not elected were GDR (Christel Hoffman), Poland (Halina Machulska), Romania (Ion Lucian), Spain (Maria Navarro), Switzerland (Santuzza Oberholzer), and Yugoslavia (Zvjezdana Ladika). Lucky, Hijikata, Luiz, and Shapiro were the only new faces on the EXCOM, and it numbered only 13 instead of the Statute approved total of 17.

In the Bureau Adolf Shapiro (USSR) was elected President, with Michael FitzGerald (Australia), Harold Oaks (USA), and Eddie Socorro (Cuba) as Vice-Presidents. The fact that Shapiro was elected on a second ballot and won by only 1 vote indicates an ambivalent note of transition was being sounded, but Europe was still in charge.

In retrospect and upon close examination of the historic details, it becomes obvious that the "old guard" in the EXCOM realized that they were losing control of the Association, and to counter that loss they erected as many road blocks as possible. Also, they kept demanding that everything must go through and be approved by the EXCOM, and finally a member of the EXCOM needed to be in charge. This last request was true! Only it was Mårtin Harrie who ended up in charge, instead of Maria Navarro!

The next three years would provide major shifts in ASSITEJ policy, as well as a most welcome rapidity in communication and response, because of the activities of the new Secretary General. Not until 1993 with the election of Michael FitzGerald as President did ASSITEJ find itself on a completely new track, steering to the rapidly changing future with confidence. The cobwebs of familiarity and suffocating precedence had been wiped away completely.

CONCLUSION

This concludes Volume II of the History of ASSITEJ from 1976–1990. The first twenty-five years are now complete, and hopefully Volume III (1991–2005) will be published by 2012, but not in time for the XVIIth World Congress in Malmo, Sweden and Copenhagen, Denmark.

In the meantime, writing this History has continued to be a marvelous experience, and the authors feel fortunate to have been able among them to have attended all the World Congresses listed, as well as most of the EXCOMs.

Materials were difficult to come by for the latter half of Volume II from 1984 on. With the exception of Shaw there were few consistent witnesses and sometimes no Minutes of the various meetings in the Arizona archives. However, Shaw's handwritten "Notes" were a tremendous help, as were Harold Oaks' archives after his election to the EXCOM in 1987. Michael Ramløse was both formidable and generous in his accuracy in editing the manuscript, and Michael FitzGerald was a tremendous help in the details during the time of his involvement. With greater stability and permanent Secretariats in ASSITEJ from 1991 to 2005, Volume III should be easier to compile and write, as well as being more accurate. Approximately half of it is already in manuscript form.

We hope this History will continue to prove to be a balanced eye-witness and recorded account of the many events which shaped the international organization, but it will be up to future witnesses and scholars to continue this history after Volume III, and perhaps to add additional material to these volumes.

The three authors

Ann Shaw

Nat Eek

Katherine Krzys

APPENDIX A
Volume II

List of Officers and Honorary Members (1965-1990)

Presidents of ASSITEJ
1965 - 1968	Gerald Tyler (Great Britain)—2 terms
1968 - 1972	Konstantin Shakh-Azizov (USSR)—2 terms
1972 - 1975	Nat Eek (USA)—1 term
1975 - 1978	Vladimir Adamek (Czechoslovakia)—1 term
1978 - 1987	Ilse Rodenberg (German Democratic Republic)—3 terms
1987 - 1990	Hildegard Bergfeld (Federal Republic of Germany)—1 term

Vice-Presidents
1965 - 1968	Vladimir Adamek (Czechoslovakia)—2 terms
	Konstantin Shakh-Azizov (USSR)—2 terms
1968 - 1972	Vladimir Adamek (Czechoslovakia)—2 terms
	Nat Eek (USA)—2 terms
	Ilse Rodenberg (GDR)—2 terms
1972 - 1975	Vladimir Adamek (Czechoslovakia)—1 term
	Ilse Rodenberg (GDR)—3 terms
	Joyce Doolittle (Canada)—1 term
1975 - 1978	Ilse Rodenberg (GDR)—1 term
	Joyce Doolittle (Canada)—2 terms
	Maria Sunyer (Spain)—1 term
1978 - 1981	Joyce Doolittle (Canada)—3 terms (resigned in 1980)
	Maria Sunyer (Spain)—2 terms
	Natalya Satz (USSR)—1 term
1981 - 1984	Ann Shaw (USA)—1 term
	Maria Sunyer (Spain)—3 terms
	Eddy Socorro (Cuba)—1 term
1984 - 1987	Ann Shaw (USA)—2 terms
	Eddy Socorro (Cuba)—2 terms
	Nena Stenius (Finland)—1 term
1987 - 1990	Mårten Harrie (Sweden)—1 term
	Maria Navarro (Spain)—1 term
	Eddy Socorro (Cuba)—3 terms

Secretary General
1965 - 1990	Rose-Marie Moudoués (France)—25 years

Treasurers
1965 - 1968	José Géal (Belgium)—3 years

1968 – 1972	Ion Kojar (Romania)—4 years
1972 – 1987	Ion Lucian (Romania)—15 years
1987 – 1993	Paul Harman (Great Britain)—6 years

Honorary Presidents

As of 1966	Gerald Tyler (Great Britain)
As of 1972	Konstantin Shakh-Azizov (USSR)
As of 1981	Vladimir Adamek (Czechoslovakia)
As of 1984	Nat Eek (USA)
As of 1988	Ilse Rodenberg (Germany)

Honorary Members

As of 1975	Leon Chancerel (France)—posthumously
	Alexander Bryantsev (USSR)—posthumously
	Mila Milanova (Czechoslovakia)—posthumously
	Victor Ion Popa (Romania)—posthumously
	Charlotte Chorpenning (USA)—posthumously
As of 1978	Caryl Jenner (Great Britain)—posthumously
	Hans Rodenberg (GDR)—posthumously
	Sara Spencer (USA)—posthumously
As of 1981	Hans Snoek (Netherlands)
	Kaoru Ota-Ai (Japan)—posthumously
As of 1987	Maria Nieves Sunyer y Roig (Spain)

APPENDIX B
Volume II

Biographies of Principal Officers, Leaders, and Members (1976–1990)

Volume II has the biographies of members who were actively involved in ASSITEJ during these fifteen years. Leaders active during 1964–1975 are listed by name in alphabetical order, but their biographies will be found in Appendix B of Volume I.

Vladimir Adamek (Czechoslovakia[150]

Dr. Vladimir Adamek was born in Prague on 1 February 1921. He studied at the Conservatory of Prague and the Theater Institute of Moscow. He was an actor and director of the Army Theatre in 1945–46 and the Realist Theatre from 1951–57. He became the Artistic Director of the Jiří Wolker Theatre in Prague from 1957 to 1974 for which he directed many productions.

He was a Professor of Directing at the Academy of Arts in Prague. He wrote many articles and presented papers at conference on children's theatre, both in Czechoslovakia and abroad. He was Editor-in-Chief of many books and publications. He traveled abroad extensively, and was the organizer of many colloquies.

Adamek was a highly respected member of the children's theatre community by both the East and West. His Jiří Wolker Theatre did plays from both the East and the West with impeccable casts, and imaginative design, giving a theatrical experience to young people that was professional in every sense. As a person he was reserved, modest, had an excellent sense of humor, and was personally dedicated to the sense of the "art" in theatre. From the Western viewpoint he was able to skate the differences in the opposing "cold war" philosophies extremely well.

He was involved from the beginning in the creation of ASSITEJ (1960–63), and was appointed to the Preparatory Committee. His country was elected as a member of the first EXCOM, and he continued as its representative through the 1970s. He hosted the Ist International Congress of ASSITEJ in Prague in 1966. He was elected Vice-President for 4 terms (1966–1975), and was President from 1975–78. With Ján Kákoš he founded the National Center of Czechoslovakia, and served as its President from 1965–1973.

He received many awards and decorations—Honored Artist of Czechoslovakia, Prize of the Capital of Prague, etc. He died in Prague on 20 March 1990.

Helge Anderson (Norway)[151]

Helge Anderson received his Doctor of Drama from the University of Oslo. He is a dramaturge/producer at the Department of Drama at the Norwegian Broadcasting Corporation, where he has worked with radio drama for children and young people for ten years.

He is a member of the Norwegian Playwrights Society (Norske Dramatikers Forbund).

He has written plays for professional puppet theatre in Norway and for radio.

He has also worked as a theatre critic at the largest morning newspaper in Norway "Aftenposten", mainly on children's theatre and literature. He has written two books for children.

Hildegard Bergfeld (FGR)[152]

Hildegard Bergfeld went to Sweden with her husband, Günter Bergfeld, and worked at Unga Klara in Stockholm, Sweden, together with Suzanne Osten.

She then returned to Germany, and founded the Children's and Young People's Theater in Essen, one of the first to be established as a state theater in the late '70s and early '80s. She then returned to Sweden where she became Artistic Director of one theatre in Sweden as well as continuing her activity with her theater in Essen (FGR). While in Sweden, she wrote many translations of plays for young people.

She was a play director, as well as a translator of many plays on a high artistic level from Swedish to German and vice-versa. She initiated many exchanges between theatre artists in the international field. She was President of the FGR Center of ASSITEJ.

She was first elected to the Executive Committee of ASSITEJ in 1983, and then was elected President of ASSITEJ, serving from 1987 to 1990.

She died in November 1994.

Benito Biotto (Italy)[153]

Benito Biotto was born on 19 November 1927 at Moriago della Battaglia, Italy, and was a resident of Milan. He began his activities in children's theatre in 1953. In collaboration with the Angelicum, he established the first permanent professional theatre for children in 1957. In 1958 he began writing theatrical transcriptions for children on Italian Radio television. Then in 1964 he started making recordings of plays for children.

He promoted national Festivals of Plays for Children, and promoted many tours to Switzerland and performed in many play festivals in Venice. He was author of plays transmitted on television. He wrote many articles and publications. He attended the Constitutional Conference in Paris, France in 1965, and with Don Raffaello Lavagna established the Italian National Center in 1965. He took over as representative of the Italian National Center for ASSITEJ from Maria Signorelli, whose profession was primarily puppetry, and Don Rafaello Lavagna from the Vatican, whose interest was youth theatre and as a playwright. Bioto was a member of the EXCOM of ASSITEJ from 1966 to 1975, and attended all the International Conferences.

Biotto had his own professional company, Teatro dei Ragazzi, which performed primarily in Milan for young people. He invited ASSITEJ to hold its 3rd Congress in Venice, Italy in 1970, and was able to able to obtain funding from the Cini Foundation to support the meeting. That same Foundation supported the Preparatory Conference of ASSITEJ in 1964 which wrote the first Constitution for ASSITEJ.

He was a respected colleague, well organized, consistently cheerful, and participated fully in all the meetings and discussions.

Andrew Kingsnorth Bleby (Australia)[154]

Andrew Bleby was born near Adelaide in South Australia, and received a Bachelor of Arts and Diploma in Education from the University of Adelaide. He received a Diploma with Distinction in 2002 from the International Center for Culture and Management (ICCM) in Salzburg, Austria, and was Head of his class at their Summer Academy in Arts Management and International Project Workshop.

He has had 30 years of experience as well as an extensive record of success in senior management of the performing arts, theatre, festivals and events.

Bleby has directed six different arts festivals, four of them international. He was founding Director of Melbourne's Next Wave Festival in 1985. In all these positions he oversaw all aspects of management, programming, and marketing.

For ten years he was Program Director of the Adelaide Festival Centre, South Australia's major performing arts complex, producing and presenting a wide array of programs including significant international seasons, subscription series of contemporary dance and world theatre, community and education programs. He was a key member of the senior management team at the AFC, managed national tours, and was Executive Producer of several major musicals including *42nd Street*, *The King and I* and *South Pacific* in Australia, New York and Hong Kong. He has also produced spectacles, commercial drama, and circus shows.

He developed and produced several of Australia's biggest festivals, including one of the biggest ever—*Festival Melbourne 2006*, the award-winning (Helpmann Award 2006 "Best Special Event"), hugely successful free 12 million dollar Cultural Festival of the Melbourne 2006 Commonwealth Games, the largest fully curated arts festival ever held in Australia. This was followed by the *Festival of the 12th FINA World Championships*, a major free international festival held in Melbourne in March 2007. In 2009 he produced the newest sensation in Tasmania, the inaugural MONA Festival of Music and Art.

He has had extensive global experience in programming international artists and with international organisations including ASSITEJ, and AAPPAC *(Association of Asia-Pacific Performing Arts Centres)*, has been an invited keynote speaker at conferences in Shanghai, Vancouver, Dunedin, and Melbourne and has studied at the International Center for Culture and Management (ICCM) in Salzburg.

He was the Australian representative on the EXCOM of ASSITEJ from 1982-1987, during which time he promoted and helped create and develop the IXth World Congress of ASSITEJ in April 1987 in Adelaide.

Bleby has also undertaken significant work as an independent consultant, including a major review of *Opera Australia*, a review of the *Australian Performing Arts Market*, the production of a manual on youth festival management, strategic planning workshops for *The Push International Performing Arts Festival* in Canada and regional festivals in Australia, planning for the *National Institute of Circus Arts*, major project management for the *Australian Centre for the Moving Image*, and project development for the *Victorian Arts Centre, Orchestra Victoria* and festivals in several states. He has been a member of over thirty boards and committees.

He is now in demand from major clients around the country and overseas to undertake arts-based consultancies: project development, reviews, feasibility studies, planning, and festival management.

He currently lives in Melbourne, Australia and operates his own company, Andrew Bleby and Associates.

João Luiz Brites (Portugal)[155]

João Luiz was born in Porto, Portugal.

He began his career as an actor in the Experimental Theatre in Porto. From 1966 to 1975 he lived in Belgium as an exile. While there he was active as an assistant director and an actor in performances for a Portuguese audience. In 1968 he helped found the company *Clou dans la Langue*, and directed various performances in the Théâtre-Poéme in Brussels.

He returned to Portugal in 1975, where he founded and directed at the theatre *"Pé do vento"*, producing over 17 plays. He also founded the theatre Bando, whose production of *Alfonso Enrique*, seen at the Lisbon EXCOM Meeting was reported by Shaw as "excellent".

As a member of the Board of ASSITEJ/Portugal, he belonged to the Theatre Arts Council (Ministry of Culture), and was the national delegate to the Lyon Congress in 1981 and the Moscow Congress in 1984.

He was a member of the EXCOM of ASSITEJ from 1981–1987.

Léon Chancerel (France), I, p. 295.

Ian Cojar (Romania), I, p. 297.

Orlin Corey (USA), I, p. 297.

Elisabeth Cozona (Switzerland)
Elisabeth Corzona was on the EXCOM from 1978-1984.

Ljubiša Djokič (Yugoslavia), I, p. 298.

Joyce Doolittle (Canada)[156]
Prof. Joyce Doolittle was born in 1928 in the USA. She first taught child drama in Indiana, Wisconsin, and North Dakota. She was appointed to the faculty of the Department of Drama at the University of Calgary, where she initiated and taught first courses in Developmental Drama, Theatre for Children, Playwriting and Studies in Canadian Drama. She has acted in and directed over 100 plays, often in collaboration with well known Canadian composer-husband Quenten Doolittle.

She is co-author, with Zina Barnieh, of *A Mirror of Our Dreams—Children and the Theatre in Canada*, and was Drama Editor of the Red Deer Press for fifteen years. In 1972, she founded the Pumphouse Theatres, saving an historic, river-edge pumping station from demolition and helping raise over a million dollars to renovate it into two performing arts spaces, one of which bears her name. She returned to acting after retirement, winning an award for best actor for her performance of Mag in *The Beauty Queen of Leenane* at Alberta Theatre Projects (ATP).

Prof. Joyce Doolittle attended her first ASSITEJ meeting in Moscow in 1968 where she was appointed as an official observer. She served as Canada's official representative on the EXCOM from 1969–1978, and as Vice-President of ASSITEJ from 1972–1978. In 1972 she was Chairman of the IVth International Congress of ASSITEJ in Montreal, Canada.

As of this writing, she lives in Calgary, Alberta, Canada with her husband Quentin, a major Canadian contemporary composer, and continues in her acting career.

Nat Eek (USA)

Nat Eek [Nathaniel S. Eek] (PhD) was born on 16 October 1927 in Maryville, Missouri (USA). He obtained his degrees from the University of Chicago (PhB), Northwestern University (BS, MA), and Ohio State University (PhD). He taught theatre arts, children's theatre, art administration, and directed plays at the University of Kansas, Michigan State University, and the University of Oklahoma. He was Director of the School of Drama at the University of Oklahoma from 1962-1975, and then Dean of the College of Fine Arts from 1975-1991. He retired from the University of Oklahoma in 1993, and was named Regents Professor Emeritus of Drama and Dean Emeritus of Fine Arts.

He was the USA representative at the Founding Congress of ASSITEJ in Paris, France in 1965, and served on the Executive Committee from 1965-1975 at which time he retired from active participation in the international Association.

He was the USA representative to ASSITEJ, was twice elected as Vice-President from 1968-1972, and was elected President serving from 1972-75. In 1984 he was made an Honorary President of ASSITEJ. From 1988-1994 he was producer and director of the professional Southwest Repertory Theatre in Santa Fe, New Mexico.

During his career he directed over 100 plays, musicals, operas, and did the *mise en scene* of several ballets. He was a Board Member of the American Theatre Association, President of their national Children's Theatre Association, and President of the International Association of Fine Arts Deans. He was named a Fellow of the American Theatre in 1985.

He continues to be active in his professional associations, and began the writing of *The History of ASSITEJ* in 2002. His current address is in Santa Fe, New Mexico.

Egmont Elschner (FGR)[158]

Egmont Elschner was born in Jena, GDR, in 1947. He received his theatre education and training in West Berlin.

He was a Dramaturge and Director starting in 1969 in West Berlin, Frankfort, Munich and Dortmund. He was Head of Theatre in Dinslaken of Landesbühne im Kreis Wesel from 1983 when he succeeded Kathrin Türks. He also served as Head of Rheinisches Landestheater in Neuss from 1987 to 1992.

From 1975 to 1983 he was a Member of the Board of ASSITEJ/FGR, attended many of the Executive Committee meetings and Congresses, and worked closely with Kathrin Türks, Head of ASSITEJ/FGR at the time.

He currently is Head of the Studio for SAEK-Chemnitz TV and Radio, and lives in Chemnitz, Germany.

John English (Great Britain)[159]

John English was born in Dudley, Worcestershire, Great Britain on 13 January 1911.

He received his M.A. degree from Birmingham University, and had been educated at the Dudley Grammar School and Bishop Vesey's Grammar School, Sutton Coldfield.

Prior to going into the professional theatre in 1948, he was Production

Manager at Chance Bros. Ltd., Glass Works in Smethwick. He was married to Alicia Randle.

He was a member of the European Culture Commission Conferences, Member of the United Kingdom and National Council for UNESCO, and Special UNESCO Commission on Cultural matters in Jordan and Australia.

He was the Founder of the Highbury Theatre Centre in Sutton Coldfield, Founder and Managing Director of the Arena Theatre Company of Sutton Coldfield, Founder and Director of Arena Children's Theatre Company of Cannon Hill Trust, Midland Arts Centre for Young People, Birmingham Founder of Midland Arts Theatre Company. Author of many plays for children, some adult plays, and several adaptations.

For ASSITEJ he was Head of the Great Britain Delegation at the Ist International Conference in Prague, Czechoslovakia, and attended several Conferences after that. From 1972 on he was the Great Britain Representative for ASSITEJ.

As a well earned honor he was granted the Order of the British Empire.

He died in the 1990s.

Michael FitzGerald (Australia)[160]

Michael FitzGerald was born in Hobart, Tasmania on the third of October in 1936.

After obtaining a BA and a Diploma of Education from the University of Tasmania in 1957, FitzGerald was a High School Teacher of English, Modern History and Social Studies for some years. Both at University and during these teaching years, FitzGerald was an actor in Tasmania in the professional/amateur theatre movement (Pro/Am) then flourishing across Australia. He won a number of Awards in both acting and later directing. In his teaching he used the new methods of drama-in-education. These early experiences shaped FitzGerald's commitment to the place of theatre in the education and the cultural development of children and young people.

In the 1960s and '70s FitzGerald lived in different countries in Europe and the Middle East where he was a Teacher of English as a Foreign Language (TEFL). Later he settled in London and obtained a Post Graduate Diploma in TEFL. At this time, he continued to use drama-in-education methods in his work as well as involving companies and artists in the then burgeoning theatre-in-education movement, particularly in Great Britain.

Upon his return to Australia in 1975, FitzGerald became an arts administrator and bureaucrat at the Australia Council, the Australian Federal Government's Arts Advisory and Funding Body. He joined the Theatre Board as the Youth/Puppetry Project Officer, and over the ten years became its Senior Project Officer and finally Director. This period was a major time in the development of a distinct Australian theatre culture which saw the establishment of major theatre companies across the country. These included Australia's first theatre-in-education companies. FitzGerald was a significant supporter of this development.

In 1985 FitzGerald was appointed Director of the IXth ASSITEJ World Congress and General Assembly which was held in Adelaide in 1987. Also in 1985 he became Australia's representative on the ASSITEJ Executive Committee, and attended his first meeting in Šibenik, Yugoslavia that year. In 1990 he became a Vice President of ASSITEJ, and in 1993 he was elected President. He was re-elected President in 1996, and held this office for a total of six years.

Concurrently with his ASSITEJ work and after the Adelaide Congress, he became Artistic Director of the *Come Out Festival*, Australia's premier youth arts festival, until 1991. He then became Director of Youth Performing Arts Australia (YPAA) and ASSITEJ Australia until his retirement in 1999. Since his retirement he has continued his involvement as a youth arts consultant.

Throughout his working life, FitzGerald has been a prime force in the promotion and development of theatre for children and young people at national and international levels. In 1989 FitzGerald was appointed as a Member of the Order of Australia (AM) for services to youth arts and arts administration.

In 1994 he was presented with The Frannie Arts for Young Audiences Award for his outstanding contribution in the field of arts for Young Audiences from The Canadian Institute of the Arts for Young Audiences, Vancouver, B.C.

In 2002 he was made an Honorary President of ASSITEJ International in recognition of his extraordinary work as President of ASSITEJ International (1993–1999) and in the service of theatre for children and young people.

Jürgen Flügge (FGR)[161]

Jürgen Flügge was born in 1944 in Darmstadt, Germany.

From 1967–1972 he studied Theatre Science and Literature in Munich. From 1972–1977 he was the Dramaturge in Frankfort (TAT, Schauspielehaus), Munich (Theater der Jugend), and Stuttgart (Staatstheater).

From 1976–1979 he was a member of the group "Rote Grütze" in Berlin; Director, Dramaturge, and co-author of "Was heisst hier Liebe"

As of 1980 he was Director of the Theater der Jugend in Munich, Art-Director of the festivals "Schauspiele 1985/86" and "Schauspiele 1988 Theatre of the World." Since 1989 he was Director of "Württembergische Landesbühne Esslingen." From 1993–1994 he was General Director of the state theater at Braunschweig.

He has directed various plays for children and young people as well as adults. He is Chairman of the German ASSITEJ, and one of the Vice-Presidents of the EXCOM of ASSITEJ International.

Jean-Yves Gaudrault (Canada)[162]

Jean-Yves Gaudrault was born on the 15 August 1943 in La Malbaie, Québec, Canada.

In 1966 he played many roles in the Théâtre Populaire du Québec, for the Théâtre du Nouveau Monde, and others. In 1968 he was Founder and Artistic Director of the Théâtre des Pissenlits, and President of the Compagnie du Théâtre des Pissenlits in Montreal. He had experience in cultural animation in Jonquière. He has toured Romania, Yugoslavia, Czechoslovakia, the Soviet Union, GDR, France, as well as other countries. He was the staging director for many plays for children.

He participated in many Congresses, was a Member of the Canadian Delegation. He attended the session of the EXCOM in Italy in 1976, and of the Bureau in Montreal in 1977. He was a member of the Canadian Center for ASSITEJ, and Co-President with Joyce Doolittle in 1977.

José Géal (Belgium), I, p. 299.

Victor Georgiev (Bulgaria)[163]

Victor Georgiev was born in Plovdiv, Bulgaria on 8 May 1919. He finished his studies at the Academy of Theatre Art, and began his acting career at the National Theater of Sophia. He was appointed Director of the Theater of Young People in Sophia in 1966. He was Founder and Host of the International Festivals of Theatres for Children and Youth in Sophia, hosting in 1968, 1972, and 1976. He has performed in many foreign countries.

He was made a Member of the EXCOM of ASSITEJ in 1968, having established the Bulgarian National Center one year before and was serving as its President. He was widely recognized and respected as an excellent actor in the National Theatre of Bulgaria.

After the political change in the late 1980s, his theatre was shut down, and perhaps because of this he died soon after.

His awards include Artist of the People, and the G. Dimitrov Prize Laureate.

Hanswalter Gossmann (FGR), I, p. 300.

Paul Harman (United Kingdom)[164]

Paul Harman was born in 1940. After four years at Birmingham University acting such parts as Laertes in *Hamlet* and Lucky in *Waiting for Godot*, he gave up studying Russian and started work as a professional actor in 1963. However, playing small character parts in the standard repertory of the time did not entirely satisfy his desire to make theatre accessible to everyone and to be of some social usefulness. By 1966 he joined the pioneering Theatre in Education (TIE) team at Belgrade Theatre, Coventry, and with them he began a 42-year career creating and directing over 100 plays for young audiences.

After similar TIE experiments in Liverpool with the Everyman Theatre, he founded and became Artistic Director of Merseyside Young People's Theatre (now Fuse Theatre) from 1978 to 1989. There he commissioned Willy Russell to write the original version of a play about the English class system, and later the highly successful musical, *Blood Brothers*.

From 1994 to his retirement in 2008 he was Artistic Director of the Cleveland Theatre Company (CTC) in Darlington, North East England, creating a repertoire of plays from improvising with actors, from new commissions, and from international sources, such as Germany, Holland, and Canada. About 250 performances are given each year, mostly in schools in the region.

CTC received invitations to take productions to nine countries during that time, and for some years there was also a successful program of theatre events for young people in museums as well as open air productions of Shakespeare in local parks with the region's resident professional actors.

Since 1994 he has, as part of the company's annual program, directed the annual Takeoff Festival of professional theatre for young audiences to celebrate the best of United Kingdom theatre for young audiences, as well as to introduce them to overseas companies with ideas new to the United Kingdom.

He has directed plays in Poland and Russia, and translated plays from both French and German. He is currently performing with Sylvie Bloch of the French company Pointure 23 in C(H)AT, a bilingual play for children about the one thousand year old love-hate relationship between France and England.

Because of his service to the United Kingdom Center of ASSITEJ, he was named Honorary Life President in 2006. He served ASSITEJ as International Treasurer from 1987–1993, and was elected again to the Executive Committee for 2008–2011.

Mårten Harrie (Sweden)[165]

Mårten Harrie received his high school diploma in 1961. As a youth he performed in theatre during the holidays at the Arena Theatre in Stockholm. After high school he practiced as a technician and Assistant Director at the Malmo Statsteater.

He studied further at Axel Witzansky's Theatre Acting School in Stockholm, with additional courses at Dramatiska Institute in Stockholm. He has had theatrical experiences at many theatres in Sweden, as well as Swedish Radio, Television, and Film.

He is a professional actor, director, playwright, technician, and dramaturge. He has directed about 80 plays for children and youth, 10 plays for theatre, and 5 scripts for film.

He has worked in the theatre for over 25 years, and for 14 years has been a Producer and Director for the Children and Youth Theatre Group at Östgötateatern in Norrköping.

He has been a member of ASSITEJ/Sweden since it was started in 1980, both as a Vice-President and President. He served as a member of the Executive Committee of ASSITEJ from 1987–1993.

Shaun Hennessey (United Kingdom)[166]

Shaun Hennessey worked for Theatre Centre for many years. Starting in 1983 he represented the United Kingdom as its ASSITEJ representative. He was elected to its Executive Committee in 1984. He continued in that capacity until he stepped down in 1987. As a member of the Executive Committee he was given the additional title and responsibility as Financial Officer, and was responsible for handling the transfer of ASSITEJ funds from the Paris Secretariat to its new bank in London. In this capacity he also saw that the Financial Statements were accurate and distributed widely.

After he left the Theatre Centre, he worked for Milton Keynes for several years as an arts officer. He was director in a range of local authority positions until his untimely death in 1989.

His wife Sue has since remarried, and their son Ben, graduated from Sheffield University, and is currently working for Milton Keynes.

Yohei Hijikata (Japan)[167]

Yohei Hijikata was born in Japan in 1927. His father, Yoshi Hijikata, was one of the leaders of the "New Play" movement, which was started around the 1990s to create modern plays in Japan, in contrast to the old style Kabuki theatre. In 1924 he founded with his colleague the Tsukiji Small Theatre in Tokyo as their pilot work, and later his young son Yohei was proud of being a member of its pioneering children's troupe.

Before long, however, Yohei had to spend much of his childhood in Russia and France with his parents who took political asylum away from Japan, which made him a trilinguist.

Through the 1950s, he worked to develop youth cultural movements in Japan. In 1966 he joined Theatre Seinen Gekijo to work in translating and producing various foreign plays for young people, such as E. Schwarz's *Dragon* and *The Naked King*. He later became this theatre's Chief Producer, and continuing in that position until 1997. He was then nominated as Advisor to the Theatre.

In 1983 he was elected to the Executive Committee of ASSITEJ/Japan, and in 1990 became a member of the Executive Committee of ASSITEJ International, remaining in that position until 1996.

In 1998 he received the Art & Culture Award Chevalier from the French Ministry of Culture for his lifelong service in the field of youth theatre.

He died of cancer on 21 January 2010 at the age of 82.

Vicky Ireland (Great Britain)[168]

Vicky Ireland was trained at the Central School of Speech and Drama, London, where she received her Teaching Diploma in English and Drama. At the University of London she received a Diploma in Dramatic Art.

She is an actress, staging director, playwright, and artistic director. After her training she joined the newly formed Theatre-in-Education team at the Belgrade Theatre. She has worked as an actress in TIE all over Great Britain. She has also appeared in various television programs for children, and presented BBC TV's award-winning schools program *Words and Pictures* for twelve years.

As a playwright she has authored over twelve original plays, as well as adapted works of other authors for the stage. She has won awards for her work both in radio and television, and received a Writer's Guild of Great Britain nomination for best children's program.

She wrote and directed original children's productions for five years at Regent's Park Open Air Theatre, and was an international guest director in Russia and Cypress. In 2001 she directed *Playing from the Heart* for the Royal Lyceum Theatre in Edinburgh, which was part of the Scottish International Children's Theatre Festival, which toured both the Highlands and the Islands of Scotland.

She has taken productions to the Ukraine, Spain, Singapore, Finland, and the United Arab Emirates, has been a guest speaker in Israel and Hungary, and held drama workshops in the Philippines and Cyprus.

She has represented Great Britain at Children's Theatre Festivals in Australia, Sweden, Russia, Cuba, Peru, Israel, Norway, Japan, Poland, Denmark, Brazil, Korea, and Canada.

From 1989-2002 she was Artistic Director of the Polka Theatre for Children where she directed and produced over 60 productions. She commissioned three original plays, all of which won Writer's Guild of Great Britain nominations.

From 1996-2002 she was International Representative of ASSITEJ/United Kingdom, and a member of the EXCOM of ASSITEJ. From 1999-2002 she served as the Treasurer of ASSITEJ.

She continues as an active panel member, was a guest of the Japan Foundation and ASSITEJ/Japan to study Children's Theatre and primary education in Tokyo and

Osaka, and in 2007 took part in a plenary seminar on Theatre and Education in Okinawa.

She also continues to write and direct plays for Polka Theatre, the Stephen Joseph Theatre, Scarborough, and the Queen's Theatre, Hornchurch. She will tour a new production for Arts Depot for three 5-year-old youngsters in the fall of 2009.

She was awarded the Member of the British Empire (M.B.E.) medal in Queen Elizabeth's Jubilee Birthday Honors list 2002 for her services to children's drama, and in 2008, she was elected a Fellow of the Royal Society for the Arts.

Currently in Great Britain she is Vice-Chair of Action for Children's Arts; Co-Director of A Thousand Cranes Theatre; Patron of the Polka Theatre for Children; and Deputy International Representative for ASSITEJ/United Kingdom.

Caryl Jenner (Great Britain), I, p. 301.

David Johnston (Great Britain)[169]

David Johnston, as a member of the British Theatre Centre, succeeded Shaun Hennessey as the Head of the British delegation to ASSITEJ, and served on the Executive Committee from 1987 to 1988 as a financial representative.

He left the Theatre Centre in 1987, free-lancing in theatre at home and abroad. He took over Roundabout at the Nottingham Playhouse from 1991–1998, and then started freelancing again.

He continued his involvement with ASSITEJ until 1998.

In 2003 he set up Tangere Arts with a group of friends, the main purpose of this group was to create work for children in Morocco. He continues his involvement in theatre working with Michael Ramløse (Denmark) and Galya Kolosova (Russia). He hopes to attend the next ASSITEJ Congress in Copenhagen/Malmo in 2011.

Inga Juul (Denmark)[170]

Mrs. Inga Juul was born in Odense, Denmark on 25 October 1928. She studied at the University of Copenhagen, and did specialized study in children's theatre in Great Britain and Scotland, and all over Europe. She came to Dansk Skolescene in 1963, and created a division that produced regular professional performances for children. From 1968 on performances were given for various age groups of young people in "Inga Juul's Børnetheater."

She gave lectures, wrote articles, and made translations of plays for children and youth. She headed workshops and seminars for teachers and students. With two others she founded the Danish Drama Teachers' Society in 1968. She also founded and built a private library with archives covering children's and youth theatres from all over the world, open to interested specialists.

She attended the Constitutional Conference in 1965, the Congresses since 1966, and many of the EXCOM meetings. She was appointed an Advisor to the EXCOM from 1968 to 1972. She died in the 1990s.

Ladislav Knižátko (Czechoslovakia)[171]

Ladislav Knižátko graduated from the High Theatre School, and later became an actor, stage director, and theatre director at the P. Bezruč Theatre, Ostrava. Since

1977 he was President of the Czech Center for ASSITEJ, and since 1981 a member of the EXCOM of ASSITEJ. He was replaced by Marián Lucky in 1990.

He currently is Deputy Director of the Cultural Center at Ostrava, responsible for the artistic and creative work of the theatre groups "Divadlo v kufru" (Luggagetheatre) and "Kruh" (The Circle) which tour permanently to schools and cultural houses in both parts of the Czech Republic, where they present their program.

The group of P. Bezruč Theatre Ostrava has been touring for several seasons with a musical play for children based on the novel of Mark Twain *Tom Sawyer's Adventures*, a successful play which was prepared and directed by Knížátko.

His professional interest is concentrated and addressed in the artistic interpretation of presentation of dramatic texts in the theatre for children and young people.

Galina Kolosova (USSR)[172]

Mrs. Galina Kolosova was born on 11 May 1940 in Moscow. She graduated in 1965 from Moscow State University majoring in the Department of Philology specializing in Romantic and Germanic Languages and Literature. She worked for the Soviet Women's Committee (International Department) as of 1969 at the Pan-Russian Theatrical Society. She functioned as Secretary and Translator for the Soviet Center of ASSITEJ from 1969, and attended many sessions of the EXCOM and Congresses from 1970 on.

In 1975 she was invited to join the Theatre Association of Russia (STD) where she was designated Secretary of the Soviet ASSITEJ Center (later ASSITEJ/Russia), whose main task was the development of international relations for 60 Russian professional repertory companies for young spectators.

While in that position she organized and coordinated the committee that was responsible for the VIIIth (Moscow) and XIIth (Rostov-on-Don) World Congresses of ASSITEJ and their corresponding Festivals. She remained in that position until 1996.

Since 1980 she has been a translator of English, American, Canadian, and French plays into Russian, and these translations have been performed in Moscow, Rostov-on-Don, Oryol, Nizhny Novgorod, and many other cities in Russia and CIS.

She initiated and coordinated the first Russian International Theatre Festivals for children and young people (MINIFEST) in Rostov-on-Don (1989, 1991, 1993, 1995, and 1996). With her Netherlands counterparts, she organized in Russia the first International Seminar for Theatre Managers which dealt with problems of marketing and management (1990, 1991, and 1992).

She created a special volume of the leading theatre magazine based in Moscow entitled *Theatre Life (Teatralnaya Zhizn)* dedicated to problems of survival of theatres for young spectators in new Russian and to ASSITEJ activities (published July 1996).

From 1996 to 2000, she was a member of the Advisor's Council of *Theatre Life* Magazine, a member of the "George Soros" Foundation (Open Society Institute) as an expert on cultural programs, a member of the editorial Board of the new Moscow Quarterly *Theatre for Children and Young People* (affiliated with *Contemporary Playwriting* Magazine), and Advisor to the EXCOM of ASSITEJ.

Since 2000 she has been Projects Coordinator with English-speaking countries for the Organizing Committee of the Moscow Chekhov International

Theatre Festival, a member of the Theatre Association of Russian, and a member of the EXCOM of ASSITEJ/Russia.

Fusako Kurahara (Japan)[173]

At the age of 5, Fusako Kurahara was taken to see a traditional *Noh* play by her grandmother, a theatre experience which became a part of her life forever.

She studied English and Psychology (counseling) at the international division of Sophia University. She then taught English at the Kyoritsu Girls' High School in Tokyo for 14 years.

During the 1970s she help translate a pamphlet "Children's Theatre in Japan" into English, which led her to become involved in the Japanese Center for ASSITEJ.

In 1983 she became the Secretary of ASSITEJ/Japan, and they were visited by a delegation from ASSITEJ/USA, which was their first formal visitation by members from another ASSITEJ Center. This eight person delegation, led by Dr. Ann Shaw as Vice-President of ASSITEJ, had just returned from China in search of a play performance to bring to the New Orleans, Louisiana World's Exposition in the USA in 1984. As a result of this visit Shaw became known to the Japanese Center as their "Shoguness"!

From this beginning ASSITEJ/Japan became very much involved in the affairs of ASSITEJ, developing international theatrical exchange through meetings, festivals, and Congresses, and as a result of their hard work, they were elected to serve on the ASSITEJ Executive Committee, with Kurahara as their translator.

In 1987 at the Adelaide International Congress of ASSITEJ, she saw the plays of David Holman (Great Britain), one was "Small Poppies", and she asked permission to do translations of his plays into Japanese. As a result of his approval many Japanese children have been enjoying his plays. "Small Poppies" performed by Theatre Nakama received the Best Children's Play of the Year Award in 1998, and had been performed 175 times by 2002.

She retired as Secretary of ASSITEJ/Japan in 1997. Currently she is helping the Kijo Picture Book Village on Kyushu Island to invite foreign theatre groups to visit each year. They also hold workshops for children and young people there.

As a result of her teaching, recently one of her students is planning to host a theatre workshop for children in his town, after being a student at her Workshop in Kijo. He is now 21 and interested in the theatre as a profession.

She feels that theatre for young people is blessed work, a joy which makes children happy, which in turn lets those children convey that joy to others "like flying seeds of a dandelion."

Kazuto Kurihara (Japan)[174]

Kazuto Kurihara graduated from the Art Division of Nihon University in 1939. He worked as an assistant and an instructor in actor-training at various colleges. While writing, dramatizing, and directing plays for children, he helped establish the Association of Children's Playwrights in 1948. Later this Association became known as the Japan Children's Theatre Association, Inc. In 1958 he became the Association's first President, and remained so until his death in 1994.

In 1955 he was appointed a Judging Committeeman for the Art Festival sponsored by the Governmental Agency for Cultural Affairs. In 1974 this same Agency appointed him a Project Commissioner for its Children's Art Theatre.

In 1979 the Japan Center for ASSITEJ was established, and he became its first President until his death. In 1984 he was elected a Member of the Executive Committee of ASSITEJ International, and continued in that capacity until 1990. Also, in 1984 he became a member of the Board of Directors for ITI, continuing until 1992.

In 1985 the first all Japan Children's Performing Arts Festival was held on Sado Island. He became Head of the Festival, and chaired the International TYA Symposium with 12 countries attending. As President of ASSITEJ/Japan, he was eager to develop international exchange, especially among Asian countries.

During his presidency the Japan Center held several TYA meetings in Japan with many Asian colleagues attending. In 1988 the first Asian TYA Meeting was held on Shoudo Island; in 1989 the 1989 Asian TYA Symposium was held in Tokyo and Koufu; in 1991 the Japan-Sea Rim TYA Meeting was held. And in 1993 to facilitate the spread of information, the Asian TYA Newsletter "CURTAINS UP!" was issued by the Japan Center.

After a rich and active life in the theatre, Kurihara died at the age of 83 in 1994.

Zvjezdana Ladika (Yugoslavia)[175]

Mme. Zvjezdana Ladika was born in Karlovac, Croatia 1921, but moved to Varazdin in her early childhood where she received her secondary-school education. At the University of Zagreb, she completed the studies of the literatures of the nations— the former Yugoslavia, French language and literature, and Russian language and literature.

After graduation, she spent a short time teaching at a secondary school, but resigned in order to study directing at the Film Studio, which she completed in 1950. In addition, she graduated in staging from the Academy of Dramatic Arts in Zagreb.

After her second graduation, she found employment at the Zagreb Theatre for Young People as both a director and theatrical educator. It was there that she staged Shakespeare's *Romeo and Juliet* as her graduation piece. Over the years, she staged more than a hundred performances for and with children and young people at the same theatre.

In the year 1956 she went on a study tour to Prague and in 1960 to France where theatre for children developed as creative dramatics for children and young people.

With her plays she took part in numerous theatre festivals throughout Europe. Her international theatre exchange also included an exchange with the professional theatre for children and young people in Brno (Prague, Bratislava, Brno, 1956).

Mme. Ladika published a large number of writings on children's dramatic creativity—in her own book *The Child and the Dramatic Art*, and as a co-author of the books *Theatrical Plays; The Child and Creativity;* and *I'm Bored, I Don't Know What to Do*. She published her writings in professional periodicals and publications in Croatia and abroad.

She was a long-standing member of the ASSITEJ Executive Committee, where she left an indelible imprint through her activity and influenced the development of the world's theatre for children and young people. As a result she was named an

Honorary Member of ASSITEJ in 1996. She was one of the founders of the *Mala Scena* Theatre in 1989, where she was active as a director, writer, and head of its drama studio.

Mme. Ladika received numerous rewards for her artistic work, the most important of them being *Young Generation* in 1972 for direction of the play *Tomcat Genghis Khan and Miki Trasi*; an award from the Dramatic Artists' Society for direction in 1984; *Dubravko Dujsin* Award in 1988 for her long productive theatrical work with children and young people at the Zagreb Theatre for Young People; and the *Vladimir Nazor* Life Achievement Award.

She died on 17 August 2004 at the age of 82.

Don Raffaello Lavagna (Vatican, Italy)[176]

Raffaello Lavagna was born on 22 October 1918 in Savona, Italy.

As a Roman Catholic priest he was responsible for the theatrical programs of the Vatican Radio, and of the recording section of the Vatican.

He was active in the field of education, organizer of religious theatre in Italy (Carro de Tespi), a staging director, and an author of numerous articles and presenter of plays.

He participated in 1963 in the early consultations on the creation of ASSITEJ, and in 1964 participated in the work of the Preparatory Committee in Venice, Italy.

He represented Italy at the Constitutional Conference of ASSITEJ in 1965, attended sessions of the Provisional Committee in 1966, and was on the EXCOM in 1968, 1976, and 1977. With Benito Biotto he co-founded the Italian Center for ASSITEJ. He attended many of the International Congresses.

Much later he was elevated to Monsignor in the Roman Catholic Church. He is currently retired in Italy at the age of 92.

Wolker D. Laturell (FGR)[177]

Wolker D. Laturell was born on 22 May 1939 in Tübingen, Germany. He attended schools in Konstanz, Rottenburg, Munich, Zurich, and Pfarrkirchen.

Since 1970 he has been a Member of the Parliament of Upper Bavaria (engaged in Cultural Affairs), as well as a member of several cultural associations, and committees. From 1969–1973 he taught at Otto Falckenberg School in Munich. Since 1974 he has lectured at the University Extension in Munich.

He is the author of plays for youth since 1956, of books *Theater und Jugend in München (1969)*, *Kinder und Jugendtheater als Sozialisztionsagentur—Emanzipation oder Manipulation?*, as well as numerous brochures, essays, articles about children's theatre and the history of Munich, Editor of *Informationen* of the Theatre for Youth Munich (1964–69. He was Administrative Director "Münchner Kammerspiele" and Theatre for Youth in Munich (1962–74). He organized International Festivals of Children and Youth Theatre in Munich (1967, 1971).

For ASSITEJ in 1968 he was a member of the ASSITEJ Committee for Exhibitions. Since 1966 he has participated in several Congresses and EXCOM Meetings. He was co-founder with Hans Gossmann of the FGR Center in 1966, and was its Secretary and Treasurer until 1974. In 1967 he was founder and director of the Central-Archives of Munich, from which structure he organized international exhibitions in 1967, 1971, etc., and publishes "Dokumente zum Theater für Kinder une Jugentliche (1973-). He was also Editor of the "Mitteilungen" form 1968-74.

Sara Lee Lewis (Canada)[178]

Sara Lee Lewis (née Levitan) was born in Montréal, Québec in 1937. In 1958 she received a BA degree in English from McGill University. She served as Features Editor for the McGill Daily campus newspaper, launching a lifetime enthusiasm for actively promoting cultural events.

Upon graduation she spent a year as editor of a community weekly, leaving to co-found Le Centre de Disque, Montreal's first commercial lending library for recordings. During her twelve-year marriage to Sam Gesser, who was to become one of Canada's leading impresarios, she partnered in presenting traditional and contemporary regional and international folk music artists, and honed her interest in ethno-musicology.

Lewis moved to Wolfville, Nova Scotia, Canada in 1971 with her three children, and married Herbert Lewis, a professor of Philosophy at Acadia University. Seeking to broaden the limited arts experiences available at that time to the children in her community, she co-founded Mermaid Theatre of Nova Scotia in 1972. Her partners in this venture were the late Evelyn Garbary, a Welsh-born Professor of Drama at the University, who sought to provide professional opportunities for her graduating students, and Tom Miller, an American arts consultant to the local school board, who wished to explore new techniques that could benefit the region's teachers.

Today Mermaid Theatre ranks among North America's most respected theatres for family audiences. Based in Windsor, Nova Scotia since 1987, the company is best known for its innovative adaptations of children's literary classics which incorprate stunning puppets, striking scenic effects, and evocative original music. Mermaid Theatre performs annually for 200,000 spectators, offers its productions in seven languages, has played for more than four million spectators on four continents, and is recognized as a leading cultural ambassador for Nova Scotia and for Canada. Lewis continues to serve as Mermaid Theatre's Managing Director, with her primary focus directed to the development of export markets as well as the promotion of unique entertainment for very young children.

During Mermaid Theatre's early years, Lewis worked with Tom Miller to co-found the Nova Scotia International Puppet Festival, based at Acadia University from 1974-1980, and has continued her involvement with UNIMA throughout her career.

She took an active role in ASSITEJ activities both nationally and internationally. She served on the Board of ASSITEJ/Canada (1977,1979), attended the VIth International Congress of ASSITEJ in Madrid, Spain in 1978 as a member of the Canadian delegation, was President of ASSITEJ/Canada from 1980-1982, and served on the Executive Committee of ASSITEJ from 1979-1984. She was also a member of the Canadian delegation to the VIIth International Congress in Lyon, France in 1981.

During her fifty-year career in arts management, Lewis has served with regional, national, and international organizations in related fields, and is active in film promotion in her community.

In recognition of her contributions, she was awarded a Canada Council "A" grant in 1989, a Cultural Life Award (Cultural Federations of Nova Scotia) in 1993, and was named a Member of the Order of Canada (her country's highest civilian honor) in April 2000. In November 2000 she received the Progress Club Women of Excellence Award in the category of Arts and Culture. Then in the Spring of 2001 received a D.Litt. (honoris causa) from Saint Mary's University in Halifax, and in the Fall of 2002 was the recipient of the Queen's Jubilee Medal. Lewis was awarded The Deep Roots Music Festival Valley Arts Award in 2005, and in 2009 accepted the Nova Scotia theatre community's Merritt Legacy Award.

Lewis continues to reside in Wolfville, Nova Scotia, Canada, a vibrant community of 6500.

Ion Lucian (Romania)[179]

Ion Lucian was born on 22 April 1924 in Bucharest, Romania. He received his Baccalaureate Degree in the Humanities from the Royale Academy of Arts.

He is a noted actor, stage director, and playwright. He was a Professor at the Royale Academy of Arts and Hyperion University in Bucharest. He is so well known as a major performer that strangers stop him on the street to praise and congratulate him.

He was Founder and Manager of the Ion Creanga Theater in 1964. Since 1965 he has been President of the Romanian Center for ASSITEJ, and continues to this day. He served ASSITEJ International as its Treasurer for fifteen years from 1972 to 1987. He was on the ASSITEJ Executive Committee from 1966 to 1990.

Since 1990 he has been the Manager of the Excelsior Theater in Bucharest, and is currently the Supervisor on the construction of a new 11-story building which will house the Excelsior Theater. He continues to perform with the National and Comedy Theaters, and has directed plays in Romania, Italy, Belgium, Canada, Japan, France, and Israel.

Plays for which he is noted include: *The Disobedient Little Cock*, *Free Voice*, *The Musketeers of Her Majesty*, *Donkey*, *Cinderella*, and *Tales With Masks* (for young people), and *Fight Against TA-GA-TA*, *Humorous Variations*, and *Humorous Sluts* (for adults). He performed in his play *Tales with Masks* at the IVth International Congress in Canada/USA to universal acclaim. He has also written translations of the plays of Moliere, Goldoni, Feydeau, and Labiche among others.

He has received many distinctions: the Title of Honored Artist of Romania, a Member of Honor of the Romanian National Theater, the Order of Cultural Merit, an Officer of the French Legion of Honor, and a Chevalier of the Cultural Order. He has also received the Cultural Merit Medal-First Class for his artistic and cultural achievements.

Marian Lucky (Czechoslovakia)[180]

Marian Lucky worked for his degree from Comenius University in Bratislava from 1969–1975. Since 1974 he has been working in the theatres for children as a dramaturge and a psychologist. His activity is concentrated on the scientific work—researches in the field of the young audience.

He is tutor to works on the theme of Children's Theatre at the High Academy of the Arts and Philosophical Faculty.

He is an actor, musician, and also the author of several plays for children presented in theatres, on radio broadcasts, and television.

He is an organizer of Festivals of Theatres for Children.

Since 1974 he has actively worked for ASSITEJ. In 1988 he became President of the Czechoslovakian Center for ASSITEJ, and has been a member of the EXCOM.

From 1991–1992 he worked in the Ministry of Culture of the Slovak Republic as Vice-Director of the Arts Department. Since November 1992 he has been the dramaturge in Theatre for Children and Deputy Director in the National Theatre Center.

João Luiz (Portugal)[181]

João Luiz was born in Porto, Portugal.

He began his career as an actor in the Experimental Theatre in Porto. From 1966 to 1975 he lived in Belgium as an exile. While there he was active as an assistant director and an actor in performances for a Portuguese audience. In 1968 he helped found the company *Clou dans la Langue*, and directed various performances in the Théâtre-Poéme in Brussels.

He returned to Portugal in 1975, where he founded and directed at the theatre *"Pé do vento"*, producing over 17 plays.

As a member of the Board of ASSITEJ/Portugal, he belonged to the Theatre Arts Council (Ministry of Culture), and was the national delegate to the Lyon Congress in 1981 and the Moscow Congress in 1984.

He was a member of the EXCOM of ASSITEJ from 1987 to 1990.

Halina Machulska (Poland)[182]

Halina Machulska, a stage director, was born on 3 April 1929 in Lodz, Poland. She graduated from the State Higher School of Pedagogy in Lodz in 1954, and in 1958 took an examination in acting in Warsaw. In 1971 she received a diploma in stage-directing from the State Higher School of Dramatic Art in Warsaw.

Since 1955 she has been performing in the theatres of Lodz and Warsaw, among others. She has played in about 50 productions of Polish and foreign plays of such authors as Zeromski, Slowacki, Durenmatt, Joyce, Brecht, Euripides, Miller, Gorki, and Dostoyevsky. She has received awards for her roles of Sybilla in *The Red Magic* by Ghelderode and of Bertha in *Exiles by Joyce*.

Together with her actor and director husband Jan, she has organized experimental studios (Reduta 61 in Lublin and the Studio Stage in Lodz). In 1970 she and Jan formed Teatr Ochoty—the Center of Theatre Culture in Warsaw, which is comprised of a professional theatre company and a 3-year studio for young drama instructors.

The professional stage of Teatr Ochoty has witnessed most of her directing achievements. They include: *Monserrat* by E. Robles, *Personal Matter* by K. Oe, *Wild Gretta* by S. Grochowiak, *I Went Straight On* by E. Stachura, *In the Garden* by Edward Albee. In Lodz, *The Maidens' Vows* by A. Fredro (Bydgoszcz). In her repertory have been plays for children: *Rasmus and the Tramp* by A. Lindgren, *The Adventures of Winnie the Pooh* and *The Search of the Little One* by A.A.Milne, *Toto* by E. Bryll, and *Fire! Fire!* by W. Chotomska. The plays for children have been presented in a run of *Children for Children* performances with children from the Drama Studio as actors.

Besides her acting and directing, she is a lecturer in The Pedagogic School in

Lublin, the Higher School of Dramatic Art in Lodz, and the Studio of Stage-Directing at the Faculty of Pedagogic, Warsaw University.

Marjorie E. MacLean (Canada)[183]

Marjorie E. MacLean was born in North Vancouver, Canada, March 2, 1953.

She obtained a BA degree in 1977 and a BFA degree in 1979 from the University of British Columbia. She practiced as a professional visual artist while also beginning a career in the performing arts—diverse work that ranged from sewing tutus for the local ballet company, to stage management, to arts administration for an alternative theatre company.

During this period, she was hired as a technician in 1978 for a new concept in presenting Canadian performing arts for children. This was the Vancouver International Children's Festival, an event that became the foremost North American showcase for children's professional theatre, music, and dance. As Artistic Director of the Festival from 1981 to 2000, she presented works that both challenged and entertained, including some commissioned pieces.

In 1992 she was named Festival Producer. She led the Festival as both Artistic Director and Producer until June 2000. She established a national touring circuit for visiting artists from across the world to children's festivals in Canada and the United States, providing significant work and new opportunities for artists, while bringing new ideas about the arts to young audiences in both small and major venues. It was an honor that festivals were established in Edinburgh and Japan that were modeled after the Vancouver Festival.

In 1997 she received a three-year appointment to the Minister of Foreign Affairs' Foreign Policy Advisory Board representing cultural interests. She willingly volunteered her time on many other cultural boards including ASSITEJ. She was head of ASSITEJ/Canada from 1993 until 1999, serving on the International Executive Committee and as International Vice-President (1993–1999) and Chair, Marketing and Communications Commission (1993–1996) as well as Chair, Artistic Commission (1996–1999). While serving in these capacities for ASSITEJ she created and wrote the MacLean Report for President Michael FitzGerald. This excellent report detailed brilliantly the artistic goals and activities of all the national centers of ASSITEJ at that time, and was used as a guide for the working program of ASSITEJ under President FitzGerald.

She returned to school after leaving the Festival in June 2000, and attended the Université de Laval, Québec, and Simon Fraser University in British Columbia where she obtain a teaching degree in Fine Arts (2003), and a Masters degree in Educational Leadership (2006). She also provided consulting services to the Canada Council for the Arts, the National Arts Centre and others, such as the 2010 Olympic Bid Committee (Cultural Division).

Currently she works in the field of early education as Principal of an independent primary school for oral deaf children, and sits on the Executive Committee of the Federation of Independent Schools of British Columbia. She continues to support the performing arts and practices as an artist, working in photography and painting.

Zdravko Mitkov (Bulgaria)
Zdravko Mitkov served on the EXCOM from 1987 to 1990. No other information was available.

Rose-Marie Moudoués (France)[184]
Mme. Rose-Marie Moudoués was born in Castejaloux, France on 28 November 1922. She did superior work in Letters, History, and History of Art at the University of Toulouse. She became a teaching professor in the Paris region as of 1945. She first worked with Léon Chancerel (1945-1965) and then with Louis Jouvet (1945-1951) at the resumption of the Society of the History of Theatre which had been interrupted during WWII. From 1948 on at this same time she served as *Engineer to the C.N.S.R. for Theatrical Sciences.*

In 1948 she left this association, and for several years helped integrate the National Center of Scientific Research and the Society of the History of Theatre. She became Director of the Documentation Center of the Library of the Society of the History of Theatre and of the Association of Theatre for Children and Young People (ATEJ), which she had helped create as an organization.

She also participated in the creation of the *Review d'Histoire du Théâtre* (she is still an editor today), and was an author and translator of programs on the theatre for the radio titled *Prestige du Théâtre.* She has published numerous articles in both French and foreign publications. She was the author of the Biography of Theatrical Arts in France, and Editor-in-Chief of the *History of Theatre Review,* and *Theatre— Children and Youth.* She has given many lectures in France and abroad.

She established and edited an annual international bibliography of shows, and was actively involved in the founding of the International Federation of Theatrical Research (FIRT) of which she became co-secretary for many years. She was also a founding member and vice-president for the Institute for Theatrical Research in Venice, Italy.

Attentive to the development of the contemporary theatre, under the Ministry of Culture she was a member of the Commission to assist local theatrical companies with the creation of theatres, and she was and is to this day an expert on the local administration of cultural affairs (DRAC). As a major reader of contemporary dramatic authors, under the Ministry of Culture from 1980 to 2000 she headed the Commission to help with the creation of dramatic works and specifically to promote the production of unpublished works.

As a collaborator with Léon Chancerel, founder in France of the first artistic theatre for children, Moudoués assisted him in his activities favoring young people's companies, and participated in the founding of the French Association of Theatre for Children and Young People (ATEJ), as well as the International Association of Theatre for Children and Young People (ASSITEJ). The first meeting she attended took place at ATEJ in Paris in 1963 which brought together representatives from Great Britain, Italy, Netherlands, Belgium, and Rumania. Later she attended the London Conference in 1964, the Preparatory Conference in Venice in 1964, and was Secretary of the Preparatory Committee in 1964-1965. As a result of these meetings, Moudoués drew up the Constitution of ASSITEJ (based on that of ATEJ) for discussion, amendment, and adoption by the Constitutional Congress in Paris organized by ATEJ in 1965. She presided at the Constitutional Congress in Paris in 1965, and was a member of the EXCOM from 1965 to 1990. In 1966 she established the French National Center for ASSITEJ.

At the 1965 Paris Conference Moudoués was elected Secretary-General, an election which was confirmed at the Ist International Congress in Prague, Czechoslovakia in 1966. She held this position for 25 years up to the Xth International Congress in Stockholm, Sweden in 1990. Leaving this position with grace, she put at the disposal of ASSITEJ the technical assistance of ATEJ and the publication of the Review of ATEJ *Théatre, Enfance, Jeaunese*.

She was named a Member of Honor of ASSITEJ at the General Assembly in Seoul, Korea, on 20 July 2002. She continues to be active in theatre research and writing.

Maria Navarro (Spain)[185]

Maria Navarro began he career in children's theatre as Assistant Director of the National Youth theatre "Los Titeres", under the direction of Angel F. Montesinos, being the first woman in Spain to fill that office.

She joined the professional theatre as Manuel Collados' Production Manager, taking part in over 30 productions, among which the most important were S.M. Trebelak's *Godspell*, Peter Shaffer's *Equus*, Ramón del Valle Inclán's *La Hija del Capitan y Las Galas del Difunto*.

She continued the experimental Teatro Benevente in Madrid, which introduces famous independent theatre groups to the commercial theatres in alternate program. They produced such well known plays as Koppit's *Oh Dad, Poor Dad, I've Hung You in the Closet and I'm Feeling So Sad*, Brecht's *The Rise and Fall of the Third Reich*, and S. Tavora's *Quejio*.

She is the founder of the Teatro Estable Castellano (TEC) together with Miguel Narros, José Carlos Plaza, Enrique Llovet, William Layton, Ana Belén, accomplishing the following productions: Lorca's *Asi Que Pasen Cinco Años*, Chekhov's *Uncle Vanya*, Schiller's *Don Carlos*, Lope de Vega's *La Dama Boba*, Alfonso Vallejos' *El Cero Transparente*, Francisco Nieva's *La Señora Tartara*, Eugene O'Neill's *Before Breakfast*, August Strindberg's *The Stronger*, and Jean Cocteau's *The Human Voice*.

Apart from her theatre activities, she also directs courses specializing in teaching expression techniques. She has been producer of the Sociedad Española de Radiodifusión, and children's theatre advisor to the Director General of Theatre in the Ministry of Culture.

She has won the following prizes: Fotogramas de Plata, Populares de Pueblo, El Espectador y La Critica, and Radio Juventud.

Currently she is Production Manager of one of the most important Spanish radio programs; her goal being the inclusion of children's theatre in this medium.

She has been President of ASSITEJ/Spain, Vice-President of ASSITEJ, and President of the Commission on Latin American Countries.

Ottorino Negri (Italy)[186]

Ottorino Negri was a native of Cremona, Italy. He served in the Italian Diplomatic Corps, and during WWII served in Africa and South America.

He was a Professor at the University of Cremona, teaching both Philosophy and Foreign Policy. He was devoted to music, and particularly treasured Respighi, who shared his first name.

He succeeded Benito Biotto and Don Rafaello Lavagna as head of ASSITEJ/Italy, and was elected to the EXCOM in 1978. While on the EXCOM he joined with Shaun Hennessey (Great Britain) attempting to modernize the direction of ASSITEJ into becoming more responsive to the needs of the membership while opening membership to all the countries of the world. In 1984 he nominated Ann Shaw to be President of ASSITEJ from 1984–1987. Shaun Hennessey seconded the nomination.

He served on the EXCOM from 1978 to 1987. He was succeeded by Franco Passatore of Italy in 1987.

He was married, and had three daughters. He died in 2009.

Harold R. Oaks (USA)[187]

Harold Rasmus Oaks was born in Provo, Utah, 20 June 1936. He completed BA and MA degrees at Brigham Young University and his PhD at the University of Minnesota. As a professor teaching at Brigham Young University, he chaired the Theatre & Film Department for 12 years, was coordinator of the Child Drama Program, and founded the Young Company which toured nationally and internationally (Šibenik, Yugoslavia, and Vienna, Austria in 1983, and Tromsø, Norway ASSITEJ Congress and Festival, 1999).

Oaks directed over 40 productions for young people and adults across the United States. The Church of Jesus Christ of Latter-day Saints commissioned him to write, design & construct puppets, and direct a series of puppet shows for Health Fairs in various countries around the world. These have been translated into over 15 languages, and have been performed in over 25 countries for thousands of young people and adults.

Oaks served ASSITEJ as a member of the Executive Committee (1988–2002), as Treasurer (1993–1999), and as President (1999–2002). He also served on the Board of Directors of the American College Theatre Festival (1974–79); as Treasurer of the American Theatre Association (1972–73); as President of the Children's Theatre Association of America (1985–86); as President of the American Alliance for Theatre & Education (1987–88); as President of ASSITEJ/USA (1988–95); and served on the Education Advisory Panel (1986–91) of the John F. Kennedy Center for the Performing Arts, Washington, DC.

Oaks has done over 80 workshops and presentations at many locations in the USA as well as in Tonga, Fiji and Western Samoa, Canada, Germany, Poland, Norway, Croatia, Sweden, Japan, Switzerland, and Brazil. He has over one hundred publications and reviews in national and international journals, newsletters and books. He was editor of The ASSITEJ/USA INTERNATIONAL HOT LINE from 1989 to 2001.

He was awarded the Gold Medallion of Excellence from the American College Theatre Festival in 1978, was given a Presidential Citation from the American Alliance for Theatre and Education in 1993, was elected to the College of Fellows of the American Theatre in April 2002, and was awarded a 2004 Medallion for Excellence by the Children's Theatre Foundation of America.

He retired from Brigham Young University as Associate Dean, College of Fine Arts & Communications in 2002. Following his retirement in 2002, Oaks and his wife,

Ima Jean, served in St. Thomas, US Virgin Islands (2002–2004) and on the island of Palawan, the Philippines (2004–2006). There they presented Health Service puppet shows to thousands of young people, delivered wheelchairs, arranged for health care for those with special needs, taught English as a Second Language, helped organize youth activities, and worked with local Church leaders on various projects.

He was named an Honorary President of ASSITEJ at the XVIth World Congress in Adelaide, Australia in 2008.

Kim Woo Ok (Korea)[188]

Kim Woo Ok was educated at New York University, receiving his PhD in Drama in 1980. On his return to Korea he became a Professor at the Seoul Institute of the Arts, and Artistic Director of the Dong Rang Repertory Company, one of the most prestigious theatre companies in Korea. In 1985 he founded the Dong Rang Theatre for Young Audiences, the first professional theatre company for the youth in Korea.

Working as the Artistic Director of the Company since 1985, he has directed 5 original plays for youth. The first piece, *The Wandering Stars*, was invited to be performed at the IXth World Congress of ASSITEJ in Adelaide, Australia. The fourth piece, *The Burning Stars*, was invited to be performed at the 2nd All-Japan Performing Arts Festival for Children on the Sado Island, Japan in 1991.

Mr. Kim is the Founder and Director of the Seoul Children's Theatre Festival, which will begin to be held in 1993. The Festival, which will be held annually, will invite the best local productions in the first year, but is planned to include foreign productions from 1994. He is very much interested not only in working hard for ASSITEJ, but in harmonious work among the increasing Asian member countries of ASSITEJ.

He currently is a co-opted EXCOM Member of ASSITEJ. Since 1991 he has been working as a member of the Artistic Commission. He was President of ASSITEJ/Korea from 1986–1991.

Sozaburo Ochiai (Japan)[189]

Sozaburo Ochiai graduated from the Aoyama Teachers College in 1929. He then took a teaching position at elementary schools. Since he came to know Mr. Takashi Saida, who was a pioneer of school drama in Japan, Ochiai became interested in school drama, and in 1932 he created the School Drama Circle with his colleagues. With the addition of more Circles, he established the School Drama League in 1937. Because of WWII, the groups disappeared one by one in the 1940s.

After the war ended in 1945, they reestablished the School Drama League in 1949, and Ochiai became their first Chief Director. In 1953 he was appointed a Commissioner for selecting the Best Children's Play of the Year by the Municipality of Tokyo.

In London in 1964 as the Head of the Japanese delegation, he attended the first International Children's Theatre Conference (which became ASSITEJ in 1965). Following this Conference, he returned to Japan and in 1967 he established a "Center of Theatre for Boys and Girls" in order to develop an international exchange in theatre for young audiences.

When he retired from teaching in 1970, he worked as a drama lecturer at various colleges. In 1976 he was appointed Professor at Tokyo Home Economics

University in order to create a Chair of Children's Theatre for the first time in the history of all senior colleges in Japan.

In 1979 when ASSITEJ/Japan was established, he became Vice-President of that Center until his death in 1995. In 1981 be was appointed Lecturer of Children's Plays at Tamagawa University until 1984. In 1990 he donated his money to the Japan Children's Association, Inc. in order to establish the Sozaburo Ochiai Theatre for Young Audiences Fund which would develop these drama activities in Japan.

He died in 1995 at the age of 85.

Franco Passatore (Italy)[190]

Franco Passatore was an actor, director, playwright, after having a career in various adult theatres in Italy.

In 1969 he founded the theatre Groco/Vita, and in 1978 the Section School for children he established the Children of the Teatro Stabile di Torino, functioning as both a playwright and a director.

He is also an author on books on children's theatre.

He was Vice President of the Italian Center for ASSITEJ, and a Member of the EXCOM from 1987 to 1993.

Luiz Velez Dos Santos Pisco (Portugal)[191]

Luiz Pisco was an actor, playwright, play director, cultural promoter, and teacher of drama. He had been a teacher of Biology and on the Faculty of Sciences at the University of Lisbon.

He was the founder of Mascara—Teatro de Grupo which based its artistic work on the prominent role of the actor. He believed that the actor was the organic material in the scene, who received and transmitted the emotions. He became the catalyst of emotions which gave truth to the art of the theatre.

He has worked for the Portuguese Center of ASSITEJ since 1981, and is a member of their Executive Committee. He was elected to serve in the Executive Committee of ASSITEJ from 1987–1990. He was replaced by João Luiz Souza on the EXCOM from 1990–1993.

Orna Porat (Israel)[192]

Mrs. Orna Porat was born in Cologne, Germany on 6 June 1924.

She attended the Drama School "Städische Bühnen der Stadt Köln" from 1940 to 1942, had various acting engagements in Schleswig, Koblenz, Eutin, and Cologne, and immigrated to Palestine in 1947. She was a permanent member of the Cameri Theatre in Tel-Aviv since 1948. She performed many major roles, and appeared in Zürich, Paris, London, and Montreal. She was the Founder and Director, with the Cameri Theatre, of the National Theatre for Children and Youth from 1970 on. In 1973 she was appointed Lecturer to the Faculty of Drama at Tel-Aviv University.

She has been considered the "grande dame" of theatre in Israel until today. In addition to her many successes on the stage, she was also noted as one of the best actresses in Israeli cinema.

She attended the Constitutional Conference in Paris in 1965. She was a Member of the EXCOM of ASSITEJ from 1970 to 1975. She participated in several

Congresses and EXCOM Meetings. In the late 1980s she was made Honorary President of ASSITEJ/ISRAEL She was made an Honorary Member of ASSITEJ in 2002.

Michael Ramløse (Denmark)[193]

Michael Ramløse was born 8 November 1949 in Copenhagen. He graduated in 1976 from the University of Copenhagen, having majored in Russian and German Languages and Literature.

From 1976–1984 he was a member of BANDEN, one of Denmark's leading free theatre companies for children in the city of Odense. Then for three years he worked freelance as a director, playwright, composer, and translator of plays for children. From 1987–1996 he served as head of TEATERCENTRUM, a semi-official office under the Ministry of Culture whose purpose is to promote professional theatre for children. TEATERCENTRUM is the organizer of the large annual Danish Children's Theatre Festival in April, performing in a new part of the country each year.

In 1983 he was one of the key-persons in re-organizing the Danish Center for ASSITEJ, and as its head made it an all-inclusive organization, taking over from Mme. Inga Juul. His involvement in ASSITEJ led him to be elected as the first new Secretary General of the organization, succeeding Mme. Rose-Marie Moudoués who had served for the twenty-five years since the founding of ASSITEJ in 1965. The national center became ASSITEJ/DENMARK-TEATERCENTRUM which served as the Secretariat for both the Danish national center and the Secretary General. Ramløse served as Secretary General for two terms, from 1990–1996.

In 1997 he became administrative director of FAIR PLAY, one of Denmark's leading children's theatre companies, and continues in that capacity to this day. In addition he has served as Chair of the Children's Theatres' Association of Denmark, was on the steering committee of "The Playwrights' Greenhouse II and III", as well as Chair of the Regional Theatre Council of West Zealand County. For two years he was director of the international children's theatre festival CARAVANEN.

He has written numerous articles and given key-note speeches on Danish children's theatre in Denmark and abroad. He has received the 25th Anniversary Prize of the Children's Theatre Association; the Cultural Prize of FTF (Denmark's second largest trade union); the Children's Theatre Award of the City of Horsens, and was made an Honorary Member of ASSITEJ in 1999.

An author of numerous plays for children, he lists among those most often performed are: Mum's the Word, The Fifth Commandment, The Earth We Walked On, Our Performance about Sarah, and A Word is a Word. He has translated other plays from English, Swedish, Russian, and German.

As Secretary General of ASSITEJ, he headed the first fully professional Secretariat of the organization, which was financed by a consortium of Ministries of Culture of Denmark, Norway, Finland, Iceland, and Sweden in cooperation with the staff of TEATERCENTRUM. His new approach to the administration of ASSITEJ improved administrative practice and procedures, improved communication among the National Centers, implemented a new subscription system, and most importantly changed ASSITEJ from a Euro-centric organization to a global association. This made it inclusive instead of exclusive, making it more manageable and visible internationally.

Ilse Rodenberg (Germany)[194]

Dr. Ilse Rodenberg was born in Düsseldorf on 3 November 1906, and died at the age of 99 on 6 January 2006 in Berlin.

She was born the illegitimate child of a serving girl in Düsseldorf. Self-supporting at an early age, she moved to Hamburg where she began her career as an actress at the left-wing Kollektiv junger Schauspieler from 1930 to 1933. Then from 1935 to 1945 she was banned from performing, but she established contacts with comrades working illegally and supported them with information from her job as switchboard operator in a hotel. From 1945 to 1947 she was Manager and actress at Kabarett "Laternenanzünder" in Hamburg. From 1949 to 1950 she was the head of the theatre in Neustrelitz, and from 1950 to 1957 of the theatre in Potsdam.

In 1959 Rodenberg became the head of "Theater der Freundschaft" (today Theater an der Parkaue) in Berlin, and through her marriage to Hans Rodenberg rose in the political establishment of the GDR. This theatre, which she now headed, had been founded by her husband in 1950.

In opposition to the provincial nature of the GDR elite, she was open to the world, and in children's and youth theatre she found a career that she loved. During her 14 years as Intendant she made the theatre an indispensable venue for children's and young people's culture due to her unprecedented competence and remarkable personality. She was Founder and Director of the Bureau for International Questions on Theater for Children and Young People in the GDR in 1973. She wrote many publications, made speeches, and traveled to countries in Europe, Asia, and America. In West Germany which she visited often she was a member of a Fraternal Party of the National Democratic Party of Germany, an association she found useful in the GDR.

She understood power but made it her own, coping emotionlessly and pragmatically with all problems, such as presenting a poor play by a politically-connected author in order to raise actor's salaries to equal those of the great Berlin theatres at the time. Outwardly she showed complete trust of her cohorts, but she never allowed anyone to question her control. She cooperated with the major GDR theatres, putting her theatre on an equal level.

She was a Member of the Preparatory Committee in 1964–65, a member of the EXCOM of ASSITEJ from 1965 on, and served three terms as President from 1978 to 1987.

As Vice-President and later as President of ASSITEJ she contributed comprehensively to the development of children's and young people's theatre on a world scale. In 1973 on her retirement the GDR Center for ASSITEJ was established as an independent office, and she was placed in charge. Refusing a salary and relying on her pension, she devoted herself full-time to the Center and later to her office as ASSITEJ President. She established the bi-annual International Directors Seminar as well as the Hallenser Workshop Meeting and Playwright's Competition. She constantly developed creative exchanges among directors, playwrights, and educational theatre artists.

In 1987 she retired as President of ASSITEJ after three terms. Then in December of 1989 after the unification of Germany, she participated in the establishment of the Children and Youth Theater Center of Germany in Frankfort, making her theatrical legacy safe for future generations.

She maintained an active interest in world affairs and children's theatre, reading three papers a day, until her death in 2006.

Susan Douglas Rubes (Canada)[195]

Susan Douglas Rubes (Zuzka Zenta) was born in Vienna, Austria in 1925. At an early age her family moved to Czechoslovakia. While there her parents took her to theatre and opera in Brno. They would also visit her maternal grandmother, who was the manager of the Burg Theater in Vienna. At the age of 8 she began studying ballet.

In 1939 her Jewish parents moved to Paris, and then to the United States. She attended high school in New York City, graduating in 1943. In 1945 she began her career in radio, television, theater and film, as an actress and a producer. Between 1946 and 1959 she appeared on hundreds of TV shows. In 1950 she married well-known Czech-Canadian opera singer Jan Rubes, and they had three children. After 59 years of marriage, Jan Rubes died in 2009.

In 1959 she moved to Toronto, Canada, and in 1963 she began introducing plays to schools. She founded the Young People's Theatre in Toronto in 1965, whose purpose was to introduce children to live theatre experiences. In 1977 they renamed the Theatre Center in her honor.

She served as the Canadian representative on the Executive Committee of ASSITEJ in 1978, succeeding Joyce Doolittle.

Among her many honors she received a Tony Award for Best Debut on Broadway, a Drama Bench Award in 1974, became a Member of the Order of Canada in 1975, and the Woman of the Year Award from B'nai Brith Women's Council of Toronto in 1979.

Currently she is retired and living in Sarasota, Florida, USA.

Natalya Ilyinichna Satz (USSR)[196]

Natalia Satz was born on 27 August 1903. Ilya Satz, her father, was a famous composer, and as a young girl she remembered hearing music being played in the room next to her bedroom. She described the music as ". . . sometimes impetuous, sometimes shimmering like water and magically glimmering as if a fairy had arrived." It was the music composed by her father to *The Blue Bird* of Maurice Maeterlinck, the famous production by the Moscow Art Theater. Her great love of music for children dates from these early childhood experiences.

By the time she was 15 in 1918, she was running the Mossovet Theatre, the first theatre for children that was born of her initiative. People would refer to her as "the Mother of all the theatres for children in the world." The Moscow Theatre for Children, the Moscow Central Theatre for Children, and the Moscow Musical Theatre for Children, named and dedicated to her, were all a result of her efforts, including the first Theatre for Young Spectators in Kazakhstan. In the early 1920s she had become known as an outstanding theatre director, and her productions of *A Little Negro and a Monkey, About Dzyuba, The Golden Key,* and *Seryozha Streitsov* were highly acclaimed by both the press and the public.

On the opera stages of the world she collaborated with conductor Otto Klemperer in productions of Verdi's *Falstaff* at the Crollopera in Berlin, Germany in 1931, and Mozart's *The Marriage of Figaro* at the Teatro Colon in Buenos Aires, Brazil that same year.

Tragically she fell afoul of the governmental authorities, and she was exiled to Siberia soon after. But even in exile she created a theatre in the gulag in which she was imprisoned. In the early 1960s she was rehabilitated under Premier Nikita Khrushchev, and began a new life in Moscow. She immediately created a musical theatre for children that had no venue at first, but by 1983 she had succeeded in building the State Musical Theatre for Children in Moscow, which was later named in her honor. After her reappearance, she immediately became involved in ASSITEJ, and during the 1980s she served as head of the USSR National Center and was elected to the Executive Committee of ASSITEJ. During her long career she was given many awards—*People's Artist of the USSR, Hero of the Socialist Labor*, and a winner of the *Lenin and State Prizes of the USSR.*
She died at the age of 100 on the 18th of December 1993.

Konstantin Shakh-Azizov (USSR), I, p. 309.

Adolf Shapiro (Russia)[197]

Adolf Shapiro is a theatre director, playwright, author, lecturer, and former Artistic Director of the famous Riga Youth theatre in Latvia. He is now a free-lance director invited to realize his productions on stages of leading Russian companies (for example: *The Cherry Orchard* of Anton Chekhov at the Big Drama Theatre in St. Petersburg in December 1992, *Boumbarash* by V. Dashkevich at the Moscow "Third Direction" Company in March, 1993, etc.)

Many companies in Russia, including Moscow and St. Petersburg, have invited Shapiro to be their leading artist.

He has been President of ASSITEJ/Russia, and has served on the EXCOM of ASSITEJ, and was elected President of ASSITEJ from 1990–1993.

Ann M. Shaw (USA)

Dr. Ann M. Shaw (EdD) was born on 26 June 1930 in Wilsonville, Nebraska, USA, and was smitten by theatre at the age of 4 when she won First Prize (a silver dollar) in an amateur contest singing and dancing to the song "I'll never say never again, again."

She studied acting and directing at Colorado Woman's College. She received degrees from Northwestern University (BA, MA) in Theatre, and Columbia University (EdD). Her dissertation was considered seminal in creative drama.

Beginning in 1952 she taught creative dramatics in the Evanston, Illinois public schools, and continued her academic career at Western Michigan University, Hunter College, and Teachers College, Columbia University. She retired in 1990 having taught for 22 years at Queens College, City University of New York.

Author of many publications on children's theatre, and on theatre by, with, and for the disabled. Her works have been translated into many languages. For the American Theatre Association (ATA) she served on their Board of Directors, key committees, organized two national conferences, and founded their program for the disabled (ATD).

Early professional theatre activities included Head, Wardrobe Department of the Central City Opera (Colorado); Box Office Manager, D'Oyly Carte Opera Co. (Colorado); costume execution of new productions (New York City Opera); and study at the Berghoff Studio, and appeared in several off-Broadway productions.

Shaw's honors include a CTAA Special Citation, Kennedy Center's Outstanding Educator Award, and Northwestern University's Award of Merit, a Medallion from the Children's Theatre Foundation, and ASSITEJ/USA named the Ann M. Shaw Fellowship Awards in her honor.

She attended her first meeting of ASSITEJ at the IVth International Congress in Canada and the USA where she programmed the Creative Drama sessions. She was the USA representative to the ASSITEJ Executive Committee from 1978–1987. In 1981 she created the new US Center for ASSITEJ, known as ASSITEJ/USA and was its President until 1987. She initiated the Pacific Rim TYA exchange (1984) and the Mexico-USA Exchange (1985). She directed the World Theatre Festival for Young Audiences and the Symposium at the New Orleans World's Fair (1984).

She was twice elected ASSITEJ International Vice President, 1981–84 and 1984–87 and served as a USA voting delegate at eight Congresses from Madrid in 1978 through Trömso in 1999. In 2002 at the XIVth World Congress in Seoul, Korea she was made an Honorary Member of ASSITEJ. She has attended every international Congress from 1972 to 2005, with the exception of the Vth Congress in Berlin, GDR in 1975.

She currently lives in Santa Fe, New Mexico, USA, and is active in St. Bede's Episcopal Church, and continues to encourage young people pursuing careers in theatre for young audiences.

Hans Snoek (Netherlands), I, p. 311.

Patricia Di Benedetto Snyder (USA)[198]

Patricia Di Benedetto Snyder (PhD) received her BA from the University of Albany, where she was named a distinguished alumna, a Master's degree from Syracuse University, a PhD from New York University, and an Honorary Doctor of Public Service Degree from the Sage Colleges, where she received The Sage Colleges Board of Trustees Community Leadership Award.

Snyder is the founding Producing Artistic Director of the New York State Theatre Institute (NYSTI) created by the New York State Legislature in 1974. In her professional theatre career, she has performed in, directed, and/or produced more than 312 productions. She directed *The Wizard of Oz*, which was the first American children's theatre production invited to perform at the Moscow Central Children's Theatre of Moscow by the Soviet Minister of Culture in 1974. She also directed the premiere, touring, and video productions of *A Tale of Cinderella*, which was released on Warner Home Video and broadcast nationwide on PBS. She is one of the adapters of Valentine Davies' *Miracle on 34th Street* published by Samuel French, Inc.

She is the recipient of two Special Recognition Citations from the John F. Kennedy Center in Washington D.C.; the Medal of the City of Milan, Italy; a Telly; an Emmy; two Audies; the Silver Award from WorldFest Charleston; and The Chicago Film Festival for *A Tale of Cinderella*. She is the recipient of an award for excellence in the performing arts by HRM Queen Noor of Jordon. Under her leadership NYSTI has been awarded the Zeta Phi Eta Award, the Jennie Heiden Award, and the AATE Sara Spencer Award for Artistic Achievement.

Snyder organized local arrangements and financing for the USA half of the

1972 International Congress of ASSITEJ held at the State University of New York (SUNY) at Albany, New York, USA. She was former Chair of the US Center for ASSITEJ and the Coordinator for the United Nations Decade of the Woman for SUNY.

She has produced on and off Broadway, has lectured in/and organized theatre exchanges with cultural agencies in Belgium, Bulgaria, Canada, Czechoslovakia, Germany, Great Britain, Hungary, Israel, Jordan, The Netherlands, Poland, Romania, USSR, Spain, Sweden, Yugoslavia, and Mantova, Italy. She was a member of the former US Center for ASSITEJ (now Theatre for Young Audiences/USA) and the American Association of Theatre in Education (AATE), the Broadway League of American Theatres and Producers where she serves on its Education Committee. She also is a member of the League of Professional Theatre Women/New York.

Eddy Socorro (Cuba)[199]

Eddy Socorro was the Artistic Director of the Teatro Nacional de Guiñol in Havana, Cuba. He is a member of the National Counsel of Scenic Artists. He is a member of the National Union of *Environs* and Artists of Cuba (UNEAC). He has been President of the Cuban Center for ASSITEJ since 1976. He was elected to the EXCOM in 1981, and served as a Vice-President.

Sara Spencer (USA), I, p. 312.

Nena Stenius (Finland)[200]

Nena Stenius was born in Helsinki in 1946.

In 1968 she graduated from the Finish Theatre School which later became the Theatre Academy Helsinki.

From 1968–1969 she was engaged as a Director and Dramaturge at the Wasa Teater. In 1969–1971 she was appointed Director and Dramaturge at the Lilia Teatern, Helsinki, and in 1970 while at this theater she directed the first performance in Finland for a teenage audience.

From 1971–1977 she directed productions for children at several free theatre groups in Finland. In 1978 she was appointed Artistic Director of the children's and young peoples' theatre *Penniteatteri* and continued in that position until 1983.

She then resumed her career as a free-lance Director, Dramaturge, and Theatre Pedagogue within the field of children's theatre.

She began her work with ASSITEJ in 1978 as President of ASSITEJ/Finland, and continued in that capacity until 1990. From 1984–1990 she was a member of the EXCOM of ASSITEJ, and served as one of the three Vice-Presidents of ASSITEJ from 1984–1987.

During 1984 to 2009 she directed plays, adaptations for professional theatres in Finland and abroad and also was consulted by children's theatre festival organizations. She worked continuously with children, young people, and adult amateurs, while writing several booklets about theatre with children.

From 1998 until 2009 she was appointed as a theater teacher at Annantalo Art Center in Helsinki, where professional artists work with children and young people.

She received the Finish Prize for Peace Education (1981), the Finish State Prize for Children's Culture (1987), and her hometown of Espoo (close to Helsinki) gave her their 2009 Pro Cultura Esbo Prize.

As of this writing she is continuing her writing and directing as a free-lance artist in children's theater.

Maria Nieves Sunyer y Roig (Spain)[201]

Sra. Maria Sunyer was born in Barcelona on 31 October 1925.

After 1942 she centered her activities in the area of theatre for children and youth. In 1960 in Madrid she organized the first professional theatre troupe called "Los Titeres" which performed only for children and young people, and has played at five national meetings of Spanish theatres. Los Titeres appeared in a special performance at the Constitutional Conference in 1965 in Paris and again at the VIth Congress of ASSITEJ in 1978 in Madrid. She has written extensively, organized numerous conferences, and travels widely abroad.

She first attended the Constitutional Conference in Paris in 1965, and then all the Congresses since then to 1975. Since 1968 she has edited and distributed free to all Spanish-speaking centers a Newsletter in Spanish that features ASSITEJ news and reviews. She was a member of the EXCOM from 1970 on, was elected Vice-President in 1975, and hosted an EXCOM meeting in Madrid in 1974 and the VIth International Congress in Madrid in 1978. She also served as the President of the Spanish National Center.

She received the Honorary Orders—Isabel the Catholic, Cisneros, and Mérite Naval. She was made an Honorary Member of ASSITEJ in 1987.

Kathrin Türks (FGR)[202]

Kathrin Türks was born in Düsseldorf as the first daughter of the main-station-pub owners. After her theatre education, she performed several acting parts in various theatres. In 1951 she founded with other actors the Burghofbühne Dislaken as a theatre for workers.

She worked there as an actress, director and Head of the Theatre for 32 years until 1983. She was called the "Mother Courage of Niederrhein", and was famous for her involvement in political theatre for children and young people.

She was awarded Order of Merit of the Federal Republic of Germany in 1982.

She served as Head of ASSITEJ/FGR from 1976 to 1983, and was elected to serve on the Executive Committee of ASSITEJ from 1978 until 1983, when she stepped down because of illness.

She died on 19 October 1983.

Gerald Tyler (Great Britain), I, p. 313

Ivan Voronov (USSR)[203]

Ivan Voronov was born in the Region of Moscow on 19 January 1915.

He graduated from the Meyerhold Theatre School, State Central Theatre for Young Spectators, the "Front" Theatre of the All-Russia Theatrical Society (during WWII), since 1944 in the Moscow Central Children's Theatre.

Besides working for 40 years as an actor in the theatre, he performed in the movies, television, and radio. He was Member for the Commission for State Prizes at the Council of Ministers of the Russian Federation, and a member of the editorial board of the magazine "Theatrical Life". He authored numerous articles for this magazine, and is also written up in the book *The Feat of the Actor*.

He was honored as People's Artist of the Russian Federation, winner of the Soviet Union State Prizes, and bearer of the order Badge of Honor.

He was member of the ASSITEJ EXCOM (1975–1978), and a Member of the Presidium of the ASSITEJ Center for the Soviet Union.

Maurice Yendt (France)[204]

Maurice Yendt was born in Lyon, France on 15 November 1937.

In 1960 at the age of 23 he founded the Théâtre des jeunes Années in Lyon as its playwright and director. He met in 1968 with Marcel Maréchal of la Compagnie du Cothurne, and together they created the new Théâtre du Huitième. From 1968 to 1980 Yendt directed 18 productions, among which were *Le pays du soleil debout (1969), Le rossignol et l'oiseau mécanique,* and *La machine à théâtre (1970), La marche à l'envers (1974)*, all of which performed at the Festival d'Avignon under the direction of Jean Vilar, and later Paul Puaux.

In 1971 Yendt was named technical advisor in the dramatic arts to the Ministry of Youth and Sports. In 1973 he traveled to Germany to direct Die Theatrespielmaschine at the Landtheatre Dortmund.

In 1980 with Michel Dieuaide he founded the Rencontres Internationales Théatre Enfance jeunesse (RITEJ), which in 1993 became the Biennale du Théâtre jeunes Publics/Lyon. About the same time Yendt was named Director of the National Drama Center by the French Minister of Culture. At that time the Théâtre des jeunes Années (TJA) moved its activities to a new theatre which featured 2 performance theatres seating 490 and 100 respectively, supported by the City of Lyon and the Ministry of Culture. The Théâtre des jeunes Années/center dramatique national became the first permanent French theatre for young audiences.

From 1980 to 2005, Yendt directed 26 plays. Among the most recent were: *Ubu Roi* by Alfred Jarry, *Candide* after Voltaire, *Le pupille veut être tuteur* by Peter Handke, *Pinocchio* from the book of Carlo Collodi and the operatic version by Sergio Menozzi for the National Opera of Lyon, and in 1999 *Ce qui couve derrière la montagne*. These productions had numerous tours in France, and also performed in Germany, Australia, Belgium, Brazil, Canada, Czechoslovakia, Spain, USA, Italy, Morocco, Portugal, Russia, and Switzerland.

Yendt has written 28 plays, of which 15 were original texts, as well as numerous articles, including an essay "Les ravisseurs d'enfants" (Actes Sud-Papiers). Many of these plays are performed regularly, as well as being translated into other languages. Part of his work has been edited in Germany (Fischer-Verlag et Theatre Stück Verlag).

Starting in 1993 Yendt was President of l'Association du Théâtre pour l'Enfance et la Jeunesse/Center français de l'ASSITEJ (ATEJ). He was an Advisor to the Executive Committee of ASSITEJ from 1981–1993, and Vice-President from 1993–1999.

Since June 2004 with the dissolution of TJA, he along with Michel Dieuaide became a Co-Artistic Director of la Biennale du Théâtre jeunes Publics/Lyon. To this day he continues his activities as author and director, most recently directing *The Marriage Proposal* by Anton Chekhov in 2005.

APPENDIX C
Volume II

List of International/World Congresses of ASSITEJ (1965–1990)

4-9 June 1965	The Constitutional Conference of ASSITEJ/Paris, France
26-30 May 1966	Ist International Congress of ASSITEJ/Prague, Czechoslovakia
27-31 May 1968	IInd International Congress of ASSITEJ/The Hague, Netherlands
19-24 October 1970	IIIrd International Congress of ASSITEJ/Venice, Italy
14-25 June 1972	IVth International Congress of ASSITEJ/ Montreal, Ontario, Canada and Albany, New York, USA
19-26 April 1975	Vth International Congress of ASSITEJ/Berlin, GDR
10-17 June 1978	VIth International Congress of ASSITEJ/Madrid, Spain
13-20 June 1981	VIIth International Congress of ASSITEJ/Lyon, France
19-27 September 1984	VIIIth International Congress of ASSITEJ/Moscow, USSR
8-16 April 1987	IXth World Congress of ASSITEJ/Adelaide, Australia
19-27 May 1990	Xth World Congress of ASSITEJ/Stockholm, Sweden

APPENDIX D
Volume II

List of Executive Committee Meetings of ASSITEJ (1965–1990)

19-26 February 1966	Executive Committee of ASSITEJ Meeting/Berlin, GDR
5-11 March 1967	Executive Committee of ASSITEJ Meeting/Nuremberg, FGR
1-10 March 1968	Executive Committee Meeting of ASSITEJ/Moscow, USSR
21-31 October 1968	Executive Committee Meeting of ASSITEJ/Sophia, Bulgaria
27 June-1 July 1969	Executive Committee Meeting of ASSITEJ/Šibenik, Yugoslavia
7-10 June 1970	Executive Committee Meeting of ASSITEJ/Bucharest, Romania
3 May 1971	Bureau Meeting of ASSITEJ/ Paris, France
17-24 October 1971	Executive Committee Meeting of ASSITEJ/Bratislava, Czechoslovakia
4-11 May 1972	Executive Committee Meeting of ASSITEJ/Berlin, Leipzig, & Dresden, GDR
10 May 1972	Executive Committee Meeting of ASSITEJ/Dresden, GDR
16-21 October 1972	Bureau Meeting of ASSITEJ/Bordeaux, France
11-17 June 1973	Executive Committee Meeting of ASSITEJ/London, Great Britain
16-22 April 1974	Executive Committee Meeting of ASSITEJ/Madrid, Spain
3-9 February 1975	Executive Committee Meeting of ASSITEJ/Zagreb & Karlovac, Yugoslavia
13-18 October 1975	Bureau of ASSITEJ Meeting /Paris, France
8-16 May 1976	Executive Committee Meeting of ASSITEJ/Milan & Rome, Italy
4-5 October 1976	Bureau of ASSITEJ Meeting/Sophia, Bulgaria
12-20 May 1977	Executive Committee Meeting of ASSITEJ/Banff, Calgary, & Montreal, Canada
October 1977	Bureau of ASSITEJ Meeting/Paris, France
26-30 March 1978	Executive Committee Meeting of ASSITEJ/Moscow, USSR
October 1978	Bureau Meeting of ASSITEJ/Paris, France
10-13 June 1979	Bureau Meeting of ASSITEJ/Moscow, USSR
25-28 June 1979	Executive Committee Meeting of ASSITEJ/Šibenik, Yugoslavia

9-14 April 1980	Executive Committee Meeting of ASSITEJ/Washington, D.C/USA
28-30 November 1980	Bureau Meeting of ASSITEJ/Dortmund/FGR
17-20 March 1981	Executive Committee Meeting of ASSITEJ/Prague, Czechoslovakia
11-13 October 1981	Bureau Meeting of ASSITEJ/Lille, France
5-11 April 1982	Executive Committee Meeting of ASSITEJ/Havana, Cuba
12-13 October 1982	Bureau Meeting of ASSITEJ/Paris, France
28-30 June 1983	Executive Committee Meeting of ASSITEJ/Lisbon, Portugal
31 October to 3 November 1983	Bureau Meeting of ASSITEJ/London, Great Britain
9-17 June 1984	Executive Committee Meeting of ASSITEJ/Munich, FGR
2-3 February 1985	Bureau Meeting of ASSITEJ/Paris, France
22-29 June 1985	Executive Committee Meeting of ASSITEJ/Šibenik Yugoslavia
4-5 October 1985	Bureau Meeting of ASSITEJ/Prague, Czechoslovakia
3-10 May 1986	Executive Committee Meeting of ASSITEJ/Helsinki, Finland and Stockholm, Sweden
6-11 January 1987	Executive Committee Meeting of ASSITEJ/Berlin, GDR
15-22 May 1988	Executive Committee Meeting of ASSITEJ/Odense, Denmark
16-18 November 1988	Bureau Meeting of ASSITEJ/Moscow, USSR
3-6 June 1989	Executive Committee Meeting of ASSITEJ/Lyon, France
4-10 November 1989	Bureau Meeting of ASSITEJ/Warsaw, Poland
4-11 February 1990	Executive Committee Meeting of ASSITEJ/Havana, Cuba

APPENDIX E
Volume II

List of Members of the Executive Committee of ASSITEJ
by Terms (1965-1990)

1965-1966 (The Provisional Committee)—12 Members
Belgium (José Géal), **Canada** (Olivia Hasler), **Czechoslovakia** (Vladimir Adamek), **FGR** (Hanswalter Gossmann), **France** (Rose-Marie Moudoués), **GDR** (Ilse Rodenberg), **Great Britain** (Gerald Tyler), **Italy** (Maria Signorelli), **Netherlands** (Hans Snoek), **Romania** (Margareta Barbutza), **USA** (Sara Spencer), and **USSR** Konstantin (Shakh-Azizov).

1966-1968 (The 1st Election)—12 Members
Belgium (José Géal), **Canada** (Betty Anderson, Florence James, Joyce Doolittle), **Czechoslovakia** (Vladimir Adamek), **FGR** (Hanswalter Gossmann), **France** (Rose-Marie Moudoués), **GDR** (Ilse Rodenberg), **Great Britain** (Gerald Tyler), **Italy** (Don Rafaello Lavagna), **Netherlands** (Hans Snoek), **Romania** (Margareta Barbutza), **USA** (Nat Eek), and **USSR** (Konstantin (Shakh-Azizov).

1968-1970—12 Members
Belgium (José Géal), **Canada** (Joyce Doolittle), **Czechoslovakia** (Vladimir Adamek), **FGR** (Hanswalter Gossmann), **France** (Rose-Marie Moudoués), **GDR** (Ilse Rodenberg), **Great Britain** (Gerald Tyler), **Italy** (Benito Biotto), **Netherlands** (Hans Snoek), **Romania** (Ian Cojar), **USA** (Nat Eek), and **USSR** (Konstantin Shakh-Azizov).

1970-1972—12 Members
Belgium (José Géal), **Canada** (Joyce Doolittle), **Czechoslovakia** (Vladimir Adamek), **FGR** (Hanswalter Gossmann), **France** (Rose-Marie Moudoués), **GDR** (Ilse Rodenberg), **Great Britain** (Gerald Tyler), **Italy** (Benito Biotto), **Netherlands** (Hans Snoek), **Romania** (Ian Cojar), **USA** (Nat Eek), and **USSR** (Konstantin Shakh-Azizov).

1972-1975—14 Members
Belgium (José Géal), **Bulgaria** (Victor Georgiev), **Canada** (Joyce Doolittle), **Czechoslovakia** (Vladimir Adamek), **FGR** (Hanswalter Gossmann), **France** (Rose-Marie Moudoués), **GDR** (Ilse Rodenberg), **Great Britain** (Gerald Tyler), **Italy** (Benito Biotto), **Netherlands** (Hans Snoek), **Romania** (Ian Cojar), **USA** (Nat Eek), **USSR** (Konstantin Shakh-Azizov), and **Yugoslavia** (Ljubiša Djokič).

1975-1978—11 Members
Bulgaria (Victor Georgiev), **Canada** (Joyce Doolittle), **Czechoslovakia** (Vladimir Adamek), **France** (Rose-Marie Moudoués), **GDR** (Ilse Rodenberg), **Italy** (Benito Biotto, Don Raffaello Lavagna, and Ottorino Negri), **Romania** (Ion Lucian),

Spain (Maria Sunyer), USA (Patricia Snyder), USSR (Natalya Satz and Ivan Voronov), and Yugoslavia (Zvjezdana Ladika).

1978-1981—15 Members

Bulgaria (Victor Georgiev), Canada (Joyce Doolittle, resigned in 1978, replaced by Susan Rubes, then Sara Lee Lewis, then Dennis Foon), Czechoslovakia (Vladimir Adamek), FGR (Kathrin Türks), France (Rose-Marie Moudoués), GDR (Ilse Rodenberg), Great Britain (John English), Israel (Orna Porat), Italy (Ottorino Negri), Romania (Ion Lucian), Spain (Maria Sunyer), Switzerland (Elisabeth Cozona), USA (Patricia Snyder, replaced by Ann Shaw in 1980), USSR (Natalya Satz), and Yugoslavia (Zvjezdana Ladika).

[At the 1981 International Congress in Lyon, France, the Statues were amended to raise the total membership of the EXCOM to 17. This now officially allowed the countries of the Secretary General and the Treasurer to be in addition to a 15 Member EXCOM.]

1981-1984—17 Members

Australia (Andrew Bleby and Geoffrey Brown); Bulgaria (Victor Georgiev); Canada (Sara Lee Lewis, Diane Bouchard, and Peter J. Gallagher); Cuba (Eddy Socorro): Czechoslovakia (Ladislav Knížátko); France (Rose-Marie Moudoués); FGR (Kathrin Türks and Hildegard Bergfeld); GDR (Ilse Rodenberg); Great Britain (Shaun Hennessey); Italy (Ottorino Negri); Portugal (João Luiz Brites); Romania (Ion Lucian); Spain (Maria Sunyer); Switzerland (Elisabeth Cozona); USA (Ann Shaw); USSR (Natalya Satz and Alexei Borodin); and Yugoslavia (Zvjezdana Ladika and Bereslav Frkič).

1984-1987—17 Members

Australia (Andrew Bleby, Michael FitzGerald as of 1985); Bulgaria (Vladimir Georgiev); Canada (Peter J. Gallagher resigned in 1987); Cuba (Eddy Socorro); Czechoslovakia (Ladislav Knížátko and Vladimir Adamek); FGR (Hildegard Bergfeld); Finland (Nena Stenius); France (Rose-Marie Moudoués); GDR (Ilse Rodenberg); Great Britain (Shaun Hennessey); Japan (Kazuto Kurihara); Portugal (João Brites); Romania (Ion Lucian); Spain (Maria Navarro); USA (Ann Shaw); USSR (Natalya Satz); and Yugoslavia (Zvjezdana Ladika and Bereslav Frkič).

1987-1990—17 Members

Australia (Michael FitzGerald); Bulgaria (Zdravko Mitkov); Cuba (Eddy Socorro); Czechoslovakia (Ladislav Knížátko and Marian Lucky); FGR (Hildegard Bergfeld); Finland (Nena Stenius); France (Rose-Marie Moudoués); GDR (Ilse Rodenberg); Great Britain (David Johnston and Paul Harman); Italy (Franco Passatore); Poland (Halina Machulska); Portugal (Luiz Pisco); Spain (Maria Navarro); Sweden (Mårten Harrie); USA (Nancy Staub and Harold Oaks); USSR (Natalya Satz and Alexei Borodin); and Yugoslavia (Zvjezdana Ladika).

1990-1993—13 Members
Australia (Michael FitzGerald), **Czechoslovakia** (Marian Lucky), **Cuba** (Eddy Socorro), **Denmark**)Michael Ramløse),**FGR** (Jürgen Flügge), **France** (Rose-Marie Moudoués), **Great Britain** (Paul Harman); **Italy** (Franco Passatore), **Japan** (Yohei Hijikata), **Portugal** (João Luiz Souza), **Sweden** (Mårtin Harrie), **USA** (Harold Oaks), and **USSR** (Adolf Shapiro).

APPENDIX F
Volume II

The Constitutions of ASSITEJ

The First Constitution (1965)
Approved at the Constitutional Conference in Paris, France, on 9 June 1965.

CONSTITUTION OF ASSITEJ

INTERNATIONAL ASSOCIATION OF THEATRE FOR CHILDREN and YOUNG PEOPLE
CHAPTER I

CREATION
Since theatrical art is a universal expression of mankind, and possesses the influence and power to link large groups of the world's peoples in the service of peace, and considering the role theatre can play in the education of younger generations an autonomous international organization has been formed which bears the name of the International Association of Theatre for Children and Young People.

ARTICLE I

1. This Association proposes to unite theatres, organizations, and individuals of the world, dedicated to theatre for children and young people.

2. This Association is free from political, religious, or racial commitment of any kind.

3. Official languages in constitutional meetings will be English, French, and Russian. On the occasion of international conferences, the languages of the inviting country will be added.

ARTICLE II—AIMS

This Association is created to facilitate the development of theatre for children and young people, on the highest artistic level. Its aims are:

1. To promote contacts and interchange of experience between all countries, encouraging theatre artists to become mutually acquainted so as to estimate their own work, and in this spirit influence their own public.

2. To promote study tours for individuals and groups, as well as engagements for producing companies traveling abroad.

3. To introduce and support, at its discretion, proposals made to competent national authorities, for the furtherance of its work.

4. To promote the formation, in countries where there is none, of national associations uniting all organizations and persons interesting themselves in theatre for children and young people.

ARTICLE III—MEANS

The means of achieving these aims are:

1. Organization of international congresses, conferences, festivals, study courses, exhibitions and other activities, and participation in such projects.

2. Assistance in the publication and distribution of books, magazines, legitimate stage plays, musical plays, and other literary works, dramatic or musical, to do with theatre for children and youth.

3. Promotion of theatre for children and young people through the press, films, radio, recording, television, and other means.

4. Encouragement of translation and exchange of plays, texts, or other literature pertaining to theatre for children and young people.

5. Foundation of institutions for research and study purpose—such as libraries, museums, collections of records, etc.—on the subject of theatre for children and young people.

6. Participation in the studies of other international organizations with related interests.

7. Acquisition of the necessary property and equipment.

CHAPTER II

ARTICLE IV—MEMBERS

Members of this Association are National Centers of Theatre for Children and Young People. The following categories of membership for National Centers are acceptable to the International Association:

1. Professional companies of adult actors playing for children and young people.

2. Adult non-professional companies, community theatre companies, college and university theatre companies playing for children and young people.

3. Institutions, organizations or individuals actively engaged in the work of theatre for children and young people.

4. Supporting organizations, institutions, associations, or persons interested in theatre for children and young people.

To qualify for Full Membership in the Association a National Center must have at least one member as defined in Category 1 or 2.

Other National Centers are Corresponding Members.

ARTICLE V—RIGHTS AND OBLIGATIONS

1. Full Members have the right to participate in activities mentioned in Article III, to make proposals in constitutional meetings, to allow their representatives to elect, to be elected, and to vote according to the rules declared in Article IX.

2. Corresponding Members have the right to participate in the activities mentioned in Article III, and have a consultative voice in the General Assembly, but have no right to vote.

3. All Members have the obligation to work to achieve the aims defined by the Association, to maintain its statutes, to act upon the decisions taken by the Association, and to pay their membership fees.

ARTICLE VI—APPLICATION, RESIGNATION, EXPULSION

1. Written applications for membership shall be addressed to the Secretary-General. In the case of a denial by the Executive Committee, the candidate may appeal to the next General Assembly.

2. Any member who wishes to resign should inform the Secretary-General in writing for it to take effect from 1st January in the following year.

3. The Executive Committee may decide, by a majority of two-thirds, on the rejection or expulsion of any member whose work conflicts with the fundamental aims of this Association, or who has failed several times in one of the obligations mentioned in Article V.

4. Any rejected or expelled member may appeal to the General Assembly.

CHAPTER III
ARTICLE VII—FINANCE

1. This Association is financed from the subscriptions of members, as well as from bequests, gifts, and subsidies accepted by the General Assembly.

2. The fiscal year of this Association runs from 1st January to 31st December.

3. Membership fees, which are determined by the General Assembly, are due to 1st January of each year, and are payable to the Treasurer.

CHAPTER IV
ARTICLE VIII—STRUCTURE

The governing body of this Association consists of:
- The General Assembly
- The Executive Committee
- The Officers

ARTICLE IX—FUNCTIONS OF THE GENERAL ASSEMBLY

1. The General Assembly consists of delegates of all National Centers.

2. Each national delegation has three (3) votes:
- Two (2) votes for its professional companies
- One (1) vote for its non-professional companies

3. Voting by proxy is permitted.

4. The General Assembly shall meet at least once every two years, and will be called at least six months in advance by the Secretary-General upon instruction of the Chairman. Normally it will decide the location where the next General Assembly shall meet – but if it should be unable to take a decision on this matter, or if a change of location should prove necessary, this decision may be left to the Executive Committee.

5. An extraordinary meeting of the General Assembly will be called by the Secretary-General three (3) months in advance on the request of two-thirds of the members or at the discretion of the officers of the Executive Committee in the case of an emergency.

6. The General Assembly has final control over the Constitution, and decides on any changes or additions necessary. Any member wishing to amend the Constitution must give notice in writing to the Secretary-General at least three (3) months before the date of the General Assembly. Any decision taken upon a proposal to amend the Constitution shall require a majority of two-thirds of the members of the Association.

7. The General Assembly establishes the broad outlines of the Association's policy.

8. The General Assembly receives for approval the report of the activities and the financial report which are submitted by the Executive Committee.

9. The Chairman of this Association is by right Chairman of the General Assembly. In the event of his absence, he will be replaced by a Vice-Chairman, or in the absence of all the Vice-Chairmen, by a member of the Executive Committee elected for this purpose by the General Assembly.

10. All decisions unless otherwise stated are taken by simple majority vote. In the case of a tie the Chairman will cast the deciding vote.

11. The General Assembly determines the membership fees and other charges to be levied on the members of the Association.

12. A meeting of the General Assembly can only be held if the delegates of half the National Centers express in writing to the Secretary-General their determination to be present and to participate, either in person or by proxy. This decision must be sent to the Secretary-General three (3) months in advance of the meeting. The General Assembly can only take decisions if half the members participate.

13. The General Assembly shall *elect* the Executive Committee and out of their members the Chairman and three Vice-Chairmen. Nominations must be submitted to the Secretary-General three (3) months before the date of the meeting of the General Assembly for circulation to the members. It appoints the Secretary-General and the Treasurer on the recommendation of the Executive Committee. The officers and members of the Executive Committee shall be chosen to represent all the interests as fairly as possible.

14. The General Assembly shall decide upon the acceptance of, and shall hold, all gifts, bequests, and subsidies made to the Association.

15. The General Assembly shall appoint two professional auditors to the Association.

ARTICLE X—FUNCTIONS OF THE EXECUTIVE COMMITTEE

1. The Executive Committee is composed of a maximum of fifteen members, having the right to vote, including:

> The Chairman and Vice-Chairmen
> The Secretary-General
> The Treasurer, appointed by the General Assembly

2. In the event of the death or resignation of one of its members, the Executive Committee shall authorize the National Center which nominated the member, to appoint a deputy for the remaining period of his office.

3. The Executive Committee has the power to co-opt up to two additional members. It also has the power to co-opt advisors.

4. Any member who cannot attend a meeting of the Executive Committee may appoint a deputy, by giving notice to the Secretary-General, in writing.

5. A meeting of the Executive Committee may be called only if at least half of the members express in writing to the Secretary-General their determination to be present and participate, either in person or represented by a deputy. The presence of half the members shall constitute a quorum.

6. The Executive Committee will meet at least once a year: the Committee will

decide by majority vote if it is necessary to hold additional meetings, and will choose the places and dates of such meetings. The Committee must be called three months in advance. Meetings will be called by the Secretary-General at the request of the Chairman.

7. The Executive Committee may decide upon urgent matters by correspondence if it proves impossible to hold a special meeting. In this case the Secretary-General, by agreement with the Chairman, shall send to each member of the Executive Committee a questionnaire, to which each member will reply in writing. Decisions will be made by two-thirds majority. The decisions will come before the Executive Committee at their next meeting for ratification. The replies will be placed in the records of the Association where they will be available for examination by members of the General Assembly.

8. Each member of the Executive Committee possesses one vote which he can use in person, or by deputy, or by letter. Voting by proxy is not permitted.

9. The Chairman of this Association is also Chairman of the meetings of the Executive Committee. In the event of his absence, he will be replaced by a Vice-Chairman, or if all Vice-Chairmen are absent, by a Chairman elected for this purpose by the Executive Committee.

10. All decisions are taken by a simple majority vote, except decisions taken by correspondence.

11. The Chairman of the meeting has the right to vote in his own right as a member of the Committee. If a majority decision cannot be established by this means, the Chairman may cast a second vote to decide the issue.

12. The Executive Committee shall deal with the affairs of the Association between meetings of the General Assembly and carry out the decisions taken by the General Assembly. The Executive Committee shall remain in office for the two years or thereabouts and its members shall be eligible for re-election.

13. The Executive Committee will accept or reject new applications for membership made to the Secretary-General.

14. The budget is administered by the Executive Committee according to a program established by the General Assembly.

15. The Executive Committee entrusts to the Treasurer the administration of funds, the preparation of the budget, and the accounts. The accounts of the Association must be audited every two years by two professional auditors, appointed by the General Assembly on the recommendation of the Executive Committee.

16. The Executive Committee may take the initiative in matters not anticipated by the General Assembly, providing that these matters are in keeping with the aims and character of this Association, and providing that the Executive Committee takes the first opportunity to report on these matters to the General Assembly.

ARTICLE XI—THE OFFICERS

The Officers of this Association are elected for two years or thereabouts and as follows:

                The Chairman, elected
                The Vice-Chairmen, elected
                The Secretary-General, appointed
                The Treasurer, appointed

1. The Officers are charge with carrying out the Association's program and rendering reports to the Executive Committee.

2. In the case of any urgent matters not foreseen by the Executive Committee, the Officers are given power to act at their discretion and will take the first opportunity to report on these matters to the Executive Committee.

CHAPTER V
ARTICLE XII—DURATION

1. This Association is created for an unlimited period.

2. This Association shall cease to function when, for any reason, three-fourths of the members (National Centers) on the basic number of votes shall express in writing to the Secretary-General, the desire to dissolve the Association. In this event, the Executive Committee shall be authorized to declare the Association dissolved, and any funds remaining in the Association's treasury shall be given to international organizations pursuing similar aims.

ARTICLE XIII—ADOPTION OF STATUTES

This Constitution shall come into force at the moment of its approval by a Constituent General Assembly of delegations from all interested countries called for this purpose. From that moment the Association may accept as members the national Centers who send their applications to the Secretary-General.

The Current Constitution (1976–1990)
This Constitution as amended served during the years documented in Volume II. Several statutes were amended at the Lyon Congress (1981). There were additional changes made at the Stockholm Congress (1990). The next major overhaul of the Constitution occurred in 1996 at the XIIth World Congress in Rostov-am-Don, Russia.

CONSTITUTION OF ASSITEJ (1990)

INTERNATIONAL ASSOCIATION OF THEATRE FOR CHILDREN
AND YOUNG PEOPLE

CHAPTER I

CREATION

Since theatrical art is a universal expression of mankind, and possesses the influence and power to link large groups of the world's peoples in the service of peace, and considering the role theatre can play in the education of younger generations, an autonomous international organization has been formed which bears the name of the International Association of Theatre for Children and Young People.

ARTICLE I

1. This Association proposes to unite theatres, organizations, and individuals of the

world, dedicated to theatre for children and young people.

2. This Association is free from political, religious, or racial commitment of any kind.

3. Official languages in constitutional meetings will be English, French, and Russian. On the occasion of international conferences, the languages of the inviting country will be added.

ARTICLE II—AIMS

This Association is created to facilitate the development of theatre for children and young people, on the highest artistic level. Its aims are:

1. To promote contacts and interchange of experience between all countries, encouraging theatre artists to become mutually acquainted so as to estimate their own work, and in this spirit influence their own public.

2. To promote study tours for individuals and groups, as well as engagements for producing companies traveling abroad.

3. To introduce and support, at its discretion, proposals made to competent national authorities, for the furtherance of its work.

4. To promote the formation, in countries where there is none, of national associations uniting all organizations and persons interested in theatre for children and young people.

ARTICLE III—MEANS

The means of achieving these aims are:

1. Organization of international congresses, conferences, festivals, study courses, exhibitions and other activities, and participation in such projects.

2. Assistance in the publication and distribution of books, magazines, stage plays, musical plays and other literary works, dramatic or musical, related to theatre for children and youth.

3. Promotion of theatre for children and young people through the press, films, radio, recording, television, and other means.

4. Encouragement of translation and exchange of plays, texts, or other literature pertaining to theatre for children and young people.

5. Foundation of institutions for research and study purpose—such as libraries, museums, collections of records, etc.—on the subject of theatre for children and young people.

6. Participation in the studies of other international organizations with related interests.

7. Acquisition of the necessary property and equipment.

CHAPTER II

ARTICLE IV—MEMBERS

Members of this Association are national centers representative of theatre for children and young people in their own country. **No theatre, organization, or individual can be refused admittance to the national center of ASSITEJ on grounds of race, religion, or political conviction.** [**1990**] The following categories of membership for national centers are acceptable to the International Association:

1. Professional companies of adult actors playing for children and young people.

2. Adult non-professional companies, community theatre companies, college and university theatre companies playing for children and young people.

3. Institutions, organizations, or individuals actively engaged in the work of theatre for children and young people.

4. Supporting organizations: institutions, associations, or persons not actively engaged, interested in theatre for children and young people.

To qualify for full membership in the Association, a national Center must have at least 3 members as defined in Category 1 or 2.

Other Centers **with only members as defined in Category 3 or 4** are Corresponding Members.

ARTICLE V—RIGHTS AND OBLIGATIONS

1. Full Members have the right to participate in activities mentioned in Article III, to make proposals in constitutional meetings, to allow their representatives to elect, to be elected, and to vote according to the rules declared in Article IX.

2. Corresponding Members have the right to participate in the activities mentioned in Article III, and have a consultative voice in the General Assembly, but have no right to vote **and to be elected.**

3. All Members have the obligation to work to achieve the aims defined by the Association, to maintain its statutes, to act upon the decisions taken by the Association, to pay their membership fees, **and to send a written report on their activities to the Secretary General once a year,**[205] **to appoint a correspondent and to give a National Center permanent address.**

ARTICLE VI—APPLICATION, RESIGNATION, EXPULSION

1. Written applications for membership shall be addressed to the Secretary General. In the case of a denial by the Executive Committee, the candidate may appeal to the next General Assembly.

2. Any member who wishes to resign should inform the Secretary General in writing for it to take effect from 1st January in the following year.

3. The Executive Committee may decide, by a majority of two-thirds, on the rejection or expulsion of any member whose work conflicts with the fundamental aims of this Association, or who has filed several time in one of the obligations mentioned in Article V.

4. Any rejected or expelled member may appeal to the General Assembly.

CHAPTER III

ARTICLE VII—FINANCE

1. This Association is financed from the subscriptions of members, as well as subsidies accepted by the General Assembly.

2. The fiscal year of this Association runs from 1st January to 31st December.

3. Membership fees, which are determined by the General Assembly, are due to 1st January of each year, and **must be sent to the Secretary General.**

CHAPTER IV
ARTICLE VIII—STRUCTURE

The governing body of this Association consists of:
The General Assembly
The Executive Committee
The Officers

ARTICLE IX—FUNCTIONS OF THE GENERAL ASSEMBLY

1. The General Assembly consists of delegates of all National Centers.

2. Each national delegation has **a maximum of** three (3) votes:
Two (2) votes for its professional companies
One (1) vote for its non-professional companies

3. Voting by proxy is permitted. **A national delegation can hold proxy for only one other National Center. [1990]**

4. The General Assembly shall meet at least once every **three years,**[206] and will be called at least six months in advance by the Secretary General upon instruction of the Chairman. Normally it will decide the location where the next General Assembly shall meet—but if it should be unable to take a decision on this matter, or if a change of location should prove necessary, this decision may be left to the Executive Committee.

5. An extraordinary meeting of the General Assembly will be called by the Secretary General three (3) months in advance on the justified request of two-thirds of the members or at the discretion of the officers of the Executive Committee in the case of an emergency.

6. The General Assembly has final control over the Constitution, and decides on any changes or additions necessary. Any member wishing to amend the Constitution must give notice in writing to the Secretary General at least three (3) months before the date of the General Assembly. Any decision taken upon a proposal to amend the Constitution shall require a majority of two-thirds of the members of the Association.

7. The General Assembly establishes the broad outlines of the Association's policy.

8. The General Assembly receives for approval the report of the activities and the financial report which are submitted by the Executive Committee.

9. The **President** of this Association is by right President of the General Assembly. In the event of his absence, he will be replaced by a Vice-**President**, or, in the absence of all the Vice-**Presidents**, by a member of the Executive Committee elected for this purpose by the General Assembly.

10. All decisions unless otherwise stated are taken by simple majority vote. In the case of a tie the President will cast the deciding vote.

11. The General Assembly determines the membership fees and other charges to be levied on the members of the Association.

12. A meeting of the General Assembly can only be held if the delegates of half the National Centers express in writing to the Secretary General their determination to be present and to participate, either in person or by proxy. This decision must be sent to the Secretary General three (3) months in advance of the meeting. The General Assembly can only take decisions if half the members participate **themselves or by proxy.**

13. The General Assembly shall elect the members of the Executive Committee as representatives of their particular countries. Each center, on its own behalf, should send to the Secretary General the name of its candidate three months before the date of the meeting of the General Assembly in order to circulate nominations to the members of ASSITEJ.

From amongst the **members of the Executive Committee the General Assembly shall elect the President and Vice-Presidents. They shall be elected in a personal capacity.**

The General Assembly appoints the Secretary General and the Treasurer on the recommendation of the *outgoing* Executive Committee.[207]

The officers and members of the Executive Committee shall be chosen to represent all the interests as fairly as possible.

The General Assembly on the recommendation of the Executive Committee can give the title of President of Honor and in a general manner the title of Member of Honor for exceptional service given to the Association. The members of honor have a consultative voice, but no right to vote and they cannot represent their country.[208]

14. The General Assembly shall decide upon the acceptance of subsidies made to the Association.

15. The General Assembly shall appoint two professional auditors to the Association **on the recommendation of the Executive Committee.**

16. Only questions which are set down on the Agenda may be voted upon[209] **in the General Assembly.**

ARTICLE X—FUNCTIONS OF THE EXECUTIVE COMMITTEE

1. The Executive Committee is composed of a maximum of ***seventeen [1984]*** members, having the right to vote, including:

The **President** and three Vice-**Presidents elected by the General Assembly**

The Secretary General **appointed by the General Assembly**

The Treasurer **appointed by the General Assembly**

2. In the event of the death or resignation of one of its members, the Executive Committee shall authorize the National Center which nominated the member, to appoint a deputy for the remaining period of his office, **except in the case of the President where the replacement shall be from amongst the Vice Presidents and in the case of the Vice Presidents where the Executive Committee is authorized either to leave the place vacant or, if it judges it necessary, to elect a replacement from amongst its own members. [1981]**

3. The Executive Committee has the power to co-opt up to two additional members. It also has the power to **appoint** advisors.

4. Any member who cannot attend a meeting of the Executive Committee can be replaced **only by a permanent deputy from his or her Center for the duration of his or her term of office** [1981]. The Secretary General must be notified of the deputy's name as soon as possible after General Assembly.

5. A meeting of the Executive Committee may be held only if at least half of the

members express to the Secretary General their determination to be present and participate, either in person or represented by a deputy **from their own national Center**. The presence of half the members shall constitute a quorum.

6. The Executive Committee will meet at least once a year: the Committee will decide by majority vote if it is necessary to hold additional meetings, and will choose the places and dates of such meetings. The Committee must be called three months in advance. Meetings will be called by the Secretary General at the request of the President.

7. The Executive Committee may decide upon urgent matters by correspondence if it proves impossible to hold a special meeting. In this case the Secretary General, by agreement with the **President**, shall send to each member of the Executive Committee a questionnaire, to which each member **of the Executive Committee** will reply in writing. Decisions will be made by two-thirds of the majority votes. The decisions will come before the Executive Committee at their next meeting for ratification. The replies will be placed in the records of the Association where they will be available for examination by members of the General Assembly.

8. Each member of the Executive Committee possesses one vote which he may use in person, or **by delegation to a member of his own National Center, [1981]** or by letter. **Voting by proxy is not permitted.**

9. The **President** of this Association is also **President** of the meetings of the Executive Committee. In the event of his absence, he will be replaced by a **Vice-President**, or if all **Vice-Presidents** are absent, by a Chairman elected for this purpose by the Executive Committee.

10. All decisions are taken by a simple majority vote, except decisions taken by correspondence **or regarding Art. VI, No. 3**.

11. The Chairman of the meeting has the right to vote in his own right as a member of the Committee. If a majority decision cannot be established by this means, the Chairman may cast a second vote to decide the issue.

12. The Executive Committee **will submit a plan of activities to the General Assembly. It manages the affairs of the Association between two meetings of the General Assembly** and carries out the decisions of the General Assembly. The Executive Committee will remain in office for the period **between one General Assembly and the next which will be three years or thereabout** and its members shall be eligible for re-election.

13. The Executive Committee will accept or reject new applications for membership made to the Secretary General. **A rejection may be appealed to the next General Assembly.**

14. The budget is administered by the Executive Committee according to a program established by the General Assembly.

15. The Executive Committee entrusts to the Treasurer the administration of funds, the preparation of the budget, and the accounts. The accounts of the Association must be audited every **three** years by two professional auditors, appointed by the General Assembly on the recommendation of the Executive Committee (**Art. IX, No. 15**).

16. The Executive Committee may take the initiative in matters not anticipated

by the General Assembly, provided that these matters are in keeping with the aims and character of this Association, and provided that the Executive Committee takes the first opportunity to report on these matters to the General Assembly.

ARTICLE XI—THE OFFICERS

The Officers of this Association are elected for **three** years or thereabouts and as follows:

>The Chairman, elected
>The Vice-Chairmen, elected
>The Secretary General, appointed
>The Treasurer, appointed

1. The Officers are charge with carrying out the Association's program and rendering reports to the Executive Committee.

2. In the case of any urgent matters not foreseen by the Executive Committee, the Officers are given power to act at their discretion and will take the first opportunity to report on these matters to the Executive Committee.

3. **The Bureau may appoint two counselors for the period of its mandate. The counselors may attend, without voting rights, meetings of the Executive Committee during their time of office. The Bureau may also invite specialists to meetings to offer advice on particular questions. These specialists may attend, without voting rights, meetings of the Executive Committee by invitation. [1981].**

CHAPTER V

ARTICLE XII—DURATION

1. This Association is created for an unlimited period.

2. This Association shall cease to function when, for any reason, three-fourths of the members (National Centers) on the basic number of votes shall express in writing to the Secretary General, the desire to dissolve the Association. In this event, the Executive Committee shall be authorized to declare the Association dissolved, and any funds remaining in the Association's treasury shall be given to international organizations pursuing similar aims.

ARTICLE XIII—ADOPTION OF STATUTES

This Constitution shall come into force at the moment of its approval by a Constituent General Assembly of delegations from all interested countries called for this purpose. From that moment the Association may accept as members the National Centers who send their applications to the Secretary General.

Amended at the Vth International Congress in Berlin, GDR, April 1975
Amended at the VIIth International Congress in Lyon, France, May 1981
Amended at the Xth World Congress in Stockholm, Sweden, May 1990
[The wording in this version of the Constitution has been revised for clarity by an unknown editor. These writers believe it was clarified by the British Center, based on the spelling of many words.]

APPENDIX G
Volume II

THE HISTORY OF THE FORMATION
and SUSPENSION OF NATIONAL CENTERS
(1975-1990)

ASSITEJ was formed with a total of twelve (12) National Centers whose representatives were elected to the Provisional Committee at the Constitutional Conference in Paris, France in May of 1965.

At the Berlin Congress in 1975 it was announced that there were 28 official Centers for ASSITEJ. However, the Czech Bulletin issued in the Fall of 1975 listed additional centers. By combining the two lists to avoid duplication, there became a total of 33 National Centers. These would be the following:

1975
ALGERIA	IRAN
ARGENTINA	ISRAEL
AUSTRALIA	ITALY
AUSTRIA	JAPAN
BELGIUM	NETHERLANDS
BULGARIA	PERU
CANADA	PORTUGAL
CUBA	ROMANIA
CZECHOSLOVAKIA	SPAIN
DENMARK	SRI LANKA
FEDERAL GERMAN REPUBLIC (FGR)	SWITZERLAND
FINLAND	TURKEY
FRANCE	USA
GERMAN DEMOCRATIC REPUBLIC (GDR)	USSR
GREAT BRITAIN	VENEZUELA
HUNGARY	YUGOSLAVIA
IRELAND	

Year	Center	Status
1976	JAPAN	Still forming
	ARGENTINA	No Statutes
	MEXICO	Had made contact
	EGYPT	Contact w/Minister of Culture
	IRELAND	No correspondence
	POLAND	Contact thru Minister of Culture
	GREECE	Asked for info
1977	ARGENTINA	All still forming according to Secy-Gen'l's Report
	BELGIUM	"
	BRAZIL	"

	DAHOMEY	"
	EGYPT	"
	GUATEMALA	"
	INDIA	"
	IRELAND	"
	JAPAN	"
	JORDAN	"
	MEXICO	"
	POLAND	"
	TUNISIA	"
	URUGUAY	"
	DENMARK	Reorganizing
	URUGUAY	Accepted as Member
	CANADA	Split into 2 centers - French & English
1978	FGR	No longer in existence
1979	JAPAN	Accepted as a new center
	ECUADOR	"
	IRAQ	"
	FGR	Was active again
1980	SWEDEN	Accepted as Member
	TURKEY	"
	ARGENTINA	"
1981	EGYPT	Would send Observer to Lyon Congress
	CHINA	Has sent Statutes to Minister
	PANAMA	Asked for info & forming
	ZAIRE	Would send Observer to Lyon Congress
	DENMARK	Continuing conflict among Members
	ECUADOR	Head of Center has left with no successor
	NORWAY	Corresponding Member
	MEXICO	Accepted as member
1982	PERU	Must clarify leadership & pay dues
1983	DENMARK	New Center accepted as Member
	GREECE	Accepted as Member
	URUGUAY	"
	VIETNAM	"
	SOUTH KOREA	"
	NORWAY	Accepted as Full Member
1984	ECUADOR	Readmitted as Member
1985	ARGENTINA	Readmitted as Member
	SWITZERLAND	Reorganizing
1987	ISRAEL	Reorganizing

All the following Centers were listed as active at the end of the ASSITEJ Congress in Adelaide, Australia.

ALGERIA	JAPAN
ARGENTINA	MEXICO
AUSTRALIA	NETHERLANDS
BELGIUM	NORWAY
BRAZIL	PARAGUAY
BULGARIA	PERU
CANADA	POLAND
CUBA	PORTUGAL
CZECHOSLOVAKIA	ROMANIA
DENMARK	SPAIN
ECUADOR	SOUTH KOREA
FGR	SRI LANKA
FINLAND	SWEDEN
FRANCE	SWITZERLAND
GDR	TURKEY
GREAT BRITAIN	USA
GREECE	URUGUAY
HUNGARY	USSR
IRAN	VENEZUELA
IRAQ	VIETNAM
ISRAEL	YUGOSLAVIA
ITALY	

1988	AUSTRIA	Accepted as Member
	IRELAND	"
	SRI LANKA	Accepted as Corresponding Center
1989	INDIA	Corresponding Center
	MADAGASCAR	Corresponding Center for 3 years
	MONGOLIA	" "
	ISRAEL	Restructuring
	TAIWAN	Accepted as Member
	KENYA	Corresponding Center for 3 years
1990	TURKEY	Reorganizing

Accepting the fact that Centers which were reorganizing were still active centers, this made for a total 46 active National Centers and 5 Corresponding Centers for a total of 51 Centers. Considering that there were 33 Centers in 1976, this showed an increase of 34% in the last 4 years as of 1990.

APPENDIX H
Volume II

The Current Election Process of ASSITEJ (2005)
Written by Nat Eek and Edited by Michael Ramløse

Over the years, an elaborate election process has emerged and been codified. This lists the process as currently used and which incorporates all the changes in the Constitution as of 2005. The initial pattern was established and codified by the first Secretary General Rose-Marie Moudoués starting in 1966.

1. In the General Assembly with the Elections on the Agenda—after presentation to the Bureau and the EXCOM, the Secretary General announces publicly those centers present and which are eligible to vote. This means that each center has had acceptable statutes in conformity with the ASSITEJ Constitution, has a corresponding delegate and address, and has paid its dues. Each center so approved may be present in person, or may give its proxy to another center. However, by the current Constitution no center can have more than one (1) proxy.
2. The President then appoints three (3) tellers with the approval of the General Assembly. They count the ballots; and report the results to the Secretary General who in turn announces them to the General Assembly.
3. Next, the delegates vote on whether the Secretary General and the Treasurer are to be retained. The President publicly announces the recommendation of the EXCOM. Nominations are accepted from the floor for replacements. If a new Secretary General is elected, then he or she immediately takes his or her place on the podium, and continues chairing the elections. In Stockholm in 1990 Rose-Marie Moudoués (France) was defeated as Secretary General and Michael Ramlöse (Denmark) was nominated from the floor and elected.
4. The Secretary General reads in English the names of the National Centers, in alphabetical order, who have nominated themselves and who are willing to stand for election. This can be any number. In 1993 Secretary General Michael Ramløse as part of the final meeting of the General Assembly introduced the custom that each candidate for office should stand up and briefly inform the Assembly of his or her qualifications, their "policies", and why they should be voted for.
5. On the day of the elections in the General Assembly the Secretary General announces any proxies and what Centers hold them. The total number of votes is announced, as well as the majority of votes required for election. In order to be elected a Center must receive at least the majority of the votes cast (51%). Also, according to the current (2005) Constitution there

can only be seventeen (17) members on the EXCOM. With the Centers of the Secretary General and the Treasurer automatic members of the EXCOM, the delegates can only vote for a total of fifteen (15) Centers. This means that by *not* voting for all 15 Centers or voting *only* for particular Centers, a Center may be defeated for election since it will not have received a majority vote (51%). Several times there has been a proposal to require all Centers to vote for a total of the current 15, but it has been defeated twice. On the positive side, this voting procedure guarantees that every Center on the EXCOM has a majority vote of confidence.

6. Three (3) identical ballots with the name of each nominated Center on them are distributed to each Center, one for each of their potential three (3) votes (2 professional and 1 amateur), again in alphabetical order. Originally each center marked the ballots accordingly, and the ballots were deposited in the ballot box, again each center being called to the ballot box for deposit in alphabetical order.

7. In 2002 at the Seoul, Korea Congress, Ramløse, as Chair of the Voting Commission, started the precedent of giving the delegates a 20-30 minute break to mark their ballots. At the end of the time period, the Secretary General would call out that the voting was over, and the members of the Voting Commission (Tellers) would collect the ballots. The Secretary General always asked if everyone had voted. Then the General Assembly resumed their discussions while the ballots were being counted. This same procedure was followed for each balloting, and continues to this day.

8. The Secretary General announces those elected by starting with the greatest number of votes received, continuing until a total of fifteen (15) Centers are reached. The number of votes received by each candidate is always announced. Ties are automatically accepted within the fifteen. If there is a tie at 15, then a run-off election is held between the two. If less than fifteen (15) Centers receive a majority vote, the EXCOM would be comprised of only that number who received a majority vote.

9. A recess is declared; the new EXCOM retires; and in executive session they select a slate of officers by name, not by country: a President and 3 Vice-Presidents from among the fifteen individuals on the new EXCOM. They may present more than one name for each office. Returning to the General Assembly in session, the Secretary General reads off the names; there can be nominations from the floor for any office as long as the person is on the new EXCOM and has agreed to the nomination; ballots are prepared; and the Centers vote on those names. They first vote for the President, then the 3 Vice-Presidents. This method allows a nominee for President who was not elected, can be possibly elected as a Vice-President. Each name

must receive at least 51% of the total eligible vote. If a name receives less than the majority vote, the EXCOM retires to come up with a new slate; or additional nominations can be made from the floor; or if it is among the Vice-Presidents, they may just have fewer than three. The Vice-Presidents become 1st, 2nd, and 3rd in order of the majority of votes received.

10. Again, the three (3) tellers count the ballots and give the vote totals to the Secretary General for announcement of the election results.

11. Only the EXCOM can co-opt a Center to sit on the EXCOM with or without vote, and it can co-opt no more than two (2) by the Constitution. However, the delegates have made their wishes known to the EXCOM, who usually follow that advice. Recently the EXCOM has also created the office of counselor without vote for a single person whose advice will be sought in their deliberations. Co-opted Centers and Counselors do not have to be appointed. If it so wishes, the EXCOM can do without, or appoint them at a later date as need arises. The EXCOM also has the right to invite any person to attend the EXCOM Meeting, if it so wishes. This has usually been used as a method to introduce leaders from new centers to the ASSITEJ process.

12. In 1996 at the Rostov-on-Don World Congress this entire election process was adopted in a series of amendments, and which were written into the Constitution. This finally codified the process as it was being practiced, but it took thirty-one years to happen! However, there have been several changes in the protocol since that time, and they have been entered into this History.

APPENDIX I
Speeches—Volume II

"Children and the Art of the Theatre"
Speech by Dr. Nat Eek, Past President of ASSITEJ, given at the Yugoslav Festival of the Child in Šibenik, Yugoslavia on 25 June 1979.

Every time the house lights dim before a play for children begins, there is a shout of anticipation from the audience accompanied by a hurried burst of applause. This has been true of every children's theatre I have had the privilege of attending around the world.

This spontaneous eager response indicates that the child regards the theatre as his friend, an experience to cherish and love. The child knows this special friendship brings wonderful sights and exciting adventures. It shows him glimpses of horizons which he did not know were there. It reveals to him people throughout the world, from countries other than his own, who have similar hopes, fears, desires, and dreams.

By witnessing plays from his own country, from his own culture, those values which his society deems worthy are passed on to him. By witnessing plays from other countries he leans about similarities and differences between cultures, and hopefully develops a healthy respect for those other cultures. Through theatre he learns a cultural history of the world.

Theatre is one of the vital living arts, and it is composed of six elements which make it particularly suitable for children.

First, the glory of the theatre is the spoken word. It is through words that ideas, thoughts, stories are told. The stage action reinforces those ideas, but it is the language that conveys them concisely. Shakespeare is undoubtedly one of our most translated English playwrights, but great writers like Boris Pasternak and André Gide have been able to transcribe successfully the Bard's English into their own languages while still maintaining the richness of the English poetry. While some writers are more difficult to translate, Sophocles and Pushkin for example, the transcribing of a play into another language emphasizes the glory of the spoken word on the stage. It also brings to that country and its child audiences an understanding of the literature and culture of that other country.

Second, theatre is a temporal art. It exists only during the time that the play is presented. Once the curtain falls, the play ceases to exist, until it is presented the next night. Also, the play can only exist in the space of the one stage on which it is presented. There may be many productions of "Cinderella", but there is only one which is presented in Seattle, Washington, USA on a particular night in a particular year with a particular cast, and with particular designers and directors. Film and television are permanently recorded mechanically. Theatre is recorded primarily in the mind of that night's audience. Theatre as an art is indeed temporal.

Third, theatre presents the subjective ideas of the playwright and the artists to the audience in an objective manner. The audience hears the words and views the actions individually. It can draw its own conclusions, but if the play is well prepared, the audience will go away principally with the ideas of the playwright well understood in concrete visual images of that particular production.

Fourth, theatre is a guide to the understanding of the world. By viewing plays like "King Midas" the child understands greed; through "The Emperor's New Clothes" he understands honesty and hypocrisy; through "Treasure Island" he understands adventure and bravery; through "Pinocchio" he understands laziness and responsibility. All these plays are from different countries, but their messages are universal.

Fifth, through theatre the child learns to enjoy group experience in a positive way. When the play is good and exciting and suspenseful, he finds all those around him responding as he responds. It is comforting to the child to find his emotional reaction reinforced by similar reactions of others. George M. Cohan, the American playwright and performer, said you come to the theatre "to laugh, to cry, to be thrilled". Hopefully the child will experience all these in the theatre in a positive way, and learn to treasure the emotional release which the theatre provides. TV is personal and solitary; film is two-dimensional and predictable. Only theatre can be affected by the reaction of the audience as the production progresses. The actor adjusts the action and the dialogue to the reacting audience; in turn the audience responds to the actor's readjustment, and quickly an artistic bond between the stage and the audience is formed which becomes indissoluble.

Lastly, theatre is the most powerful of the visual arts, because it happens "live" right before your eyes. The actor is in direct proportion to each member of the audience. He is not shrunk as in TV, or enlarged as in film. He is just the right size. Note how a child audience always responds with enthusiasm when it sees real children on stage. They are just like him, and therefore more believable.

Theatre is strong, pertinent, and unique. Therefore, we must show certain ideas which should be common to all children from all countries through this vital medium. While there are many such ideas, let me mention just four and give you examples of each.

First, let theatre for children show both good and evil. Only by seeing the effects of both can the child judge that good is better. By seeing the evil actions of Macbeth as the King, obsessed by ambition, ruthlessly pursuing his way, are we able to appreciate Macduff's daring and courage in opposing and ultimately killing Macbeth.

Second, let theatre for children show both justice and injustice. In Sara Spencer's version of Mark Twain's "Tom Sawyer" during the trial scene we see Tom free the Negro Jim from the suspicion of murdering Dr. Anderson through the courageous testimony in court. This is just, and the court wisely accepts Tom's evidence. But at the same time the child sees that Tom may seriously endanger his own life by giving that testimony, since Injin Joe may try to murder him. However, justice is more important, and Tom must take that chance.

Third, let theatre for children show both freedom and bondage. This can be both in idea as well as body. Musically there is no greater chorus than the Prisoner's Chorus from Beethoven's opera "Fidelio", as it expresses their need for freedom. "Pinocchio" is kept a virtual prisoner by the wicked puppeteer where the boy slaves for a living. The child audience easily sees the agony of such restraint. Unfortunately, once free Pinocchio takes some time to learn what the best choices are that he must make to use his freedom properly. But like Pinocchio the child sees the importance and responsibility of freedom as opposed to the security and debilitation of bondage.

Fourth and last, let children's theatre show the importance of individuality as opposed to group conformity. Let him see that one of the functions of the artist is to show his own intimate view of a private world. While the crowd agrees that the Emperor's new clothes are indeed beautiful, it is the child that identifies them for what they are—nothing! The individual suddenly stands up and speaks honestly, and sees the world as it is to him. Individual integrity is important, and it is this unique quality that makes Ivo Andric and Miroslav Krleza of your country [Yugoslavia] stand out as unique literary artists recognized around the world. Let theatre always show that individuality.

I have discussed theatre's uniqueness as an art, and mentioned four ideas which I hope good children's theatre will present. Let me finish by citing six examples of plays in productions which demonstrate that the art of children's theatre is indeed international. It will always form a bridge of understanding and friendship among countries.

First, a production of H.G. Wells' "The Invisible Man" in Leningrad in Russian showed incredible suspense, courage, and imagination. Second a production of "The Firebird" in Prague gave the Russian fairy tale an artistic brilliance and beauty that was breathtaking. Third, a production of the German fairy tale "Rumplestilskin" in Chicago had all the grumpy fun of a guessing game, and visually showed the dwarf with a delightfully long green beard. Fourth, the Danish tale of "The Emperor's New Clothes" done in Paris with stylized Chinese decor and mannerisms showed the formality of the tale while underlining the realism of its truth. Fifth, a production of scenes from "Romeo and Juliet" in Zagreb showed the poignancy of young love and deep devotion along with personal sacrifice. Sixth, a production of "Pinocchio" in Germany showed the outrageous fun of the original Italian while portraying the puppet as an awkward creature that was a misfit in society who ultimately found himself.

In these six productions we have seen plays, languages, cultures, and ideas from the following countries: Great Britain, USSR, Czechoslovakia, Germany, USA, Denmark, France, China, Italy, and Yugoslavia—a total of eleven different countries. What a wealth, and what a learning experience for the child!

We are indeed fortunate that we are able to work in the theatre for children. It is an awesome responsibility, but it is one of the few careers where we are able to see the results instantly. When the houselights dim and the shout of the children goes up, there is our reward. May we all continue to receive such riches!

"Welcoming Speech"
Speech by Dr. Ilse Rodenberg, President of ASSITEJ, given at the VIIIth International Congress of ASSITEJ in Moscow, USSR on 20 September 1984.

I would like to extend a warm welcome to you all. May I say how pleased I am that as many countries are represented here at the 8th ASSITEJ World Congress.

First, may I extend our hearty thanks to the USSR Ministry of Culture and the host city, Moscow, for their hospitality as well as the USSR ASSITEJ Center, which has put a great deal of effort into preparing this Congress.

Dear friends, I believe that this Congress is particularly significant—firstly for historical reasons. The country which is the birthplace of our professional children's theatres and which bore witness to the founding of ASSITEJ nearly 20 years ago has welcomed us back today. It was here in the Soviet Union, shortly after the 1917 October Revolution, that instructions were given for the founding of professional children's theatres. Today, not only can such theatres be found all over the world but also alongside them their paternal international organization, ASSITEJ, which [is] committed to the [same] humane causes.

It is impossible to speak of children's theatre without mentioning two names, one of which is Alexander A. Bryantsev, who has left us his works and the theatre for children and youth named after him. We are, however, lucky to have in our midst an actual eye-witness, Natalya Satz, whose whole life has been connected with work in the professional children's theatre. She recently received tribute from her country on the occasion of her 80th birthday. As yet, we regret to say, ASSITEJ has no such award for Natalya Satz [who] was to be the first to receive an honor of this kind.

Let us leave history now and turn to the present.

Our work can only flourish in peace. It seems to me to be no coincidence that at this critical and troubled time our Congress is taking place in the country whose first message to the world in 1917 was the call for peace.

We feel ourselves committed to preserving peace in the world. We need peace for the sake of art and of our young audiences as well as for ourselves. This is why the will for peace is the guiding force of our theatre work.

We can look back with justification at a healthy and positive development within our organization since our last World Congress in Lyon [in 1981].

First, I ask that we spare a minute's thought to a member of our Executive Committee, our friend Kathrin Türks, who following a serious illness in October 1983, had to leave us for good, after many years service as President of the FRG ASSITEJ Center.

Thank you.

Since the 7th World Congress in Lyons and now that more countries have joined us, our organization has grown in strength. [There were 41 official national centers at this time.] ASSITEJ centers now enjoy even greater influence in many of the member countries. The proof of this is that the theatre for children and young people no longer takes a side-line position but has become an important part of public awareness. The necessary role it plays cannot be disputed. Similarly, the self-confidence of our theatre members has grown considerably, and so has their reputation in many countries.

This, however, brings with it the demands which are set before ASSITEJ. In the period preceding this Congress and the 20th founding anniversary of our organization a variety of proposals have been made of all that ASSITEJ could and should do.

The fact is, dear friends, that we must be realistic. ASSITEJ is not a rich organization and as yet has been unable to be granted UNESCO status. Our sole source of income consists of yearly contributions from member countries amounting to 150 US$ [each], costs which many centers have extreme difficulty in meeting.

This meant that ASSITEJ has to rely on the activities of the individual national centers for its existence. ASSITEJ can only grow in strength if the national centers themselves play a strong and active role and if they make a contribution to the international development of the theatre for children and young people.

In my opinion, such important activities include the following:

- the organization of our Congresses, general assemblies and Executive Committee meetings through the national host centers;
- the BOLETINO IBERO-AMERICANO has for many years been published through the Spanish Center, since this center is in a position to establish better contact with the many Spanish speaking countries;
- the publication of the international bibliography by the Czechoslovakian Center, which provides us for the first time with a general idea of the literature available for children's theatre;
- the INTERNATIONAL INFORMATION CENTER established by the US Center to provide information about the THEATER FOR YOUNG AUDIENCES;
- the publication of the book KINDER UND JUGEND THEATER DER WELT in four languages by the GDR center;
- the holding of the THEATRES DU MONDE ASSITEJ festival every two years by the French center;
- the annual Bryantsev seminar, organized by the USSR Center and whose international attraction could be extended;
- and the annual international seminar held for theatre directors by the GDR center.

This list is by no means exhaustive. It is aimed not so much at praising national activities, which contribute to an international development, but rather should be seen as a list of proposals. These suggest that everyone should examine ways possible of making an influential mark on the international development of the theatre for young audiences through their own activities.

A new stage of international development has begun which ASSITEJ must adapt itself to. In many countries, the theatre for young audiences has found its way to becoming a permanent institution, even though it may not receive the support it deserves. The emphasis of the discussion has shifted from the necessity of a theatre for children and young adults to what such a theatre can achieve and how, and [what] are the most effective means for fulfilling its function. Unfortunately educational points of view are frequently considered to be more important than artistic ones.

ASSITEJ is not an educational organization but rather comprises eight autonomous international theatre organizations. For this reason, our main priority both now and in future must be to concentrate on the artistic development of our theatre. The goal of our organization is the same as that written in the statutes resolved 20 years ago, namely "to facilitate the development of theatre for children and young people on the highest artistic level".

This means that an increasing number of artistic problems must be brought to the forefront of our meetings and councils.

It is my intention to mention only a few such questions. Good theatre work depends primarily on the performance abilities of its actors, dancers, and singers.

For a variety of reasons, it is mostly only young people who perform in the theatre for young audiences. This places a great responsibility on our shoulders. As well as putting their young talent to good use, we must also assign them tasks which will enable them to grow and develop further, so that later they will be able to play other roles and perform in other theatres. Without the [assignment] of such tasks, the theatre for children and young people will be unable to cultivate talented young artists for itself and will become no more than a second-rate theatre.

There is another question in connection with this.

Good dramatic literature and plays are a prerequisite if any theatre is to be considered as important. Plays written by the theatre will most certainly remain part of the future program. However, while it may be true that such plays make a useful contribution to creating a lively and modern theatre, we must not overlook the fact that using them to the exclusion of everything else will limit the theatre's scope considerably. It will lack the true-to-life experiences of the dramatist transposed into his literary work; it will lack the artistic production of speech and the challenge which the dramatic text presents to the performers and the audience. Without good literature new capabilities cannot be acquired, neither can the feeling for art and art's own special language. Good dramatic literature is essential if the children's theatre is to lose its "provincial" character.

Many theatres designed for children and young people tend to underestimate their young audience. They do not see them as partners in their activities, but instead behave towards them exactly as a benign old uncle would, bending down to them, proffering a little advice and sharing some fun with them. This has little to do with art and such performances are responsible again and again for bringing our theatre into discredit. This is especially so in those countries which do not have a good theatre for children.

I think the time has come to open up discussions within the national ASSITEJ Centers concerning questions of an artistic nature which the theatre for young audiences is faced with. It is also time that standards were set and tenaciously represented. It is up to us to separate the wheat from the chaff, a task that we cannot push aside.

It is no longer sufficient for ASSITEJ Centers merely to be the organization for those with an interest in questions concerning youth and the theatre, even if this does remain one of today's prerogatives. At the same time, the Centers must strengthen their own authority and influence. Public meetings should help them and their audiences assess the theatre for children and young people not only by the good intentions of the theatre and the material offered by it, but by their artistic performance. This will enable us to create the [venue] for an international discussion concerning questions of an artistic nature raised during our Congresses, festivals, and colloquia. In doing so, we will help to achieve at least some of these objectives, the most important of which were highlighted by MONDIACULT, the UNESCO world conference held in Mexico in 1982 and which are included in the Mexico Cultural Policy Declaration. We should apply this important document to our activities all the more so, since it has been adopted unanimously by representatives from more than 120 nations. It constitutes something like a guide for topical problems concerning our work, such as the cultural identity of peoples, cultural activities, international cultural cooperation, and the struggle for world peace.

Let us, together with UNESCO, approach the International Youth Year with this in mind.

Last but not least, I would like to extend, my hearty thanks to you all for continuing to fight for a high standard of theatrical work for our young audiences. I would also like to thank all those who have supported me during my term as president of ASSITEJ.

I wish you all the best for the next few days and hope that some good experiences will emerge from them.

On this finishing note, I now declare the Congress as open.

NOTES
Volume II

Introduction
1. Ann M. Shaw, *The Formation of ASSITEJ*, ASSITEJ Annual 1996/97. (Ed. Wolfgang Schneider, Druckerei Heinrich, Frankfurt am Main.)

The World at the Time
2. The World Almanac and Book of Facts (Annual). (Pharos Books, Scripps Howard Company, New York, NY, USA.)

The Status of ASSITEJ in June 1975
3. "Information Bulletin—ASSITEJ, 1975 (3)" (Edited by the Theatre Institute, 118 00, Prague 1, Valdštejnské. č.3 for the Czechoslovak National Center of ASSITEJ.) Special Collections. Dept. of Archives and Manuscripts, University Libraries, Arizona State University, Tempe, AZ, USA.

4. Nat Eek, letter to Executive Committee, US Center for ASSITEJ, undated (probably August, 1975).

Bureau Meeting, October 1975
5. "Information Bulletin—ASSITEJ, 1975-1976 (1)" (Edited by the Theatre Institute, 110 01, Prague 1, Celetná ul. č.17 for the Czechoslovak National Center of ASSITEJ.) Special Collections, University Libraries. ASU, AZ, USA.

EXCOM Meeting, May 1976
6. Joyce Doolittle, ASSITEJ/Canada, *A Report Upon Meetings of the Executive Committee of ASSITEJ, Milan and Rome, Italy, May, 1976*. Special Collections, University Libraries. ASU, AZ, USA.

7. Ibid.

8. This also meant more control from the Secretariat.

Bureau Meeting, October 1976
9. "Information Bulletin—ASSITEJ, 1976 (3)" (Edited by the Theatre Institute, 118 00, Prague 1, Valdštejnské. č.3 for the Czechoslovak National Center of ASSITEJ.) Special Collections, University Libraries. ASU, AZ, USA.

Also, Patricia B. Snyder, *Report to the Executive Committee of the US Center for ASSITEJ, 15 October 1976*. Special Collections, University Libraries. ASU, AZ, USA.

10. Australia, Israel, and Sri Lanka had all attended various EXCOM Meetings since 1965.

11. Snyder Report, Ibid, 2.

12. Eek presented the speech "Children and the Art of the Theatre" at the VIth International Congress of ASSITEJ, 1978.

13. In 1978 seventy-eight delegates came from the USA. Spain had sent 22 delegates to the IVth International Congress in Canada/USA in 1972.

14. See discussion in EXCOM Meeting in Milan, Italy, 8-16 May 1976

EXCOM Meeting, May 1977
15. Patricia Snyder, *Report to the Executive Committee of the US Center for ASSITEJ*, 22 May 1977, 11 pages; and "The "Information Bulletin—ASSITEJ, 1977" (Edited by the

Theatre Institute, 118 00, Prague 1, Valdštejnské. č.3 for the Czechoslovak National Center of ASSITEJ); both in Special Collections, University Libraries. ASU, AZ, USA.

16. Francisco Franco had died in November 1975, and Juan Carlos had been sworn in as King and he had dissolved the institutions of the Franco regime. In the free elections of June 1977 moderates and democratic socialists emerged as the largest parties making the 1978 Congress in Madrid secure in its funding and support.

17. These changes in the Statutes were never approved by the General Assembly. However, both changes were reworded and were adopted later as amendments to the Statutes.

18. Joyce Doolittle, 4 November 2008 and 29 September 2009, e-mail to Nat Eek.

19. Joyce Doolittle, 21 September 2009, e-mail to Nat Eek.

Bureau Meeting, October 1977

20. "Information Bulletin—ASSITEJ, 1977-2" (Edited by the Theatre Institute, 110 01, Prague 1, Celetná 17 for the Czechoslovak National Center of ASSITEJ.) Special Collections. University Libraries. ASU, AZ, USA.

EXCOM Meeting, March 1978

21. "Information Bulletin—ASSITEJ, 1978-1" (Edited by the Theatre Institute, 110 01, Prague 1, Celetná 17 for the Czechoslovak National Center of ASSITEJ.) Special Collections. University Libraries. ASU, AZ, USA.

22. Joyce Doolittle, 29 September 2009, Notes taken at the time mailed in a letter to Nat Eek.

VIth International Congress, June 1978

23. In part from the Minutes in French provided by the Paris Secretariat (undated). Special Collections. University Libraries. ASU, AZ, USA. Also "Information Bulletin—ASSITEJ, 1978-2" (Edited by the Theatre Institute, 110 01, Prague 1, Celetná 17 for the Czechoslovak National Center of ASSITEJ.) Special Collections. University Libraries. ASU, AZ, USA.

24. "US Center for ASSITEJ Newsletter", No. 2, 1978. Special Collections. University Libraries. ASU, AZ, USA.

25. Japan was admitted as a Center in 1969 according to Volume I. This is 1978. Perhaps its Center had become inactive in this interim.

26. The election results were taken from the notes of Ann Shaw as well as the French Minutes of the VIth Congress. Special Collections. University Libraries. ASU, AZ, USA.

27. According to the *Secretary General's Report to the General Assembly* in 1981, Adamek and Snyder were appointed as Advisors. This contradicts the Minutes of the Madrid Congress. These appointments must have been made after Shaw took over from Snyder as head of ASSITEJ/USA, and when Karl Richter was appointed head of the Jiří Wolker Theatre and the Czech Center.

28. The majority required for election was listed as 33. Satz had only 31. It is assumed that the majority number had changed by the absence of a voting delegation.

29. ASSITEJ-REPORT FROM MADRID, by Kenneth R. McLeod. *Children's Theatre Review*, Vol. XXVIII, No. 1, Winter, 1979. 12. Special Collections. University Libraries. ASU, AZ, USA.

30. For a more complete series of play critiques of performances at the Madrid Congress see "US Center for ASSITEJ Newsletter", No. 2, 1978. Special Collections. University Libraries. ASU, AZ, USA.

Summary, 1975-78
31. Nat Eek, Letter to Executive Committee, U.S. Center for ASSITEJ, undated (probably August, 1975).

32. The names of these Commissions varied in the Minutes, but for the sake of clarity the above six (6) titles have been used consistently, since their responsibilities covered the exact same territory.

33. Joyce Doolittle, ASSITEJ/Canada, "A Report Upon Meetings of the Executive Committee of ASSITEJ, Milan and Rome, Italy, May, 1976" Special Collections. University Libraries. ASU, AZ, USA.

34. Ibid.

35. A *paseo* is a ritual promenade accompanied by street musicians on Saturday evenings in a village's central plaza where the unmarried men stroll in a circle around the unmarried women in an inside circle going opposite directions, so that the members can properly converse with each other under the eyes of the older villagers seating at tables and benches around the plaza.

Interim, 1976-79
36. Ann Shaw, personal narrative, 2005.

37. "Who's Who in ASSITEJ", (Edited by the Theatre Institute, 110 01 Prague 1, Celetná 17, for the Czechoslovakia Center for ASSITEJ.) 45 pages.

38. US Center Newsletter, William Gleason, editor, 20 November 1979. Special Collections. University Libraries. ASU, AZ, USA.

Bureau Meeting, October 1978
39. "Information Bulletin—ASSITEJ, 1978.3" (Edited by the Theatre Institute, 110 01, Prague 1, Celetná 17 for the Czechoslovak National Center of ASSITEJ.) Special Collections. University Libraries. ASU, AZ, USA.

40. The Bulletin does not mention what these problems were, probably non-payment of dues.

Bureau Meeting, June 1979
41. "Information Bulletin—ASSITEJ, 1979 (2)" (Edited by the Theatre Institute, 110 01, Prague 1, Celetná 17 for the Czechoslovak National Center of ASSITEJ.) Special Collections. University Libraries. ASU, AZ, USA.

42. "Information Bulletin—ASSITEJ, 1979 (1)" (Edited by the Theatre Institute, 110 01, Prague 1, Celetná 17 for the Czechoslovak National Center of ASSITEJ.) Special Collections. University Libraries. ASU, AZ, USA.

43. The Šibenik Program, 1979. Special Collections. University Libraries. ASU, AZ, USA.

44. Nat Eek, "Musings", a column in *The Norman, OK Transcript*, dated July 1979 as quoted in the "U.S. Center for ASSITEJ Newsletter: Vol. III, No. 2", October, 1979. Nat Eek Archives, Special Collections. University Libraries. ASU, AZ, USA.

EXCOM Meeting, April 1980
45. "Information Bulletin—ASSITEJ, 1980 (1)" (Edited by the Theatre Institute, 110 01, Prague 1, Celetná 17 for the Czechoslovak National Center of ASSITEJ.) Special Collections. University Libraries. ASU, AZ, USA.

46. "Information Bulletin—ASSITEJ, 1979 (1)" (Edited by the Theatre Institute,

110 01, Prague 1, Celetná 17 for the Czechoslovak National Center of ASSITEJ.) Also from the "U.S. Center for ASSITEJ Newsletter: Vol. III, No. 2" dated October 1979. Both in Special Collections. University Libraries. ASU, AZ, USA.

47. Pat Hale Whitton, "Impressions of Washington, D.C.; 11-13 April 1979" as printed in the "U.S. Center for ASSITEJ Newsletter: Vol. IV, No. 1", July 1980. Special Collections. University Libraries. ASU, AZ, USA.

Bureau Meeting, November 1980

48. "Information Bulletin—ASSITEJ, 1980 (2)" (Edited by the Theatre Institute, 110 01, Prague 1, Celetná 17 for the Czechoslovak National Center of ASSITEJ.) Special Collections. University Libraries. ASU, AZ, USA.

EXCOM Meeting, March 1981

49. Ann Shaw, Notes taken at the March 1981 EXCOM Meeting. Ann Shaw Archives, Special Collections. University Libraries. ASU, AZ, USA. Also, see Czech Bulletin—1981.

VIIth International Congress, June 1981

50. Michael Ramløse, 30 November 2008, e-mail to Nat Eek.

51. The French Minutes of the "ASSITEJ General Assembly, Lyon 1981", translated by ASSITEJ/Canada. Special Collections, University Libraries. ASU, AZ, USA; and the Secretary General's Report to the General Assembly "INTERNATIONAL ASSOCIATION OF THEATRE FOR CHILDREN AND YOUNG PEOPLE—REPORT—GENERAL MEETING—LYON, JUNE 1981". Ann Shaw Archives, Special Collections. University Libraries. ASU, AZ, USA.

52. Pat Hale Whitton, "International Congress—ASSITEJ/Lyon/1981", the *Children's Theatre Review*, Fall 1981, 13-14. Ann Shaw Archives, Special Collections. University Libraries. ASU, AZ, USA.

53. Michael Ramløse, 30 November 2008, e-mail to Nat Eek.

54. While this does not conform to the required 38 vote majority, it clearly elected Socorro over Satz.

55. The French Minutes of the "ASSITEJ General Assembly, Lyon 1981", translated by ASSITEJ/Canada, 10. Special Collections. University Libraries. ASU, AZ, USA.

56. Report by Secretary General Rose-Marie Moudoués titled "INTERNATIONAL ASSOCIATION FOR YOUTH AND CHILDREN'S THEATRE/ GENERAL MEETING—MOSCOW, USSR / SECRETARY'S REPORT," August 1984, 7 pages. Special Collections. University Libraries. ASU, AZ, USA. This was apparently the Secretary General's Report for 1981-1984 presented at the Moscow Congress in 1984.

57. By the 1984 Congress in Moscow a new Danish Center had been established.

58. Michael Ramløse, 30 November 2008, e-mail to Nat Eek.

59. Michael Ramløse, 4 December 2009, e-mail to Nat Eek.

60. Whitton, see Note 52.

61. "Information Bulletin—ASSITEJ, 1981 (2)" (Edited by the Theatre Institute, 110 01, Prague 1, Celetná 17 for the Czechoslovak National Center of ASSITEJ.) Special Collections, University Libraries, ASU, AZ, USA.

The World of 1981-90

62. The World Almanac, Ibid.

Bureau Meeting, October 1981

63. The French Minutes "Meeting of the Bureau, Lille, 11-13 October 1981". Special Collections. University Libraries. ASU, AZ, USA.

EXCOM Meeting, April 1982
64. Sara Lee Lewis, President, ASSITEJ/Canada, *Report of the EXCOM Meeting, April 1982*, and sent to her membership, 26 April 1982, 9 pages. Ann Shaw Archives, Special Collections. University Libraries. ASU, AZ, USA.

65. Sara Lee Lewis, Ibid, describes the productions so well that she is quoted almost verbatim.

66. Lewis, Ibid.

Bureau Meeting, October 1982
67. Taken from the German Minutes, dated 4 November 1982, 3n, E-mail, 13 May 2010, Meike Fechner to Nat Eek. Berlin Archives.

EXCOM Meeting, June 1983
68. The French Minutes of the EXCOM Meeting (undated) 8 pages. Also, Ann Shaw, Unofficial Minutes of the EXCOM Meeting, June 1983, and reported to ASSITEJ/USA Membership (undated), 9 pages. Also, Bereslav Frkič (Yugoslavia), handwritten notes, 15 July 1983. All three in the Ann Shaw Archives, Special Collections. University Libraries, ASU, AZ, USA.

69. Michael Ramløse, 30 November 2008, e-mail to Nat Eek.

70. In fact eventually the title became the exclusive property of the Festival in Lyon every two years.

71. This comment contradicts the Statutes which specify three official languages: French, English, and Russian. However, in practice the Russian speaking Centers always brought their own interpreters.

72. Australia finally agreed to host the IXth International Congress in 1987 in Adelaide, Australia.

Bureau Meeting, November 1983
73. Ann Shaw, Unofficial Minutes from the Bureau Meeting, June 1983, and reported to ASSITEJ/USA Membership (undated) 9 pages. Special Collections. University Libraries. ASU, AZ, USA.

74. Ann Shaw, Personal Notebook during the period of the meeting. Shaw Archives, Special Collections. University Libraries. ASU, AZ, USA. Also taken in part from the Offical French Minutes of the meeting, the German Archives, courtesy of Meike Fechner.

75. Shaun Hennessey, 22 August 1983, Letter to Ann Shaw. Hennessey wrote "The main business of the meeting will be the Moscow Congress [1984], the Theatre of Nations, and the 20th Anniversary [of ASSITEJ].

EXCOM Meeting, June 1984
76. Ann Shaw, 9-12 June 1984, handwritten notes taken at the Munich EXCOM Meeting, and her Unofficial Minutes reported to ASSITEJ/USA Membership (undated) 9 pages. Special Collections. University Libraries. ASU, AZ, USA.

77. This comment was necessary since ASSITEJ was demanding to view only "professional" theatre, and the Yugoslav Festival had many companies that used children as performers.

VIIth International Congress, September 1984
78. *The World Almanac and Book of Facts—1994*, 522.

79. Nena Stenius (Finland) was a newcomer to ASSITEJ, who had studied in Moscow,

and had been active with the Cuban theatre program. She was elected to the Bureau and EXCOM at this Congress, but had been serving as Maria Sunyer's (Spain) replacement for the past year. 80. Ann Shaw, *Report on the Moscow Congress—1984*. Ann Shaw Archives, Special Collections. University Libraries. ASU, AZ, USA.

    81. Ann Shaw, handwritten notes on the Moscow Congress, taken at the time in September 1984. Ann Shaw Archives, Special Collections. University Libraries. ASU, AZ, USA.

    82. Michael Ramløse, 30 November 2008, e-mail to Nat Eek.

    83. Ann Shaw Archives, Special Collections. University Libraries. ASU, AZ, USA.

    84. English text of Ilse Rodenberg's Welcoming Speech, 20 September 1984, Moscow, USSR. Ann Shaw Archives, Special Collections. University Libraries. ASU, AZ, USA.

    85. Rodenberg, Ibid.

    86. English text of the *Secretary General's Report, August 1984*. Ann Shaw Archives, Special Collections. University Libraries. ASU, AZ, USA.

    87. This essentially codified the Commissions and realigned some of their duties. Over the years they continued to be modified in both terminology and usage.

    88. Harold Oaks, Personal Notes, September 1984. Harold Oaks Archives, Special Collections. University Libraries. ASU, AZ, USA.

    89. Ann Shaw, Personal Note, 14 June 1995. Ann Shaw Archives, Special Collections. University Libraries. ASU, AZ, USA.

    90. Since each center is given 3 paper ballots, one for each vote, a center can easily mark them differently thus splitting their vote, or by leaving them blank which is called a "white ballot".

    91. Harold Oaks, Note 88.

    92. Ann Shaw, 10 August 2006, conversation with Nat Eek, Santa Fe, NM, USA.

Addendum

    93. All the following correspondence came from the Ann Shaw Archives, Special Collections. University Libraries. ASU, AZ, USA.

Summary—1978-84

    94. Ann Shaw, Notes on the Prague 1979 EXCOM Meeting. Ann Shaw Archives, Special Collections. University Libraries. ASU, AZ, USA.

    95. "Information Bulletin—ASSITEJ, 1981 (2)" (Edited by the Theatre Institute, 110 01, Prague 1, Celetná 17 for the Czechoslovak National Center of ASSITEJ.) Special Collections. University Libraries. ASU, AZ, USA.

    96. Ann Shaw, 10 August 2006, conversation with Nat Eek, Santa Fe, NM, USA.

Bureau Meeting, February 1985

    97. Taken from the French Minutes of the Bureau Meeting, undated, from the Paris Secretariat. German Archives, E-mail, 23 April 2010, to Nat Eek from Meike Fechner.

EXCOM Meeting, June 1985

    98. Ann Shaw, informal notes on the EXCOM Meeting, June 1985. Ann Shaw Archives, Special Collections. University Libraries. ASU, AZ, USA.

    99. June Fawkner arrived unannounced as a replacement for Diane Bouchard who represented French Canada who had failed in communication. Actually the Canadian Center was a "ghost center" at the time. E-mail, 21 April 2010, to Nat Eek from Michael FitzGerald.

    100. List of Centers was taken from the list of addresses of National Centers of

ASSITEJ, May 1985, distributed by the French Secretariat. Special Collections. University Libraries. ASU, AZ, USA.

101. "Report to ASSITEJ Executive [Committee] Meeting in Šibenik, June 1985 on Non-Member Countries in Asia" by Yasuo Fukushima, ASSITEJ/Japan. Special Collections. University Libraries. ASU, AZ, USA.

Bureau & EXCOM Meeting, May 1986

102. Ann Shaw, handwritten notes of the EXCOM Meeting of 3-10 May 1986. Ann Shaw Archives, Special Collections. University Libraries. ASU, AZ, USA.

103. Ann Shaw, Letter to "The Executive Committee of ASSITEJ & Observers Who Attended the 1986 Executive Committee Meeting in Stockholm, Sweden", January 1987, 3 pages. Ann Shaw Archives, Special Collections. University Libraries. ASU, AZ, USA.

EXCOM Meeting, January 1987

104. Ann Shaw, "REFLECTIONS ON ASSITEJ EXCOM MEETING—EAST BERLIN—JAN 6-11, 1987". Ann Shaw Archives, Special Collections. University Libraries. ASU, AZ, USA.

105. Ibid.

106. Ibid.

IXth World Congress, April 1987

107. Report of the "9th WORLD CONGRESS AND GENERAL ASSEMBLY/APRIL 1987/ADELAIDE AUSTRALIA", 34n. Special Collections. University Libraries. ASU, AZ, USA.

108. Harold Oaks, Personal Notes, 9th WORLD CONGRESS, April 1987. Special Collections. University Libraries. ASU, AZ, USA.

109. Report of the 9th WORLD CONGRESS. Ibid.

110. Rose-Marie Moudoués, *The Activities Report of the Secretary General* presented at the IXth World Congress in Adelaide, Australia, April 1987. Harold Oaks Archives, Special Collections. University Libraries. ASU, AZ, USA.

111. Ibid.

112. E-mail, 22 April 2010 to Nat Eek from Michael FitzGerald.

113. Ann Shaw, handwritten MS, spoken at the Adelaide, Australia Congress, April 1987. Special Collections. University Libraries. ASU, AZ, USA.

114. Ian Chance, "DIVIDED WE STAND; the Ninth ASSITEJ World Congress, Adelaide, 1987", published in "Lowdown", May 1987, Adelaide Australia. Ann Shaw Archives, Special Collections. University Libraries. ASU, AZ, USA.

115. "TYA Today" Vol. 3, No. 1, 1987. Ann Shaw Archives. Special Collections. University Libraries. ASU, AZ, USA.

116. E-mail, 22 April 2010 to Nat Eek from Michael FitzGerald.

117. A change in the Statutes in 1990 now allows only one proxy per country.

Commission on Themes Meeting, November 1987

118. The French Minutes and its English translation of the Meeting in Modena, Italy, 3-8 November 1987. Harold Oaks Archives, Special Collections. University Libraries. ASU, AZ, USA.

EXCOM Meeting, May 1988

119. The French Minutes of the EXCOM Meeting in Odense, Denmark, 15-22 May 1988. Also, The English Minutes, translated by the USSR Center, and distributed by the Secretariat, 17 March 1989. Also, Harold Oaks, Notes taken at the EXCOM Meeting in May

1988. All three in the Harold Oaks Archives. Special Collections, University Libraries, ASU, AZ, USA.

120. Michael Ramløse, 28 February 2010 and 12 March 2010, e-mails to Nat Eek.

121. There is nothing in the Odense Minutes to indicate what these corrections were.

122. To the best of the knowledge of these writers, this was the first time that such a complete balance sheet had been presented. Undoubtedly this was partly because of the transfer of ASSITEJ funds to a bank in Great Britain.

123. In reality neither the Commission nor the Secretariat ever sought grants from UNESCO. All the ground work and all the money came from the Nordic Centers. Michael Ramløse, 28 February 2010, e-mail to Nat Eek.

124. Harold Oaks, Personal Notes, 29 May 1988. Harold Oaks Archives, Special Collections. University Libraries. ASU, AZ, USA.

Bureau Meeting, November 1988

125. Minutes of the sessions in English (author unidentified), 16-18 November 1988, seven pages. Harold Oaks Archives, Special Collections. University Libraries. ASU, AZ, USA.

126. Ibid.

127. In reality no other fund raising was done, and the Nordic Centers paid the bills.

128. The money for the Symposium was gotten as follows: DANIDA (Danish) paid for the Africans; NORAD (Norway) paid for the Asians; FINNIDA (Finland) paid for the Latin American delegates; and SIDA (Sweden) paid for them all to attend the Congress. The entire phenomenal events of Symposium and Congress for non-members of ASSITEJ was carried out by the Nordic Centers as originally planned—a one week Symposium with the Africans in Denmark, the Asians in Norway, and the Latin Americans in Finland, and then everyone went to Stockholm, Sweden. Michael Ramløse, 28 February 2010, e-mail to Nat Eek.

EXCOM Meeting, June 1989

129. Rose-Marie Moudoués, Letter to Harold Oaks undated. Harold Oaks Archives, Special Collections. University Libraries. ASU, AZ, USA.

130. The English Minutes of the EXCOM Meeting, June 1989, author unknown and undated. Harold Oaks Archives, Special Collections, University Libraries. ASU, AZ, USA.

Bureau Meeting, November 1989

131. The English Minutes of the Bureau Meeting, distributed by the Paris Secretariat. No date and no author. Harold Oaks Archives, Special Collections. University Libraries. ASU, AZ, USA.

Bureau & EXCOM Meeting, February 1990

132. The Official Minutes of the Meeting in English. The Secretariat, 98, Boulevard Kellermann, 75013 Paris, France. 8n.

Xth World Congress, May 1990

133. The Official Minutes of the 10th General Assembly of ASSITEJ, 19th-27th May 1990, Stockholm, Sweden, 10 September 1990, ed. Michael Ramløse, Secretary General of ASSITEJ. Special Collections. University Libraries. ASU, AZ, USA.

134. Flora B. Atkin, "Rune Kapsyl of Plattvagan 11 Review", Theatre for Young Audiences Today (5) 2, Fall 1990, 24-26.

135. There is confusion in times and dates between the advance program, the meeting Agendas, the General Assembly, and the elections. The authors have included all the necessary

information under the General Assembly, but have put some items in an arbitrary chronological order. Also, since the EXCOM and the General Assembly covered the same agenda, the authors have combined them into one narrative of the General Assembly. Wherever appropriate, if the discussion occurred in the EXCOM Meeting that is indicated.

     136. This statement is inaccurate. In 1966, one year after the Constitutional Conference, only 18 official centers were listed, which led to some amusement that the EXCOM of 12 outnumbered the remainder of the electorate!

     137. Apparently Iraq and Mexico had not paid their dues, and consequently could not vote.

     138. This was no longer true. The new Danish Center had been accepted officially at the Moscow Congress in 1984.

     139. In fact this subsidy was continued for three years more when Ramløse was re-elected as Secretary General for 1994-1996, and then six (6) more years (1997-2002) while Niclas Malmcrona (Sweden) was Secretary General.

     140. The following is quoted in its entirely, since the replacement of the Secretary General was a cataclysmic event after Moudoués' 25 years of service to ASSITEJ. Michael Ramløse, 30 November 2008, e-mail to Nat Eek.

     141. Michael Ramløse, 30 November 2008, e-mail to Nat Eek, in which he comments: ". . . there was no other candidate than me, [but] it took the EC more than 1 1/2 hours to discuss the issue and end up with a split decision on the recommendation!"

     142. The Minutes of the MEETING OF THE EXECUTIVE COMMITTEE—STOCKHOLM MAY 27 1990, ed. Michael Ramløse, Secretary General, 3n. Special Collections. University Libraries. ASU, AZ, USA.

     143. Margaret McKerrow, "ASSITEJ-STOCKHOLM THEATRE FESTIVAL MAY 19-27, 1990", published in *TYA Today*, Vol. 5, No. 2, Fall 1990. Special Collections. University Libraries. ASU, AZ, USA.

     144. Nat Eek, 1 June 1990, Letter to Mârten Harrie. Special Collections. University Libraries. ASU, AZ, USA.

Summary, 1985-1990
     145. Nena Stenius, 10 February 2010, e-mail to Nat Eek, titled "A MEMORY".
     146. E-mail, 22 April 2010 to Nat Eek from Michael FitzGerald.
     147. Michael Ramløse, 10 March 26, 2010, e-mail to Nat Eek.
     148. Ibid.
     149. Ibid.

Appendix B
     150. *History*, Volume I, 294.
     151. The Form for CANDIDATE FOR EXECUTIVE COMMITTEE for the ASSITEJ General Assembly in Havana, Cuba, February 1993. Nat Eek Archives, Special Collections. University Libraries. ASU, AZ, USA. And also Meike Fechner, ASSITEJ/Germany, 23 September 2009, e-mail to Nat Eek.

     152. The Form for CANDIDATE FOR EXECUTIVE COMMITTEE for the ASSITEJ General Assembly in Adelaide, Australia, 1987.

     153. *History*, Vol. I, 295.
     154. Andrew Bleby, 2 April 2009, e-mail to Nat Eek.

155. Taken from the Form for CANDIDATE FOR EXECUTIVE COMMITTEE for the ASSITEJ General Assembly in Adelaide, Australia dated 1987, and from the "List of Candidates for Executive Committee", Stockholm Congress, 1990. Harold Oaks Archives.
156. *History*, Vol. I, 298
157. *History*, Vol. I, 299.
158. Egmont Elschner, 21-22 September 2009, e-mail to Nat Eek.
159. *"Who's Who in ASSITEJ."* The Czech Bulletin, 1977 (3). (Edited by the Theatre Institute, 110 01 Prague 1, Celetnà 17, for the Czechoslovak Centre for ASSITEJ.) Mimeographed.
160. Michael FitzGerald, 13 November 2006, e-mail to Nat Eek.
161. The Form for CANDIDATE FOR EXECUTIVE COMMITTEE for the ASSITEJ General Assembly in Havana, Cuba, February 1993. Nat Eek Archives, Special Collections. University Libraries. ASU, AZ, USA.
162. *"Who's Who in ASSITEJ."* The Czech Bulletin, 1977 (3). (Edited by the Theatre Institute, 110 01 Prague 1, Celetnà 17, for the Czechoslovak Centre for ASSITEJ.) Mimeographed.
163. *History*, Vol. I, 300.
164. Paul Harman, 6 November 2008, e-mail to Nat Eek.
165. The Form for CANDIDATE FOR EXECUTIVE COMMITTEE for the ASSITEJ General Assembly in Adelaide, Australia, 1987. Nat Eek Archives, Special Collections. University Libraries. ASU, AZ, USA.
166. David Johnston, 22 January 2010, e-mail to Nat Eek.
167. The Form for CANDIDATE FOR EXECUTIVE COMMITTEE for the ASSITEJ General Assembly in Havana, Cuba, February 1993. Nat Eek Archives, Special Collections. University Libraries. ASU, AZ, USA. . Also The Japan Center for ASSITEJ (Mr. Shinji Ishizaka, General Secretary), 27 January 2010 and 2 February 2010, e-mails to Nat Eek, translated by Fusako Kurahara.
168. Vickie Ireland, 12 December 2008, e-mail to Nat Eek.
169. David Johnston, 22 January 2010, e-mail to Nat Eek.
170. *History*, Vol. I, 301.
171. The Form for CANDIDATE FOR EXECUTIVE COMMITTEE for the ASSITEJ General Assembly in Adelaide, Australia, 1987.
172. *History*, Vol. I, 302.
173. Fusako Kurahara, 5 February 2010, e-mail to Nat Eek.
174. Japan Center for ASSITEJ (Mr. Shinji Ishizaka, General Secretary), 27 January 2010, e-mail to Nat Eek, translated by Fusako Kurahara.
175. *History*, Vol. I, 303.
176. *"Who's Who in ASSITEJ."* The Czech Bulletin, 1977 (3). (Edited by the Theatre Institute, 110 01 Prague 1, Celetnà 17, for the Czechoslovak Centre for ASSITEJ.) Mimeographed. Also Patricia Snyder, 19 February 2010, e-mail to Nat Eek.
177. *"Who's Who in ASSITEJ."* The Czech Bulletin, 1977 (3). (Edited by the Theatre Institute, 110 01 Prague 1, Celetnà 17, for the Czechoslovak Centre for ASSITEJ.) Mimeographed.
178. Sara Lee Lewis, 1 February 2010, e-mail to Nat Eek.

179. *History*, Vol. I, 304.
180. The Form for CANDIDATE FOR EXECUTIVE COMMITTEE for the ASSITEJ General Assembly in Havana, Cuba, February 1993. Nat Eek Archives, Special Collections. University Libraries. ASU, AZ, USA.
181. The Form for CANDIDATE FOR EXECUTIVE COMMITTEE for the ASSITEJ General Assembly in Adelaide, Australia, 1987, and "List of Candidates for Executive Committee", Stockholm Congress, 1990. Harold Oaks Archives, Special Collections. University Libraries. ASU, AZ, USA.
182. Taken from the Machulska Biography submitted in the 1987 form for Election.
183. Marjorie MacLean, 16 November 2008, e-mail to Nat Eek.
184. *History*, Vol. I, p. 305.
185. The Form for CANDIDATE FOR EXECUTIVE COMMITTEE for the ASSITEJ General Assembly in Havana, Cuba, February 1993. Nat Eek Archives, Special Collections. University Libraries. ASU, AZ, USA.
186. Patricia Snyder, 22 January 2010 and 19 February 2010, e-mails to Nat Eek.
187. Harold Oaks, 10 September 2006, e-mail to Nat Eek.
188. The Form for CANDIDATE FOR EXECUTIVE COMMITTEE for the ASSITEJ General Assembly in Havana, Cuba, February 1993. Nat Eek Archives, Special Collections. University Libraries. ASU, AZ, USA.
189. The Form for CANDIDATE FOR EXECUTIVE COMMITTEE for the ASSITEJ General Assembly in Adelaide, Australia, 1987. Also The Japan Center for ASSITEJ (Mr. Shinji Ishizaka, General Secretary), 27 January 2010 and 2 February 2010, e-mails to Nat Eek, translated by Fusako Kurahara.
190. The Form for CANDIDATE FOR EXECUTIVE COMMITTEE for the ASSITEJ General Assembly in Adelaide, Australia, 1987.
191. The Form for CANDIDATE FOR EXECUTIVE COMMITTEE for the ASSITEJ General Assembly in Adelaide, Australia, 1987.
192. *History*, Vol. I, 306.
193. Taken from an E-mail to Nat Eek from Michael Ramløse.
194. *History*, Vol. I, 307.
195. Susan Rubes, 5 February 2010, Letter to Nat Eek.
196. *History*, Vol. I, 308.
197. The Form for CANDIDATE FOR EXECUTIVE COMMITTEE for the ASSITEJ General Assembly in Havana, Cuba, February 1993. Nat Eek Archives, Special Collections. University Libraries. ASU, AZ, USA.
198. Patricia Snyder, e-Mail to Nat Eek.
199 The Form for CANDIDATE FOR EXECUTIVE COMMITTEE for the ASSITEJ General Assembly in Havana, Cuba, February 1993. Nat Eek Archives, Special Collections. University Libraries. ASU, AZ, USA.
200. Nena Stenius, 10 February 2010 and 15 February 2010, e-mails to Nat Eek.
201. *History*, Vol. I, 313.
202. Egmont Elschner, 22 September 2009, e-mail to Nat Eek, and Meike Fechner, ASSITEJ/Germany, 23 September 2009, e-mail to Nat Eek. .
203. "*Who's Who in ASSITEJ.*" The Czech Bulletin, 1977 (3). (Edited by the

Theatre Institute, 110 01 Prague 1, Celetnà 17, for the Czechoslovak Centre for ASSITEJ.) Mimeographed.

204. Maurice Yendt, 10 October 2006, e-mail to Nat Eek, translated by Nat Eek.

Appendix F

205. See Vol. I, *The History of ASSITEJ*, 264.
206. Ibid.
207. Ibid.
208. Ibid.
209. Ibid.

BIBLIOGRAPHY
Volume II

Works Cited

ASSITEJ International, 15th General Assembly and World Congress, Montreal, Canada, September 20th-30th 2005 (Agenda, enclosures and other material) published by the Secretariat, ASSITEJ International, Box 6033, S-121 06 Johanneshov, Sweden.

Eek, Nat, Ann Shaw, and Kathy Krzys, *The History of ASSITEJ*, Volume I. Santa Fe, NM, The Sunstone Press. 2008.

Shaw, Ann M. *The Formation of ASSITEJ*, ASSITEJ Annual 1996/97, (Ed. Wolfgang Schneider, Druckerei Heinrich, Frankfurt am Main, Germany.)

The ASSITEJ Book 2004/2005, Ed. by Wolfgang Schneider and Tony Mack, Published in Germany, Printing in Croatia, 182-197.

World Congress materials distributed by ASSITEJ/Canada at the Congress, 20-30 September 2005.

References

The Encyclopedia Britannica. Encyclopedia Britannica, Inc., Chicago, Illinois, USA.

The World Almanac and Books of Facts (Annual). Pharos Books, Scripps Howard Company, New York, NY, USA

Archives

ASSITEJ International Archives, Dept. Information and Documentation, Children's and Young People's Theatre Centre in the Federal Republic of Germany, Frankfurt (Main), Germany

(Everything listed below is available in the Special Collections, Dept. of Archives & Manuscripts, University Libraries, Arizona State University, Tempe, Arizona, USA.)

Doolittle, Joyce, *A Report Upon Meetings of the Executive Committee of ASSITEJ, Milan and Rome, Italy, May, 1976.* Special Collections, University Libraries. ASU, AZ, USA.

Eek, Nat, Notes, 15th General Assembly and World Congress, Montreal, Canada, 20-30 September 2005; edited by Kim Peter Kovac, President, ASSITEJ/USA, Ann Shaw, and Joyce Doolittle.

Frkič, Bereslav, Handwritten notes, 15 July 1983. Ann Shaw Archives, Special Collections. University Libraries, ASU, AZ, USA.

Lewis, Sara Lee, President, ASSITEJ/Canada, *Report of the EXCOM Meeting, April 1982*, 9n. Ann Shaw Archives, Special Collections. University Libraries. ASU, AZ, USA.

McLeod, Kenneth R. ASSITEJ-REPORT FROM MADRID, *Children's Theatre Review*, Vol. XXVIII, No. 1, Winter, 1979. 12.

Oaks, Harold, Personal Notes, September 1984. Harold Oaks Archives, Special Collections. University Libraries. ASU, AZ, USA.

_____. Personal Notes, 9th WORLD CONGRESS, April 1987. Special Collections. University Libraries. ASU, AZ, USA.

_____. Notes, EXCOM Meeting, May 1988. Harold Oaks Archives. Special Collections, University Libraries, ASU, AZ, USA.

_____. Personal Notes, 29 May 1988. Harold Oaks Archives, Special Collections. University Libraries. ASU, AZ, USA.

Shaw, Ann. Notes, VIth International Congress, Madrid, Spain, May 1972.

_____. Notes, EXCOM Meeting, Prague, Czechoslovakia, 1979. Ann Shaw Archives, Special Collections. University Libraries. ASU, AZ, USA.

_____. Notes, EXCOM Meeting, Prague, Czechoslovakia, 17-20 March 1981. Ann Shaw Archives, Special Collections. University Libraries. ASU, AZ, USA.

_____. Unofficial Minutes, the Bureau Meeting, November 1981, 9n. Special Collections. University Libraries. ASU, AZ, USA.

_____. Personal Notebook during the period of the meeting, November 1981. Shaw Archives, Special Collections. University Libraries. ASU, AZ, USA.

_____. Unofficial Minutes, EXCOM Meeting, Lisbon, Portugal, 28-30 June 1983, 9n. Ann Shaw Archives, Special Collections. University Libraries, ASU, AZ, USA.

_____. Handwritten notes, Munich EXCOM Meeting, 9-12 June 1984, Unofficial Minutes reported to ASSITEJ/USA Membership (undated) 9n. Special Collections. University Libraries. ASU, AZ, USA.

_____. *Report on the Moscow Congress—1984*. Ann Shaw Archives, Special Collections. University Libraries. ASU, AZ, USA.

_____. Handwritten notes on the Moscow Congress, September 1984. Ann Shaw Archives, Special Collections. University Libraries. ASU, AZ, USA.

_____. Informal notes, EXCOM Meeting, June 1985. Ann Shaw Archives, Special Collections. University Libraries. ASU, AZ, USA.

_____. Handwritten notes, EXCOM Meeting, May 1986. Ann Shaw Archives, Special Collections. University Libraries. ASU, AZ, USA.

_____. "REFLECTIONS ON ASSITEJ EXCOM MEETING—EAST BERLIN—JAN 6-11, 1987". Ann Shaw Archives, Special Collections. University Libraries. ASU, AZ, USA.

_____. Handwritten MS, spoken at the Adelaide, Australia Congress, April 1987. Special Collections. University Libraries. ASU, AZ, USA.

_____. A Personal Note, 14 June 1995. Ann Shaw Archives, Special Collections. University Libraries. ASU, AZ, USA.

Snyder, Patricia B., *Report to the Executive Committee of the US Center for ASSITEJ, 15 October 1976*. Special Collections, University Libraries. ASU, AZ, USA.

_____. *Report to the Executive Committee of the US Center for ASSITEJ*, 22 May 1977, 11n.

Whitton, Pat Hale, "International Congress—ASSITEJ/Lyon/1981," the *Children's Theatre Review*, Fall 1981, 13-14. Ann Shaw Archives, Special Collections. University Libraries. ASU, AZ, USA.

Documents (in chronological order)

(**1978**) French Minutes of the VIth International Congress in Madrid, Spain, June 1978. Distributed by the Paris Secretariat (undated). Special Collections. University Libraries. ASU, AZ, USA.

(**1979**) "Who's Who in ASSITEJ", (Edited by the Theatre Institute, 110 01 Prague 1, Celetná 17, for the Czechoslovakia Center for ASSITEJ.) 45n.

The Šibenik Program of the 19th Yugoslav Child's Festival, 21 June-7 July 1979. Special Collections. University Libraries. ASU, AZ, USA.

(**1981**) Moudoués, Rose-Marie. *Secretary General's Report to the General Assembly*, VIIth International Congress in Lyon, France, June 1981.

The French Minutes of the "ASSITEJ General Assembly, Lyon 1981", translated by ASSITEJ/Canada. 10n. Special Collections, University Libraries. ASU, AZ, USA.

The Secretary General's Report to the General Assembly "INTERNATIONAL ASSOCIATION OF THEATRE FOR CHILDREN AND YOUNG PEOPLE - REPORT—GENERAL MEETING—LYON, JUNE 1981". Ann Shaw Archives, Special Collections. University Libraries. ASU, AZ, USA.

The French Minutes "Meeting of the Bureau, Lille, 11-13 October 1981". Special Collections. University Libraries. ASU, AZ, USA.

(**1983**) The French Minutes of the EXCOM Meeting, Lisbon, Portugal, 28-30 June 1983, (undated) 8n.

(**1984**) Report by Secretary General Rose-Marie Moudoués titled "INTERNATIONAL ASSOCIATION FOR YOUTH AND CHILDREN'S THEATRE/ GENERAL MEETING—MOSCOW, USSR / SECRETARY'S REPORT," August 1984, 7n. Special Collections. University Libraries. ASU, AZ, USA.

The Secretary General's Report, August 1984, English text. Ann Shaw Archives, Special Collections. University Libraries. ASU, AZ, USA.

(**1985**) Addresses of National Centers of ASSITEJ, May 1985, distributed by the French Secretariat. Special Collections. University Libraries. ASU, AZ, USA.

"Report to ASSITEJ Executive [Committee] Meeting, in Šibenik, June 1985 on Non-Member Countries in Asia" by Yasuo Fukushima, ASSITEJ/Japan. Special Collections. University Libraries. ASU, AZ, USA.

(**1987**) The Form for CANDIDATE FOR EXECUTIVE COMMITTEE for the ASSITEJ General Assembly in Adelaide, Australia, 1987.

Report of the "9th WORLD CONGRESS AND GENERAL ASSEMBLY/APRIL 1987/ ADELAIDE AUSTRALIA", 34n. Special Collections. University Libraries. ASU, AZ, USA.

Moudoués, Rose-Marie, *The Activities Report of the Secretary General*, IXth World Congress, Adelaide, Australia, April 1987. Harold Oaks Archives, Special

Collections. University Libraries. ASU, AZ, USA.

Chance, Ian, "DIVIDED WE STAND; the Ninth ASSITEJ World Congress, Adelaide, 1987", published in "Lowdown", May 1987, Adelaide, Australia. Ann Shaw Archives, Special Collections. University Libraries. ASU, AZ, USA.

The French Minutes and its English translation, Meeting of the Themes Commission, Modena, Italy, 3-8 November 1987. Harold Oaks Archives, Special Collections. University Libraries. ASU, AZ, USA.

(**1988**) The French Minutes, EXCOM Meeting, Odense, Denmark, 15-22 May 1988. The English Minutes, translated by the USSR Center, and distributed by the Secretariat, 17 March 1989. Harold Oaks Archives. Special Collections, University Libraries, ASU, AZ, USA.

Minutes of the Bureau Meeting, 16-18 November 1888, in English (no author), 7n. Harold Oaks Archives, Special Collections, University Libraries, ASU, AZ, USA.

(**1989**) The English Minutes, EXCOM Meeting, June 1989 (no author, no date). Harold Oaks Archives, Special Collections, University Libraries. ASU, AZ, USA.

The English Minutes, Bureau Meeting, November 1989, distributed by the Paris Secretariat (no author, no date). Harold Oaks Archives, Special Collections. University Libraries. ASU, AZ, USA.

(**1990**) The Official Minutes (in English), Bureau & EXCOM Meeting, February 1990, Havana, Cuba. The Secretariat, 98, Boulevard Kellermann, 75013 Paris, France. 8n.

"List of Candidates for Executive Committee", Stockholm Congress, 1990. Harold Oaks Archives, Special Collections. University Libraries. ASU, AZ, USA.

The Official Minutes of the Xth General Assembly of ASSITEJ, 19-27 May 1990, Stockholm, Sweden, 10 September 1990, ed. Michael Ramløse, Secretary General of ASSITEJ. Special Collections. University Libraries. ASU, AZ, USA.

The Minutes of the MEETING OF THE EXECUTIVE COMMITTEE—STOCKHOLM MAY 27 1990, ed. Michael Ramløse, Secretary General, 3n. Special Collections. University Libraries. ASU, AZ, USA.

(**1993**) The Form for CANDIDATE FOR EXECUTIVE COMMITTEE for the ASSITEJ General Assembly in Havana, Cuba, February 1993. Nat Eek Archives, Special Collections. University Libraries. ASU, AZ, USA.

(**1996**) The Official Minutes of the 12th General Assembly of ASSITEJ, 1996, Rostov-am-Don, USSR, 1 November 1996, ed. Michael Ramløse, Secretary General of ASSITEJ. Special Collections. University Libraries. ASU, AZ, USA.

<u>Newsletters (in chronological order)</u>

"Information Bulletin—ASSITEJ, 1975-1976 (1)" (Edited by the Theatre Institute, 110 01, Prague 1, Celetná ul. č.17 for the Czechoslovak National Center of ASSITEJ.) Special Collections, University Libraries. ASU, AZ, USA.

"Information Bulletin—ASSITEJ, 1975 (3)" (Edited by the Theatre Institute, 118 00, Prague 1, Valdštejnské. č.3 for the Czechoslovak National Center of ASSITEJ.) Special Collections. Dept. of Archives and Manuscripts, University Libraries, ASU, AZ, USA.

"Information Bulletin—ASSITEJ, 1976 (3)" (Edited by the Theatre Institute, 118 00, Prague 1, Valdštejnské. č.3 for the Czechoslovak National Center of ASSITEJ.) Special Collections, University Libraries. ASU, AZ, USA.

"Information Bulletin—ASSITEJ, 1977" (Edited by the Theatre Institute, 118 00, Prague 1, Valdštejnské. č.3 for the Czechoslovak National Center of ASSITEJ); both in Special Collections, University Libraries. ASU, AZ, USA.

"Information Bulletin—ASSITEJ, 1977-2" (Edited by the Theatre Institute, 110 01, Prague 1, Celetná 17 for the Czechoslovak National Center of ASSITEJ.) Special Collections. University Libraries. ASU, AZ, USA.

"Information Bulletin—ASSITEJ, 1978-1" (Edited by the Theatre Institute, 110 01, Prague 1, Celetná 17 for the Czechoslovak National Center of ASSITEJ.) Special Collections. University Libraries. ASU, AZ, USA.

"Information Bulletin—ASSITEJ, 1978-2" (Edited by the Theatre Institute, 110 01, Prague 1, Celetná 17 for the Czechoslovak National Center of ASSITEJ.) Special Collections. University Libraries. ASU, AZ, USA.

"Information Bulletin—ASSITEJ, 1978-3" (Edited by the Theatre Institute, 110 01, Prague 1, Celetná 17 for the Czechoslovak National Center of ASSITEJ.) Special Collections. University Libraries. ASU, AZ, USA.

"US Center for ASSITEJ Newsletter", No. 2, 1978. Special Collections. University Libraries. ASU, AZ, USA.

"Information Bulletin—ASSITEJ, 1979 (1)" (Edited by the Theatre Institute, 110 01, Prague 1, Celetná 17 for the Czechoslovak National Center of ASSITEJ.) Special Collections. University Libraries. ASU, AZ, USA.

"Information Bulletin—ASSITEJ, 1979 (2)" (Edited by the Theatre Institute, 110 01, Prague 1, Celetná 17 for the Czechoslovak National Center of ASSITEJ.) Special Collections. University Libraries. ASU, AZ, USA.

"US Center for ASSITEJ Newsletter: Vol. III, No. 2", ed. William Gleeson, October 1979. Special Collections. University Libraries. ASU, AZ, USA.

"US Center for ASSITEJ Newsletter, Ed. William Gleeson, 20 November 1979. Special Collections. University Libraries. ASU, AZ, USA.

"Information Bulletin—ASSITEJ, 1980 (1)" (Edited by the Theatre Institute, 110 01, Prague 1, Celetná 17 for the Czechoslovak National Center of ASSITEJ.) Special Collections. University Libraries. ASU, AZ, USA.

US Center for ASSITEJ Newsletter: Vol. IV, No. 1, July 1980.

"Information Bulletin—ASSITEJ, 1980 (2)" (Edited by the Theatre Institute, 110 01, Prague 1, Celetná 17 for the Czechoslovak National Center of ASSITEJ.) Special Collections. University Libraries. ASU, AZ, USA.

"Information Bulletin—ASSITEJ, 1981 (2)" (Edited by the Theatre Institute, 110 01, Prague 1, Celetná 17 for the Czechoslovak National Center of ASSITEJ.)

Special Collections, University Libraries, ASU, AZ, USA.

Magazines

Atkin, Flora B. "Rune Kapsyl of Plattvagan 11 Review", Theatre for Young Audiences Today (5) 2, Fall 1990, 24-26. Special Collections. University Libraries. ASU, AZ, USA.

McKerrow, Margaret. "ASSITEJ-STOCKHOLM THEATRE FESTIVAL MAY 19-27, 1990", published in *TYA Today*, Vol. 5, No. 2, Fall 1990. Special Collections. University Libraries. ASU, AZ, USA.

TYA Today Vol. 3, No. 1, 1987. Ann Shaw Archives. Special Collections. University Libraries. ASU, AZ, USA.

Newspaper Articles

Eek, Nat, "Musings", a column in *The Norman, OK Transcript*, July 1979. Nat Eek Archives, Special Collections. University Libraries. ASU, AZ, USA.

Whitton, Pat Hale, "Impressions of Washington, D.C.; 11-13 April 1979", "U.S. Center for ASSITEJ Newsletter: Vol. IV, No. 1", July 1980. Special Collections. University Libraries. ASU, AZ, USA.

Correspondence (in chronological order)

Eek, Nat, letter to Executive Committee, US Center for ASSITEJ, undated (probably August 1975).

Eek, Nat, 1 June 1990, Letter to Mårten Harrie. Special Collections. University Libraries. ASU, AZ, USA.

Hennessey, Shaun, 22 August 1983, Letter to Ann Shaw.

Moudoués, Rose-Marie, Letter to Harold Oaks (undated). Harold Oaks Archives. Special Collections, University Libraries, ASU, AZ, USA.

Rubes, Susan, 5 February 2010, Letter to Nat Eek.

Shaw, Ann, January 1987, Letter to "The Executive Committee of ASSITEJ & Observers Who Attended the 1986 Executive Committee Meeting in Stockholm, Sweden", 3n. Ann Shaw Archives, Special Collections. University Libraries. ASU, AZ, USA.

Interviews (in chronological order)

Shaw, Ann, August 2005, personal narrative by telephone.

_____. 10 August 2006, conversation with Nat Eek, Santa Fe, NM, USA.

Speeches

Eek, Nat, "Children and the Art of the Theatre", VIth International Congress of ASSITEJ, Madrid, Spain, 1978.

Rodenberg, Ilse, 20 September 1984, Welcoming Speech, VIIIth International Congress, Moscow, USSR. Ann Shaw Archives, Special Collections. University Libraries. ASU, AZ, USA.

E-mail

Bleby, Andrew, 2 April 2009, E-mail to Nat Eek.
Doolittle, Joyce. 16 November 2005, E-mail to Nat Eek.
_____. 4 November 2008, E-mail to Nat Eek.
_____. 21 September 2009, E-mail to Nat Eek.
_____. 29 September 2009, E-mail to Nat Eek.
Elschner, Egmont, 22 September 2009, E-mail to Nat Eek.
Fechner, Meike, ASSITEJ/Germany, 23 September 2009, E-mail to Nat Eek.
FitzGerald, Michael, 13 November 2006, E-mail to Nat Eek.
Harman, Paul, 6 November 2008, E-mail to Nat Eek.
Ireland, Vickie, 12 December 2008, E-mail to Nat Eek.
Japan Center for ASSITEJ, 27 January 2010, E-mail to Nat Eek.
Johnston, David, 22 January 2010, E-mail to Nat Eek.
Kurahara, Fusako, 5 February 2010, E-mail to Nat Eek.
Lewis, Sara Lee, 1 February 2010, E-mail to Nat Eek.
MacLean, Marjorie, 16 November 2008, E-mail to Nat Eek.
Oaks, Harold, 10 September 2006, E-mail to Nat Eek.
Ramløse, Michael. 30 November 2008, E-mail to Nat Eek.
_____. 4 December 2009, E-mail to Nat Eek.
_____. 28 February 2010, E-mail to Nat Eek.
_____. 10 March 2010, E-mail to Nat Eek.
_____. 12 March 2010, E-mail to Nat Eek.
Snyder, Patricia, 19 February 2010, E-mail to Nat Eek.
_____. 22 January 2010. E-mail to Nat Eek.
Stenius, Nena, 10 February 2010, E-Mail to Nat Eek.
_____. 15 February 2010, E-mail to Nat Eek.
Yendt, Maurice, 10 October 2006, E-mail to Nat Eek.

www.ingramcontent.com/pod-product-compliance
Lightning Source LLC
Chambersburg PA
CBHW020941230426
43666CB00005B/112